# THE RYLANDS
# HAGGADAH

INTRODUCTION
NOTES ON
THE ILLUMINATIONS
TRANSCRIPTION
AND ENGLISH
TRANSLATION BY
RAPHAEL LOEWE

Goldsmid Professor of Hebrew Emeritus
University College London

# THE RYLANDS HAGGADAH

## A Medieval Sephardi Masterpiece in Facsimile

AN ILLUMINATED

PASSOVER COMPENDIUM

FROM MID-14TH-CENTURY

CATALONIA

IN THE COLLECTIONS OF

THE JOHN RYLANDS

UNIVERSITY LIBRARY

OF MANCHESTER

WITH A COMMENTARY

AND A CYCLE

OF POEMS

PUBLISHED BY

HARRY N. ABRAMS, INC.,

NEW YORK

Reproduced, by kind permission of the Director and
University Librarian, from Rylands Hebrew MS 6 in the Department of Manuscripts,
The John Rylands University Library of Manchester.

ENDPAPERS *Front:* enlargement of the decorative micrography on f.41a, discussed on page 21; and
*Back:* enlargement of the decorative micrography on f.42b, discussed on page 21.

**Library of Congress Cataloging in Publication Data**

Haggadah. English & Hebrew.
   The Rylands Haggadah.

   English and Hebrew.
     1. Haggadot—Texts.   2. Seder—Liturgy—Texts.
   3. Judaism—Liturgy—Texts.   4. Illumination of books
and manuscripts, Jewish.   5. Manuscripts, Hebrew—
Facsimiles.  I. Loewe, Raphael.  II. Title.
BM675.P4Z55693 1988     296.4'37    88–3290
ISBN 0–8109–1568–5

Texts © 1988 Thames and Hudson Ltd, London

Reproductions © 1988 Thames and Hudson Ltd, London, and The John Rylands University Library of Manchester

Published in 1988 by Harry N. Abrams, Incorporated, New York

A Times Mirror Company

Printed and bound in Japan by Dai Nippon

# CONTENTS

FOR
MY GRANDCHILDREN
IN THE HOPE
THAT THEIR PARENTS
MAY MAKE
PASSOVER
MEAN AS MUCH TO THEM
AS MINE
DID FOR ME

דור לדור ישבח מעשיך

Psalm 145, 4

# PREFACE

The ceremonial for the first night of Passover, perhaps more than any other Jewish institution, exercises an emotional pull over a wide spectrum of Jewry. Irrespective of whether spirituality is shallow or profound, it serves to enunciate a sense of ethnic identity which, even where it is not consciously 'religious', cannot be considered a merely secular manifestation. It is an old Jewish tradition that Passover draws together history (the original exodus), Jewish experience ('the Passover of the generations'), and messianic aspiration ('the future Passover'); and a *Haggadah* manuscript such as this from the John Rylands Library (Hebrew MS 6), is eloquent of the sense of cohesiveness, geographical and historical alike, of the Jewish people – in Israel, across the Diaspora, and back through Europe to the Roman Empire (in echoing the dining conventions of which one still drinks the four cups of wine reclining on the left elbow). On Passover night my own table carries, in addition to the statutory shank-bone, egg, unleavened bread and other symbols, a jar from Ur of the Chaldees dating from the 18th century BCE; an enormous locust, found in Egypt in about 1838; a medal struck to commemorate the Israeli air-rescue from Entebbe in 1976; and a black stone, picked up by me near the crematorium in Theresienstadt. No Jew who is conscious of belonging to a community of fate can be other than moved when he recites the climactic thanksgiving to God 'who hast redeemed us, did redeem our fathers from Egypt, and hast brought us to celebrate this night'; and the physical presence of such things as a facsimile of a *Haggadah* first used and treasured by Sephardi Jews nearly 600 years ago will surely, on such a night as this, serve to focus one's emotions.

The form and content of the manuscript will be discussed in the introduction, but a preliminary word is apposite in regard to the substantial quantity of material that appears here supplementary to the text of the *Haggadah* proper. It consists of hymns (or other, more reflective religious poems) – eighty-three in all – for insertion at highlighted points in the established liturgy, running from the Saturday preceding Passover (*Shabbath ha-gadol*, 'the Great Sabbath') to the eighth and last day of the Festival. Most of these works are now forgotten, having been squeezed out of local rites in which they had a place, by print and demographic change. As compared with the relative sobriety of, say, the Grace after the Meal, these items open a window onto Jewish concern with the meaning of Jewish distinctiveness, history and exile. Occasionally, correlation is possible with a known historical event or custom, as for instance with the confinement of Jews during Holy Week (poem 70 on f.50b). More frequently, it is rather a reflection of atmosphere and attitude, even though allowance may have to be made for their literary intensification, that may not always correspond with social reality. Thus, some of the poets most forthright in rejecting the political legitimacy of 'Edom', or Christendom, and 'Ishmael', or the world of Islam, shared in the cultural heritage at any rate of the latter, and will have maintained social relations with their Gentile environment which, if generally self-conscious, will not invariably have been strained. The *Sehnsucht* in these poems may indeed be a reliable thermometer for the spiritual temperature induced by the rhythm of the Jewish calendar; but that does not mean that it is necessarily also valid evidence for the social history of the Jewish minority, even though it was not infrequently victimized.

Of these eighty-three poems, not more than a handful – perhaps ten or twenty – can be considered great, or even memorable; of the remainder, a few are quite undistinguished. Important as they are for the study of Hebrew literary history, one must acknowledge that, save in a few cases, the lay consensus that consigned them to oblivion was understandable. A number of them, resting on extreme subtleties of *double entendre*, or juxtaposition of common and rare homonyms, are – frankly – far too difficult for congregational use. But if they were sometimes composed (albeit within the conventions of liturgical framework) rather like Torquemada-style crossword puzzles intended for a coterie of fellow devotees, that is not to deny them a spiritual validity: they were still composed *ad majorem Dei gloriam*. The problem is how to translate them for the average reader. No translation could possibly do justice to all their subtleties. A straight prose rendition, as close to the original as possible, might be of some use to the specialist student, but would fail entirely to convey the spiritual and aesthetic interplay, much of which is achieved through skilful use of biblical quotation and allusion. I have, within I hope reasonable measure, provided the key to this last element in the footnotes. The translation itself has (in my view) necessarily to be done into poetic form and archaic diction; I, at any rate, could not possibly achieve a meaningful rendering in modern idiom. However, I cherish no illusions as to the result. In my own judgement, I may have produced perhaps about a dozen reasonably successful verse renderings. But if they all satisfactorily serve the reader as a crutch, and challenge him to make himself competent to address the originals for himself, they will have served their purpose.

While some of these hymns can stand up as poems in their own right without regard to their setting, in many cases an understanding of the liturgical function that the piece fulfils will enhance appreciation of its form and content: and indeed, sometimes that understanding is indispensable in order to account for some specific feature, such as the repetition at the beginning of every stanza of the words 'the breath of . . .' in a poem designed to link *Nishmath* with its sequel, *We-'ilu phinu*. In order to provide a key to their correct interpretation, a skeletal outline has been provided of the relevant parts of the morning and other services, that also explains the corresponding liturgical titles (such as *Me'orah*, *'Ophan* and *'Ahabah*) which head the poems in the hymnic supplement (see p. 17).

Two items in particular call for some further explanation here: the versified institutional regulations for Passover, by Judah Hallevi (no. 82) and Zeraḥyah Hallevi (no. 3) respectively (ff.5bf, main text and margin), both examples of the *'Azharah* genre. To the uninformed reader the inclusion of such material might understandably appear somewhat bizarre, until it has been appreciated that in Judaism ritual is itself a symbolic language that can generate its own aesthetic dimension. Some elaboration of this theme will also be found below, p. 18, where it is explained that Jewish scholasticism impregnates tradition with a conviction that the dedicated study of procedure, concerning any particular Jewish institution, is itself almost as much a re-affirmation of Jewish identity as is the implementation of the institution itself.

It is a pleasure to me to acknowledge the help which I have received from others in preparing this edition of the *Rylands Haggadah*. I am grateful to Dr Leila Avrin for permitting me to use information supplied by her regarding the decorative micrography, of which she has made a particular study. In regard to the planning of production and the technical challenges, it has been a privilege to work with Shalom Schotten and Jeremy Schonfield; the fact that both of them are, quite apart from their specialisms, embued with an understanding of Hebrew values, traditions and art forms, combined with the appreciation of the significance of these by the publishing house, has meant that our collaboration has been in every sense a labour of love.

*Raphael Loewe*

# INTRODUCTION

## The Passover Festival

It is hardly surprising that the origins of the spring festival called in Hebrew *pesaḥ* (and thus in French *Pâques*, 'Easter') should seem, to those who observe the occasion or know it by repute, to call for no further explanation that that it commemorates the departure of the Children of Israel from Egyptian bondage. The main biblical account (*Ex.* 12–15) comprises a historical narrative so graphic that it appears to render any further enquiry superfluous. Indeed, the significance of the event, equally for popular Jewish sentiment, for Jewish theological and philosophical endeavour (to say nothing of mysticism), and for latter-day secularizing Jewish self-account, is so emotionally charged that for many Jews a scholarly examination of the source-material on modern academic premisses is felt to be irrelevant or possibly insidious. But Jewish appreciation of the intellect as a God-given faculty, and regard for the truth, do not admit one to ignore the relevant evidence; and even the biblical sources themselves are not as self-consistent as popular enthusiasm assumes them to be. The *Exodus* account itself betrays awareness that the feast antedates the historical events it purports to commemorate,[1] and that the meaning 'pass over' has, in the narrative,[2] been artifically grafted onto the verbal stem *psḥ*, whence *pesaḥ* is derived. The root means not 'cross' or 'pass over', but 'limp' or 'hop'. In rabbinic Hebrew *pesaḥ* means specifically the lamb or kid offered on the festival.

Such circumstances in themselves should be sufficient to prompt a closer investigation; and since the beginnings of a modern academic approach to matters Jewish, some 150 years ago, the question of passover origins has attracted a great deal of interest. The study has been greatly enriched during the last half-century by the increasing availability of sources, both written and other, concerning the culture, institutions and myths of Middle Eastern peoples – including Sumerian, Babylonian, Ugaritic and Hittite documents – and the correlation of new material with what was already known regarding the religious institutions of the Greco-Roman world. Its relevance insofar as Passover is concerned has been exhaustively examined, most recently by J. B. Segal.[3] All that need be said here by way of summary is the following. As the biblical sources present it, Passover is clearly the result of conflating two discrete spring festivals – a firstlings and/or lambing feast, and a feast to

mark the beginning of the first cereal crop (barley) of the agricultural year. Virtually all the institutions connected with Passover – those prescribed in the Hebrew Bible or the rabbinic law-codes, as well as the non-prescriptive customs maintained by Jewish folk-tradition – can be paralleled in one or other of the culture-areas referred to above, where they constitute elements of, for instance, new-year ritual, pilgrimage, purification and adult initiation-rites. But even though it is likely enough that at an early period within Israel *Pesaḥ* and the Feast of Unleavened Bread (*Ḥag ha-maṣṣoth*) may have been celebrated by the populace on a plane not noticeably different from that of any other Middle Eastern ritual in which the unsophisticated and spiritually insensitive participated alongside others, two considerations stamped Passover with the unique character that it has subsequently retained: and both of them are already attested in the biblical sources.

The first of these is the historicization of the festival, or festivals, as an annual commemoration of Israel's departure from Egypt. The second is the investing of that historical event with theological meaning as an act of deliverance, and indeed of redemption, consequent upon the divine election of Israel and the covenant with the patriarchs. Rabbinic Judaism would later reinforce this reading of the story by the prominence that it attached to the motif of redemption from Egypt not merely in the context of Passover itself, but throughout the liturgy: spiritual consciousness of the continuing significance of God's redemption is to be reinforced by reciting scriptural references to it every morning and night. And other notions, some of them appealing particularly to the minority of marked spiritual sensitivity, such as the symbolic connection of leaven with sin and the consequent treatment of its avoidance during Passover as a type of spiritual spring-cleaning, in some cases link back to institutional observances in the myth-and-ritual pattern of surrounding Middle Eastern cultures of which Jewry has been, for two millennia at least, blithely ignorant.

## The '*Haggadah*' and the *Passover Haggadah*

The central feature of the Passover feast was originally the eating, by family groups on the first night, of a lamb or kid slaughtered in

the Temple area and roasted whole. Despite the abrogation of the sacrificial cult with the destruction of the second Temple by the Romans in 70 CE, the celebratory meal has been maintained ever since with certain features on the table representing symbolically the sacrifices no longer offered. The order of proceedings as detailed in the *Mishnah*,[4] a legal code edited in about 200 CE, no doubt represents traditional practice that ascends considerably earlier – one view, probably incorrect, would have it that Jesus' Last Supper was just such a celebration. Except for hymnic embellishments, added customs reflecting the social experience of later diaspora Jewry, and the fleshing out of the mishnaic prescriptions with near-contemporary benedictions, and so on, the ceremony remains unchanged to this day; save where it has been modified or rewritten, either by proponents of reform Judaism motivated by theological and ethical considerations, or by propagandists of a doctrinaire secularism determined to purge the account of any divine participation, no less rigorously than rabbinic ordinance directs that the house itself must be purged of any residual leaven matter. For the great mass of Jewry the traditional text is retained.

The ceremonial involves the prescribed drinking of four cups of wine, the formal tasting of unleavened bread and other items, prayers of sanctification and thanksgiving, and a central element where, in response to a child's set questions, the basic facts of the exodus from Egypt are recited and elaborated (ff.22a– 32a). This element is called the *Haggadah* – 'recounting', in the sense of 'the story' – a term that has been extended to cover the whole order of ceremonies otherwise termed *seder*, 'order [of proceedings]', together with the prescribed text that accompanies them. Hence the term *Haggadah (shel pesaḥ)* to describe manuscripts and printed editions that contain the relevant text and instructions.

But the term *Haggadah* also has a wider frame of reference, the significance of which needs to be understood, since it is pertinent to the understanding of certain items contained within the Passover *Haggadah* itself that sometimes occasion puzzlement or even ridicule. The root of the noun *Haggadah* (*n–g–d*, verb *higgid*) is very common in biblical Hebrew (and also in modern speech), meaning simply 'narrate', 'inform'. In rabbinic Judaism the noun *Haggadah* has come to constitute a whole theological category within the overarching umbrella of

Torah. Torah ('instruction', rather than 'law') in its fullest sense means the revelational encounter between God and mankind. For purposes of schematization everything within that field is reckoned to fall within two areas, not water-tight, but rather impinging on and occasionally interpenetrating each other. One of these, called Halakhah ('procedure'), is concerned with the expression of one's awareness of the presence of God in practical matters (religious institutions, civil law, public and private hygiene, and so on), together with their corollary negative aspect that derives from spiritually motivated self-discipline (such as the avoidance of forbidden foods). Approximately speaking, therefore, Halakhah corresponds to the sphere of 'law'. The other category, (H)aggadah (the unaspirated form is Aramaic rather than Hebrew), tends to be treated as if it were of secondary importance alongside Halakhah. The fact that in current Hebrew speech haggadah is generally used to mean 'old wives' tale' is eloquent of the extent to which contemporary Jewry is out of touch with its own spiritual heritage.

Haggadah is so called because it consists largely of the free elaboration ('information') of the biblical history, and of anecdotes based on it, in a manner calculated to make them the vehicles of a theological, ethical or aesthetic message, very much in the way, for example, that Aeschylus treated the Homeric account of the Trojan Wars in order to produce the Agamemnon; or Shakespeare handled his historical sources to write Julius Caesar or Macbeth. Haggadah, then, far from constituting 'old wives' tales', is (or may be) myth, in the strict sense of the word: an imaginative story designed to encapsulate truth, analogous to a molecular model or the diagram of an electrical circuit. Thus the body of the Haggadah, comprising the Midrash or elaborative commentaries on the biblical text, constitutes the source-material out of which a theology of Judaism has to be constructed. Some examples, connected with the Passover story and its own particular Haggadah, may help to make this clear.

In one passage (ff.28a–29a) the number of Egyptian plagues is extrapolated, by reference to the 'finger'[5] and 'hand'[6] of God, and to the four or five aspects of the divine anger visited upon the Egyptians listed in Psalm 78, 49. The casuistic discussion as to whether a total of 10 plus 50, or 40 plus 200, or 50 plus 250 plagues is implied, appears to be but a piece of schoolboy-ish gloating hardly appropriate to the three distinguished sages to whom it is credited. It is necessary to appreciate that scarcely even a fanciful, let alone a factual, reconstruction of the historical events is here intended. The object is to highlight, in terms that even the least sophisticated can appreciate, the divine interven-tion that secured Israel's deliverance from Egypt by means not explicable from natural causes or human endeavour.

More impressive are two other examples which did not find their way into the Passover Haggadah. Commenting on the words in the

'Song of Moses': 'This is my God and I will glorify Him',[7] Rabbi Eliezer said that: 'At the Red Sea, the very serving-maid saw what was never seen by Ezekiel or any other prophet'.[8] And cumulative legend has it that at the Red Sea Pharaoh himself did not perish, but, having been saved in order to promulgate God's might, became king of Nineveh, where, in response to Jonah's preaching, he led his subjects in penitence; and, since his death, has been sitting at the gateway to Hell as the door-keeper, where he reproaches prospective entrants for having failed to profit from his own career of sinful defiance, punishment, penitence and, ultimately, faith.[9] If one wonders why a conceit of such spiritual power failed to be taken up into the text of the Passover Haggadah, there are no doubt adequate answers based on text-historical considerations. But perhaps the essential answer is provided by Rabbi Eliezer's dictum regarding the spiritual insight of the common folk at the Red Sea (an experience which, in some measure, was realized in our own days as we watched the outcome of the Six Days' War of 1967). For participants in the Passover meal who succeed in achieving that sense of historical identity which enables them to feel as if they personally have come out of Egypt (f.31b), even so sublime a lesson as that provided by the alleged spiritual progress of Pharaoh is superfluous.

## Illuminated Haggadoth

The Passover Haggadah, if excerpted from the larger liturgical compendia and written in a volume of convenient format for use at the table, constitutes a relatively short text for a ceremony which, with much incidental discussion, is often continued into the small hours. This, combined with the spectacular quality of the historical events that it relates, has invited its illustration in order to satisfy both an aesthetic need and a pedagogical purpose; various devices were evolved for retaining the interest and attention of small children late into the night. Since the story is contained in the Bible, there is naturally enough a link-up (which we shall discuss below) with the history of Jewish biblical iconography.

Surviving medieval Hebrew Bibles carrying illustrations are antedated by a millennium by the famous frescoes from the Dura Europos synagogue on the Euphrates, completed in 244/5 CE;[10] and C. Roth argued[11] that a link between the two is to be postulated, based on the unattested existence of a Jewish tradition of Bible-illustration, sometimes drawing on ac-cretional midrashic lore, in late antiquity – a tradition which supposedly contributed also to the evolution of Bible-illustration in Eastern and Western Christianity. That thesis, although non-proven, is not to be dismissed as pure fantasy. But whatever the origins of medieval Jewish biblical iconography, there developed alongside it a tradition (or rather traditions) of Haggadah-illustration; indeed, after the Bible itself the Haggadah is the most popular object of the illuminator's interest. The genre was carried

forward into the age of print, and enjoyed something of an amateurish manuscript revival in the 18th century. For the medieval period, the most comprehensive treatment of Haggadah-illustration and decoration is that by Metzger, who (limiting himself to the period between the 13th and 16th centuries) surveys and reproduces monochrome specimens of seventy-three illumi-nated Haggadoth;[12] he mentions several others that were not accessible to him, and to these may be added two more, both in Cambridge – one complete and the other but a fragment of a single leaf.[13] The quality of some of these, and their lavish use of gold leaf in some cases, indicates that they will have been commissioned by wealthy patrons, most likely to have been in touch, through service in the court or other Gentile connections, with circles where richly executed psalters and books of hours might have been seen during an age when the techniques employed in their production were advancing so strikingly. It is consequently not surprising that the influences of Western book-art and décor can be traced in these Hebrew counterparts. Approximately twenty 14th-century illuminated Haggadoth are known to survive.

Medieval illuminated Haggadoth can be classified in three main groups: SEPHARDI, emanating from the Iberian peninsula or its Jewish cultural extension into Provence, and perhaps occasionally (as a result of migrations by scribes and illustrators) from the south-Mediterranean seaboard; ASHKENAZI, from Northern France, the Rhineland or Southern Germany; and ITALIAN. It is the first group only that concerns us here.

The Sephardi type[14] to be considered here is characterized by relatively sparse illustration of the Haggadah text itself, which is nevertheless lavishly decorated with foliage, drolleries and so on. But that sparseness is compensated by an illustrative supplement collected at, or (as in the case of the Rylands MS) near the beginning of the codex, or sometimes at the end. The supplement comprises scenes from the Bible story – either that of the exodus, from Moses' birth and Israel's slavery in Egypt, or starting from the creation; in each case representations of the original Passover in Egypt merge into those of the preparation for the feast, and its domestic celebration at dinner, depicted in contemporary idiom. The inclusion of such a picture-cycle is hardly surprising, given the Jewish notion of providential history, and the tradition which sees 'the Passover of successive generations' as a chain linking 'the Passover of Egypt' with the messianic 'Passover of the future'. Curiously, while the eschatological climax is not a regular feature of Sephardi Haggadah-illustration, the Ashkenazi tradition (which does not evince the biblical-illustration supplement) tends to include, towards the end, the figure of Elijah, in whom Jewish tradition identifies the never-dying harbinger of the Messiah.[15]

The Rylands MS belongs to a substantial subgroup among the Sephardi Haggadoth; this is to be regarded as Catalan, in distinction from the Castilian subgroup which is more archaizing, and evinces Hispano-Moresque features.[16] The Catalan *Haggadoth* are characterized by an artistic eclecticism that blends French-Gothic composition with the gesturing postures typical of Spanish-Gothic art, with Italian-style architecture and costume, while landscape and colouring suggest Byzantine models. Doubtless the primary factor here is European influence flowing through cultural opportunities arising out of upper-class contacts between Jews and Christians; but one ought not to ignore the impact of the Jewish Mediterranean cosmopolitanism that characterized the community as a whole – particularly in the environs of Barcelona, at a period when, as an international entrepôt, Barcelona was vying with Genoa and Venice.

Specific decorative features met with in the Catalan subgroup are initial word-panels (e.g. Rylands ff.22b, 27a) either painted in magenta, blue and with burnished gold, or consisting of very delicate penwork (e.g. f.47a). Floral or geometrical extensions of these panels, embodying drolleries and so on, flow into the margin (e.g. ff.21b, 27b); this type of decoration being integrated with a columnar arrangement for the *dayyenu*-litany (ff.29b–30a).

Individual *Haggadoth* identified as constituting the Catalan subgroup are here tabulated. A prefixed asterisk* indicates that a facsimile in colour of the whole MS has been published (except for IX, which limits itself to reproducing the illuminated *Haggadah* only, omitting the hymnic supplement).

  * I London, British Library Add. 27210 (the 'Golden' *Haggadah*). Barcelona, *c.* 1320.[17]

  II London, British Library Or. 2884. A 'Sister-*Haggadah*' to I, neither its parent nor its derivative. Barcelona, mid-14th century.[18]

  III London, British Library Add. 14761. Barcelona, mid-14th century.[19]

  * IV Manchester, The John Rylands Library Heb. MS 6. Catalonia, mid- and late 14th-century: the subject of the present publication.

  V London, British Library Or.1404. Styled by Narkiss a 'Brother-*Haggadah*' to IV and possibly its parent. This question is discussed in detail below, p. 16. Catalonia, 3rd quarter of the 14th century.[20]

  * VI Cambridge, University Library Taylor-Schechter K 10. 1. A *genizah* fragment (single leaf). Catalonia, early 14th century.[21]

  VII Cambridge, University Library Add. 1203. Catalonia, late 14th–early 15th century.[22]

  VIII Jerusalem, Israel Museum 181/41 (the Sassoon *Haggadah*, previously MS Sassoon 514). 14th century.[23]

  * IX Sarajevo, National Museum. Second half of the 14th century.[24]

  X Bologna, University 2559 (incomplete: included within a prayerbook). According to Roth, this MS belongs to the group.[25]

  XI Parma, Biblioteca Palatina 2411 (or de' Rossi 1107). Early 14th century (Metzger's date). Similar to II, but less profusely illustrated.[26]

  * XII Budapest, Hungarian Academy of Sciences Oriental 422 (the Kaufmann *Haggadah*). Late 14th century.[27]

  XIII Privately owned (previously Rome, L. Pollack; and named Prato *Haggadah*), in New York, Jewish Theological Seminary of America. Unfinished; 3rd quarter of the 14th century (Metzger's date).[28]

  XIV New York, Jewish Theological Seminary of America Adler 1337. Early 14th century (Metzger's date). According to Roth, a composite codex (ff.1–13, 14→).[29]

These fourteen codices again vary according to the extent of the historical coverage in their illustrated biblical supplements. Those which start with, or near to, the creation are I, II, XII and XIII. Those which begin with the story of Moses and the events leading up to the exodus are the Rylands MS (i.e. IV), together with V, X, XI and XII. Roth furthermore conjectured that the first portion of XIV, the hand of which is calligraphically similar to those of I and IX, will at one time have included a cycle of illustrations similar to the full one found in I.[30]

# THE BOOK AND ITS HISTORY

## PHYSICAL DESCRIPTION

The description of Rylands Heb. MS 6 furnished by Narkiss[31] is so detailed that one can expect to add little to it, and it is here condensed, omitting, however, much of what the reader, with a full facsimile in front of him, may be reasonably expected to observe for himself, such as the range of colours. On the other hand, technical matters difficult or impossible to reassemble from the facsimile have been repeated.

PROVENANCE The MS includes no colophon, or owners' or other identificatory marks. It was purchased by the John Rylands Library in 1901, having previously belonged to the Earl of Crawford and Balcarres. There is no available record of his own acquisition of it. The brief English description on the 2nd fly-leaf by the Revd A. Löwy was presumably made for the 26th Earl (James Ludovic Lindsay, 1847–1913).

The first parchment fly-leaf bears an erased inscription, apparently in Hebrew, but illegible even under infra-red; and also a note, possibly related to a sale-price, which includes the figures

$$\frac{68\,000}{49}$$

58 xii d.

The second unnumbered paper guard-sheet in the binding contains on the verso a pencil scribble, partly, probably, in Arabic, partly in a European language, and, in Hebrew characters, *memirah yaphathi*. I cannot find any meaning in the Arabic.

BINDING In Narkiss' words: '17th-century red morocco … with green inlaid centrepiece. Gold tooled with two frames, the inner with black bands. Motif of small garlands round the centrepiece, larger foliage motifs in the inner corners of the black frame, and single motifs in its outer corners and at the middle of each side. Two brass clasp-plates on each cover, the clasps … missing.'

CODICOLOGY Vellum, i + 57 + ii leaves, *c.* 280 × 230 mm. Square Sephardi script throughout, except for rubric in rabbinic characters on f.54a, preceding the Grace after the Meal. Brown ink, in some places very light. For the quality of the scribe, see below p. 15. Two hymns for Passover eve (nos 1 and 2, ff.2a–4b) and the Grace after the Meal (ff.54a–57b) were added in a later, 14th-century Sephardi hand. The first stage was mid-14th century.

Ruling by stylus, 2 + 24 + 3 or 2 + 30 + 3 horizontal and 1 + 1 vertical lines. Pricking observable in all margins.

Eight quires of eight leaves, except for I⁴, VII¹⁰, VIII³; the seventh quire is disordered: f.45 should follow f.53. Corrective catchwords at the foot of f.44b and f.53b only. In this facsimile, the error has been rectified. Consequently what are in MS as bound ff.46–53 are here numbered 45–52, and MS f.45 becomes here f.53. From f.54 the foliation of the MS is retained.

## THE ILLUMINATIONS AND THE SCRIBE

The writing and decoration of the Rylands *Haggadah*, Heb. MS 6, was undertaken in two stages: the poems (except the first two), the cycle of miniatures and the *Haggadah* proper were written and illuminated in the mid-14th century, the rest before the 15th. The detailed description that follows is arranged in the following order: the miniature cycle; the painted word-panels; the penwork word-panels; the *Haggadah*-text illuminations; the decorative micrography; and the illuminations to the Grace after the Meal.

THE MINIATURE CYCLE The under-drawing can be observed where the paint has flaked off, e.g. f.14a. The composition is directed from right to left (e.g. the sheep in f.13b), with minor movement left to right (e.g. f.18a); the sequence of episode-compartments is similarly arranged. All the drapery has black outlines and fold lines, but the blue garments are more obviously modelled than are the remainder (see e.g. the lower part of f.13b).

The captions, which were copied by a later hand in the margins, are translated in sequence (p. 31).

f.13b (*Above right*) Moses as shepherd. (*Left*) Moses and the burning bush (*Ex.* 3, 2f). Narkiss[32] claims that traces of an angel's face can be seen in the flames. (*Below right*) Moses with his staff (shepherd's crook). (*Left*) The crook turned into a serpent and then reconstituted (*Ex.* 4, 2f).

f.14a (*Above*) Moses' hand turned leprous inside his garment, and then restored (*Ex.* 4, 6f). Although the incident is unitary, Moses' robe is represented as brown, red, blue and again red. (*Below right*) Moses and his family return to Egypt (*Ex.* 4, 20). A woman looks out from Midian's walls; a man on the walls of Egypt blows a horn. (*Left*) Zipporah circumcises her son (*Ex.* 4, 25).

f.14b (*Above right*) Moses and Aaron meet (v. 27). (*Left*) Moses recounts his divine call to Aaron (v. 28). (*Below*) Aaron repeats the miraculous signs before the Israelites (v. 30).

f.15a (*Above*) Moses and Aaron before Pharaoh (*Ex.* 5, 1). To their rear, Egyptian magicians. (*Below*) A taskmaster supervises Israelites cutting clay (v. 9). (*Right*) Gathering straw (v. 12). (*Left*) Making bricks (v. 18).

f.15b (*Above right*) Aaron's staff turned into a serpent before Pharaoh (*Ex.* 7, 10). (*Left*) It devours the magicians' staffs, in serpent form (v. 12). (*Below*) Aaron strikes the Nile, turning it into blood (vv. 15, 20f).

f.16a (*Above*) Aaron touches the Nile with his staff and the frogs swarm (*Ex.* 8, 1f). (*Below*)

Aaron extends his staff to the ground, producing lice on Pharaoh, his magicians and domestic animals (v. 13).

f.16b (*Above*) The fourth plague, interpreted in Jewish tradition[33] as hordes of wild beasts ('*arob*), which attack Pharaoh and magicians (*Ex.* 8, 20 [24]). (*Left*) The walls of Goshen with Israelites in front (v. 19 [23]). (*Below*) Cattle-plague (*Ex.* 9, 3). Moses and Aaron before Pharaoh, with attendants. (*Left*) Unaffected cattle of the Israelites (v. 7).

f.17a (*Above right*) The plague of boils. Moses and Aaron before Pharaoh and attendants, stricken (v. 10). (*Left*) Flock and shepherd affected. (*Below right*) The plague of hail (v. 25). Moses and Aaron before Pharaoh. (*Left, upper*) A shepherd with dead sheep. (*Lower*) A shepherd with his flock intact. In MS British Library 1404 the corresponding scene is identified with a God-fearing Egyptian (v. 20).

f.17b (*Above*) The plague of locusts (*Ex.* 10, 14). Moses and Aaron before Pharaoh, attended. (*Below*) The plague of darkness (v. 22). (*Right*) Egyptians seated in darkness. (*Left*) Israelites in full daylight (v. 23), with Moses and Aaron to the fore.

f.18a (*Above*) The death of the firstborn (*Ex.* 12, 29f). (*Right*) Pharaoh rising at night (v. 30). (*Centre*) Six death-scenes, including a chained prisoner and animals (v. 29). (*Left*) Moses and Aaron summoned to Pharaoh

(v. 31). (*Below*) Israelites spoiling the Egyptians before leaving (v. 36).

f.18b (*Above*) The exodus from Rameses (vv. 34f, 37f). (*Right*) Egyptians watch from window and roof. (*Centre*) Israelites march out armed (*hamushim*, see *Ex.* 13, 18), carrying sacks and a kneading-bowl (v. 34). (*Left*) Moses and Aaron encourage them onward. (*Below*) Pharaoh's pursuing army (cavalry and infantry, *Ex.* 14, 6f) arrives at the Red Sea (v. 9).

f.19a (*Full-page panel*) Two columns of Israelites, armed and carrying sacks, gold and silver spoil, and so on, march on dry land through the Red Sea, in which Egyptian soldiers and horses are drowning (not, however, Pharaoh, as discussed on p. 12).

f.19b (*Above right*) Slaughter of the paschal lamb (*Ex.* 12, 6). (*Centre*) The daubing of the lintel with the lamb's blood (v. 22). (*Left*) Roasting the paschal lamb whole (v. 9). (*Below*) The contemporary Passover meal. (*Right*) An elderly man prepares to recite the Sanctification (*qiddush*) (f.20a). A servant brings wine. (*Left*) In a separate room, a young couple, attended by servant-boy. Metzger conjectures[34] that they are eating celery-sticks as the bitter herb.

PAINTED WORD-PANELS These occasionally contain more than one catch-word, e.g. f.35a (cf. the juxtaposition in f.36a). Sometimes the panel

*Right* The call of Moses and the return to Egypt. *Left* Death of the firstborn and the Spoiling of the Egyptians. Two pages (f.2a, f.6a) from a manuscript closely related to the present one (f.14a, f.18a). For a discussion of MS British Library Or.1404, see p.16. (Courtesy of the British Library.)

is integrated with marginal illustration (e.g. f.31ab). The human figures, animals and grotesques enclosed within the cusped corners and curls are listed by Narkiss:[35] attention may be drawn to the hare, shot from below by a (legless) man (f.27b), and, among the substantial aviary, the parrot (f.35b).

PENWORK WORD-PANELS The panels consist of scrollwork, enclosing palmettes. They are sometimes divided by colour into rectangular sections (ff.5b, 8a), triangles (f.8a) or lozenges (f.8b). The rectangular frame may bulge into the margins, or be linked with the margin by flourishes (f.37b).

*HAGGADAH*-TEXT ILLUMINATIONS Regarding the nine figures the following points call for explanation or note.

f.20a The servant may be rinsing the cup (see accompanying text) rather than pouring out the wine. Although his skin is dark, the features are not negroid.

f.21b The bowl-like vessel raised by the reclining figure is probably a basket (cf. commentary, f.20b, below, line 1).

f.22b The book held by Rabbi Eleazar ben Azariah contains the text of the end of *Deut.* 16, 3, quoted in the corresponding paragraph. Similarly, on f.23a the Wise Son's book shows the beginning of the citation of his question. The sword, dripping with blood, wielded by the Wicked Son (figured as a moorish soldier) is of oriental design.

f.28a Rabbi Jose the Galilean's book displays the beginning of the paragraph referring to him; that held by Rabbi Eleazar (f.28b, *above*) the quotation from *Ps.* 78, 49; and that of Rabbi Akiba (*below*) the text of the relevant paragraph, as also in the case of Rabbi Gamaliel (f. 30b).

f.31b The bitter herb represented is intended to be lettuce, despite its artichoke-like compactness (*Mishnah, Pesaḥim* II, 6, see f.6a, p.27).

DECORATIVE MICROGRAPHY Narkiss[36] lists the motifs as confronting peacocks and foliage (f.5b), interlacing geometrical motifs (e.g. ff.6a, 40b, 49b, 50a), palmette scrolls (f.43a), dogs chasing hares and stags (ff.41a, 42b), a scroll-like procession of a fox, a grotesque bird, a dog and a stag (f. 46a), and confronting winged dragons with foliated tails (f.38a).

Dr Leila Avrin, who has generously acquainted me with the contents of a forthcoming paper of hers,[37] points out that no other medieval Sephardi *Haggadah* is known that includes micrographic decoration – not even MS Or.1404 in the British Library, which is in many respects so similar to the Rylands *Haggadah*. Moreover, the fact that the text utilized in the decorative micrography is from the *Talmud* (or, more strictly, from a digest) is unprecedented. Dr Avrin has been able to identify the hand (which is also responsible for the main text of the *Haggadah* itself, its liturgical appendage, and the micrographic non-illustrative texts in the upper and lower margins) with the hand of the scribe of two other mid- or late-14th-century MSS

from Barcelona, and now in Jerusalem: Heb. 28°–6527 (a Catalan *Maḥzor* for the New Year and Day of Atonement), and Heb. 8°–5127, the Nahum MS (a complete Hebrew Bible). Dr Avrin's identification of the scribe as the micrographer of all three MSS was made on the basis of his draughting style and of the similar, unusual micrography. Although the micrographic script in the Rylands *Haggadah* is square and in the *Maḥzor* it is rabbinic, occasionally in the *Haggadah* the scribe uses a rabbinic *shin* identical with that found in the *Maḥzor*. From the scribe's proclivity to pick out the name 'Jacob' in the micrography of the Catalan *Maḥzor* it may be inferred that that was his own name.

In the hymnic appendix, decorative micrography was planned for each opening where the beginning of a poem occurred at the top of a page (ff.5b–6a, 37b–38a, 40b–41a, 42b–43a, 46b–47a, 49b–50a). Some of the motifs were repeated in the Catalan *Maḥzor*, where the dominant theme is pursuit by men, animals and birds. The micrographic texts themselves are described and summarized below on pp. 20–2.

ILLUMINATIONS TO THE GRACE AFTER THE MEAL The text and decorations were added in the late 14th century. On f.54a a seated figure holds a cup of wine in his left hand: the manner in which an open prayer-book (or *Haggadah*) is secured under his right arm invites comment.

CONCLUSIONS REGARDING THE DECORATION[38] The style of the decoration of the Rylands *Haggadah* goes back to French and Italian origins, the French elements predominating in the illumination of the text-pages and their panels. The Italian element is more clearly seen in the full-page illustrations. The roundness and softness of the human figures is an archaizing French element, typical of Spanish conservatism.

The style of illustration in the *Haggadah* shows affinities with Western MSS from Spain around the middle of the 14th century, and it is possible that the artist may have been influenced by one identifiable manuscript: the *Chronicles* of Jaime I of Aragon ('el conquistador', 1208–76), MS Barcelona 1, dated 1343, f.1a.

The fact that a poem by Isaac ben Judah of Mont Ventoux, preserved in the Carpentras rite (no. 70, f.50b) is included, although it is not found in the associated MSS, may suggest that this *Haggadah* was commissioned by a patron from Provence.[39]

## The Scribe

In her forthcoming article[40] Dr Avrin will state her opinion that the hand responsible for the main texts as well as for the micrography is identical with that of 'Jacob', the scribe to whom the micrography of two other MSS is attributed. He was certainly a first-rate calligrapher: but a Jewish scribe needs also to be a fairly competent Hebrew scholar (whether scholastically trained or amateur) and a very conscientious copyist.

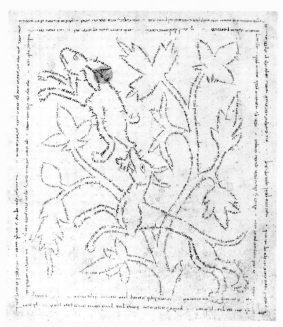

An example of micrographic decoration by 'Jacob' the scribe, possibly also responsible for the present manuscript. It is from the Catalan *Maḥzor*, MS Hebrew University Library 28°–6527 f.5a. (Courtesy of the Jewish National Library, Jerusalem.)

Unfortunately, on both counts our scribe is to be faulted. It is probable that the vocalization of the MS is to be credited to him as well, but even if it should be proved that it was the work of another, the charge must stand on the evidence of the consonantal text (see below). Where he is copying familiar material, even the vocalized marginal texts of Scripture that include also the cantillation accents, he is amazingly accurate. True, where non-biblical texts were concerned he may have taken a more relaxed view of his responsibilities. Nevertheless, some of his errors here are such that they not only expose his lack of understanding of the massoretic rules for vocalization (which are, in their complexity, comparable in difficulty to standard English spelling), but they also make it clear that he could not always differentiate the particular sense apposite to an ambivalent consonantal form – which he may very well have understood: the average Israeli Hebrew-speaker today is in the same situation. However, even those who might be inclined to consider such shortcomings venial would have to concede that his consonantal text shows him up as a not particularly proficient Hebrew scholar when he was dealing with less familar material. A crucial test here is afforded by the hymnic appendix to the *Haggadah*, the language of which is admittedly difficult for the layman, but less so for one deeply steeped in Jewish tradition, symbolism, allegory and so on; and a Hebrew *sopher*, 'scribe', was hardly expected to be a 'layman'. The footnotes to the translations of these poems reveal him perpetrating such howlers as to write *dor*, 'generation', for *dod*, 'friend', in defiance of the context. The fact that errors of this kind were very rarely corrected either by him or by the owner(s) of the MS perhaps tells us at least as much about their own command of Hebrew as about their aesthetic sensibilities where a superb piece of book-production was concerned. De-

Two pages from the closely related MS British Library Or. 1404. These pages may be compared with parallel ones from the present manuscript. (*Right*) f.9b, to be compared with Rylands f.22b and (*left*) f.32b. (Courtesy of the British Library.)

spite this scribe's capacity for 'short burst' accuracy in copying scriptural texts, one must wonder whether – in the light of his general performance – patrons would have risked giving him important commissions where accuracy was paramount, not merely in regard to biblical texts (a pentateuchal scroll, after all, represents a very substantial capital outlay), but also in regard to such civil instruments as a bill of divorce, where an error of one letter in the spelling of a name could invalidate the whole document.

## The Rylands *Haggadah* and MS Or.1404 in the British Library

The compelling similarity between these two *haggadoth* has long been remarked; but fate has dealt more kindly with the Rylands MS, whose state of preservation is much superior. Helen Rosenau's study[41] is still of value, although in part superceded by the work of B. Narkiss and the forthcoming article by L. Avrin; but, as will be seen below, H. Rosenau's conclusion that the London MS is a 'free copy' of the Rylands MS must now be definitely abandoned. Narkiss, who calls them 'brothers', concludes: 'The differences in iconography are minute, but it is impossible to state with accuracy whether one was copied from the other. It is most likely that a similar model, now lost, was used for both.'[42] While the assumption of a common ancestor seems to me to be the most probable explanation, Narkiss'

formulation can now be refined, on the basis of textual evidence: while it is virtually impossible for the Rylands *Haggadah* to be the archetype of the London MS, the reverse cannot be excluded, as will be seen.

The evidence is supplied by the hymnic appendix. As indicated in the previous section, the textual readings (vocalization is for present purposes largely ignored) are not infrequently poor, and are occasionally absurd. The collation of between thirty and forty such readings with those of the London MS (MS Or. 1404 in the British Library, henceforth styled L) yields the following results. The folio references are to the Rylands *Haggadah*.

### i Poor Readings Occurring in both MSS

The readings are either identical, or, where so indicated, equally inferior.

1 f.6a l.17 *qerusah* (probably read *harusah*).
2 f.6b l.17 *shello* is superfluous.
3 f.7b upper margin, l.1 *mephalleah*: L *mi-le-phalleah*.
4 f.9a l.10 *li-shemo nissim* (read *le-samu missim*).
5 f.10a l.2 *ka-hasoth* (*ba-hasoth* more probable).
6 f.38a l. 3 of *'ophan, mey 'ayin* (read *me-'ayin*).
7 f.38b 1st piece, l.7 *u-mizrahekh* (read *u-marzahekh*): L *u-madduhekh*.
8 f.40a 1st piece, l.12 *be-yom* (read *ke-yom*): L *yom* (*be-* erased).
9 f.41b 1st piece, l.6 first *niphle'tha* (? read *niphleytha*).
10 f.43b 2nd piece, l.2 *mi sur* (read *miy[e]sur*).
11 f.49b *ge'ullah*, l.8 *le-sophi* (with sin).
12 f.51a penultimate line *bi-debirekha* (superfluous prefix).
13 f.50b l.3 *yashub* (read *yashib*).
14 f.50b 1st piece, l.8 *'ulay* (read *'ulam*).
15 f.51a 2nd piece, l.7 *yahellu* (read *yah lo*). After l.8, both MSS omit the stanza beginning *mesharethaw*.
16 f.52a 1st piece, l.5 first *he'ekhilanu* (read *he'ebilanu*): L *he'ekhilanu . . . 'aris she-'akhalanu*.
17 f.52a 2nd piece, 3rd line from foot *u-le-hared* (possibly corrected to *u-le-harer*?): L *u-le-heder*.

### ii Readings in which L is Inferior to Rylands

It must be pointed out that the text of L has not been collated throughout, but merely compared where readings in Rylands are poor or questionable. In the course of that limited collation the following instances have been noted where Rylands is superior to L. Conceivably, a thorough check might enlarge this section.

1 f.6a upper margin, l.1 *be-borhakha*: L *be-bodqekha*.
2 f.38b 1st piece, l.5 *qumi we-he'ali mi-nuhekh* (read *mi-gohekh*): L omits.
3 f.50a 3rd piece, l.7 *ma'asay* (sic: vocalize *me-'osi* or *-say*): L *ma'asim*.

### iii Readings in which L is Superior to Rylands

1 f.6a upper margin, l.2 *salseloth*: L *salseloth*.
2 f.6a l.5 *muzhab*: L *mushab*.
3 f.6a l.3 from foot, *le-tarnogelim*: L *le-tarnegolim*.
4 f.6b l.6 L concludes the section with citation from *Ez.* 28, 15, and not, as Rylands, from *Deut.* 18, 13; see poem 3, n.58.
5 f.7a last line, the citation from *Il Sam.* 22, 23 in L needed no correction, as in Rylands; see poem 3, n.114.
6 f.9a lower margin, l.1 *timsa*: L *tisma*.
7 f.37b 1st piece, l.4 *dor*: L *dod*.
8 f.41a last piece, 4th line from foot, *me'unneh*: L *me'unney*.
9 f.42b last piece, l.5 *'ebkeh*: L *'ebneh*.
10 f.46b 1st piece, penultimate line, after *mishkenoth*, L includes *qehillah* (sic) *ke-'az beneh*.
11 f.47b 1st piece, l.6 *tashub we-lo' tashub* [*reyqam*]: L *tashib we-lo' tashub*.
12 f.50b 1st piece, after the 8th line, L includes the missing stanza commencing *hith'azzeri*.
13 f.51b l.2 *le-dor*: L *le-dod*.
14 f.52a 1st piece, penultimate line, *mi-leb* [ + *leb*, erased] *te'aseb*: L *mi-leb 'eth te'aseb*.

The implications of the foregoing comparison seem to me to be as follows:

The most spectacular difference between Rylands and L is the inclusion by the latter (see iii, 12 above) of a stanza in a poem by Abraham Ibn Ezra missing in Rylands, although the two codices share the lacuna of a stanza in a poem by Moses Ibn Ezra (see i, 15 above). This in itself is sufficient to prove that Rylands cannot have served as the archetype of L (arguments based on the assumption that the hymnic appendix was a later addition seem to me to be insubstantial).

The equivalence of L and Rylands for a substantial number of poor readings (see i above) indicates that even if Rylands had been L's archetype, the scribe of L did not command sufficient Hebrew scholarship to correct Rylands' shortcomings. A trial test (see ii above) – admittedly not an adequate sampling – suggests that he rarely perpetrated worse howlers than did the scribe responsible for the Rylands *Haggadah*.

L's superior readings (see iii above) reflect more faithful use either of the same archetype as that used by the scribe of Rylands, or of another codex very close to it. The common archetype must have already evinced the lacuna of the stanza of Moses Ibn Ezra, and may well have also suffered from other defects, such as the shared poor readings of Rylands and L (see i above): if that were the case, the scribe of Rylands could be relieved of some of the gravity of the charge levelled against him in the previous section. But in view of the weight of 14 superior readings in L (see iii above), against 17 common poor readings (see i above), it would seem to me that the Rylands scribe cannot be acquitted of some carelessness. It would be pleasant to be able to suggest, in mitigation, that he had ruined his eyesight in executing the micrography; unfortunately it is clear, from f.47a, that the micrographic ornamentation was added after the main text had been completed.

## THE RITUAL AND THE TEXTS
### The *Haggadah* and the Grace after the Meal

Minor variants in the text of the *Haggadah* proper call for little comment here. The omission of *Psalm 136* and *Nishmath* ('the breath of all that lives shall bless thy name', etc., for a definition see p. 17) after the *Hallel*-psalms that end on f.36a is not surprising. The identification of the 'blessing over psalmody' ordained in the *Mishnah*[43] is disputed in the talmudic discussion:[44] according to Rabbi Judah it means *yehallelukha* ('let all thy works praise Thee', etc.), as found in the Rylands *Haggadah*, f.36a–b; according to Rabbi Yohanan it means *Nishmath*. Modern *Haggadoth*, following the entrenched Jewish liturgical practice of hedging one's bets, include both.

The Grace after the Meal (ff.54a–57b), however, is of considerable interest as it evinces a mixture of recensions. Basically, as one would expect, it is of a Sephardi type, but it contains a number of features taken from parallel recensions, as these have been set out for critical comparison by L. Finkelstein.[45] A few details correspond to features specific to the Sephardi text-form in a MS in the Jewish Theological Seminary of New York, dated 1380, of the

*Manhig* of Abraham of Lunel – in other words to the very period to which, on art-historical grounds, this portion of the Rylands *Haggadah* is referred.[46] Other details reflect textual traditions preserved by Maimonides, or the *Mahzor Romania*, and others again the Ashkenazi recension as represented, for instance, by the *'Es hayyim* of Jacob of London.[47] Indeed, from the foot of f.56b onwards the text effectively presents an Ashkenazi Grace-form, merely reverting to cite some of the biblical verses which close the Sephardi form (f.57b).

The formula of invitation to the company to say Grace (f.54a) includes the divine epithets [*barukh*] *masbia' re'ebim* [*barukh*] *mashqeh seme'im* known from the Qaraite Grace-form (Venice, 1528, with *marweh* for *mashqeh*), but according to Finkelstein this is also known in some rabbanite rites. The short *ha-rahaman*-series (f.56b) contains some unfamiliar petitions in the context of the Grace after Meals. But the most striking thing about this order of the Grace is the abnormality of sequence on ff.54b–55b: apparently deliberate – an error in preparing these supplemental leaves could have been easily (and cheaply) remedied. Between the second benediction, concluding *'al ha-'ares we-'al ha-mazon*, and the beginning of the third (*rahem*), there has been located (f.54b, l.3 from foot) the additional paragraph for use on the Sabbath, that normally stands immediately preceding the concluding benediction of this section. That its unfamiliar preamble: *nahamenu ... tahazirennah li-meqomah*, *reseh*, etc., was intended as a shortened equivalent of the *rahem* paragraph, seems to be confirmed by its concluding with a built-in benedictional formula: *barukh ... menahem 'ammo yisra'el be-binyan yerushalayim 'amen* (f.55a, l.6). It would be interesting to know whether this arrangement is attested in any other source. The paragraph is followed by the regular *rahem* section, and then by the festival addition (*ya'aleh we-yabo'*) (f.55b), concluding with the benedictional formula *barukh ... boneh yerushalayim*. To say the least, it is a curious arrangement; it may even be of dubious canonicity. What happens when Sabbath and festival coincide? Were *both* concluding benedictions recited, and is their difference in meaning ('blessed ... who wilt console thy people Israel by the rebuilding of Jerusalem', and 'blessed ... who wilt build Jerusalem') sufficient to avoid the impropriety of vain repetition (*berakhah le-battalah*)?

## The Poems: Liturgical Setting

Most of the poems in the Rylands Sephardi *Haggadah* bear titles descriptive of their position in the liturgy. As regards the contents, the position which each poem is designed to occupy dictates its theme, yet the poet's development of that theme is as free as is the dramatist's licence in dealing with a historical character. Thus the location, or genre, of the hymn is perhaps comparable to an indication to a musician that a particular key – such as E major, or C minor – is

to be used in a new composition. In order to clarify the function of each, there follows a bare skeleton of the relevant parts of the statutory liturgy, together with the possible 'stations' for the introduction of a hymn. Only those parts of the service for which poems are preserved in the present MS are discussed, representing a large proportion of the poetic genres traditional in Jewish liturgical poetic writing. Examples appearing here are listed by the number indicating their position in the translation.

THE MORNING SERVICE
The early part of the morning prayers – consisting of study-passages and psalms, and ending with the Song of Moses (*Ex.* 15) – was originally restricted to private devotion. On Sabbaths and festivals its completion is marked by *Nishmath*, which may, however, be preceded by a poem of the *Reshuth* genre.

RESHUTH, *'Permission'*, *'Authorization'*. *A general term describing a poem that introduces a statutory liturgical item of particular prominence. The title reflects a social situation in which the prayer-leader, who would not normally be an officially employed cantor, and who might himself be competent to introduce liturgical compositions of his own, asks the congregation's permission to proceed to the recitation of a particularly significant passage in the liturgy. Examples of Reshuyyoth to be found in this MS include the following intended to introduce* Nishmath: 6, 23?, 24? 33, 34?, 35, 55?, 66?, 67?

*Nishmath*, 'Breath'. This prominent prayer is sung communally even though, strictly speaking, congregational worship has not yet commenced. It begins: 'The breath of all living shall bless thy Name, O Lord, and the spirit of all flesh shall continually glorify'; and ends: 'It is to Thee alone that we give thanks'.

NISHMATH. *The generic title of a poem for insertion after the* Nishmath *prayer, and before its appendix beginning:* We-'ilu phinu. *Examples here are:* 8, 25, 37, 38, 58, 70.

*We-'ilu phinu*, 'And were our mouth'. This prayer follows upon the theme of *Nishmath*: 'And yet, were our mouth as full of song as the sea ... we should still be inadequate to render thanks unto Thee ... from Egypt didst Thou deliver us ... all my bones shall say, Lord, who is like unto Thee?' This prayer completes the opening sequence, and the beginning of congregational worship is heralded by the reader's recitation of the Aramaic *Kaddeesh* doxology, itself often prefaced by a *Reshuth*.

RESHUTH to KADDEESH. *Introductory poems of this type resemble those related to* Nishmath *in function only, since their themes are drawn from their proximity to the sanctification motif of the Kaddeesh. Those in the present MS are:* 39, 59, 71.

*Kaddeesh*. The text opens with its main theme: 'Magnified and sanctified be his great Name in the world that He created according to his will'. It serves here to introduce the beginning of communal prayer.

*Barekhu*, 'Bless ye the Lord'. This summons to communal prayer is followed by the first benediction. This, recited after daybreak, introduces the theme of light, that is linked particularly with the imagery of the angelic world, through reference to such biblical passages as *Ez*. 1.

*Yoṣer 'or*, 'Creator of light'. This, the first blessing, begins: 'Blessed art Thou, O Lord, our God, king of the cosmos, who formest light, createst darkness, makest peace, and createst all things. Let all give thanks unto Thee ... who dost daily open the gates of the east, causing the sun to issue from its place ... The luminaries that our God created ... perform with awe the will of their Creator ... all the heavenly host praise Him, Seraphim, Ophanim, and Holy Beings ... They all declare in awe, "holy, holy, holy is the Lord of Hosts, the whole world is full of his glory".'

*'OPHAN*, *'Wheel'*. *Poetic insertions at this point are named after a term taken to indicate an angel, in the context of the description of the angel-borne chariot-throne of God in Ez. 1, 15f. Such poems are inserted in the benediction on light just after the 'Ophanim are mentioned. Examples in this MS are: 9, 26, 40, 60?.*

The statutory prayers then continue on the same theme, describing the angelic praise of God in *Ez*. 3, 2: 'And the Ophanim and Holy Beings raise themselves with a vast quaking, to affirm, "Blessed is the glory of the Lord from his place". To the blessed God the angels offer melodious praise, to Him who ... made the great luminaries, for his mercy endureth for ever.'

*ME'ORAH*, *'Luminary'*. *Poems on the theme of light may be inserted before the climax of the benediction on the creation of light. Examples are: 10, 11, 27, 28, 29, 41, 57?, 61, 73, 74, 75, 77.*

The first blessing – on light – then concludes: 'And He did so adjust the luminaries to gladden the world which He created: blessed art Thou, O Lord, who didst form the luminaries.'

*'Ahabath 'olam*, 'Everlasting love'. The second benediction, on the election of Israel, begins: 'With everlasting love hast Thou loved us, O Lord our God ... for the sake of thy Name ... Thou didst teach our fathers the statutes of life, to do thy will with a perfect heart ... for Thou art a God who dost effect acts of deliverance, and didst make us thy choice over all peoples, bringing us near in love ...' The blessing may here include an *'Ahabah*.

*'AHABAH*, *'Love'*. *Poems may be inserted here, before the climax of the benediction on the election of Israel. Examples to be found in this MS are: 12, 30, 42, 44, 45, 46, 47, 62, 63, 76, 77.*

The second benediction then continues where it broke off (with the words: 'bringing us near in love'), and concludes as follows: 'to give thanks unto Thee ... Blessed art Thou, O Lord, who dost choose thy people Israel in love.'

The second benediction introduces the recitation of the *Shema'*: 'Hear, O Israel, the Lord is our God, the Lord is one', the central credal statement of Judaism (*Deut*. 6, 4–9; 11, 13–21; *Num*. 15, 37–41).

*'Emeth*, 'True'. The credal passage after the *Shema'* begins: 'True and certain ... is this for ever and ever. It is true that the everlasting God is our King ... his words are living, enduring and faithful ...' The first part concludes: 'There is no God except for Thee' (*zulathekha*).

*ZULATH*, *'Except [for]'*. *Poems may be inserted here, before the prayer continues with the recital of the salient facts of Israel's providential history, leading up to the exodus. Examples in this MS are: 13, 31, 48, 64, 78.*

*'Ezrath 'abotheynu*, 'The help of our fathers'. The credal passage continues: '... Who is like Thee, glorious in holiness, revered in praises, working miracles?'

*GE'ULLAH*, *'Redemption'*. *Poems may be inserted before the climax of the benediction on the redemption of Israel. Examples in this MS are: 14, 49, 50, 51, 52, 53, 56, 65, 69?, 79, 80, 81.*

The credal passage then concludes: 'A new song, redeemed on the seashore, did they sing unto thy Name, in unison giving thanks they asserted thy sovereignty, saying: "The Lord shall reign for ever and ever". And it is said: "Our redeemer, the Lord of Hosts is his Name, is the Holy One of Israel". Blessed art Thou, O Lord, who didst redeem Israel.'

*'Amidah*, 'Standing [prayer]'. The sequence that follows is often called *tephillah*, 'prayer [*par excellence*]', and forms the core of each service on every day of the year. On a few occasions its first three benedictional paragraphs are highlighted by the interposition of hymns preceding the climactic points. One such occasion is on the first morning of Passover, in the *Musaph* (additional service read on Sabbaths and festivals), when in place of the reference to the divine gift of rain ('Thou causest the wind to blow, and the rain to fall') that has been recited during the winter months, reference to the divine gift of dew ('Thou causest the dew to descend') is introduced for the duration of the summer. The link of the ideas of dew, spring revival, resurrection[48] and ethnic deliverance explains why that service is enriched by the introduction of hymns into the statutory framework.

*'Aboth*, 'Patriarchs'. The first blessing opens as follows: 'Blessed art Thou, O Lord, our God and our fathers' God ... who possessest all things: who, remembering the loving devotion of the patriarchs, wilt in love bring a redeemer for their descendants, for thy Name's sake.'

*MAGEN*, *'Shield'*. *Poems may be inserted into the 'Aboth benediction in the Additional Service, before its climax. One example appears in the present MS: 15.*

*Magen 'abraham*, 'Shield of Abraham'. The first blessing ends: 'Blessed art Thou, O Lord, the shield of Abraham.'

*'Attah gibbor*, 'Thou art mighty'. The second blessing, *Geburoth*, '[Divine] powers', begins: 'Thou, Lord, art mighty for ever: thou revivest the dead.'

*MEHAYYEH*, *'Resurrector'*. *Poems may be inserted into the second benediction, Geburoth, in the Additional Service. One example appears in the present MS: 16.*

*Mekhalkel*, 'Sustainer'. The *Geburoth* blessing continues: 'Thou sustainest the living, revivest the dead, healest the sick, releasest those bound, and dost fulfil thy faithful promise to them that sleep in the dust. Who is like unto Thee, Lord of mighty acts, who dost kill, restore to life, and cause deliverance to spring forth? Faithful art Thou to revive the dead: blessed art Thou, O Lord, who revivest the dead.'

*RESHUTH to ṬAL, 'Dew'*. *As for the Nishmath, discussed earlier, Reshuyyoth ('introductions') have been written for the prayer for dew introduced into the Additional Service on Passover (see above). The present MS contains a single example: 17.*

The *'Amidah* then concludes with prayers for the acceptance of petitions, and praise.

## THE EVENING SERVICE

The structure of the evening service evinces an analogous arrangement of benedictions astride the *Shema'*, beginning: 'Blessed art Thou ... who bringest on the evening twilight', save that after the benediction: 'blessed ... who didst redeem Israel', there follows another, beginning: 'Cause us to lie down in peace, O Lord, our God, and raise us up ... to a happy and peaceful life ... blessed art Thou, O Lord, who spreadest the tabernacle of peace over us and all thy people Israel, and over Jerusalem.' The hymns for the eve of the Festival on ff.8a–10b slot into that pattern on the same principle. They are referred to as *Ma'araboth*, 'Evening [hymns]'.

## OTHER TERMS

In addition to the statutory prayers and their insertions described above, three genres, less closely linked to the liturgy than these, and one technical term appearing in the MS, require clarification if the translations are to be understood correctly.

*'AZHAROTH*, literally 'warnings', is here translated as 'Laws for Passover'. For readers unfamiliar with Hebrew poetry, the two examples of this genre in the present MS call in particular for some explanation. They present, in versified form, the institutional regulations for Passover, in this case by Judah Hallevi (poem 82) and Zerahyah Hallevi (poem 3) respectively (ff.5bf, main text and margin). Since in Judaism ritual is itself a symbolic language, it can generate its own aesthetic dimension. In these *'azharoth* the writers have produced a brilliantly woven fabric of words with a quality reminiscent of shot silk: through the reapplication of biblical phrases, generally lifted from contexts entirely discrete to the subject-matter, paradoxes are created (of course, close familiarity with the Hebrew Bible is taken for granted) that can suddenly refract the light, throwing into relief the poetic and sometimes mystical quality of the institution itself, and revealing the brilliance of its handling by a master of the Hebrew language. Those who find the subject-matter itself jejune, and are inclined to regard it as reflecting a Jewish preoccupation with institutional extern-

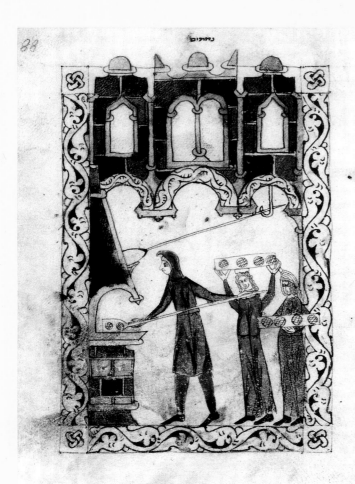

Two pages (ff.87b–88a from MS British Library Or. 2737 written in Castile during the late 13th or 14th century) showing the preparation of unleavened bread, as described by Judah Hallevi (on ff.8a–b of the present MS, pp.69–70) and Zeraḥyah Hallevi (f.6b, p.28). (Courtesy of the British Library.)

alities, are liable to miss the point. The reader of these poems is in a position not unlike a viewer who is watching a television discussion between the adjutant of a battalion of the Household Brigade, a regimental sergeant-major and a military historian, as to the niceties and historical origins of the detailed procedure for the Trooping of the Colour. That ceremony, in so far as it enunciates both loyalty and an identity encapsulated in tradition, provides a suggestive analogy to the celebration of Passover night. Perhaps in no other category of poetry included here, is the impossibility of adequately rendering the beauty of the original in translation more clearly demonstrated.

MUḤARRAKH. This word is a Hebraized version of the Arabic *muḥarrikh*, meaning 'agent' or 'instrument' of 'movement' or 'agitation'. It is apparently not a technical term known to Arabic poetics. In Jewish usage it designates a poem with a refrain – perhaps regarded as an 'opening movement' – in which the rhyme-scheme of the first short stanza dictates the rhyme of the concluding members of each successive stanza, in which the rhyme-schemes are otherwise individually self-contained. Most of the poems headed *Muḥarrakh* are introductions similar to those of the *Reshuth* genre discussed above. Examples are: 7, 36, 56, 57?, 68, 69?

PIZMON, translated here as 'Hymn', derives from the Greek *psalmon*. This term was originally used to indicate the refrain only, but later came to be applied to the whole poem. Although the name is not restricted to any particular functional class of poem, of those to be found in the present MS all but two are on the theme of dew: 4, 18, 19, 20, 22, 83.

JAMIA', abbreviated in Hebrew spelling to *gimel mem*, is a transcription of the Arabic *jamia'*, 'collectivity', in the sense of congregation. Placed at the end of a stanza, it is an indication that after the first stanza has been intoned or sung by the leader in prayer, the last phrase or line is to be repeated, as a refrain, by the whole group of worshippers at the end of each following stanza. The term is not transcribed in the translation. It appears at the end of the first line of poem 7, and in many others, in order to indicate the refrain, which is here identified by typographic means.

## The Poets

The poems are listed here according to author, on whom a few salient facts are given wherever possible. More biographical details concerning most of the poets are to be found in the *Encyclopaedia Judaica* (published in Jerusalem). In the case of patronymics, the entry appears there under the Arabic Ibn ('son of'). Where appropriate other sources are given.

It needs to be borne in mind that although probably all these poets could have carried on some sort of a conversation in Hebrew, Hebrew was the vernacular of none of them. Jacob

ben Me'ir Tam, and Me'ir ben Isaac Nehorai, spoke Norman French; the others spoke Arabic, although many of them will have commanded some Spanish as well. Some of them, including Abraham Ibn Ezra, composed prose writings (such as biblical commentaries) in Hebrew; but for the most part, even where matters of specifically Jewish interest were concerned, as a prose medium they preferred to use Arabic (as in Judah Hallevi's *Cuzari*).

In view of the close relationship between the Hebrew and Arabic languages, their literary situation invites comparison with such medieval writers in the West as Petrarch, who was equally at home in Italian and Latin. There is, however, a significant difference. When these Christian writers were dealing with political philosophy, or other abstract matters, they used Latin; for poetry, they either restricted themselves to their vernacular, or, if they wrote poetry in both languages, were acclaimed for what they wrote in their mother tongue. (The same applies, for example, to Milton, save that English is less intimately linked to Latin than is Italian, or Hebrew to Arabic.) To the Jews, on the other hand, their Arabic vernacular was but a medium of convenience, not appropriate as a vehicle for the emotional level inherent in poetry, be it specifically liturgical, or composed to serve some social purpose; to label this genre 'secular' is to superimpose inappropriate categories. In their view, the appropriate emotional register could only be attained in a rigorously classicizing

Hebrew that could evoke, at every turn, reminiscence of the biblical text.

The numbers refer to those appearing before each translation.

ANONYMOUS. 1, 2, 13, 25, 37, 68, 71, 78.

ABRAHAM BEN ME'IR IBN EZRA (Aben Ezra). 1089–1164. Born in Spain (Tudela). Bible-commentator, mathematician, astronomer, traveller (he visited England) and poet. (His son Isaac, rather than Abraham himself, probably, was son-in-law to Judah Hallevi.) His poems have been critically edited by I. Levin. 27, 31, 47, 48, 52, 53, 57?, 63, 69.

(ABRAHAM) ḤARIZI, see ḤARIZI.

DAVID BEN ELIEZER. According to Zunz (*Lit. synag. Poesie*, p. 546) he lived in Istambul. Davidson (iv, p. 375) distinguishes him from David ben *Eleazar* Ibn Paquda (Spain, early 12th century). 36.

ḤARIZI (possibly the same as Abu Isḥaq Abraham Ḥarizi). *c.*1100. Spain (Toledo). 46.

ḤIYYA IBN AL-DA'UDI. Died Castile, 1154. *Jewish Encyclopedia* vi, p. 431. S. Bernstein, *Sinai* 19, 1946, pp. 99–104, 208–17, 313–37. 56.

ISAAC BEN JUDAH IBN GHAYYAT (Ghiyyat). 1038–89. Spain (Lucena). Halakhic authority, biblical commentator and poet; friend of Samuel Ha-nagid. Schirmann, *Genizah*, pp. 187f lists all of his poems published to 1966, and prints a further five items. 6, 7, 9, 10, 23, 26, 32, 62, 65, 67, 74, 75, 76.

ISAAC (acrostic יצחק, as for the foregoing) 19, 20, 39.

ISAAC (acrostic ישחק), perhaps Isḥaq. 12th–13th century Spain. Translator from Arabic of *Mishley 'Arab*. 58.

ISAAC BEN JUDAH 'HA-SENIRI'. 13th century (active in 1208 and 1220). Provence (*Senir* probably stands for Mont Ventoux, near Carpentras and Avignon). His poetry was praised by Judah Al-ḥarizi. Schirmann, ii, pp. 275f. 70.

ISAAC (HA-YIṢHARI) BEN ZERAḤYAH HALLEVI. 12th century. Spain (Gerona). Father of Zeraḥyah Hallevi (see below). 22.

JACOB BEN ME'IR (TAM) (*Encyclopaedia Judaica* under 'Tam'). *c.*1100–71. France (Ramerupt); grandson of Rashi. Leading halakhic authority of his generation, and the first French-Jewish scholar to compose rhymed Hebrew poetry; exchanged poems with Abraham Ibn Ezra. 59.

JACOB 80.

JOSEPH IBN ABITUR BEN ISAAC ('Ibn Shatanash'). 10th–11th century. Spain, born Merida, studied in Cordoba. Settled in Palestine and environs, died in Damascus. Author of rabbinic responsa, biblical commentary and poetry. Schirmann, *Genizah*, pp. 150–1 lists all of his poems published to 1966, and prints three further items. 8.

JOSEPH (asterisked numbers with acrostic spelled יושף). 12*, 14, 28, 29, 38*, 45, 49.

JUDAH BEN SAMUEL HALLEVI. Before 1075–1141. Spain, possibly born in Tudela. Royal physician in Toledo. Travelled to Egypt with the intention of settling in Palestine, where he probably died. Poet and Jewish apologist (designated in popular sentiment a philosopher). Collected editions of his poems by H. Brody and D. Yarden. 82, 33, 40, 41, 43, 44, 51, 54, 61, 64, 82, 83.

LEVI BEN JACOB IBN AL-TABBAN (Abulfahm). Late 11th-century Spain (Saragossa). Grammarian and poet. A critical edition has been published by Dan Pagis. 55.

ME'IR BEN ISAAC NEHORAI (*Sheliaḥ Ṣibbur*, 'congregational cantor'). Died before 1096. Rhineland (Worms). Liturgical authority and poet. 5.

MOSES BEN JACOB IBN EZRA (Abu Harun). *c.*1055 – after 1135. Spain, born Granada; pupil of Isaac Ibn Ghayyat (see above) in Lucena; encouraged Judah Hallevi's early poetry. Poet, literary critic and neoplatonic philosopher. His sacred poems were published in a critical edition by S. Bernstein. 72.

MOSES. 42.

(MOSES?) BEN SHESHETH. 79.

NAHUM BEN JACOB MA'REBI. 13th-century Spain and North Africa (Fez). Translator and poet. Yonah David, *Shirey Nahum*, 1974. 50, 73, 77, 81.

SOLOMON BEN JUDAH IBN GABIROL (Avicebrol, -bron) (*Encyclopaedia Judaica* under 'Gabirol'). *c.*1020–*c.*1057. Spain (born Malaga, lived in Saragossa, died in Valencia). Friend of Samuel Ha-nagid. Neoplatonic philosopher and poet. His sacred poems have been published in a critical edition by Dov Yarden. 15, 16, 17, 18?, 21, 24, 30, 34, 35, 66.

YAHYUN. His identity is doubtful, but he is thought to have lived in Daroca, a province of Saragossa. 60.

ZERAḤYAH BEN ISAAC HALLEVI GERONDI (*Encyclopaedia Judaica* under 'Gerondi'). 12th century. Born in Spain (Gerona), settled in Provence (Narbonne and Lunel). Halakhic authority and poet; author of *Ha-ma'or* (on Al-fasi's digest). Son of Isaac ben Zeraḥyah Hallevi (see above). A critical edition has been published by I. Meiseles. 3, 4.

## The Decorative Micrographic Texts

The text utilized here for decoration is not, as has previously been claimed, that of the *Babylonian Talmud*, since on f.46b the text contains the remark that a particular argument appears *bi-gemara di-beney ma'araba*, 'in the *Jerusalem Talmud*', a comment that could not possibly come from the *Babylonian Talmud*.

It is in fact derived from the digest of the *Babylonian Talmud* by Isaac ben Jacob of Fez (1013–1103), known as Al-fasi or Rif. Close examination of the minute hand has made possible the identification of all the external and several of the internal passages, that have been compared with the Wilna edition of 1860, and partially transcribed here and located in the design in order to aid further research. Al-fasi combines with his abstract of the tractate dealing with Passover relevant matter drawn from elsewhere in the *Talmud*, but parallels to the text of tractate *Pesaḥim* only have been indicated. Where the text can be easily completed by reference to the talmudic source it has been abbreviated, and marked.... Turning-points in the design are indicated by arrows in the course of the text, and the 'route' it takes is described in the introductory paragraph to each.

Only a summary of the extremely complex material is offered here, to aid the identification of the text in question. The interested reader can find the subject-matter in full in the translation of the *Babylonian Talmud*. Al-fasi's work has itself not been translated.

f.5b BORDER: The text is Al-fasi f.20b, on *Pesaḥim* 102a (f.102b begins from the asterisk); the same as f.49b. It discusses the correct procedure for reciting the Grace and the Sanctification (*Qiddush*), when a convivial gathering is overtaken by the onset of Sabbath or Festival. It is read from the left, level with the initial word *we-'im* in the main text. INTERIOR: The text enters the design opposite the initial word *gerarta* in the main text, and is read up the inside of the animal's right foreleg.

תנו רבנן חבורה שהיו מסובין ··· ברכת המזון ‏| Border
דברי → יהודה ר יוסף או׳ אוכלין ושותי ‏| הולכין
עד שתחשך ··· * ··· הא מתניתא כבר
אידחיה לה ··· אין הלכה לה דאמ׳ ר׳ יהודה
אל ← א אמר יוסף אלא פורס מפה ‏| ואעג דשני
ר נחמן לר׳ יצחק לא סמכינן

תניא לילי שבת ולילי יום טוב יש בה קדוש לו(!) ‏| Interior
על הכוס ויש בהן הזכרה בברכת המזון ··· ···

f.6a BORDER: The text is Al-fasi f.20a, on *Pesaḥim* 101b. It discusses the circumstances in which temporary adjournment from table in order to greet a bridal party need not involve first reciting the Grace after the Meal and subsequently beginning *de novo*. It is read from the bottom right. INTERIOR: The text is Al-fasi f.19b, on *Pesaḥim* 101a. It begins slightly below the word *u-le-ma'lah le-ba'*, appearing at the end of a line of the main text, and continues round the chevron. At the asterisk it jumps to the parallel strap above.

אין טעונין ברכה ובערבי שבת במד״א בזמן ← Border
‏| שהניחו זקן [או?] חולה כשהן יוצאין טעונין
ברכה למפרע וכשהן חוזרין ··· במקומן עסקינן
ודהניחו → שם זקן או חולה כשהן יוצאין טעונין
ברכ׳ למפרע ‏| וכשהן יוצאין חוזרין (!) טעונין
ברכה לכתחלה וקשיא ··· הלכתא כרב ששת
דתניא כותה

← דאמר שמואל אין קדו[ש] * אלא במקום ← Interior
סעודה

f.37b BORDER: The text is Al-fasi f.1a, on *Pesaḥim* 2a (at the double asterisk, f.3a). It discusses whether the search for leaven at the 'light' ('*or*) of 14 Nisan means in the light of morning, or the previous twilight. The first passage begins at the bottom left, from the extreme point of the flower. Oblique lines mark the beginnings or ends of flowers, and asterisks their tips. The second passage contains the continuation of the text from the bottom left, along the inner line at the foot. INTERIOR: Al-fasi f.1b, on *Pesahim* 4a, appears in the lower leaf-spray, below the initial word *tishmor* in the main text, opposite the leaf pointing to 10 o'clock in the whorl.

Border ⎤ אור לארבעה עשר בודקין את/החמץ *
בית שמאי אומרין שתי שורות במרתף(!) ובית
הלל · · · · החצ ונות/שהן עליונות מאי אור רב *
הונא אמר נגהי ורב/יהודה לילי דכולי עלמא
בין רב הונא/ובין לרבי יהודה אור* אורתא היא
ולא פליגין / מר כי אתריה · · · · לישנא **
מעליא · · · לעולם אל/יוציא אדם דבר מגונה
מפיו שהרי עקם הכתוב שמ/ונה אותיות
מגונה/מפיו שנא' מן הבהמה? · · · ·

Interior → אשר איננה טהורה ותנא דבי ר' ישמעאל
לעולם יספר אדם · · · הנהו תרי תלמידי דהוו
יתבי → קמיה דר' · · · חד אמ' מפני מה בוצרין
בטהרה ומוסקין בטומאה · · · מורה הלכה
בישראל ⎤ עד שמורה הלכה בישראל ומנו

Interior → וישכם אברהם בבקר אל המקום אשר עמד שם
את פני ייי אף על פי שכל היום כשר למילה
א[ל]א שהזריזין מקדימין למצות נבדוק מצפרא
אמר רב נחמן בר יצחק · · ·

**f.38a BORDER:** The text is Al-fasi f.2a (from the asterisk, f.3a), on *Pesahim* 6a. It discusses the handling of leaven casually encountered on one's property during Passover and the procedure regarding abjuration of title to ownership of leaven by those setting out on a long journey before, or within thirty days of, Passover. The first passage begins from the top left and is read along the outer line. The second passage contains the continuation of the text from the top left (from the asterisk, *Pesahim* 6b), along the inner line and into the interior loops at the foot. INTERIOR: The text is Al-fasi f.2a, on *Pesahim* 5a. It begins at the centre of the foot, at 6 o'clock.

Border → חמץ ביום טוב כופה עליו את הכל[י]ן] דאמ'
רב ⎤ יהודה חמצו של גוי · · · המפרש והיוצא*
בשיירה · · · שלשים יום זקוק לבער אמר רבא
הא דאמרת → קודם שלשים יום זקוק לבער
ואזדא רבא ⎤ לטעמיה · · · אפי' · · · קודם שלשים
יום זקוק לבער · · ·

שלשים יום מאי עיבידתיהו דתניא ⎤
שואלין · · · * ומ ז היר על פסח שני אמ' רב
יהודה הבודק צריך שיבט ל → ל היכי מבטל
דאמר הכי כל חמירא דאיכא ברשותי ⎤ ולא
ידענא ביה ליבטל · · · וליבטלה כי משכח לה

Interior → דילמ' משכח לה בתר איסורא ולא ⎤ מצי
מבטיל לה דלאו ברשותי

מה(?) שא ו] ימים שאור לא ימצא בבתיכם מה
תלמוד לומר והלא כבר נאמר · · ·

**f.40b BORDER:** The text is Al-fasi f.4b, on *Pesahim* 10b. It discusses dealing with crumbs observed after the search for leaven has been conducted: whether dropped by children, who may be deemed to finish up their morsel, or by vermin, that must be deemed to secrete food in their holes. The first text begins from the top left, and is read along the inner line. The second text is Al-fasi f.4b, on *Pesahim* 11b, it begins near the top left at *yah*, and is read along the outer line. Note that the corner flowers are not

---

read in sequence. INTERIOR: The text is Al-fasi f.4a, on *Pesahim* 7b. The first text begins in the bottom right, and is read diagonally from the corner. The second text reads from the upper circumference of the lowest 'maze'.

Border → מי פיתא דנהמא אעג דעאל לההוא ⎤ ביתא
ואשכח פירורין · · · פיתא דעכברא דאמר →
רבא תינוק נכנס וככר בידו ונכנס אחריו ⎤ ומצא
פירורין אינו צריך בדיקה שדרכו של תינוק →
עכבר לפרר מתניתין דעל לביתא ובפיו · · ·

אוכלין כל חמש ושורפי' ⎤ בתחלת שש · ר'
יהודה אומר אוכלי' כל ארב' | ותולין כל
חמש · · · אפלו כל ארבע נמי לא ⎤ ניכול אמ'
רב פפא ארבע זמן סעודה לכל | הוא ולא אתי
למטעא · · · ושורפין תרומות תלויות

Interior · · · ולא לאור האבוק ⎤
לדבר שנא שבעת ימים שאור לא ימצא →
בבתי · · ·

**f.41a BORDER:** The text is Al-fasi f.5b, on *Pesahim* 21b. It discusses the legitimacy of usufruct of leaven after the time-limit for actually eating it. The psychological attitude of various types towards the material outlay involved in religious observances, and emergency circumstances warranting relaxation, are also covered. The first text begins in the bottom left. The single asterisk marks substantial lacunae, and the double asterisk *Pesahim* 25a. The second text contains the continuation, from the bottom left, along the inner line. The single asterisk marks Al-fasi f.6a, and the double asterisk substantial lacunae. INTERIOR: The first text begins at the bottom left, and is read along the back of the left hind leg of the animal. The second text – Al-fasi f.4a, on *Pesahim* 9a and 11b – is read along the top of the stag's back.

Border ⎤ ומותר בהנאתו· פשיטא לא צריכא · · · אפי'
לאחר זמנו* אמר חזקיה מנין לחמץ בפסח
שאסור בהנאה · · · התר אכילה אמ' ⎤ ר'
**יעקב אמר ר' יוחנן בכל מתרפין במקום סכנה |
חוץ מעצי אשירה דתניא · · · לכך נאמר בכל
מאדך → ואם יש לך אדם שגופו חביב עליו
ממממונו לכך

→ בכל נפשך · כי אתא רבין אמ' ר' יוחנן בכל ⎤
מתרפין · חוץ מעבודה זרה · · · תא [צ"ל תניא]
ר' אומ' · · · וכי מה ענין רוצח → אצל נערה
המאורסה אלא הרי זה בא ללמד | ונמצא למד
מקיש ** נערה מאורסה לרוצח מה רוצח יהרג
ואל יעבר אף נערה · · · לקמיה דרבא אמ' ליה

Interior → הא תנן אין חוששין שמא גררה
חולדה · · ·

⎤ ושורפין תחלת שש

**f.42b BORDER:** The text is Al-fasi f.21b, on *Pesahim* 106b. It discusses the propriety of reciting the *habdalah*-benediction, which marks the end of Sabbath or Festival, as late as the following morning. The first text is read from the bottom left, along the inner line. The second text contains the continuation from the bottom left, along the outer line. The asterisk marks Al-fasi f.22a. INTERIOR: The text begins from the tip of the dog's tail at the top right.

Border ⎤ בעא מניה רבא(!) מר נחמן בר יצחק מי שלא
קדש בערב שבת · · · מי שלא קדש בערב שבת
מקד—ש והולך כל היום כולו ומי שלא הבדי[ל

---

במוצאי שבת · · · מיהא שמעי' דאי לא אבדיל
אבסא (צ"ל אבסא) · · · טעם מקדש טעם
מבדיל מאי דלא טעם אמימר

⎤ ומידי · ובת תות למחר אבדיל · · · לא שנא
בליליא · · · ולא שנא ביממא דאמרי אמרי(!) ליה
מר | ינוקא ומר קשישא · · · ואיתינא חמרא
ואבדיל → וטעם מידי שמע מנה תלת שמע מ"י

Interior מדליקין תנא בין שאמרו להדליק ובין שאמרו
שלא להדליק שניהם

**f.43a BORDER:** The text is Al-fasi f.8a, on *Pesahim* 30b (from the asterisk, Al-fasi f.8b). It discusses the admissibility or otherwise, according to the type of glaze, for the use on Passover of earthenware vessels that have contained leaven. Also how earthenware vessels used during the year for cold foodstuffs only may be used on Passover. The first text is read along the inside line, from the top right. The second passage contains the continuation of the text along the outer line, from the top left. INTERIOR: The text begins on the left, above the lowest leaf-spray that breaks the inner line, around the hairpin bend of the curve.

Border ⎤ דודאי אסירי כי תבעי לך * דשיעי מאי
אמר · · · מדלענגין יין נסך דדרש מרימר →
קוניא בו[ין] אוכמ י בין חוארי בין ירוקי שרי | אמר
ליה זה תשמישו · · · כרב זביד דאמ' ירוקא
אסיר משום → דמצריף וככר בר ירנא ליה
במסכ' עבודת

→ ודרא מקשין הכא מדרמימר לאו מירקוקא
אל[א] מחוארי ואוכאמי מקשינן · · · חוץ מבית
השאור הואיל וחמוצו → קשה ואמר אביי ובית
חרוסת כבית השאור | שחמוצו קשה ראמי אמר
רבא · · · ושליט' בהו אוירא אסירי והאידנא

Interior ואין טהורין דברים שנשתמש בהן על ידי צונן
כגון כוסות וצליחיות וקיתונות מדיחן ומטבילן
והם טהורין · · ·

**f.46b BORDER:** The text is Al-fasi f.12b, on *Pesahim* 42b. It discusses various fermented liquids that may not be retained unopened through Passover, and the crucial factor of their dilution with water, and their constituting 'juice' only. The first text is read along the outer line, from the bottom left. The second passage contains the continuation of the text along the inner line, from the bottom right (from the first asterisk, Al-fasi f.14a, and from the second asterisk, *Pesahim* 43a). INTERIOR: The text is read from the head of the fox at the foot, and along its back.

Border ⎤ הא דתנן שכר המדי · · · ובגמרא דבני מערבא
אמרי וכולהו על ידי מוי כתה הבבלי משום
קומניתא דאומא דאית בהו → חמץ האדומי
דרמו ביה שערי זיתוס | המצרי תאני רב
יוסף · · · על פי קדירה ושואבת את → הזוהמא
וקולן של סופרן[י]ם מהכא

⎤ אמרי רבנן נמי דלא לאקל (צ"ל לקי) הני מלי
היכא דליכא כזית · · · * מתניתין בצק שבסדקי
ערבה אם יש ב— · · · כזית במקום אחד חייב לבער
| על חמץ דגן גמור · · · * ועל עירובו בלא
כלום א"ע"ג דאמור רבנן על עירובו ולא כלום
מילקא הוא דלא

Interior כתה הבבלי ושכר המדי וחמץ האדומי וזיתוס
המצרי · · ·

f.47a BORDER: The text is Al-fasi f.14a, on *Pesaḥim* 46a. It discusses the complications on the eve of Passover regarding disposal of *ḥallah* (the priestly portion of dough) that may have become ritually unfit for consumption by priests; and the difference in status of the relevant law in Palestine, where it is a biblical ordinance, and elsewhere, where its application rests on rabbinical authority only. The first text is read along the outer line, from the bottom left. The second passage contains the continuation of the text along the inner line, from the bottom left (the asterisk marks Al-fasi f.14b). INTERIOR: The text continues at the bottom right, from the point of the leaf-spray.

Border | כיצד מפרישין חללה(!) בטומאה · · · ובל
ימצא אלא מפר—ישה ומנחתה עד הערב ואם
החמיץ[ה החמיצה· תניא ר' אומר · · ·]דהא דר'
אליעזר שיבא בהך → אחריתי דר' אליעזר
דאמ' אף הרוד'

→ ונותן לתוך הסל הסל מצרפ(י)ן | לחלה וחד
טעמ' היא וכבר פסק · · · ואמ' ר' חנינ' בעני)
(צ"ל כעבין) →· · דאין נושכות זו בזו הסל מצרפן
| לחלה אלא מידהו הני מלי בארץ ישראל · · ·
לא לגדול ולא לגדול(!) ולפי

Interior | אלא מידהו הני מילי בארץ ישראל דחלה
דאוריתא היא וכיון שהיא · · ·

f.49b BORDER: The text is Al-fasi f.20a, on *Pesaḥim* 100a–b; paralleling the material on f.5b. The first passage is read along the inner line, from the top left. The second contains the continuation of the text along the outer line, from the top left. INTERIOR: The text begins at the foot, to the left of the dark-edged 'nipple'.

Border | תנו רבנן בני חבורה שהיו מסבין · · · אוכלין
והולכי' עד שתחשך → גמרו כוס ראשון מברך
עליו ברכ' | המזון והשני · · · אין הלכה לא כר'
יהודה ולא כר' יוסי אלא · · · מידהו מידהו(!) אע"ג
דאדחיא → לא גמרינן מינא הא דגמור'

→ סעודתידהו מקמיה וקדיש יומא ואו[דמשו ידהו
קדיש יומא מדקדמינן(!) ומברכ' · · · אומר עליו
→ קדוש היום אמאי ונמרינהו אחד | כסא אמ'
ר' הונא · · · חבילות חבילות ואי קשיא לך יום
טוב

Interior | חברי מסובי ועקרו רגליה

f.50a BORDER: The text is Al-fasi f.20b, on *Pesaḥim* 103b (from the asterisk, Al-fasi f.21b). It discusses sundry benedictional formulae, and the accompanying light-ceremony, of *habdalah*, to mark the conclusion of Sabbath or Festival. It is read along the outer line, from the top left. INTERIOR: The text continues round three rectangular patterns. A *Upper rectangle*: The text begins near the top at the left, at the apex of the highest complete chevron. B *Central rectangle*: The text begins at the bottom right, and continues into the indents. C *Lower rectangle*: The text appears to begin at the top left.

Border | → והמבדיל לא יפחות משלש [והמוסיף לא
יוסיף] על | שבע אמ' שמואל המבדיל · · · הוה
אמרינן המבדיל → בין קדש לחול * ואפכינן
סילתי | אפילו הכי הא נהגו העם · · · מעין
חתימ'

---

Interior | אבוקה להבדלה מצ—וה מן המובחר
והמבדי|ל בין קדש משלש (?· צ"ל וא"ר) יוסי
עד שבע ואעג דאמר ר—ב בין דאמר קדושת
שב[ת לקדשת יום טוב הבדלת והלכתא

| אמימר ומר זוטרא ורב אשי הוו יתבי
בסעודת(!) וקאי עלוהי רב אחא בריה דרב—א
אמימר בריך על כל כסא | וכסא מר זוטרא בריך
אבסא קמא ואבסא דברכתא (צ"ל דבתרא) רב
אשי בריך אבסא קמא — ותו לא בריך אמ' רב
[אחא] בריא דרבא

— א מריה אנא בי | המבדיל בין קדש לחול בין
אור לחשך בין ישראל לגוים — בין יום השביעי
לש[שת ימי המעשה זאת היא הבדלתו של ר
יהודה הנשיא

## The Commentary

In the upper and lower margins of ff.20a–36b there is a commentary, written in a minute but beautifully clear hand, headed *Perush ha-hallel le-rabbeynu shelomoh*, 'Commentary on the "*Hallel*" [in the sense of *Haggadah*][49] by Rabbenu Solomon'. The title *rabbenu* ('our master'), as opposed to *rabbi* ('my master'), paying posthumous respect to an outstanding juridical authority, was closely restricted in the Middle Ages. Among those to whom it was applied – indeed, the only one whose name was Solomon – is 'Rashi' (Solomon ben Isaac of Troyes, 1040–1105), and Rashi did, indeed, comment in passing on a number of matters in the *Haggadah*.[50] However, had this commentary been a genuine work of Rashi, his own celebrity would surely have kept it in the public domain along with his other works, instead of allowing it to be neglected; but certain comments in it can hardly be credited to Rashi himself. The same considerations would equally deny its authorship to Rashi's grandson, Samuel ben Me'ir, under whose name the second part of it was ultimately to appear in print.[51] Rosin[52] denies it to Samuel ben Me'ir on grounds of language, style and some of its content. But what must be regarded as conclusive evidence against his authorship, as also that of his grandfather, occurs in the unpublished first part which Rosin will not have known. On f.21b, in the lower margin, the reason given for the preference of spits made of pomegranate-wood for the roasting of the paschal lamb is because of the taste that it imparted to the meat. Neither Samuel, nor his grandfather, could possibly have been ignorant of the talmudic discussion of the *Mishnah*,[53] where it is made clear that the reason for the choice is because pomegranate-wood does not sweat.

At the end of the first part (f.27b) a statement, formulated in the first person singular, declares that the author intends to proceed with a commentary on the text of the *Haggadah* itself, as distinct from the foregoing explanation of the ceremonial. What then follows is a commentary that has been printed under the name of Samuel ben Me'ir. We must consequently assume that – unless the author of the first part was a plagiarist – the same person is responsible for both. In the sentence here

---

referred to, six letters carry a flourish. The first, over the word *nishlemu*, might be a glance at the name of an unidentifiable Solomon. The sequence of letters, *shin* (or *lamed*: the flourish is midway), *kaph*, *waw*, *taw* (or *he*), *shin*, *gimel*, yields neither a name nor any obvious abbreviation.

While we must resign ourselves for the time being to the author's unidentifiability, two of his comments might point the road for further enquiry. On f.20b, in the lower margin, he explains the custom of using parsley (Hebrew: *KaRPaS*) for the first herb by its being an anagram of *PeReKh*, 'hard labour' and *s[amekh]*, the initial letter of *Sebaloth*, 'burdens'. With the substitution of *siman* (borrowed from Greek, *sēmeion*), 'sign', 'miracle', this is found in the *Manhig*[54] of Abraham ben Nathan Yarhi (i.e. of Lunel), *c*.1155–1215, who was born in Avignon. The second comment (f.33a) relates to Rabbi Judah's tripartite grouping of the ten plagues according to their initials (f.28a). The author explains this as being because the first three plagues ('blood', 'frogs' and 'lice') were ecological, the next three ('wild beasts', 'cattle-plague' and 'boils') 'accidental', implying 'epidemic', while the last triad ('hail', 'locusts' and 'darkness') were climatic, the tenth plague ('death of the firstborn') being appended, as itself asymmetrical. It should be noted that the motive credited to Rabbi Judah is a purely taxonomical one, with no hint at any non-miraculous causes. Even so, the comment is redolent of the more speculative atmosphere of Spanish and Provençal Jewry rather than of the down-to-earth attitude of the Jewish communities of the Rhineland and Northern France. A quite superficial search has not run the notion to earth in the Jewish philosophers;[55] conceivably it is an original idea.

[1] *Ex.* 5, 1; 8, 23; 10, 9, etc. [2] *Ex.* 12, 12–13. [3] *The Hebrew Passover* (1963), especially chaps 3–6. [4] *Mishnah, Pesaḥim* X. [5] *Ex.* 8, 15(19). [6] *Ex.* 14, 31. [7] *Ex.* 15, 2. [8] *Mekhilta, Shirta* 3, ed. I. H. Weiss, f.44a, English translation by J. Z. Lauterbach, ii, p. 24. [9] *Pirqey de-Rabbi Eliezer*, chap. 43; *Midrash Gan 'eden we-Gehinnam*, ed. A. Jellinek, *Beth Ha-midrash* 5, p. 51, and associated texts; L. Ginzberg, *The Legends of the Jews*, 3, p. 30, 6, p. 10, n. 54. [10] See *Encyclopaedia Judaica* (hereafter: *Enc. Jud.*) 6, 275–98 (coloured illustrations following 300), with profuse illustration, and bibliography. [11] 'Jewish Antecedents'; 'Rylands Haggadah', pp. 131, 148f, 153f; Narkiss, *Golden Haggadah*, pp. 43f. [12] *La Haggada enluminée*, index, pp. 500–5. [13] Cambridge University Library, MS T.-S. K. 10.1 (*genizah* fragment, Catalonia, early 14th century), and Add. 1203 (Catalonia, 14th–15th century); Narkiss, pp. 99–101. [14] Roth, *BJRL* 43, 1960, pp. 134f; Narkiss, pp. 42f. [15] *Mal.* 3, 23–4 (4, 5–6). [16] Narkiss, pp. 44, 56f. In this whole chapter, as in the detailed description of MS Rylands below, my reliance upon Narkiss' work in particular will be obvious, and my debt to him is gratefully acknowledged. For a specimen of the Hispano-Moresque type, see the Mocatta *Haggadah*. [17] Narkiss, pp. 58–67, pls XXVI–XLV (figs 123–54); Metzger, index, p. 502; *Enc. Jud.* 7, 1084, fig. 7, 1099. [18] Narkiss, pp. 67–9, pls XLVI–LIX (figs 155–208), pl. LI (figs 173–88); Metzger, pp. 415–24. [19] Narkiss, pp. 78–84, pls LX–LXXIV (figs 209–45), LI (figs 211, 233); Metzger, pp. 424–30; *Enc. Jud.* 7, 1081, fig. 2, 1199. [20] Narkiss, pp. 93–9, pls. LXXXIX–CIV (figs 283–305); Metzger, pp. 414–15; *Enc. Jud.* 7, 1083, fig. 4. [21] Narkiss, pp. 99–100, pl. CV (figs 306–7). [22] Narkiss, pp. 100–101, pl. CV (figs 308–9). [23] Sassoon Catalogue ('*Ohel Dawid*), i, pp. 303–4, with monochrome plates; Metzger, p. 478, index p. 501, pl. LIX (figs 336, 339); *Enc. Jud.* 7, 1084, fig. 5. [24] Müller-von Schlosser; Roth, *Sarajevo*; Metzger, index, p. 505; *Enc. Jud.* 7, 1086, fig. 10, 1099, facing p. 1132. [25] Roth, *BJRL* 43, 1960, p. 137; Sierra, pp. 229–43. [26] Metzger, pp. 407–8. [27] Scheiber; *Enc. Jud.* 7, 1086, fig. 9, 1099–1100; Metzger, index.

p. 500. [28] Metzger, p. 19, n. 5. Described by M. Narkiss in *Ha-Aretz* (Hebrew), 26 March 1956. [29] Metzger, pp. 413–14; Roth, *BJRL* 43, 1960, p. 145. [30] *BJRL* 43, 1960, p. 145. [31] *Catalogue*, pp. 86–93. [32] *Catalogue*, p. 88. [33] See e.g. *Midrash Rabbah, Ex.* 11, 3 (ed. Wilna, f.23a); Ginzberg, *Legends*, 2, p. 343. [34] Metzger, p. 81. [35] *Catalogue*, p. 91. [36] *Catalogue*, pp. 91f. [37] 'The Micrography of the Catalan *Maḥzor* and its Symbolism', to appear shortly in Ulrich Ernst and Jeremy Adler (eds), *Changing Forms of Visual Poetry*, Wolfenbütteler Forschungen. A further study by her, of the relationship of the *Haggadah* micrography to that of the other two MSS, will appear in a future issue of the *Bulletin of the John Rylands Library*. She also contemplates a study of the micrography in the Mocatta Library *Haggadah* (MS 1), in University College London. [38] I must again emphasize my dependence on (and gratitude to) Narkiss, whose fuller presentation should be studied (pp. 92f). [39] Roth, *BJRL* 43, 1960, p. 142. [40] See above, n. 37. [41] *BJRL* 36, 1953–4, pp. 468–83, see especially p. 473. [42] Narkiss, pp. 95f, 98. [43] *Pesaḥim* X, 7. [44] *Pesaḥim* 118a. [45] *JQR New Series* 19, 1929, pp. 243f. [46] Thus f.54a, l.5 (ignoring rubric), *be-ṭob* (Finkelstein, p. 245, n. 21); f. 54b, l.4, *torathekha she-limmad[tanu]*, p. 249, n. 20; l.7, *'al* (not *we-'al*), p. 250, n. 22; f.56a, l.2, *boneh yerushalayim*, p. 256, n. 46. [47] For these see Finkelstein, pp. 240–1. [48] See Loewe, p. 358f. [49] See p. 76, n. 1. [50] See Buber, *Sepher ha-'orah*; S. Hurwitz, *Maḥzor Vitry*, pp. 283f; *Enc. Jud.* 7, 1092. [51] In Ḥabib Toledano's *Haggadah (Derekh 'emunah)*, Leghorn, 1838; subsequently also in *Haggadah shel Pesaḥ*, Stettin, 1865; *Haggadah 'im 'asarah perushim*, Wilna, 1875; and Kasher, *Haggadah shelemah*. [52] pp. 11f. [53] *Pesaḥim* VII, 1, f.74a. [54] Goldberg, f.82b. David Abudarham, writing in Seville in 1340, has a third version: *samekh* (numerical value 60) for the 60 myriads (600,000) Israelites who left Egypt (*Ex.* 12,37). Ed. Venice, 1506, f.47a, col.ii. [55] An abbreviated version is given by Yom Ṭob ben Abraham of Seville (Riṭba'), *c.* 1250–1330; Kasher, p. 51 (Hebrew pagination), n. 558.

# Index and Bibliographies

## Index of the Poems

The Hebrew titles of the eighty-three poems in the present MS are here listed alphabetically, together with the number of the folio on which each appears, and the number of its translation.

## Bibliography of the Poems

The following list provides the basic reference-literature for the detailed textual study of each of the poems. The majority have been printed, but in many cases are of extreme rarity. The entry in Israel Davidson's *'Oṣar Ha-shirah we-ha-piyyuṭ* indicates, in the case of well-known poems, the earliest printed source; a number were known to Davidson from manuscripts only. Where the existence of a modern critical edition is known to me, it is cited, and should obviously be the starting-point for any further study.

The Rylands *Haggadah* is related to a group of other *Haggadah* manuscripts listed by C. Roth (*Bulletin of the John Rylands Library*, 43, 1960, pp. 135–7):

i   The Sarajevo *Haggadah*.
ii  The Kaufmann *Haggadah* (Budapest, Academy of Sciences MS 422).
iii British Library MS Add. 27210.
iv  British Library MS Or. 2884.
v   British Library MS Or. 1404.
vi  British Library MS Or. 2737.
vii Bologna University MS 2559.
viii A manuscript in private ownership (in 1960) in Jerusalem, *olim* Prado *Haggadah* (Pollack, Rome).
ix  Parma, Biblioteca Palatina MS 2411.

In addition to these are:

x   The Sassoon *Haggadah*, now in the Israel Museum, pressmark 181/41 (Sassoon Catalogue no. 514, vol. i, pp. 303–4; Sotheby's Sale Catalogue, 5 November 1975, no. 11, pp. 31–6).
xi  The Mocatta Library *Haggadah* (MS 1), University College London.

The majority of the MSS contain supplementary poems – in some cases one or two only, in others on a scale similar to the Rylands *Haggadah*. Although I have not been able to collate the individual texts, I indicate the presence of any of the poems (indicated here by the numerals assigned them in this edition) in those MS which I have been able to survey, namely: i, iii, iv, v, vi and xi. Most of the items may be found in numerous other MSS outside the aforementioned group, and what is here provided merely assists full collation. For similar reasons I have noted, where relevant, the inclusion of poems in MSS of the former Sassoon Collection as indexed in its *Catalogue* ('*Ohel Dawid*, D. S. Sassoon, here abbreviated to 'Sassoon') and have stated how many MSS in that great collection contain it.

1   f.2a. ANONYMOUS. Davidson, iii, *pe*, 144; *i* f.40a; *iii* f.95a; *iv* f.64a; *vi* f.32b; *x* before f.163; *xi* f.54a; Sassoon, 2 copies.

2   f.3a. ANONYMOUS. Davidson, iii, *mem* 166; *i* f.42b; *iii* f.96a; *vi* f.33b; *x* before f.163; *xi* f.57b (beginning only); Sassoon, 2 copies.

3   ff.5b–7b. ZERAḤYAH BEN ISAAC HALLEVI GERONDI. Davidson, i, *'aleph* 5950; Isaac Mar-'Eli, *Ha-me'asseph* (ed. Ben-Zion Abraham Cuenca, Jerusalem), 13 part ii, 1908, pp. 1–8; *iii* f.18b; *v* f.23b; Meiseles, pp. 85f.

4   f.7b. ZERAḤYAH BEN ISAAC HALLEVI GERONDI. Davidson, ii, *zayin* 263; Isaac Mar-Eli (see no. 3), p. 9a; *iii* f.21b; *v* f.25b; Meiseles, pp. 97f.

5   f.8a. ME'IR BEN ISAAC NEHORAI. Davidson, iii, *lamed* 726; *i* f.101a; *iii* f.22b; *iv* f.20a; *v* f.27b; Sassoon, 7 copies. MS exhibits the poem in the form known from the *Romania* rite: Wallenstein, *BJRL* 43, 1960, p. 248, n. 5.

6   f.37b. ISAAC IBN GHAYYAT. Davidson, ii, *yod* 2044; *i* f.56a; *iii* f.56b; *v* f.30b; Sassoon, 5 copies.

7   f.37b. ISAAC IBN GHAYYAT. Davidson, ii, *kaph* 229; *i* f.23a; *iii* f.57a; *v* f.30b; Sassoon, 4 copies.

8   f.37b. Possibly JOSEPH IBN ABITUR. Davidson, iii, *nun* 766; *i* f.64b; *iii* f.71a; *v* f.31a. Not listed among his poems by Schirmann, *Genizah*, pp. 150–1.

9   f.38a. ISAAC IBN GHAYYAT. Davidson, ii, *yod* 2577; *i* f.65b; *iii* f.71b; *v* f.32b.

10  f.38b. ISAAC IBN GHAYYAT. Davidson, ii, *yod* 2367; A.M. Habermann, *Mishor* 6, nos 245/6, 1945, p. 6; *i* f.69a; *iii* f.80a; *v* f.32b.

11  f.38b. JUDAH HALLEVI. Davidson, ii, *yod* 3819; Brody, 3, pp. 15–16; Yarden, 2, pp. 343–5; *iii* f.60b; *v* f.333; Sassoon, 5 copies.

12  f.38b. JOSEPH (acrostic יוסף). Davidson, ii, *yod* 2052; *i* f.58a; *iii* f.61a; *v* f.33b; Sassoon, 5 copies.

13  f.39a. ANONYMOUS. Davidson, i, *'aleph* 2202; *i* f.58b; *iii* f.62a; *v* f.34b.

14  f.39a. JOSEPH. Davidson, ii, *yod* 1887; *i* f.59a; *iii* f.62b; *v* f.34b; Sassoon, 9 copies.

15  f.39b. SOLOMON IBN GABIROL. Davidson, iii, *shin* 776; Yarden, 2, p. 337, no. 106; *i* f.59b; *iii* f.66a; *v* f.37a; Sassoon, 9 copies.

16  f.39b. SOLOMON IBN GABIROL. Davidson, iii, *shin* 1350; Yarden, 2, p. 337, no. 107; *i* f.59b; *iii* f.66a; *v* f.37a.

17  f.39b. SOLOMON IBN GABIROL. Davidson, ii, *beth* 407 (cf. no. 15); Yarden, 2, pp. 338–44, no. 108; *i* f.66b; *v* f.37b; Sassoon, 4 copies.

18  f.40a. Possibly SOLOMON IBN GABIROL. (Not included by Yarden.) Davidson, ii, *mem* 145; *i* f.60b; *iii* f.37b; *xi* f.10b; Sassoon, 3 copies.

19  f.40a–b. ISAAC. Davidson, iii, *shin* 776 (cf. no. 15).

20  f.40b. ISAAC. Davidson, ii, *yod* 994; *i* f.61b; *iii* f.68a.

21  f.40b. SOLOMON IBN GABIROL. Davidson, iii, *shin* 776; Yarden, 2, pp. 344–6; *iii* f.68a.

22  f.40b. ISAAC BEN ZERAḤYAH HALLEVI. Davidson, ii, *yod* 1682; *i* f.62a; *iii* f.68b; *v* f.38b; Sassoon (possibly), 4 copies.

23  f.41a. ISAAC IBN GHAYYAT. Davidson, ii, *yod* 662; Schirmann, i, p. 304, no. 114; *iii* f.70b; *v* f.39a; Sassoon, 1 copy.

24  f.41a. SOLOMON IBN GABIROL. Davidson, iii, *shin* 2046; Yarden, 2, p. 469, no. 145; *i* f.68a; *iii* f.78b; *v* f.39b; Sassoon, 1 copy.

25  f.41a. ANONYMOUS. Davidson, iii, *nun* 687; *i* f.57a; *iii* f.77b; *v* f.39a; Sassoon, 4 copies; Wallenstein, *BJRL* 43, 1960, p. 250, n. 2.

26  f.41b. ISAAC IBN GHAYYAT. Davidson, ii, *yod* 3668; Schirmann, i, pp. 306–7, no. 116; *i* f.57a; *v* f.40b.

27  f.41b. ABRAHAM IBN EZRA. Davidson, i, *'aleph* 8161; Levin, i, p. 334; *v* f.49a; Sassoon, 1 copy.

28  f.42a. JOSEPH. Davidson, ii, *yod* 3198; *i* f.77b; *iii* f.80a; *v* f.48b; Sassoon, 13 copies.

29  f.42a. JOSEPH. Davidson, iii, *shin* 1840; *i* f.66a; *iii* f.72a.

30  f.42a–b. SOLOMON IBN GABIROL. Davidson, ii, *yod* 96; Yarden, 2, pp. 519–20, no. 180; *i* f.94a; *v* f.41a.

31  f.42b. ABRAHAM IBN EZRA. Davidson, i, *'aleph* 1905; Levin, i, pp. 254–6; *v* f.44a; Sassoon, 7 copies.

32  f.42b. ISAAC IBN GHAYYAT. Davidson, ii, *kaph* 332; *v* f.44b; Sassoon, 3 copies.

33  f.43a. JUDAH HALLEVI. Davidson, ii, *gimel* 159; Brody, 3, pp. 3–4; Yarden, 2, p. 325; *i* f.71a; *iii* f.83a.

34  f.43a. SOLOMON IBN GABIROL. Davidson, iii, *shin* 1224; Yarden, 2, p. 324, no. 96; *i* f.56b; *i* f.56b; *v* f.42a; Sassoon, 11 copies.

35  f.43a. SOLOMON IBN GABIROL. Davidson, iii, *shin* 2103; Yarden, i, p. 20, no. 12; *i* f.71a; Sassoon, 22 copies.

36  f.43a. DAVID BEN ELIEZER (possibly David ben Eleazar Ibn Paquda). Davidson, ii, *daleth* 334.

37  f.43a. ANONYMOUS. Unique? Wallenstein, *BJRL* 43, 1960, pp. 250, 253.

38  f.43b. JOSEPH (acrostic יוסף). Wallenstein, *BJRL* 43, 1960, p. 250, n. 4; *i* f.79b; *v* f.47b.

39  f.43b. ISAAC. Davidson, ii, *yod* 197; *v* f.42b; Sassoon, 1 copy.

40  f.43b. JUDAH HALLEVI. Unique? Wallenstein, *BJRL* 43, 1960, pp. 253–65.

41  f.44a. JUDAH HALLEVI. Davidson, ii, *yod* 4136; Brody, 3, pp. 152–3; Yarden, 1, pp. 218–20; *i* f.69b; *iii* f.61a; Sassoon, 2 copies.

42  f.44a. MOSES. Unique? Wallenstein, *BJRL* 44, 1961, pp. 239–45.

43  f.44b. JUDAH HALLEVI. Davidson, ii, *yod* 945; Brody, 3, pp. 18–19; Yarden, 2, pp. 350–1; *i* f.69b; *iii* f.61a; *v* f.48b.

44  f.44b. JUDAH HALLEVI. Davidson, *BJRL* 43, 1960, pp. 265–71; *i* f.43b.

45  f.45a. JOSEPH. Davidson, ii, *yod* 3222; *i* f.85b; Sassoon, 1 copy.

46  f.45a. (possibly Abraham) ḤARIZI. Davidson, ii, *heth* 87; *iii* f.81a; Sassoon, 1 copy.

47  f.45b. ABRAHAM IBN EZRA. Wallenstein, *BJRL* 44, 1961, pp. 245–56; Levin, ii, pp. 558–60.

48  f.45b. ABRAHAM IBN EZRA. Davidson, iii, *ṣade* 189; Levin, i, pp. 78–80; *v* f.44a.

49  f.46b. JOSEPH. Davidson, ii, *yod* 658; *i* f.80b; *v* f.44b.

50  f.46a. NAHUM BEN JACOB. Davidson, iii, *nun*, 602; Schirmann, ii, pp. 461–2, no. 398; David, pp. 12–13; *iii* f.73b; Sassoon, 3 copies.

51  f.46a. JUDAH HALLEVI. Davidson, ii, *yod* 3934; Brody, 3, pp. 182–3; Yarden, 1, pp. 185–7; Sassoon, 2 copies.

52  f.46b. ABRAHAM IBN EZRA. Davidson, ii, *yod* 1489; Levin, i, pp. 347f; *iii* f.97a; *v* f.41b; Sassoon, 4 copies.

53  ff.46b–47a. ABRAHAM IBN EZRA. Davidson, i, *'aleph* 2596; Levin, i, pp. 269–70; Sassoon, 3 copies.

54  f.47a. JUDAH HALLEVI. Davidson, ii, *yod* 3667; Brody, 3, p. 40; Yarden, 2, p. 378; *iii* f.70b; Sassoon, 4 copies.

55  f.47a. LEVI IBN AL-TABBAN. Davidson, iii, *lamed* 1192; Pagis, p. 62; *iii* f.83a; *v* f.45a; Sassoon, 1 copy.

56  f.47a. ḤIYYA IBN AL-DA'UDI. Davidson, ii, *kaph* 312; *i* f.71a; *iii* f.83b; *v* f.44b; Sassoon, 5 copies.

57  f.47b. (Attributed to ABRAHAM IBN EZRA.) Davidson, iii, *shin* 1414; iv, *'aleph* 637*; excluded by Levin, even from doubtful attributions; *v* f.45a.

58  f.47b. ISAAC (acrostic ישחק). Davidson, iii, *nun* 732; *v* f.45b.

59  f.48a. JACOB BEN ME'IR (TAM). Davidson, iii, *shin* 987; i, *'aleph* 4007; *i* f.72b; *iii* f.84b; *v* f.45b; Sassoon, 1 copy.

60  f.48a. Possibly YAḤYUN. Davidson, ii, *yod* 2505; *iii* f.84b; *v* f.46a; Sassoon, 3 copies.

61  ff.48b, 51b. JUDAH HALLEVI. Davidson, ii, *yod* 2413; Brody, 3, pp. 15–16; Yarden, 2, pp. 345–7; *iii* f.59b; Sassoon, 8 copies.

62  f.48b. ISAAC IBN GHAYYAT. Davidson, ii, *yod* 3356; *i* f.73a; *iii* f.59b; *v* f.46b.

63  f.49a. ABRAHAM IBN EZRA. Davidson, iii, *mem* 1132; Levin, i, pp. 191–3.

64  f.49a. JUDAH HALLEVI. Davidson, ii, *yod* 1865; Brody, 3, pp. 52–3; Yarden, 2, pp. 392–5; *i* f.67a; *iii* f.73a; *v* f.47a; Sassoon, 1 copy.

65  f.49b. ISAAC IBN GHAYYAT. Davidson, ii, *yod* 2954; D. Yarden, *Hadoar* 40, 1961, p. 351; *v* f.50a.

66  f.50a. SOLOMON IBN GABIROL. Davidson, iii, *shin* 2214; Yarden, 2, p. 334, no. 103; *i* f.64a; *iii* f.56b; *v* f.47b.

67  f.50a. ISAAC IBN GHAYYAT. Davidson, ii, *yod* 177; A. M. Habermann, *Ha-Aretz* 31 March 1961; *iii* f.78b; Sassoon, 1 copy.

68  f.50a–b. ANONYMOUS. Wallenstein, *BJRL* 44, 1961, pp. 263–4; *v* f.42a.

69  f.50b. ABRAHAM IBN EZRA. Davidson, i, *'aleph* 5843; Levin, i, pp. 245–7; *v* f.42a; Sassoon, 7 copies.

70  f.50b. ISAAC BEN JUDAH 'HA-SENIRI'. Davidson, iii, *nun* 678.

71  f.51a. ANONYMOUS. Wallenstein, *BJRL* 44, 1961, pp. 263–4. Unique?

72  f.51a. ISAAC IBN EZRA. Davidson, ii, *yod* 1136; Bernstein, pp. 28–9, no. 26; *i* f.69a; *iii* f.58b; *v* f.48a; Sassoon, 3 copies.

73  f.51a–b. NAHUM BEN JACOB. Davidson, ii, *he*, 944; Schirmann, ii, p. 460, no. 397; David, pp. 7–9; *v* f.50a; Sassoon, 3 copies.

74  f.51b. ISAAC IBN GHAYYAT. Davidson, ii, *yod* 1954; *iii* f.60b; *v* f.46b; Sassoon, 6 copies.

75  f.52a. ISAAC IBN GHAYYAT. Davidson, i, *'aleph* 8559; *i* f.57b; *iii* f.59b; *v* f.41a.

76  f.52a. ISAAC IBN GHAYYAT. Davidson, ii, *he* 416; *iii* f.62a; *v* f.48a.

77  f.52b. NAHUM BEN JACOB. Davidson, iii, *nun* 20; David, pp. 10–11; *i* f.73a; *iii* f.93b; Sassoon, 1 copy.

78  ff.52b–53a. ANONYMOUS. Davidson, i, *'aleph* 2571; *i* f.79a; *iii* f.94b; *v* f.49b.

79  f.53a. MOSES(?) BEN SHESHETH. Davidson, iii, *resh* 832; Sassoon, 1 copy.

80  f.53a. JACOB. Davidson, ii, *yod* 1086; *i* f.67b; *iii* f.73a.

81  f.53b. NAHUM BEN JACOB. Davidson, iii, *nun* 2966; David, pp. 14–15; *i* f.80a; *iii* f.62b; Sassoon, 1 copy.

82  ff.5b–9a (margins). JUDAH HALLEVI. Davidson, i, *'aleph* 7806; Brody, 4, pp. 57–63; Yarden, 2, pp. 315–22. The MS exhibits a few lacunae: essential corrections (from collation with *'ayyeleth ha-shaḥar*, liturgical supplement, Mantua, 1612, ff.101–104) are included between [ ]. *i* f.53b; *iii* f.16b; *v* f.26a.

83  f.9b (margins). JUDAH HALLEVI. Davidson, ii, *yod* 3134; Brody, 4, pp. 63–4; Yarden, 2, pp. 322–4; *i* f.55b; *iii* f.18a; *v* f.27a; Sassoon, 1 copy.

## Bibliography

The Bible is cited according to the Hebrew chapter- and verse-division. Where that of the King James' Version differs, this is added in brackets.

ABUDARHAM, DAVID *Tephilloth kol ha-shanah*, Venice 1506

AL-FASI, ISAAC *Hilkhoth Rab Alphas*, ed. Wilna 1860

AVRIN, LEILA *Micrography as Art*, Paris-Jerusalem 1981

—'The Micrography of the Catalan *Maḥzor* and its symbolism', in Ulrich Ernst and Jeremy Adler (eds), *Changing Forms of Visual Poetry*, Wolfenbütteler Forschungen (forthcoming)

*BABYLONIAN TALMUD see Talmud, Babylonian*

BERNSTEIN, SHIMEON MOSHEH IBN 'EZRA. *Shirey ha-qodesh*, Tel Aviv 1957

BIALIK, Ḥ N., and Y. Ḥ. RAWNITZKI *Shirey Shelomoh ben Yehudah Ibn Gabirol*, 2nd ed., 7 vols, Tel Aviv 1928–32

BOHIGAS, P. *La ilustración y la decoración del libro manuscrito en Cataluña*, 2 vols, Barcelona 1965

BRAUDE, WILLIAM G. *see Midrash Psalms; Pesikta de-Rab Kahana*

BRODY, Ḥ. *Diwan . . . Yehudah ben Shemu'el Ha-levi*, 4 vols, Berlin 1894–1930; reissue, with introduction, etc., by A. M. Habermann, Farnborough (England) 1971

BUBER, SALOMON *Sepher Ha-'orah*, Lemberg 1905

—*see Midrash Psalms*

DAVID, ABRAHAM *see Encyclopaedia Judaica ('Piyyut')*

DAVID, YONAH *Shirey Nahum*, Jerusalem 1974

DAVIDSON, ISRAEL *'Oṣar ha-shirah we-ha-piyyut. Thesaurus of Mediaeval Hebrew Poetry*, 4 vols, New York 1924–33

DOMÍNGEZ BORDONA, J. 'Miniatura', *Ars Hispaniae*, 18, Madrid 1962, pp. 17–242

*ENCYCLOPAEDIA JUDAICA* Articles 'Haggadah, Passover: Illuminated Manuscripts' (B. Narkiss), 'Commentaries' ([E.] D. Goldschmidt), 7, 1095–9, 1092–3; 'Piyyut' (E. Fleischer; includes alphabetical list of poets by A. David), 13, 573–602, Jerusalem 1971

FINKELSTEIN, LOUIS 'The Birkat Ha-mazon', *Jewish Quarterly Review*, New Series 19, 1929, pp. 211–62.

—'The Oldest Midrash: Pre-rabbinic Ideals and Teachings in the Passover *Haggadah*', *Harvard Theological Review* 31, 1938, pp. 291–317

FLEISCHER, EZRA *see Encyclopaedia Judaica ('Piyyut')*

FREEDMAN, H. *see Midrash Rabbah; Talmud, Babylonian, The Soncino Talmud*

FRIEDLANDER, H. *see Pirqey de-Rabbi 'Eli'ezer*

GESENIUS, W. *Gesenius' Hebrew Grammar*, ed. E. Kautzsch, revised by A. E. Cowley, 2nd ed., Oxford 1910

GINZBERG, LOUIS *The Legends of the Jews*, 7 vols, Philadelphia 1913–38

GOLDBERG, J. M. *Sepher Ha-manhig . . . 'Ibn Yarḥi*, Berlin 1855

GOLDSCHMIDT, ERNST DANIEL *see Encyclopaedia Judaica ('Haggadah, Passover: Commentaries')*

GOLDSTEIN, DAVID *Hebrew Manuscript Painting*, London 1985

GUTMANN, J. *Hebrew Manuscript Painting*, New York 1978

HABERMANN, A. M. *see Brody, Ḥ.*

HURWITZ, S. *Machsor Vitry*, Nuremberg 1923

KAPSTEIN, ISRAEL J. *see Pesikta de-Rab Kahana*

KASHER, MENAḤEM M. *Haggadah Shelemah*, Jerusalem 1956

LAUTERBACH, J. Z. *see Mekhilta de-Rabbi Yishma'el*

LEVIN, ISRAEL *Shirey ha-qodesh shel 'Abraham 'Ibn 'Ezra*, 2 vols, Jerusalem 1976–80

LOEWE, RAPHAEL '"Salvation" is not of the Jews', *Journal of Theological Studies*, New Series 32, 1981, pp. 341–68

MANDELBAUM, BERNARD *see Pesikta de-Rab Kahana*

MEISELES, ISAAC *Shirath Ha-Ma'or. Piyyuṭey Rabbi Zeraḥyah Ha-Levi*, Jerusalem 1984

*MEKHILTA DE-RABBI YISHMA'EL*, ed. I. H. Weiss, Vienna 1865;

English translation by J. Z. Lauterbach, 3 vols, Philadelphia 1933–5

METZGER, MENDEL *La Haggada enluminée. I Étude Iconographique et Stylistique des manuscrits enluminés et décorés de la haggada du xiii* au xvi* siècle. Études sur le judaisme médiéval*, ii, Leiden 1973

*MIDRASH PSALMS* ed. Salomon Buber, Wilna 1891; English translation by William G. Braude, 2 vols, New Haven 1959

*MIDRASH RABBAH (The Soncino Midrash)* Translated by H. Freedman and Maurice Simon, 9 vols, London 1939

*MISHNAH The Mishnah.* Translated by H. Danby, Oxford 1933

MÜLLER, DAVID HEINRICH, and JULIUS VON SCHLOSSER *Die Haggadah von Sarajevo*, 2 vols, Vienna 1898

NARKISS, BEZALEL *Hebrew Illuminated Manuscripts*, New York 1969

—*The Golden Haggadah*, 2 vols, London 1970

—*see Encyclopaedia Judaica ('Haggadah, Passover: Illuminated Manuscripts')*

—*Hebrew Illuminated Manuscripts in the British Isles. A Catalogue Raisonné*, 2 vols, Oxford 1982

PAGIS, DAN *Shirey Levi 'Ibn 'al-tabban*, Jerusalem 1968

*PESIKTA DE-RAB KAHANA* ed. Bernard Mandelbaum, 2 vols, New York 1962; English translation by William G. Braude and Israel J. Kapstein, London 1975

*PIRQEY DE-RABBI 'ELI'EZER*, ed. David Luria, Warsaw 1852; English translation by Gerald Friedlander, London 1916, reprinted New York 1971

RAWNITZKI, Y. Ḥ. *see Bialik, Ḥ. N.*

RIF *see Al-fasi, Isaac*

ROSENAU, HELEN 'Notes on the Illuminations of the Spanish *Haggadah* in the John Rylands Library', *Bulletin of the John Rylands Library*, 36, 1953–4, pp. 468–83

ROSIN, DAVID R. *Samuel b. Meïr als Schrifterklärer*, Berlin 1880

ROTH, CECIL 'Jewish Antecedents of Christian Art', *Journal of the Warburg and Courtauld Institutes*, 16, 1953, pp. 24–44

—'The John Rylands *Haggadah*', *Bulletin of the John Rylands Library*, 43, 1960, pp. 131–59

—*The Sarajevo Haggadah*, London 1963

SASSOON, DAVID *'Ohel Dawid, Descriptive Catalogue of the Hebrew and Samaritan Manuscripts in the Sassoon Library*, London, 2 vols, Oxford 1932

SCHEIBER, ALEXANDER *The Kaufmann Haggadah*, Oriental Library of the Hungarian Academy of Sciences, I, Budapest 1957

S(C)HIRMAN(N), ḤAYIM *Ha-shirah ha-'ibrith bi-sepharad u-ba-provanz*, 2 vols, Jerusalem 1954–6; 2nd ed., 4 vols, 1961

—*Shirim ḥadashim min ha-genizah*, Jerusalem 1966

SCHLOSSER, JULIUS VON *see Müller, David Heinrich*

SEGAL, J. B. *The Hebrew Passover from the earliest times to AD 70*, London Oriental Series 12, London (Oxford University Press) 1963

SIERRA, SERGIO J. 'Hebrew codices with miniatures belonging to the University of Bologna', *Jewish Quarterly Review*, New Series 43, 1953, pp. 229–48.

SIMON, MAURICE *see Midrash Rabbah*

*TALMUD, BABYLONIAN (The Soncino Talmud)*, Translated (ed. I. Epstein), *Pesaḥim*, by H. Freedman, 2 vols, London 1938

TOLEDANO, ḤABIB *Derekh 'emunah*, Leghorn 1838

WALLENSTEIN, ME'IR 'Hebrew MS. 6 in the John Rylands Library, with special reference to two hitherto unknown poems by Yehudah (Halevi?)', *Bulletin of the John Rylands Library*, 43, 1960, pp. 243–72

—'Four unpublished poems in Rylands Hebrew MS. 6 – One by Abraham (Ibn Ezra)', *Bulletin of the John Rylands Library*, 44, 1961, pp. 238–64.

YARDEN, DOV *Shirey ha-qodesh le-rabbi Shelomoh Ibn Gabirol*, 2 vols, Jerusalem 1971–3

—*Shirey ha-qodesh le-rabbi Yehudah Ha-levi*, 4 vols, Jerusalem 1978–86

ZUNZ, L. *Die Ritus des synagogalen Gottesdienstes*, Berlin 1859

—*Literaturgeschichte der synagogalischen Poesie*, Berlin 1865

# TRANSLATION OF THE MAIN TEXTS

f.2a **[Hymns for the First Night of Passover**

I[1] This and the following poem, added later to the MS, properly belong to the order of prayers for the first night of Passover beginning on f.8a. The author is unknown. There is an alphabetical acrostic.]

In Egypt, Passover did mean
    My sires, their fetters loosed, went free:
But down the years has seen
    Ill-tempered masters holding me in fee.

In Egypt, Passover did mean
    Strong-armed redemption for thy folk:
But down the years has seen
    Me silent, underneath thine anger's stroke.

In Egypt, Passover did mean
    That Thou their firstborn sons didst slay:
But down the years has seen
    My children's plots caused trouble all the way.

In Egypt, Passover did mean
    Lamb on each board, for festive meal:
But down the years has seen
    Ravening steppe-wolves, searching flocks to steal.

In Egypt, Passover did mean
    They ate in haste, all set to go:
But down the years has seen
    Me writhe as if in childbed, fraught with woe.

In Egypt, Passover did mean
    As sign upon my lintel, blood:
But down the years has seen
    My heart whirl, tossed about in trouble's flood.

In Egypt, Passover did mean
    An angel barred death from our door:
But down the years has seen
    None to protect us from the lions' roar.

f.2b In Egypt, Passover did mean
    Death's tread my threshold did avoid:
But down the years has seen
    How tyrants' will would have us all destroyed.

In Egypt, Passover did mean
    Our ransomed ones released in haste:
But down the years has seen
    The foe at us alone for battle braced.

In Egypt, Passover did mean
    Us viewed, as holy men, with grace:[2]
But down the years has seen
    Oppressors grind in poverty our face.

In Egypt, Passover did mean
    Wives from Egyptian wives asked gold:[3]

But down the years has seen
    Jewels of the mistress in her handmaid's hold.

In Egypt, Passover did mean
    Unleavened bread and herbs: bring near
The year when shall be seen
    Thy call to captives – freedom's hour is here.

As it is written: 'Because the Lord has anointed me to bring good news to the humble, He has sent me . . . to proclaim liberty to captives and release to those in prison';[4] 'Rise up, my beloved; my fairest, come away'.[5]

---

[1] The translations of all poems, other than those in the *Haggadah* text itself, have been numbered for ease of reference. [2] *Ex.* 11, 2; 12, 36; see miniature on f.18a. [3] *Ex.* 11, 2; 12, 36. [4] *Is.* 61, 1. [5] *S. of S.* 2, 10.

---

f.3a **2**

[The *Song of Songs*, breathing the air of spring, is associated with Passover in Jewish tradition, which reads the *Song* as an allegory of God's idyllic love for Israel. In this poem the concluding words of *S. of S.* 2, 10 form a refrain, and each couplet culminates in a biblical reference to the Land of Israel, some drawn from the classical 'Praise of the Land' in *Deut.* 8, 7–10. The author is unknown. There is an alphabetical acrostic.]

From a house of vain show, from a realm judged[1] by Me – 'away'
To the Land God entailed, his own ever to be,[2]
    'Come away, my beloved, away.'

From a house by a taskmaster's wiles sore oppressed – 'away'
To the Land of Canaan, and Lebanon's crest,[3]
    'Come away, my beloved, away.'

From the house of a nation that bends thy back low – 'away'
To the Land throughout which milk and honey streams flow,[4]
    'Come away, my beloved, away.'

From a house of wrath, raging in furious heat – 'away'
To the Land of the vine and the barley and wheat,[5]
    'Come away, my beloved, away.'

From a house of astrologers scouring the skies – 'away'
To the land where clear fountains and rivulets rise,[6]
    'Come away, my beloved, away.'

From the house whose lord argues, as loth to let go[7] – 'away'
To the Land of Canaan, that Hittites did know,[8]
    'Come away, my beloved, away.'

From the house where the stranger would fain seek thine end – 'away'
To the Land that thou needest no labour to tend,[9]
    'Come away, my beloved, away.'

f.3b From the house where the hypocrite robs from the poor – 'away'
To the Land from whose rocks thou canst mine iron ore,[10]
    'Come away, my beloved, away.'

From a house that spreads lies, treating truth with despite – 'away'
To the Land that to Gilead's acres has right,[11]
　'Come away, my beloved, away.'

From the house where the proud plough the furrows of wrong – 'away'
To the Land thy God watches with care, the year long,[12]
　'Come away, my beloved, away.'

From the house where grim, grilled walls a prison confine – 'away'
To the Land where for bread there grows corn, and the vine,[13]
　'Come away, my beloved, away.'

From the house where oppressors constrict, to give pain – 'away'
To the Land with more milk than its pails can contain,[14]
　'Come away, my beloved, away.'

From the house where my judgement[15] did Memphis reject – 'away'
To the Land that the Lord for his own did elect,[16]
　'Come away, my beloved, away.'

From the house where a prey-gorging beast slyly feeds – 'away'
To the Land of rich pastures, of Gilead's meads,[17]
　'Come away, my beloved, away.'

f.4a From the house of the devious haunter of ill – 'away'
To the Land of fair views from each valley and hill,[18]
　'Come away, my beloved, away.'

From the house where one plots to drag down into filth – 'away'
To the Land of fair acres, a land of rich tilth,[19]
　'Come away, my beloved, away.'

From the house where thy neck-bones are stretched, till it cracks – 'away'
To the Land of Canaan, the Perizzite's tracks,[20]
　'Come away, my beloved, away.'

From the house that, next door to death's shadow, must dread – 'away'
To the Land where thou needest not stint to eat bread,[21]
　'Come away, my beloved, away.'

From the house son and father-in-law[22] did disgust – 'away'
To the Land which, to give thee, thy God gave his trust,[23]
　'Come away, my beloved, away.'

From a house pledged to hurt, where deception abounds – 'away'
To the Land of Canaan, to beat there the bounds,[24]
　'Come away, my beloved, away.'

From a house where the grapes of wrath smother the soil – 'away'
To the Land with abundance of corn, wine and oil,[25]
　'Come away, my beloved, away.'

f.4b From the house whose lord mocks, whilst his cruelty reigns – 'away'
To the Land of Menasseh, and Ephraim's domains,[26]
　'Come away, my beloved, away.'

From the house in which darkness is doubled, may we
Next year in Jerusalem Passover see –
　'Come away, my beloved, away.'

As it is written: 'The fig-tree putteth forth green figs, and the
vines with tender grapes give a good smell. Arise, my love, my
fair one, come away.'[27]

THE END
Praise be to God in perpetuity AMEN
Courage

[1] Ex. 12, 12. [2] Josh. 22, 19. [3] Deut. 1, 7. [4] Ex. 3, 8. [5] Deut. 8, 8. [6] Deut. 8, 7. [7] Ex. 13, 15. [8] Ex. 3, 17. [9] Josh. 24, 13. [10] Deut. 8, 9. [11] Num. 39, 29. [12] Deut. 11, 12. [13] II Kings 18, 32. In the original context this refers to Assyria, not to the Land of Israel. It is doubtful whether the author was conscious of the irony. [14] Ex. 3, 17. [15] Ex. 12, 12. [16] Josh. 22, 19. [17] Cf. Num. 32, 1.

[18] Deut. 11, 11. [19] Ex. 3, 8. [20] Cf. Deut. 7, 1. [21] Deut. 8, 9. [22] The reference is apparently to Moses and Jethro; the latter, according to the Midrash (Ex. Rabbah 1, 9, on Ex. 1, 10), had been a councillor of Pharaoh, and subsequently became a proselyte to Judaism (Ex. 18, 10f). [23] Ex. 20, 12. [24] Num. 34, 2. [25] Gen. 27, 28. [26] Deut. 34, 2. [27] S. of S. 2, 13.

f.5b
# 3 Laws for Passover, to be read on the 'Great Sabbath' preceding the Feast
### By Zeraḥyah Hallevi, of blessed memory.

[This 'Azharoth is an example of a poetic genre discussed on p. 18. It may be compared with its model (direct or indirect), by Judah Hallevi, poem 82, that is written in the margins (see p. 69). Judah Hallevi's diction, as is usual in Spanish Hebrew poetry, is almost entirely biblical. Zeraḥyah Hallevi, on the other hand, uses much rabbinic vocabulary – the connective particles in particular give the flavour of halakhic (procedural and jurisprudential) Hebrew – no doubt because of his concern to include rather more explicitly technical matter than Judah Hallevi had done. The rhyme-scheme is principally intended to aid the reader in identifying the clause-division and period. But a poetic dimension is present in the tension (often resting on a double entendre) between the meanings of the climactic biblical quotations in their original contexts, and when reapplied. An approximation to the Hebrew scheme has been embodied in the rendering of the first two paragraphs only: were it to be maintained throughout, it would make for tedious reading in English. Consequently the end of the last clause only has been rhymed to match the biblical punch line. The translation is much indebted to the commentary on the poem by Isaac Mar-Eli for source identification. The alphabetical acrostic is followed by: אני זרחיה הלוי ברבי יצחק, 'I am Zeraḥyah Hallevi, son of Rabbi Isaac'.]

Pure is the Word of God, for whom reverence shall for aye
endure, serenely bright; who instructed me to search out leaven
on the fourteenth day, by night; the search
　To be lit not by sun,[1] moon, nor flaring torch to aid the sight,
　But with a lamp – the 'lamp' that 'is God's precept, Torah's light'.[2]

Pronounce benediction on God's Name ere you annul your
leavened hoard;[3] Then search[4] the storehouses and granaries that
furnish the fare to deck your board: Declare what remains undetected
　To be worthless,[5] as eluding your efforts though not ignored:
　'And so may you find favour with your Lord'.[6]

Be not concerned should a weasel drag leaven from one room to
another;[7] but on your property[8] let no leaven be found, seen,
deliberately put out of view, or accepted on deposit from any
Gentile over whom you exercise some control. However, leaven
reserved for God's service, or which belongs to others without
your having accepted any responsibility for it, for which you
have designated separate accommodation –
　All these have licence on your land to stay;
　Their ban, like 'sundered shackles, falls away'.[9]

The law requires that holes[10] between your property and that of
a fellow-Jew be searched as far as the arm can reach, but the
law exempts courtyards because of the presence there of crows
to scavenge the scraps. It is sufficient to examine moderately
accessible holes:
　High up or low – such holes are hard to find;
　'For these, concern need not weigh on your mind'.[11]

What is left for the next morning's breakfast you are to deposit,
secreted from interference by vermin, so that a further search
will not be necessary afterwards.[12] If, during the holy days of the
festival, one comes across any leaven, one should isolate it by
placing on top of it an inverted bowl.[13] If a Gentile deposits
leaven with you, wall it off by a barrier ten handbreadths high,
　Or in some store-pit keep it deep, apart,
　Then 'shall no qualms with trembling touch your heart'.[14]

If you go off on a journey more than thirty days before
Passover,[15] and do not expect to return home during the festival,
or if you turn your house into a grain-store, you have no need
to get rid of leavened matter provided that you have no

intention of clearing out the barn before or during the feast. If, however, you depart less than thirty days beforehand, or you intend to return in time, or to empty the barn,

> Then be not slack to rid you of ferment:
> 'So shall you save your soul from punishment'.[16]

If, on the morning preceding Passover, one recalls while out of the house that one has left a roll of dough[17] at home and is apprehensive lest it rise, one is obliged to abjure it (as being valueless) while it is not yet in a forbidden state, being still unleavened: that is, if one is afraid that

> He has no time back to his house to go
> 'Twixt kneading and the rising of the dough'.[18]

If, after the search for leaven has been carried out, a child[19] has come rushing in holding a piece of bread, and you detect crumbs, forbear from further search: it is a child's nature to finish a morsel up, and not to secrete it for later consumption. However, if any vermin are seen introducing leaven, carry out a careful search:

> No crumbs a mouse drops from the bread he stole,
> But 'hoards it carefully inside his hole'.[20]

f.6a  Any leaven buried beneath a collapsed structure[21] is considered disposed of, and its owner should mentally abjure title to any of it deeper than three handbreadths into the heap – as far as a dog might dig out. Culinary vessels[22] are to be purified in boiling water, since they thus reject what they have absorbed,

> Just like the wicked, 'whose ill-gotten gain
> Once swallowed, he must vomit forth again'.[23]

Cauldrons,[24] kettles and large boiling-pans – any vessels that can be exposed to naked flame – are to be rinsed, each by being immersed in a larger vessel; likewise iron spits and vessels of burnished copper. Similarly deal with wooden ladles[25] and knives,

> In fireproof pots, in boiling water laid,
> 'The handle following hard upon the blade'.[26]

Place wooden or metal spoons and dishes in a bowl, and pour boiling water over them.[27] Anyone anxious to avoid breakage[28] of earthenware pots and pans that have been used for leaven, betrays a niggardly attitude, but when the period of Passover is done,

> Forbidden-use, Passover passed will make
> Licit again: 'of these none need you break'.[29]

Although you may eat leaven on 14 *Nisan* through the fourth hour, be prompt to refrain therefrom during the fifth, and to burn it at the beginning of the sixth,[30] or scatter it to the wind (first cutting it up and crumbling it[31]), or throw it into the sea in order that it may not be found:

> Scattered, considered worthless, not the same
> In form, 'dispersed abroad without a name'.[32]

After the time-limit it is still permissible to derive advantage from leaven, provided that, before the material time, one has scorched[33] it sufficiently to alter its taste and character. Leaven which, during Passover, has been Gentile property, may after the festival be eaten, or be occasion of other advantage to a Jew; but in order that a Jew who deliberately and visibly retains his leaven during the feast may be mulcted, usufruct of it is declared prohibited, except for such as has been indistinguishably mingled into some other substance:[34]

> To flout the law, ignoring what is due
> Means 'ill must those who will offend pursue'.[35]

A vessel which has been used for leaven in a cold state only may on Passover be used for unleavened stuff,[36] except, as is well known, for bowls in which dough is left to rise, and earthenware vessels with a leaden glaze: the ruling that these are prohibited is clearly decided. Anyone who on the day preceding Passover eats unleavened bread after the sixth hour (i.e. midday) is comparable to a man who

> Lustful, takes his betrothed too soon to bed:[37]
> 'Lover of sin, strife and unleavened bread'.[38]

Sponge-cakes, honey fritters and griddle cakes are excluded, as too luxurious for fulfilment of the precept to eat unleavened bread:[39] reject them. But it is permissible to use the finest-quality flour, such as that with which King Solomon's own unleavened bread will have been baked; but equally second-grade flour may be used.[40] Syrian cakes baked in divers shapes ought not to be made on Passover,

> But 'poor-man's bread', the mendicant's dull fare:
> 'All vainglory before the King forswear'.[41]

The dough is not to be kneaded with oil, honey or wine[42] – absolutely not for the first night. But from the second day onwards dough made with milk may be used, but solely for small unleavened wafers no bigger than the eye of an ox. When the eating of 'poor-man's bread' is of the essence,

> On the first day, use of all these decline:
> 'God's love confers a sweeter taste than wine'.[43]

Make your unleavened bread of wheat,[44] barley, spelt, goat's wheat or oats. Look for lettuce,[45] endive, chickory, pepperwort or some very bitter herb to set alongside your dainties. You may take half-baked wafers that are breakable without fissuring,[46] in order to make the blessing on Him

> Who gives you food, with seasoning to dress:
> 'So may He, too, your bread and water bless'.[47]

You are bidden not to soak bran[48] in cold or warm water for chickens on Passover, but you may stir it into boiling water. If a woman goes to the bath-house[49] taking bran with her for scrubbing herself, she should not let it soak in the runnels; she should stick it with some detergent onto her skin without water, and then rub it over her body. One may not chew[50] wheat in order to make

> A salve, to place on sores that cause you pain:
> 'These are the statutes God's will did ordain'.[51]

f.6b  Dough baked and subsequently boiled is acceptable, likewise flour that has been stirred into boiling water, since fermentation is thereby prevented.[52] Meal into which a trickle of water off the roof causes constant dripping is permissible for use. But the fathers of later rabbinic tradition have established a precautionary prohibition of the rinsing or stirring of any meal.[53]

> 'The fence they built one may not breach – a norm
> 'To which in practice people now conform'.[54]

One can fulfil the obligation of eating unleavened bread with a thin wafer that has been soaked,[55] but do not trip up as regards procedure by letting it boil, any more than the paschal lamb itself may be eaten boiled. Be alert to find unleavened bread made specially for Passover,[56] and to have those possessed of the necessary competence dispose in advance, by sale, of any wheat that has begun to ferment,[57] in quantities too small to stockpile. Refrain from making a mush of meal and vinegar; nor put flour into *haroseth* or mustard[58] – such mixture

> Where you as master move, you should not see:
> 'Let not your love of God half-hearted be'.[59]

Pour away down an inclined drain water used by a baker to rinse his hands and implements[60] since it ferments if left stagnant, by permitting which you would transgress the precepts of God in heaven. For kneading the dough-mixture seek for water not recently drawn:[61] to the people whom God has sustained from their very birth

> He gave this precept: say, then, '"ours the right
> To water", for we drew it yesternight'.[62]

A woman should be careful not to knead the dough in sunlight,[63] or with warm water, or with water slightly warmed through standing in the sun. She should avoid kneading in the open air on a cloudy day, or using water from the bottom of a cauldron that may retain residual heat; nor should she let her hand leave the oven (i.e. interrupt her kneading) until the work is completed. She should provide herself with two bowls of cold water, one for cooling her hands and the other from which to moisten the lump of dough. If she disregards any of the foregoing prescriptions and kneads as she ought not,

> She must endure what comes of her offence
> 'Of knowing not, nor using common sense'.[64]

Retention of any of the following on Passover is a transgression: four items[65] being cereal-based stuff, used by the man in the street, and three by artisans only. You must destroy Babylonian curd-pudding, Median ale, Egyptian beer and vinegar made of barley from Idumea. Dyer's pulp must be used up, as also cook's starch-wadding and scribe's glue, which also serves as a depilatory

> Their needy daughters' skin to beautify,
> Flour-based cosmetic pastes 'to catch the eye'.[66]

Should cracks in a kneading-trough[67] contain an olive's bulk of old dough at any single point – acting as a plug to stop leakage – or a lesser quantity outside the area where the kneading takes place, it must be removed. A lesser quantity within the kneading area[68] may be left, being considered part of the material of the vessel. If a tanner[69] has put flour into his tan-vat, as a curing agent, within three days before Passover

> He must destroy what is as leaven classed:
> Although 'its title goes off very fast'.[70]

The flour may be disregarded as 'leaven' if the tanner also tosses skins into the vat one day, or even one hour, before Passover. A patient may leave alone any plaster,[71] compress or emollient containing flour that has become putrid; likewise any in collyrium for the eye. Bread that has gone mouldy[72] –

> But by a drooling dog is not yet spurned
> As foul – 'by human kind such must be burned'.[73]

A team of three women is to be assigned to each oven to engage in the correct method of handling the dough:[74] one kneads, the second pulls portions off the mass to shape into wafers, while the third fulfils the essentially womanly precept of baking for the festival. They successively change roles,[75]

> Till each has baked what her household requires:
> ''Tis woman's task to keep alight the fires'.[76]

The appropriate quantity for a single batch of kneading is seven quarters, or more, of a Sidonian *kab*[77] – the minimum quantity subject to deduction, for the priestly entitlement, from the first portion of all dough.[78] Should a woman, while kneading, experience the onset of menstrual uncleanness,[79] and thus be precluded from baking the priestly dues which, if left as dough, would ferment, she should not separate it off: dough does not become technically *hallah* ('priest's loaf') until the baking is completed. Her first act in declaring it *hallah* (when in a state to do so) is to recite, with due reverence, the blessing[80] of God

> Who, by his precepts, Israel sanctifies;
> Thus 'from her mouth words issue that are wise'.[81]

The dough of a wafer that is 'dumb'[82] (i.e. which may be sad), is to be considered as leaven if another wafer baked with it has risen; or if, after the eighteen minutes necessary to walk a mile have elapsed since the kneading stage was completed, its state is still obscure. Dough beginning to ferment[83] has streaks in it, like the antennae of a locust; at the next stage it is marbled with cracks, and the eating of either involves the heavenly penalty of being cut off. If 14 *Nisan* falls on Sabbath,[84] both priestly dues paid in kind and common foodstuffs are to be declared void at the same moment of time

> If leaven they contain: 'one who is true
> To God's commandments, will discharge each due'.[85]

f.7a A man who is out of his house while concerned with the fulfilment of some religious obligation on the morning preceding Passover, and recalls that he has left some leaven at home, should mentally abjure ownership of it if time does not suffice for him to return before the latest moment for its destruction.[86] He should proceed to the Temple to slaughter his paschal lamb, and not linger, until he reaches Jerusalem. Analogous errands are to attend to the circumcision of one's own son, or to visit one's prospective father-in-law

> To share his board upon the trysting-day:
> 'The righteous man will hold fast to his way'.[87]

If, however, a voluntary errand takes you to a different house, you must return forthwith and destroy it in due form. If you are on the way to save people from marauding bands, from a river in flood, a collapsed building or a fire, abjure the leaven mentally: it is entirely unnecessary for you to return.

> Although thereto no flame you have applied,
> Yet 'in God's eyes will you be justified'.[88]

On 14 *Nisan*, being the day preceding Passover, carry out such work only as your sages declare permissible.[89] Tailors,[90] laundry-men and barbers are allowed to work as usual until midday, as a public service. If your forefathers were accustomed to refrain from work in the forenoon, adhere to their local practice:[91]

> 'My son, the code thy sire prescribed, obey,
> Thy mother's teaching do not thrust away'.[92]

On the eve of Passover,[93] towards the latter part of the afternoon, one should refrain from eating until it gets dark. One should not begin the meal until one is comfortably seated – in a position to recline on the left elbow in the ancient manner of those who felt free as kings[94] – nor drink less than four cups of wine at table during the formal celebration:

> As they upon each cup my name confess
> 'Those whom I set about my hill I bless'.[95]

The appropriate quantity for each cup is a quarter of a *log* (i.e. the liquid capacity of one and a-half eggs), diluted to taste, from your winestore.[96] While drinking the cups all must recline – you yourself, your wife, children and any Jewish servants in attendance.[97] The bitter herb, recalling slavery, should not be eaten reclining,[98]

> For so our ancient sages did declare:
> 'Eat, and within thy gates enjoy thy fare'.[99]

Over the first cup of wine, arrange the series of benedictions so as to commence with that over the wine itself, followed by that for the Sanctification of the day.[100] Next comes the first occasion of the dipping of greenstuff into its condiment; one does this using any edible herb from the garden, and reciting the blessing of God as creator of what grows in the soil.[101] The table (or central dish) is then removed[102] for a short while, so as to stimulate questions from the four types of son

> Each asking as described in Holy Writ,
> 'Like olive saplings round thy board they sit'.[103]

When the table or central dish has been replaced, with its unleavened bread, lettuce, haroseth and two cooked dishes, as the ordinance prescribes,[104] the second cup is poured out; and it is at this point that the son asks questions, formulating them according to his intellectual capacity. The celebrant replies, expounding the text until he reaches the end of the central explanatory part of the Haggadah; beginning the account with matters occasioning shame,

> That after, praise triumphant shall transcend:
> 'What starts with ill is better at its end'.[105]

At the points (f. 31a–b) where the significance of the unleavened bread and bitter herbs is formally declared,[106] the celebrant should raise each aloft,[107] but not the dish of roast meat that symbolizes the paschal lamb, lest he appear to be profanely offering a holy sacrifice outside the Temple. Then follow (f. 32a–b) psalms of praise and thanksgiving to God – the first two psalms (113 and 114) of the Hallel.

> Our thanks to God and praises thus we bring
> 'Extolled in hymns my lips shall sweetly sing'.[108]

Then say the blessing of God 'who redeemed us and our fathers' (ff. 32b–33a).[109] Prior to the second dipping of herbs in condiment the celebrant is to wash his hands, and, on the occasion of this second[110] washing, to recite the appropriate blessing. He is then to say two blessings – that of God who makes bread grow, and that of God who commanded the eating of unleavened bread. Of the wafer previously divided (in order to lay one half aside) he is now to put the other half within (that is, beneath) the whole wafer.

> This to the company he gives to share;
> 'For upright men this plan did God prepare'.[111]

He is then to reach for the lettuce, and to recite over it the blessing of God who commanded the eating of bitter herbs; he is to dip it (this being the second dipping of the ceremony) in the haroseth,[112] being careful not to immerse it enough for the bitterness to be nullified. The basis of haroseth is a tart conserve[113] worked into a thick consistency reminiscent of mud, as used in brick-making;

> Spices one adds, to make the flavour sweet:
> 'I stamp it firm, like mire crushed in the street'.[114]

f. 7b The celebrant is then to wrap some unleavened bread and lettuce together as a sandwich.[115] Thereafter comes the meal, and when all have had their fill, no one, be they old or young, is to disperse after the last taste of unleavened bread to join in revelry.[116] The celebrant then washes his hands and pours out the third cup:[117]

> With this he thanks the One who spread his board,
> 'His Name be blessed, now and for aye, the Lord'.[118]

It is God's behest that I reserve the fourth cup for the reciting of the remaining psalms (115–118) of the Hallel (ff. 33b–36a) and the subsequent blessing regarding psalmody;[119] and thereafter (f. 36b) the final grace after wine, which covers all four cups.[120] Between the first three of these, one is permitted also to drink at will, but not between the third and the fourth:[121]

> One's thirst for liquor then one must repress:
> 'Thee, Lord, throughout my life so will I bless'.[122]

Thus I look for the fulfilment of those divine acts of consolation in store, the promises laid down long since for my ultimate solace. New every morning are God's mercies, manifold his faithful support of those who set their hope on Him. Mayest Thou dress me in new garments, the raiment of our ultimate deliverance, that will outshine the deliverance from Egypt;[123] for, in the light of

> The gathering of those world-wide dispersed
> 'Things long ago will scarcely be rehearsed'.[124]

Do Thou gather the scattered ones of Judah and Ephraim to the holy mountain, in the Beauteous Land. For those that languish amid the dunghills, cause Thou salvation to spring forth, even as our seers have proclaimed,[125] as when from Egypt

> Thou camest forth, wonders will I display:
> 'See Zion prosper till thy latest day'.[126]

[1] Babylonian Talmud, Pesaḥim (henceforth: BT) 7b, foot. [2] Prov. 6, 23. [3] BT 7a. [4] BT 8a. [5] BT 6b. [6] II Sam. 24, 23. [7] Mishnah, Pesaḥim (henceforth: Mishnah) I, 2; BT 9a. [8] BT 5b, 6a. [9] Judg. 15, 14. 'Bonds', 'asuraw, in the original context, is here transmuted into 'prohibitions', 'issuraw. [10] BT 8a. [11] I Sam. 9, 20. [12] BT 9b. [13] BT 6a. [14] I Sam. 25, 31. [15] BT 6a. [16] Ez. 3, 19. [17] BT 7a. [18] Hos. 7, 4. [19] BT 10b. [20] Nahum 2, 13. [21] Mishnah II, 3; BT 31b. [22] BT 30b. [23] Job 20, 15. [24] BT, 'Abodah Zarah 75b. [25] BT (Pesaḥim) 30b. [26] Judg. 3, 22. The biblical text concerns a dagger-hilt disappearing into a wound; the Talmud (see n. 25) considers the cleansing of knives with handles made of material different from the blades. [27] Isaac Al-fasi, Hilkhoth Ḥameṣ u-maṣṣah, under Nequṭ ha'i kelala (on II, 2). [28] BT 30a. [29] Ps. 34, 21. [30] 11 a.m.; Mishnah I, 4; BT 11b. [31] Mishnah II, 1; BT 28a. [32] Job 18, 17. [33] BT 21b, top. [34] BT 29a, 30a. [35] Prov. 13, 21. [36] BT 30b. [37] Jerusalem Talmud, Pesaḥim X, 1. [38] Prov. 17, 19. Maṣṣah, which in the biblical context means 'contention', is homonymous with the common maṣṣah, 'unleavened bread'. [39] BT 119b. [40] BT 36b, 37a. [41] Prov. 25, 6. [42] BT 36a. [43] S. of S. 1, 2. [44] Mishnah II, 5. [45] Mishnah II, 6. [46] BT 37a. [47] Ex. 23, 25. [48] Mishnah II, 7. [49] Mishnah II, 8. [50] Mishnah II, 8. [51] Deut. 4, 45. [52] BT 39b. [53] Cf. BT 40a; the interdiction is gaonic. [54] Eccles. 2, 12. [55] BT 40a. [56] BT 38b. [57] BT 40b. [58] Mishnah II, 8. [59] Ez. 28, 15. In the closely related London Haggadah (MS British Library Add. 27210), the concluding text is: 'Perfect art thou in thy ways', from Ez. 28, 15. The copyist of our MS was confused by his greater familiarity with Deut. 18, 13, which also begins with the word tamim; but the rhyme (derakheykha) shows that the Ezekiel verse is correct. [60] BT 42a. [61] BT 42a. [62] Gen. 26, 20. Lanu, in the biblical context meaning 'belonging to us', is a homonym of lanu, 'passed the night'. [63] BT 42a. [64] Prov. 9, 13. [65] Ps. 73, 7. [66] Mishnah III, 2. [67] Mishnah III, 2. [68] Shello is to be omitted, as in MS British Library Add. 27210, as is confirmed by the author's own commentary (Ha-ma'or ha-qaṭan) to Isaac Al-fasi in loc. BT 45a. [69] BT 45b. [70] Ps. 147, 15. The biblical text concerns (God's) 'word'. The author, in reapplying it, apparently equates 'word' with 'name' or 'description'. The point of the quotation is borne out by the next paragraph. [71] Tosefta, Pesaḥim III, 1, Al-fasi on BT 45b. [72] BT 45b. [73] Is. 45, 15. [74] Mishnah III, 4. [75] BT 48b. [76] Is. 27, 11. The biblical context refers to gathering firewood from deserted parkland. [77] BT 48b. [78] Num. 15, 20. [79] Mishnah III, 3. [80] Mishnah, Ḥallah II, 3. [81] Prov. 31, 26. [82] Mishnah (Pesaḥim) III, 2. [83] Mishnah III, 5. [84] Mishnah III, 6. [85] Eccles. 7, 18. The author has credited the verb yaṣṣa, 'go out', with an idiomatic nuance current in rabbinic Hebrew: 'to be free of further obligation'. Conceivably this was the meaning already intended by the author of Ecclesiastes itself. [86] Mishnah III, 7. [87] Job 17, 9. [88] Deut. 24, 13. [89] Mishnah IV, 1. [90] Mishnah IV, 6; BT 55b. [91] BT 50b, foot. [92] Prov. 1, 8. [93] Mishnah X, 1. [94] Mishnah X, 1; BT 108a. [95] BT 109b; Ez. 34, 26. The author reads into the biblical reference to berakhah (here meaning God's blessing of man) a pointer towards benedictional formulae. Once this has been appreciated, the word gibʿah, 'hill', becomes evocative of gebiaʿ, 'goblet'. [96] BT 108b. [97] BT 108a. [98] BT 108a. [99] Deut. 12, 21. [100] Mishnah X, 2. [101] BT 114b. [102] BT 115b. [103] Ps. 128, 3. [104] Mishnah X, 3–4; BT 114b, 116a. [105] Eccles. 7, 8. [106] Mishnah X, 5. [107] BT 116b. [108] Ps. 63, 6. [109] Mishnah X, 6. [110] The first was prior to serving the first herb (f. 20b). [111] Prov. 2, 7. [112] BT 114b, 115b. [113] BT 116a; Jerusalem Talmud, Pesaḥim X, 3. [114] II Sam. 22, 23. The scribe has corrected his original 'ariyqem (as in the parallel Ps. 18, 43, where the following 'erqa'em is missing) into 'adiqqem. [115] BT 115a. [116] Mishnah X, 8. [117] Mishnah X, 7. [118] Ps. 113, 2. [119] BT 118a. [120] Mishnah X, 6. [121] Mishnah X, 7. [122] Ps. 63, 5. [123] BT, Berakhoth 13a. [124] Is. 65, 17. [125] Cf. Micah 7, 15. [126] Ps. 128, 5.

## 4 Hymnic Sequel

[This poem concludes the 'Laws of Passover', also written by Zeraḥyah Hallevi, whose name appears here in an acrostic: זרחיה, 'Zeraḥyah'.]

Sing, my people, crushed in spirit: thou whose arm enfeebled lies
Sing to God on high, transcendent, who in triumph rides the skies,
For He destines thee for glory that all splendour shall excel,
    When God's light beams forth from Zion, see, Jerusalem is well.

Lord, thy son – from his own sire's correction sick – with grace regard:
O my people, be yet patient in thy prison under guard;
Though with scorn of foemen sated, though good fortune thou dost lack,
God shall speedily relieve thee of his scourge upon thy back.
Swift as the deer there comes one bearing tidings glad to tell:
    When God's light beams forth from Zion, see, Jerusalem is well.

He will free thee from taskmasters at whose bidding thou must run,
As his slave shall God acquire thee but to treat thee as his son;
And thy priests restored again shall be in linen robes arrayed,
Then shall holiness and glory thy camp's air once more pervade,
But all worshippers of idols He shall smite, and sound their knell;
    When God's light beams forth from Zion, see, Jerusalem is well.

For the mercies of the Lord of Hosts shall shield thee with his might
From the archers who would pierce thee with the arrows of their spite.
His Messiah He shall send, so fleet he shall with deer compare,
For thy thirsty soul a draught of wondrous saving to prepare.
As in Egypt once, my miracles shall lay on thee their spell:
    When God's light beams forth from Zion, see, Jerusalem is well.

As it is written: 'According to the days of thy coming out of Egypt I will show unto him marvellous things';[1] and it is said: 'The Lord shall bless thee out of Zion; and thou shalt see the good of Jerusalem all the days of thy life';[2] and it is said: 'For behold, I create new heavens and a new earth: and the former things shall not be remembered nor come into mind';[3] and it is said: 'But be ye glad and rejoice for ever in that which I create: for behold, I create Jerusalem a rejoicing, and her people a joy'.

    Then *Kaddeesh* is said to its conclusion.

[1] *Micah* 7, 15.  [2] *Ps.* 128, 5.  [3] *Is.* 65, 17–18.

## 5 Order of Passover[-Eve Prayers]

f. 8a

[Insertions by Mei'r ben Isaac, Sheliaḥ Ṣibbur.]

On the day preceding Passover, when the afternoon service is read, the supplicatory psalm (said with the head inclined over the arm) is to be omitted, and the service terminates with *kaddeesh tithkabbal* ('may our prayers be accepted', etc.). At the beginning of the evening service the Reader intones: 'Bless ye the Lord', etc. as on the Sabbath; and when, in the following prayer, he has read the phrase: 'and Thou dost mark the difference between day and night', he reads the following insertion:

[Incomplete alphabetical acrostic.]

A WATCH-NIGHT, THIS: when God, at midnight's hour,
Went out o'er Egypt with doom-laden power.
With might befriend us, Lord; the West destroy,
In factions split: then shall we sing for joy
    Blessed art Thou, O Lord, who bringest on the evening twilight.

Then follows: 'With everlasting love', etc.

A WATCH-NIGHT, THIS: God, who rules light and dark,
Predestined it, at midnight's stroke – a mark
Of love, that He remembers for the seed
Of Abraham, whose night-march[1] captives freed.
f. 8b    Blessed art Thou, O Lord, who lovest thy people Israel.

Then follows: 'Hear, O Israel', etc., 'True and steadfast', etc. as far as: 'and thy sovereignty did they most willingly acknowledge'. The following is then inserted:

[Complete alphabetical acrostic.]

A WATCH-NIGHT, THIS:

Eating their lambs, an anxious band,
Wonders they watched divinely planned    on that First Passover;
    Ours down the years to mark the day:
    Turn, wonders yet again display    as once at Passover.

This day[2] thy faithful sons decreed
Must serve four hundred years till freed    on that First Passover;
    This day the seventh ten-fold week[3]
    Will end, when God will vengeance wreak    as once at Passover.

This day all Ham's firstborn He slew,
His own firstborn in mercy knew[4]    on that First Passover;
    This day shall see felons condemned
    And champions to Zion send[5]    as once at Passover.

f. 9a  This day trimmed Egypt's pride, to see
Abraham's sons redeemed and free    on that First Passover;
    This day my perfect knight,[6] the Lord,
    Shall put the wicked[7] to the sword    as once at Passover.

This day saw dusky hordes' blood shed:
God's folk with booty forth He led    on that First Passover;
    This day foes from their crags[8] shall fling,
    Our scattered people home shall bring    as once at Passover.

This day taskmasters'[9] grip God broke,
From Pharaoh's lands released his folk    on that First Passover;
    This day shall see oppressors feel
    God's hand, our battered limbs will heal    as once at Passover.

This day, that rabble-rule did foil,
God moved his vine[10] to richer soil    on that First Passover;
f. 9b    This day shall mute the boaster's voice,
    With doubled joy[11] God's folk rejoice    as once at Passover.

This day the proud to plagues consigned,
God's people healed in flesh and mind    on that First Passover;
    This day is marked: heathen must dread;
    'Vengeance is mine',[12] our God has said    as once at Passover.

This day, when Egypt panic saw,
God knew their hurt[13] who kept his law    on that First Passover;
    This day Hell[14] claims the foeman's crest:
    Bring home those on thy palms impressed[15]    as once at Passover.

This day the tyrant's fall God schemed,
His loved ones from chain-gangs redeemed    on that First Passover;
    This day, the arrogant o'erthrown,[16]
    Thou wilt in wedlock[17] take thine own    as once at Passover.

f. 10a  This day, on each house mourning broke
At thine approach on[18] midnight's stroke    on that First Passover;
    This day was fixed for us, that we
    Wonders henceforth each day might see    as once at Passover.

This day all praise to Him on high
Whose might affects both far and nigh,
Which at the sea to glorify
Laughing and singing, all did vie.

One continues with the text of the prayer: 'Moses and the Children of Israel sang to Thee a song', etc., as far as: 'Thou who didst cleave the sea before Moses'.

[Continuation of the sequence of insertions begun on f. 8a.]

A WATCH-NIGHT, THIS: symbol of things to be,
That the Most High shall come: then shall we see
How for his folk He cares, his nearest stock,
Even as we rejoice in Him, our Rock.

One continues: 'They sang "this is my God", and said', etc.

f. 10b    A WATCH-NIGHT, THIS: God, who thus styled it,[19] snapped
With might the chains Isis[20] upon us clapped;
He will bring down the beast that rends to eat,
This night will He redemptive deeds repeat.

One continues: 'Blessed art Thou, O Lord, who didst redeem Israel', [and the following prayer: 'Cause us to lie down in peace', etc.].

A WATCH-NIGHT, THIS: its fame rehearsed by those
Beloved of God, who saved them from their foes,
From Egypt's spawn;[21] daughter of noble line,
She may, *sans* fear, in peace this night recline.

'Spread over us the tabernacle of thy peace, and over Jerusalem thy holy city: blessed art Thou, O Lord, who dost spread the tabernacle of peace', etc.

---

[1] *Gen.* 14, 15. [2] *Gen.* 15, 13; *Pirqey de R. Eliezer* 28. [3] *Dan.* 9, 24; *Is.* 63, 4; *Babylonian Talmud, Rosh Hashanah* 11a. [4] *Ex.* 2, 25. [5] *Obad.* 21. [6] *S. of S.* 5, 10. [7] The text specifically mentions *Edom* – a covert reference in earlier rabbinic texts to the Roman Empire, and subsequently to Christendom (viewed as a secular power). [8] *Obad.* 4. [9] *Li-shemo nissim* should read *le-samu missim*. [10] *Ps.* 80, 9(8). [11] *Is.* 61, 7. [12] *Deut.* 32, 35; *'ammo* should be pointed *'immo*. [13] *Ex.* 2, 25. For the almost meaningless *mi-beyn ṣiwwui* read *mebin 'innui*. [14] *Prov.* 30, 15–16. [15] *Is.* 49, 16. [16] For *ḥerasta, we-ra'yathi, 'erasta*, read *teḥares, ra'ayathekha, te'ares.* [17] *Hos.* 2, 21. [18] For *ka-ḥaṣoth* read *ba-ḥaṣoth.* [19] *Ex.* 12, 42. [20] Egypt is described as a *heifer* by Jeremiah (46, 20), in allusion to the Isis-cult. [21] *Gen.* 10, 13.

## [The Miniature Cycle: Captions

The text of each caption appears twice: once integrally to the illumination itself, and a second time repeated (except for matter in square brackets) by a cruder hand in the margin. The illustrations are described in detail on pp. 13f.]

f. 13b    (*Above*) Moses was acting as shepherd (*Ex.* 3, 1); Remove thy shoes from thyfeet (v. 5); [And the bush was not consumed (v. 2)].
(*Below*) What is that in thy hand? (4, 2); And it became a serpent (v. 3); And it became a staff in his hand (v. 4).

f. 14a    (*Above*) Place thy hand in thy bosom; Behold his hand was leprous (v. 6); Return thy hand; And behold it had returned like the remainder of his flesh (v. 7).
(*Below*) Midian (*right*); And Moses took the staff of God in his hand (v. 20); And Zipporah took a flint (v. 25); Egypt (*left*).

f. 14b    (*Above*) And he met him at the mountain of God and kissed him (v. 27); And Moses told Aaron all the words of the Lord (v. 28).
(*Below*) And he performed the signs in the sight of the people (v. 30); And they bowed down and worshipped (v. 31).

f. 15a    (*Above*) Pharaoh (*right*); Thus saith the Lord God of Israel: 'Let my people go' (5, 1); Magicians (*left*).
(*Below*) Let the work be heavy (v. 9); Taskmaster (*centre*); And let them gather straw for themselves (v. 7); Bricks (*left*).

f. 15b    (*Above*) Pharaoh (*right*); And Aaron's rod swallowed their rods (7, 12); Magicians (*left*).
(*Below*) Pharaoh going out to the river (*right*; v. 15); Blood (*centre*); Moses, Aaron (*left*).

f. 16a    (*Above*) Pharaoh, Magicians (*right*); And frogs came up and covered the land of Egypt (8, 2).
(*Below*) And Aaron stretched out his hand with his rod and smote the dust of the earth, and it became lice (v. 13).

f. 16b    (*Above*) Very grievous beasts of divers kinds in the house of Pharaoh and his servants (v. 20); And I will set a redeeming mark between my people and thine (v. 19); Goshen (*left*).
(*Below*) A very grievous plague upon the horses, asses, camels, cattle and flocks (9, 3).

f. 17a    (*Above*) And it became blistering boils burgeoning on man and beast (*right*; v. 10); Soot from the furnace which Moses shall fling (*left*; v. 8).
(*Below*) And the hail smote everything in the field in the land of Egypt (v. 25).

f. 17b    (*Above*) And locusts came up over the whole land of Egypt and settled throughout the borders of Egypt (10, 14).
(*Below*) And there was thick darkness; but for all the Children of Israel there was light in their dwellings (vv. 22, 23).

f. 18a    (*Above*) And there was a very great crying in Egypt, for there was no house without one dead therein (12, 30).
(*Below*) And the Lord gave the people favour in the sight of Egypt, so that they lent to them: and they despoiled Egypt (v. 36).

f. 18b    (*Above*) Rameses (*right*); (Kneading-troughs) bound up in their garments upon their shoulders (v. 34); And the children of Israel went out armed (13, 18).
(*Below*) And Pharaoh harnessed his chariotry and took his forces with him (14, 6).

f. 19a    And God shook the Egyptians into the sea (v. 27); But the Children of Israel went on dry land in the midst of the sea (v. 29).

f. 19b    (The Children of Israel to take) a lamb for each family household (12, 3); And they shall take some of the blood and put it on the two doorposts (v. 7); (They shall eat it) roasted over the fire (v. 8).

f. 20a

## The Haggadah

THEY COME from the prayer-gathering, rinse a cup and mix (i.e. pour out) wine,[1] and recite the following benedictions:

BLESSED art Thou, O Lord, our God, king of the cosmos, creator of the fruit of the vine.

    BLESSED art Thou, O Lord, our God, king of the cosmos, who didst choose us out of every people, exalt us above every tongue, and sanctify us with thy commandments: giving us in love, O Lord, our God, fixed seasons for gladness, pilgrim feasts, and set occasions for joy; even this feast of unleavened bread, the occasion of our liberation, given in love as an holy convocation in remembrance of our coming forth from Egypt. For it is us whom Thou hast chosen, and us whom, out of all peoples, Thou hast sanctified: and Thou hast given us as an inheritance in gladness and joy thy holy appointed seasons. Blessed art Thou, O Lord, who didst pronounce Israel and the appointed seasons to be holy.

    BLESSED art Thou, O Lord, our God, king of the cosmos, who hast maintained us alive, and brought us to reach this season.

f. 20b    [The company] then drink, reclining on the left elbow; they wash their hands, and say the benediction concluding '[who hast commanded us] to wash the hands'. [The celebrant] then takes some of the parsley, dips it into the *ḥaroseth*, and says this benediction:

    Blessed art Thou, O Lord, our God, king of the cosmos, creator of the fruit of the soil.

He then eats some, and serves the members of his family with it. Taking two unleavened wafers, he divides one of them in half, placing one half on top of the intact wafer, and laying the other aside beneath a napkin. He proceeds to remove from the central display-basket the two cooked items, namely, the roasted lamb's shank and the egg. The second cup is poured out, and they begin the recitation of the text of the *Haggadah*.

SHOULD the evening coincide with the onset of the Sabbath, the following is said:

THUS[2] the heavens and the earth were finished, and all the host of them. And on the seventh day God ended his work which He had made; and He rested on the seventh day from all his work which He had made. And God blessed the seventh day, and sanctified it; because that in it He had rested from all his work which God created and made.

BLESSED art Thou, O Lord, our God, king of the cosmos, who didst choose us out of every [people[3]], exalt us above every tongue, and sanctify us with thy commandments: giving us in love, O Lord, our God, Sabbaths for rest and fixed seasons for gladness, pilgrim feasts, and set occasions for joy; even this Sabbath day and this feast of unleavened bread, the occasion of our liberation, given in love as an holy convocation in remembrance of our coming forth from Egypt. For it is us whom Thou has chosen, and us whom, out of all peoples, Thou hast sanctified: and Thou hast given us as an inheritance in gladness and in joy the Sabbath and thy holy appointed seasons. Blessed art Thou, O Lord, who didst pronounce the Sabbath, Israel and the appointed seasons to be holy.

Blessed art Thou, O Lord, our God, king of the cosmos, who hast maintained us alive, and brought us to reach this season.

Should the evening coincide with the outgoing of the Sabbath, one says the benedictions over the wine and over God's election of Israel, [and then continues]:

Blessed art Thou, O Lord, our God, king of the cosmos, creator of the light of fire.

Blessed art Thou, O Lord, our God, king of the cosmos, who hast made a distinction between what is holy and what is free for common use; between light and darkness; between Israel and the other peoples; between the seventh day and the six days of construction; Thou hast distinguished the degree of holiness inherent in the Sabbath from that inherent in a festive day, and hast pronounced them to be holy.[4] Blessed art Thou, O Lord, who hast made a distinction between degrees of holiness.

Thereafter the benediction: 'who hast maintained us alive'; the mnemonic [for the order of benedictions on a Saturday night being] *Y" Q" N" H" Z"*.[5]

[The company] then drink, reclining on the left elbow. They wash their hands, raise the display-basket above the table, and begin the recitation of the text of the *Haggadah*.

f. 21b THIS[6] IS POOR [MAN'S] BREAD WHICH our forefathers ate in the land of Egypt. Let anyone who is hungry come and eat; let anyone who has need of hospitality come and celebrate Passover. This year here we are slaves; in the coming year we [hope to be] in the Land of Israel as free men.

IN[7] WHAT RESPECT IS THIS NIGHT DIFFERENT from other nights? Inasmuch as on other nights we may eat either leaven or unleavened bread, whereas everything tonight is f. 22a unleavened; on other nights we may eat other greenstuffs, whereas on this night bitter herbs only; on other nights we do not dip the herbs in condiments at all, whereas on this night we do so twice; and whereas on other nights we may either sit or recline at ease while eating, on this night we are all of us reclining.

SLAVES were we to Pharaoh in Egypt: but the Lord, our God, brought us out thence with a strong hand and an outstretched arm. And had the Holy One, blessed be He, not brought our fathers out of Egypt, then we, our children, and children's children would still have been of servile status under Pharaoh in Egypt.

AND EVEN THOUGH we may all be scholars, all of mature understanding, all of advanced years, or all of us possessed of knowledge of the Torah, it is a precept incumbent upon us to recount the story of the exodus from Egypt; and everyone who does so [at length[8]] is to be commended.

f. 22b ON ONE[9] occasion Rabbi Eliezer, Rabbi Joshua, Rabbi Eleazar son of Azariah, Rabbi Akiba and Rabbi Tarphon were reclining round the table on Passover night in Beney Berak. They continued discussing the exodus from Egypt all night long, until their disciples arrived, saying: 'Masters, the time for the morning recitation of the *Shema*' has come'.

RABBI ELEAZAR[10] son of Azariah said: I am virtually seventy years old; but could never convince my colleagues that the exodus from Egypt must be mentioned nightly, until Ben Zoma expounded it on the basis of the text: 'that thou mayest remember the day when thou camest out of the land of Egypt all the days of thy life'.[11] As a form of words, 'the days of thy life' is adequate indication of the necessity to refer to the exodus each day; the fact that 'all' is prefixed, is a pointer to the extension of the obligation to include nightly reference as well. However, the main body of the sages was of the opinion f. 23a that whereas 'the days of thy life' refer explicitly enough to this temporal world, the effect of the prefixed 'all' is to extend the obligation into the messianic age.

BLESSED is God, the Infinite Place within which the world exists, blessed be He. Blessed is He that gave the Torah to Israel, blessed be He.

[In connection with the pedagogical treatment of the exodus theme] the Torah uses language appropriate to the instruction of four kinds of son – one of them intelligent, another who reprehensibly endeavours to dissociate himself, a third who is unsophisticated, and one who is unable to ask questions at all.

HOW DOES THE INTELLIGENT ONE frame his question? He says: 'What mean the testimonies and the statutes and the judgements which the Lord our God has commanded us?'[12] Do you, for your part, therefore talk to him in accordance with all the procedural rules for the passover meal, including that which directs us not to break up after the passover meal to join in revelry.[13]

f. 23b THE WICKED son says: 'What is this service to you?'[14] Mark that he says 'to you' – not to himself, thereby dissociating himself from the corporate identity, and thus, in effect, repudiating the cardinal principal of Jewish theology. Do you, therefore, blunt his teeth by replying: 'Because of that which the Lord did unto me when I came out of Egypt'[15] – unto 'me', not to him; had he been there, he would not have been redeemed.

THE UNSOPHISTICATED ONE is represented as saying merely: 'What is this?'[16] So say to him, in the words of the scriptural continuation; 'By strength of hand the Lord brought us out from Egypt, from the house of bondage'. And with regard to the one incapable of asking questions at all, you must take the initiative; for the text says: 'And thou shalt tell thy son on that day, saying, this is because of that which the Lord did unto me, when I came forth out of Egypt'.[15]

AND THOU SHALT TELL thy son. One might assume[17] that instruction should start from the beginning of the month; but this is countered by the explicit directive of the text to tell him 'on that day'. If, then, instruction is to be given 'on that day', why not start during the daytime? Again, the text excludes this by its phrasing: 'because of that which' (literally, 'because of this'): the only point of so graphic a use of the demonstrative 'this' is to indicate the moment when unleavened bread and bitter herbs are actually in front of you.

f. 24a

ORIGINALLY our ancestors practised idolatry: but now God, the Infinite Place of the world, has brought us near to his own exclusive worship. As it said: 'And Joshua said unto all the people, thus saith the Lord God of Israel: Your fathers dwelt on the other side of the River [Euphrates] in old times, even Terah, the father of Abraham and the father of Nahor; and they served other gods. And I took your father Abraham from the other side of the River, and led him throughout all the land of Canaan, and multiplied his seed, and gave him Isaac. And I gave unto Isaac, Jacob and Esau; and I gave unto Esau, Mount Se'ir to possess it: but Jacob and his children went down to Egypt.'[18]

f. 24b

BLESSED be He that keeps his promise to Israel, blessed be He. For the Holy One, blessed be He, calculates the period that will lead to the messianic climax of Israel's history, in order to carry out that which he said to Abraham our father [at the covenant] between the pieces; as it is said: 'And He said unto Abram: Know of a surety that thy seed shall be a stranger in a land that is not theirs, and shall serve them; and they shall afflict them four hundred years. And also that nation whom they shall serve will I judge; and afterward shall they come out with great substance.'[19]

THAT promise it is which has stood firm, both for our forefathers and for us: because it is not one enemy only who has taken a stand against us to annihilate us, but in every single generation there have been those who have stood out to eliminate us; and the Holy One, blessed be He, delivers us from their hand.

GO and find out[20] what Laban the Aramaean [here meaning Syrian] endeavoured to do to our father Jacob; for whereas Pharaoh's decree affected males only, Laban attempted to extirpate the whole clan. As it says: 'An Aramaean ready to

f. 25a

perish[21] was my father, and he went down into Egypt and sojourned there, [his group consisting] of a small number of persons; and became there a nation, great, mighty and populous.'[22]

AND HE WENT DOWN into Egypt: Inevitably, because of the divine utterance.[23]

And sojourned there: Indicating that Jacob did not go down to Egypt with the intention of becoming absorbed into its population, but regarded himself as a temporary resident. As it is said: 'And they said to Pharaoh, for to sojourn in the land are we come; for thy servants have no pasture for their flocks, for the famine is sore in the land of Canaan: now therefore, we pray thee, let thy servants dwell in the land of Goshen.'[24]

A SMALL NUMBER OF PERSONS: As it is said: 'Thy fathers went down into Egypt being threescore and ten persons; and now the Lord thy God hath made thee as the stars of heaven for multitude.'[25]

AND BECAME there a nation: Indicating that Israel remained

f. 25b

a distinct entity there.

Great and mighty: As it is said: 'And the Children of Israel were fruitful, and increased abundantly, and multiplied, and waxed exceeding mighty: and the land was filled with them.'[26]

AND POPULOUS: As it is said: 'I have caused thee to multiply as the growth of the field, and thou hast increased and

waxen great, and thou art come to full womanhood: thy breasts are formed, and thine hair is grown; whereas thou wast naked and bare.'[27]

AND THE EGYPTIANS EVIL ENTREATED US:[28] As it is said: 'Come on, let us deal wisely with them, lest they multiply, and it come to pass that when there falleth out any war, they join also unto our enemies and fight against us, and so get them up out of the land.'[29]

AND AFFLICTED US:[30] As it is said: 'Therefore they did set

f. 26a

over them taskmasters to afflict them with their burdens, and they built for Pharaoh store-cities, Pithom and Rameses.'[31]

And laid upon us hard bondage: As it is said: 'And the Egyptians made the Children of Israel serve with rigour.'[32]

AND WHEN WE CRIED OUT to the Lord God of our fathers: As it is said: 'And it came to pass in process of time that the king of Egypt died; and the Children of Israel sighed by reason of the bondage, and they cried, and their cry came up unto God by reason of the bondage.'[33]

THE LORD HEARD our voice: As it is said: 'And God heard their groaning, and God remembered his covenant with Abraham, with Isaac and with Jacob'.[34]

AND HE LOOKED ON our affliction: This refers to the

f. 26b

enforced abstinence from conjugal life, as it is said: 'And God looked upon the Children of Israel, and God understood their plight'.[35]

AND OUR TOIL: This refers to the male offspring, as it is said: 'Every son that is born ye shall cast into the Nile, and every daughter ye shall save alive'.[36]

AND OUR OPPRESSION: This refers to the extreme pressure to which they were exposed, as it is said: 'And I have also seen the oppression wherewith the Egyptians oppress them'.[37]

'And the Lord brought us forth out of Egypt with a mighty hand, and with an outstretched arm, and with great terribleness, and with signs, and with wonders.'[38]

AND THE LORD BROUGHT US FORTH out of Egypt: Not by means of any angel or seraph, or through the agency of the [alleged] emissary.[39] Rather, the Holy One, blessed be He, effected it by his own direct and glorious intervention, as it is

f. 27a

said; 'For I will pass through the land of Egypt this night, and I will smite all the firstborn in the land of Egypt, both man and beast; and against all the gods of Egypt I will execute judgement: I am the Lord.'[40]

FOR I WILL PASS through the land of Egypt: I myself, and not an angel; 'and I will smite all the firstborn': I myself, and no seraph; 'and against all the gods of Egypt I will execute judgement': myself, and not the [alleged] emissary; 'I am the Lord': I am He, none other.

WITH A MIGHTY HAND: This refers to the cattle-plague, as it is said: 'Behold, the hand of the Lord is upon thy cattle which is in the field, upon the horses, upon the asses, upon the camels, upon the oxen, and upon the sheep: there shall be a very grievous murrain.'[41]

AND WITH AN OUTSTRETCHED ARM: This refers to the

f. 27b

sword, as it is said: 'Having a drawn sword in his hand, stretched out over Jerusalem'.[42]

AND WITH GREAT TERRIBLENESS:[43] This refers to the revelation of the divine Presence, as it is said: 'Or hath God essayed to go and take Him a nation from the midst of another nation, by signs,[44] and by wonders, and by war, and by a mighty hand, and by an outstretched arm, and by great terrors, according to all that the Lord your God did for you in Egypt before your eyes?'[45]

AND WITH SIGNS: This refers to (Moses') staff, as it is said: 'And thou shalt take this rod in thine hand, wherewith thou shalt perform the signs'.[46]

AND WITH WONDERS: This refers to the plague of blood, as it is said: 'And I will shew wonders in the heavens and in the earth, blood, and fire, and pillars of smoke'.[47]

An alternative construction of the foregoing text[48] is as follows:

f. 28a
'With a mighty hand'     represents two
'With an outstretched arm'     represents two
'And with great terribleness'     represents two
'And with signs'     represents two
'And with wonders'     represents two,

corresponding to the ten plagues that the Holy One, blessed be He, brought upon the Egyptians in Egypt, namely:

Blood  Frogs  Lice    Wild beasts  Cattle-plague  Boils
Hail  Locusts  Darkness prolonged  Slaying the Firstborn

Rabbi Judah used to abbreviate them, grouped by their Hebrew initials,[49] (as if in English one grouped them) BFL BCB HLDS.[50]

RABBI JOSE the Galilean said:[51] It may be deduced[52] that whereas in Egypt itself the Egyptians suffered ten plagues, at the Red Sea they suffered a further fifty. In connection with the plagues in Egypt the text says: 'Then the magicians said unto Pharaoh, this is the finger of God'.[53] Regarding Israel's experience at the Red Sea it says: 'And Israel saw the great hand of the Lord in what the Lord did upon the Egyptians: and the people feared the Lord and believed the Lord, and his servant Moses.'[54]

f. 28b
IF THE TOTAL number of plagues suffered through God's finger was ten, one must conclude that in Egypt itself they suffered ten plagues, and at the sea a further fifty.

RABBI ELIEZER said: It may be deduced furthermore that each several plague which the Holy One, blessed be He, inflicted on the Egyptians in Egypt consisted of four individual plagues. As it is said: 'He cast upon them the fierceness of his anger, wrath, and indignation, and trouble, by sending evil angels among them'.[55] 'Wrath', 'indignation', 'trouble' and 'the sending of evil angels' constitute four items; hence in Egypt itself they must have suffered forty plagues, and at the sea no less than two hundred.

RABBI AKIBA said: The deduction is rather that each several
f. 29a
plague that the Holy One, blessed be He, inflicted on the Egyptians in Egypt consisted of five individual plagues. As it is said: 'He cast upon them the fierceness of his anger, wrath, and indignation, and trouble, by sending evil angels among them'. 'Anger', 'wrath', 'indignation', 'trouble' and 'the sending of evil angels' constitute five items. Consequently in Egypt itself they must have suffered fifty plagues, and at the sea as many as two hundred and fifty.

HOW MANIFOLD are the good things conferred by God, the Infinite Place within which the world exists, upon us!

HAD[56] He brought us out of Egypt
    WITHOUT executing judgements on them,
    Enough for us!

HAD He executed judgements on them
    WITHOUT executing it on their gods,
    Enough for us!

f. 29b
HAD He executed it on their gods
    WITHOUT killing their firstborn,
    Enough for us!

HAD He killed their firstborn
    WITHOUT giving us their wealth,
    Enough for us!

HAD He given us their wealth
    WITHOUT dividing the sea for us,
    Enough for us!

HAD He divided the sea for us
    WITHOUT taking us through it on dry ground,
    Enough for us!

HAD He taken us through it on dry ground
    WITHOUT drowning our foes in its waters,
    Enough for us!

HAD He drowned our foes in its waters
    WITHOUT supplying our needs in the wilderness for forty years,
    Enough for us!

HAD He supplied our needs in the wilderness for forty years
    WITHOUT feeding us on manna,
    Enough for us!

f. 30a
HAD He fed us on manna
    WITHOUT giving us the Sabbath,
    Enough for us!

HAD He given us the Sabbath
    WITHOUT bringing us near to Mount Sinai,
    Enough for us!

HAD He brought us near to Mount Sinai
    WITHOUT giving us the Torah,
    Enough for us!

HAD He given us the Torah
    WITHOUT taking us into the Land of Israel,
    Enough for us!

HAD He taken us into the Land of Israel
    WITHOUT building us the Temple,
    Enough for us!

HOW MANIFOLD, how many times redoubled, are the good things conferred on us by God, the Infinite Place within which
f. 30b
the world exists! He brought us out of Egypt; He executed judgement on the Egyptians, and on their gods; He killed their firstborn; He gave us their wealth; He divided the sea for us; He took us through it on dry land; He drowned our foes in its waters; He supplied our needs in the wilderness for forty years; He fed us on manna; He gave us the Sabbath; He brought us near to Mount Sinai; He gave us the Torah; He took us into the Land of Israel; and He built for us the House in Jerusalem, the place of his own choice, in order to effect atonement there for all our sins.

RABBI GAMALIEL used to say that anyone who neglects to refer specifically to the following three things on Passover fails to fulfil his religious obligation, namely: the paschal lamb, unleavened bread and bitter herbs.[57]

The paschal lamb used to be eaten by our ancestors during the period when the Temple was standing, for the following reason: because the Holy One, blessed be He, passed over[58] the

f. 31a houses of our forefathers in Egypt, as it is said: 'Ye shall say, it is the sacrifice of the Lord's Passover, who passed over the houses of the Children of Israel in Egypt, when He smote the Egyptians, and delivered our houses: and the people bowed down and worshipped.'[59]

THIS UNLEAVENED BREAD WE EAT for the following reason: because there had been no time for the dough of our forefathers to rise when the Supreme King of kings, the Holy One, blessed be He, revealed Himself to them, and redeemed them forthwith; as it is said: 'And they baked unleavened cakes of the dough which they brought forth out of Egypt, for it was not leavened; because they were thrust out of Egypt, and could not tarry, neither had they prepared for themselves any victual.'[60]

f. 31b THIS BITTER HERB WE EAT for the following reason: because the Egyptians embittered the lives of our ancestors in Egypt, as it is said: 'And they made their lives bitter with hard bondage, in mortar and bricks, and in all manner of service in the field; all their service, wherein they made them serve, was with rigour.'[61]

In every generation a person is in duty bound to regard himself as having personally participated in the exodus from Egypt;[62] as it is said: 'And thou shalt tell thy son on that day, saying, this is because of that which the Lord did unto me, when I came forth out of Egypt.'[63] It was not just our forefathers whom the Holy One, blessed be He, redeemed, but us also did f. 32a He redeem together with them, as it is said: 'And us did He bring forth from thence, that He might bring us in, to give us the land which He sware unto our fathers.'[64]

Therefore we are in duty bound to give thanks,[62] to utter praise, to extol, to magnify, glorify, exalt and lay our worship before Him who performed, equally for our ancestors and ourselves, all these miracles: He brought us forth from slavery to freedom; from sorrow to joy; from mourning to a festive day; and from darkness into a great light. Let us then say before Him, Praise ye the Lord.

[Psalm 113] PRAISE YE THE LORD. Praise, O ye servants of the Lord, praise the name of the Lord. Blessed be the name of the Lord from this time forth and for evermore. From the rising of the sun unto the going down of the same the Lord's name is to be praised. The Lord is high above all [nations],[65] and his glory above the heavens. Who is like unto the Lord our God, who dwelleth on high, who humbleth himself to behold the things f. 32b that are in the heaven and in the earth? He raiseth up the poor out of the dust, and lifteth the needy out of the dunghill; that He may set him with princes, even with the princes of his people. He maketh the barren woman to keep house, and to be a joyful mother of children. Praise ye the Lord.

[Psalm 114] WHEN ISRAEL WENT OUT of Egypt, the house of Jacob from a people of strange language; Judah was his sanctuary, and Israel was his dominion. The sea saw it, and fled: Jordan was driven back. The mountains skipped[66] like rams, and the little hills like lambs. What aileth thee, O thou sea, that thou fleddest? Thou Jordan, that thou wast driven back? Ye mountains, that ye skipped like rams, and ye little hills, like lambs? Tremble, thou earth, at the presence of the Lord, at the presence of the God of Jacob; which turned the rock into a standing water, the flint into a fountain of waters.

BLESSED[67] art Thou, O Lord, our God, king of the cosmos, f. 33a who hast redeemed us and didst redeem our fathers from Egypt,

and hast brought us to reach this night on which to eat unleavened bread and bitter herbs. Even so, O Lord, our God and God of our fathers, mayest Thou enable us to reach other festive seasons and pilgrim feasts yet to come upon us in peace: joyful in the building of thy city, and exulting in the worship of Thee. And there will we partake of the paschal lambs and other sacrifices, when[68] their blood shall touch the side of thine altar as we seek thy good will: and we will give thanks to Thee with a new song for our redemption, and for the ransoming of our souls. Blessed art Thou, O Lord, who hast redeemed Israel.

BLESSED art Thou, O Lord, our God, king of the cosmos, creator of the fruit of the vine.

[The company] then drink, reclining on the left elbow: thereafter they wash their hands, and say the benediction concluding: '[who hast commanded us] to wash the hands'. [The celebrant] then takes the complete unleavened wafer and the divided one from the display-basket, and recites over the divided one the benediction of God who makes bread grow from the earth, and over the intact wafer the benediction of God who has enjoined the eating of unleavened bread on Passover. He then f. 33b takes some of the lettuce, dips it into the *haroseth*, and says: 'Blessed art Thou, O Lord, our God, king of the cosmos, who hast sanctified us by thy commandments and hast commanded us regarding the eating of bitter herbs.' He then takes both some unleavened bread and some lettuce,[69] and wraps them round each other. No benediction is called for [on eating them thus].

[The company] then eat their meal. After they have finished, they wash their hands; [the celebrant] takes that [portion of an] unleavened wafer which he had previously placed in a napkin, and all present eat an olive's bulk of it each: after which they do not break up the party to join in revelry.[70] They then recite the Grace after the Meal [see f. 54a]; the fourth cup of wine is poured out, over which the remainder of the *Hallel*-psalms are recited.

POUR OUT thy wrath upon the heathen that have not known Thee, and upon the kingdoms that have not called upon thy Name.[71]

[Psalm 115] NOT UNTO US, O Lord, not unto us, but unto thy name give glory, for thy mercy, and for thy truth's sake. Wherefore should the heathen say, where is now their God? But our God is in the heavens: He hath done whatsoever he hath pleased. Their idols are silver and gold, the work of men's hands. They have mouths, but they speak not: eyes have they, f. 34a but they see not: they have ears, but they hear not: noses have they, but they smell not: they have hands, but they handle not: feet have they, but they walk not: neither speak they through their throat. They that make them are like unto them; so is everyone that trusteth in them. O Israel, trust thou in the Lord: he is their help and their shield. O house of Aaron, trust in the Lord: he is their help and shield. Ye that fear the Lord, trust in the Lord: he is their help and shield.

THE LORD HATH BEEN MINDFUL OF US: He will bless us; He will bless the house of Israel; He will bless the house of Aaron. He will bless them that fear the Lord, both small and great. The Lord shall increase you more and more, you and your children. [Ye][72] are blessed of the Lord which made heaven and earth. The heavens, even the heavens, are the Lord's: but the earth hath He given to the children of men. The dead praise not the Lord, neither any that go down into silence. But we will bless the Lord from this time forth and for evermore. Praise ye the Lord.

f. 34b [Psalm 116] I LOVE the Lord, because He hath heard my voice and my supplications. Because He hath inclined his ear unto me, therefore will I call upon Him as long as I live. The sorrows of death compassed me, and the pains of hell gat hold upon me: I found trouble and sorrow. Then called I upon the name of the Lord; O Lord, I beseech Thee, deliver my soul. Gracious is the Lord, and righteous; yea, our God is merciful. The Lord preserveth the simple: I was brought low, and He helped me. Return unto thy rest, O my soul; for the Lord hath dealt bountifully with thee. For Thou hast delivered my soul from death, mine eyes from tears, and my feet from falling. I will walk before the Lord in the land of the living. I believed, therefore I have spoken, that[73] [I] was greatly afflicted: I said in my haste, all men are liars.

f. 35a WHAT SHALL I RENDER unto the Lord for all his benefits toward me? I will take the cup of salvation, and call upon the name of the Lord. I will pay my vows unto the Lord now in the presence of all his people. Precious in the sight of the Lord is the death of his saints. O Lord, truly I am thy servant; I am thy servant, and the son of thine handmaid: Thou has loosed my bonds. I will offer to Thee the sacrifice of thanksgiving, and will call upon the name of the Lord. I will pay my vows unto the Lord now in the presence of all his people, in the courts of the Lord's house, in the midst of thee, O Jerusalem. Praise ye the Lord.

[Psalm 117] O praise the Lord, all ye nations: praise Him, all ye people. For his merciful kindness is great toward us: and the truth of the Lord endureth for ever. Praise ye the Lord.

[Psalm 118] O GIVE THANKS unto the Lord; for He is good: because his mercy endureth for ever. LET ISRAEL now say, that his mercy endureth for ever. LET THE HOUSE OF AARON now say, that his mercy endureth for ever. LET THEM NOW that fear the Lord say, that his mercy endureth for ever.

f. 35b FROM DIRE STRAITS I called upon the Lord; the Lord answered me and set me in a large place. The Lord is on my side; I will not fear: what can man do unto me? The Lord taketh my part with them that help me: therefore shall I see my desire upon them that hate me. It is better to trust in the Lord than to put confidence in man. It is better to trust in the Lord than to put confidence in princes. All nations compassed me about: but in the name of the Lord will I destroy them. They compassed me about; yea, they compassed me about: but in the name of the Lord I will destroy them. They compassed me about like bees; they are quenched as the fire of thorns: for in the name of the Lord I will destroy them. Thou hast thrust sore at me that I might fall: but the Lord helped me. The Lord is my strength and song, and is become my salvation. The voice of rejoicing and salvation is in the tabernacles of the righteous: the right hand of the Lord doeth valiantly. The right hand of the Lord is exalted: the right hand of the Lord doeth valiantly. I shall not die, but live, and declare the works of the Lord. The Lord hath chastened me sore: but He hath not given me over unto death.

f. 36a Open to me the gates of righteousness: I will go into them, and I will praise the Lord: this is the gate of the Lord, into which the righteous shall enter. I will praise Thee: for Thou hast heard me, and art become my salvation. 'I will praise Thee', etc. The stone which the builders refused is become the head stone of the corner. 'The stone', etc. This is the Lord's doing; it is marvellous in our eyes. 'This is', etc. This is the day which the Lord hath made; we will rejoice and be glad in it. 'This', etc. SAVE NOW, I beseech Thee, O Lord: O LORD, I beseech Thee, send now prosperity. BLESSED be he that cometh in the name of the Lord: we have blessed you out of the house of the Lord. God is the Lord, which hath shewed us light: bind the sacrifice with cords, even unto the horns of the altar. Thou art my God, and I will praise Thee: Thou art my God, I will exalt Thee. O GIVE THANKS unto the Lord; for He is good: for his mercy endureth for ever.

f. 36b Let[74] all thy works, O Lord, praise Thee, and let thy devoted ones, together with the righteous who fulfil thy will, bless Thee:

and let thy people Israel give thanks to Thee in song, let them praise, glorify and exalt thy Name, O our King. For unto Thee it is good to give thanks, and to thy Name it is sweet to sing: for from everlasting unto everlasting Thou art God. Blessed art Thou, O Lord, a King whom it is due to extol with praises.

[The celebrant] then takes the cup and recites the benediction:

Blessed art Thou, O Lord, our God, king of the cosmos, creator of the fruit of the vine.

Everyone then drains his cup, and they say the following grace:

Blessed art Thou, O Lord, our God, king of the cosmos: for the vine and the fruit of the vine; for the produce of the field; and for that desirable, rich and ample Land which Thou didst give unto thy people Israel, that they might eat of its fruit and be satisfied out of its richness. Have mercy upon thy people, and upon thy Temple: for Thou art good, and doest good unto all. Blessed art Thou, O Lord, for the vine and for the fruit of the vine.

Thereafter the company are not to eat, nor drink anything save water. Except that anyone who wishes to drink an [optional] fifth cup should recite over it the 'Great Hallel'[75] in the following manner. One begins from verse 1: 'O give thanks unto the Lord', and continues to the last verse: 'O give thanks unto the God of heaven', etc.; furthermore, after each single verse one should say: 'Let all thy works, O Lord … a King whom it is due to extol with praises'. Then one says: 'Blessed … creator of the fruit of the vine', [after which one drinks the cup] and says the grace over the vine and its fruit.

[THE END]

---

[1] The introductory direction is expressed up to this point not in Hebrew but in Aramaic; save that the word *firqa*, translated 'prayer-gathering', is Arabic (literally, 'flock', 'gathering', 'sect'). In contemporary Jewish usage from North Africa it means a small, semi-domestic gathering for communal worship, not assembled in a synagogue building. Conceivably the word was adopted in order to avoid the conventional Arabic terminology of Islam. [2] *Gen.* 2, 1–3. [3] This word (*'am*) is omitted, as is also the preceding benediction over the wine. [4] There is here a lacuna (rather than a genuine variant): 'Thou hast distinguished and pronounced thy people Israel to be holy with thine own holiness.' [5] Vocalized *YaQNeHaZ*; this is formed from the initials of the words for the subject of each of the benedictions: *Yayin* ('wine'), *Qiddush* ('Sanctification'), *Ner* ('lamp'), *Habdalah* ('distinction') and *Zeman* ('season', referring to the thanksgiving for having reached the festive date). [6] This paragraph is in Aramaic. [7] *Mishnah, Pesaḥim* X, 4, the last question being substituted to suit a post-Temple age in which sacrifices are not offered. [8] *Ha-marbeh* has been omitted by the scribe. [9] Outside the *Haggadah* itself there is no ancient source for this anecdote; but a parallel story concerning Rabbi Gamaliel and 'the elders' is found in *Tosephta, Pesaḥim* X, 12. [10] *Mishnah, Berakhoth* I, 5. [11] *Deut.* 16, 3. [12] *Deut.* 6, 20. The Massoretic text here reads *'ethkhem*, 'you', and since, in the sequel, the 'wicked' son is criticized for using the second-person plural instead of the first, the change (which is found in many *Haggadah* texts, including the Sarajevo *Haggadah* and the text of Maimonides) may be tendentious. Such boldness, however, in connection with the biblical text would be remarkable. No biblical Hebrew MSS attest the variant *'othanu*, 'us', but that is the reading that underlies the Greek rendering in the *Septuagint*, a translation which dates from the 3rd century BCE. It may therefore be the case that this *Haggadah* variant represents the survival of a different Hebrew textual tradition. [13] *Mishnah, Pesaḥim* X, 8. The rendering agrees, approximately, with the traditional interpretation of *'afikoman*, the etymologies offered for which in the Rabbinic texts are clearly contrived. The word is obviously Greek, but its identification is uncertain. To the suggested explanations summarized in the *Jewish Encyclopedia* I, p. 224, may be added the possibility that *'afiqoman* is no more than a transcription of *(n)a phikome*, which in medieval Greek (stretching back to late antiquity) means 'let's go' – an expression that might be judged too casual a conclusion to a festive occasion of such momentous significance. [14] *Ex.* 12, 26; 13, 14. [15] *Ex.* 13, 8. [16] *Ex.* 13, 14. [17] The following construction of the text is taken from the *Mekhilta*, the halakhic commentary to *Exodus, in loc.* (section 17); the sequel is embodied in the explanation (already given) of the reply to be proffered to the 'wicked' son. [18] *Josh.* 24, 2–4. [19] *Gen.* 15, 13–14. [20] In 1938 Louis Finkelstein argued (*Harvard Theological Review*, 31, pp. 291–317) that this exegetical section of the *Haggadah*, with its anti-Aramaean ('Syrian') slant and its toning down of hostility towards Egypt, must ante-date the final loss of control of Palestine by the Ptolemies to the Seleucids of Syria in 198 BCE. The subsequent discovery of the Dead Sea Scrolls renders it doubtful (not least for linguistic reasons) that the present text of the section is so old; but it is not impossible that the germ of the idea goes back to the political propaganda of the time. [21] In the biblical context Jacob is (rather curiously) described as an Aramaean, and *'obed* is a participle of the *qal* form ('about to perish'). But the reapplication which would make Laban the villain of the piece has been achieved by recognizing in *'obed* the past of the rare *po'el* form, the force of which is the notion of *tentative imposition* ('an Aramaean [Laban] attempted to destroy my father [Jacob]'). [22] *Deut.* 26, 5–8. [23] *Gen.* 15, 13. [24] *Gen.* 47, 4. [25] *Deut.* 10, 22. [26] *Ex.* 1, 7. [27] *Ex.* 16, 7. [28] *Deut.* 26, 6. [29] *Ex.* 1, 10. [30] The MS adds: 'the Egyptians', erroneously repeated from the previous heading. [31] *Ex.* 1, 11. [32] *Ex.* 1, 13. [33] *Ex.* 2, 23. [34] *Ex.* 2, 24. [35] *Ex.* 2, 25. [36] *Ex.* 1, 22. [37] *Deut.* 3, 9. [38] *Deut.* 26, 9. [39] The inclusion of the definite article (*ha-shaliah*), as in the Sarajevo *Haggadah* and many printed editions, is remarkable. It appears to be an indirect repudiation of Christian (or possibly Gnostic) claims. [40] *Ex.* 12, 12. [41] *Ex.* 9, 3. [42] *I Chron.* 21, 16; the incongruity of this proof-text is probably due to the exegete's insistence that the actuality of each phrase's reference must be demonstrated. There is no scriptural reference to the divine wielding of a sword either at the exodus or at the crossing of the Red Sea. [43] The following exegesis implies that in place of *mora'*, 'fearfulness', *mar'eh*, 'vision' (meaning 'visible effects'), was either read or understood; the latter sense corresponds to the rendering in the Aramaic *Targum* of 'Onqelos. [44] *Be-massoth*, 'by challenging acts', which in the biblical text precedes, is omitted in the MS. [45] *Deut.* 4, 34. [46] *Ex.* 4, 17. [47] *Joel* 3, 3 (English 2, 30). [48] *Deut.* 26, 9. [49] דצ״ך עד״ש באח״ב. [50] רצ״ך עד״ש באח״ב. [51] *Mekhilta, Beshallaḥ*

6, on *Ex.* 14, 31. ⁵² The following exegetical extrapolation from the literal statements of the texts concerned is probably intended as no more than an exercise in casuistry. But it does reflect a general rabbinic reluctance to admit that the inspired biblical writers may have permitted themselves some licence with factual truth for the sake of metaphor, rhetoric or poetic effect. ⁵³ *Ex.* 8, 15. ⁵⁴ *Ex.* 14, 31. ⁵⁵ *Ps.* 78, 49; the psalm includes a detailed account of Israel's experiences in Egypt. ⁵⁶ Some of the links in this chain are illogical, since, for example, being conducted to Mount Sinai would have been pointless without the subsequent gift of the Torah. Some commentators rebut this criticism by arguing that it would have been adequate had each step, as a preliminary to the next, taken a less spectacular form; see the commentary to f. 34b, p. 75. ⁵⁷ *Mishnah, Pesaḥim* X, 5. ⁵⁸ *PSḤ*, the root of *pesaḥ*, means literally to 'limp', or by extension 'hop'. In *Ex.* 12, 11–13; 12, 27, it is paraphrased by 'passing (i.e. 'hopping') over [the Israelite houses]', but the word itself is apparently linked to a lambing festival celebrated long before Israel ever entered Egypt. ⁵⁹ *Ex.* 12, 27. ⁶⁰ *Ex.* 12, 39. ⁶¹ *Ex.* 1, 14. ⁶² *Mishnah, Pesaḥim* X, 5. ⁶³ *Ex.* 13, 8. ⁶⁴ *Deut.* 6, 23. ⁶⁵ *Goyim* inserted in margin. ⁶⁶ MS *tirqedu* for *raqedu*, by anticipation. ⁶⁷ *Mishnah, Pesaḥim* X, 6. ⁶⁸ MS *li-ke-she-yaggia'* (cf. *Sarajevo Haggadah*: '*ad she-yaggia'). ⁶⁹ The Aramaic *ḥassa* ('lettuce') here replaces the Hebrew word *ḥazereth*. ⁷⁰ See n. 13. ⁷¹ *Ps.* 79, 6; the inclusion of this verse, immediately after the Grace and before the 'psalms of praise', seems to reflect a situation in which, because of anti-Jewish agitation (often occasioned by Holy Week preceding Easter), it was too dangerous to spend Passover evening in noticeably large dining-groups. Parties may therefore have dispersed to eat, only to find, on reconvening, that their number was depleted. ⁷² '*Attem* omitted in MS. ⁷³ MS *ki*, 'that', by error for '*ani*, 'I'. ⁷⁴ *Babylonian Talmud, Pesaḥim* 118a. ⁷⁵ I.e. *Psalm* 136.

f. 37b   [Hymns for the First Day]

# 6 Introduction [to Nishmath]¹ for the First Day of Passover

By Rabbi Isaac [Ibn Ghayyat], of blessed memory

[The acrostic reads: יצחק חזק. 'Isaac, Courage'.]

How may thy dove,² with troubles fraught,
Storm-fluttered, sing thy praise,
Recalling joy Passover brought
In those long distant days?

The righteousness of God who lives
For aye, must calm her fears,
Hope in whose justice courage gives
Down her unending years.

In place of sacrificial gift
Or wine-libations, she
Would fain her palms to heaven lift,
Offering prayer to Thee.

She rose,³ hearing her Lover's voice,
And on her door his knock;
Her hand, in opening, dripped choice
Unguents about the lock.

While down her ledger ruled by time,
Months and years onward roll,
Thee she aspires in hymns sublime
With each breath⁴ to extol.

---

¹ Literally a '*Reshuth*' to *Nishmath*. For a discussion of this poetic genre, see p. 17. ² *S. of S.* 1, 14; for its significance on Passover, see poem 2, introductory note. ³ *S. of S.* 5, 2–6; for MS *dor* ['*al peiḥaḥekha*] read *dod*. ⁴ *Nishmathah*, leading into the established doxology, *Nishmath*, discussed on p. 17.

# 7 Muḥarrakh¹

[By Isaac Ibn Ghayyat. The acrostic reads: יצחק. 'Isaac'.]

As this day, all life long, whilst thy world numbers days,
    All that lives to thy Name with each breath shall give praise.

Shewing forth thy great deeds day and night they compete,
From thy praises to fashion a throne, as thy seat:²

Each one made by Thee, finished, thy judgement obeys:
    All that lives to thy Name with each breath shall give praise.

By Intelligence, past all sharp sophistry keen,
All sustaining – Thyself unsustained – Thou art seen,
The world's Place,³ Thee the world in no place ever lays;
    All that lives to thy Name with each breath shall give praise.

Hid all visions of Thee, for man's eyesight too fine,
Of thine essence each act is an hundredfold sign,
Since, proceeding from Thee, thy seal each one displays:
    All that lives to thy Name with each breath shall give praise.

If from sickness one rises, or ever one rides
On a royal mount, no constellation decides
When man rises or couches: who Thee, Lord, could raise?
    All that lives to thy Name with each breath shall give praise.

Thou man, think of his greatness at bread that He gives
Morn and eve, from whose life thine own body's blood lives,
Made thy mother a vine⁴ that with fruit He arrays:
    All that lives to thy Name with each breath shall give praise.

Lord, thy son – called thy vineyard⁵ – from hurricanes shield:
Without Thee, who shall dare with raised arm sword to wield,
And say: 'of thy peoples, the choice vine⁶ erase'?
    All that lives to thy Name with each breath shall give praise.

---

¹ A 'link-poem', in this case between the introduction (*Reshuth*) and *Nishmath* itself. For a fuller discussion of the terms, see p. 19. ² *Ps.* 22, 4(3). ³ The *midrash* to *Psalm* 90, 1 (ed. S. Buber, f. 195b, English translation by W. G. Braude, ii, p. 93, and parallel texts) emphasizes that God, one of the surrogates for whose name is *Ha-maqom*, 'The Place', contains the cosmos rather than being Himself located in it. The exegesis – and possibly the use of the surrogate itself – seems to be aimed at combatting Stoic notions. ⁴ Cf. *Ps.* 128, 3. ⁵ *Is.* 5, 7. ⁶ *Ps.* 80, 9(8), 15(14).

# 8 Nishmath¹

[By Joseph ben Isaac (possibly Ibn Abitur). The acrostic reads: יוסף בר יצחק (*sic*). 'Joseph bar Isaac', repeated internally and with the opening of each culminating biblical quotation.]

The breath of Israel's remnant, thy care-laden folk,
Hails Thee sole God this day, their captor's rigour broke:
    'Men shall tell how He wrought his will;
    Those not yet born his deeds shall thrill'.²

The breath of those redeemed from realms of heathen kings
Greets Thee: new songs³ they sing, in place of offerings:
    'Like those whose hearts' joy beats along
    With the pipe's note, in festive throng'.⁴

f. 38a   The breath of those left – once an awe-inspiring sight –
Exalts with sweet-sung psalms thine over-towering might:
    'Thy word fills me with joy, possessed
    Like one who finds a treasure-chest'.⁵

The breath of those ransomed from emptiness in hell
Hymns Thee: in place of music's strains, their voices swell.
    'My soul in peace Thou hast brought back,
    Redeemed from all who would attack'.⁶

The breath of those tested, mid crowds by laws unchecked,
Blesses Thee, who from rude assailants did protect;
    'They voice their thanks in song, while they
    Progress along the pilgrims' way'.⁷

The breath of princely stock upon this paschal morn
Sings to Thee, who in Memphis slayed all those firstborn,
    'Those who, descended in Ham's line,

37

Of their sires' manhood were the sign'.[8]
Their breath, who – well beloved – Scripture read this day,
Owns Thee unique, on Passover conjoined to pray,
  'For mercies, thanks to God they bring,
    Wonders He wrought for men they sing'.[9]

The breath of Israel's hosts with music's descant spells
Thy righteousness, O Rock, of which each poet tells:
  'North, south Thou madest: Thee to praise
    Tabor and Hermon voices raise'.[10]

The breath of those that daily con thy laws, to learn,
Declares thy might: the day's complete rules all discern,
  'Detailing how all must be fed
    For seven days unleavened bread'.[11]

Their breath, whose psalmody marks out this wondrous date,
Proclaims Thee holy, who new wonders wilt create:
  'Hark, to their gratitude outpoured:
    O Lord of Hosts, we thank Thee, Lord!'[12]

Their breath, who long to make thy will their own life's aim,
Praises the living Lord, who saves, for aye the same:
  Saying: 'Our mouths could not match Thee,
    Though full of praise as rolls the sea'.[13]

---

[1] A poem to be inserted after the standard *Nishmath* prayer, and before *We-'ilu phinu*. For a discussion of this and other genres. see p. 17. [2] *Ps.* 22, 32 (31). [3] The 7th word of the bottom line on f. 37b, is to be corrected to *we-ron* (see British Library MS 1404, f. 31a). [4] *Is.* 30, 29. [5] *Ps.* 119, 162. [6] *Ps.* 55, 19(18). [7] *Ps.* 42, 5(4). [8] *Ps.* 78, 51. [9] *Ps.* 107, 8. [10] *Ps.* 89, 13(12). [11] *Ex.* 13, 6, and 12, 15 (combined). [12] *Jer.* 33, 11. [13] The opening words of the prayer following *Nishmath* are: 'Were our mouth as full of song as the sea', a theme introduced by the last line of this and other poems of this genre.

---

## 9 'Ophan[1]

[By Isaac Ibn Ghayyat. The acrostic reads: יצחק, 'Isaac'.]

One, unique – Thou dost predate
  Time: thy wonders fascinate,
Since revealed to all mankind
  Who to silence are resigned.
Mysteries intense, too deep,
  Make them reticent. We sleep;
Living, we are dead; each day,
  Like a shadow slips away.
Not one honour that men prize
  With the glow of rubies vies:
Gold or ruby, nought is there
  Can with God on high compare;
Nor shall angels, standing near
  God's throne, claim to be his peer.
View thy Maker's wonders: know
  Whence thou camest, whither go.[2]
Why trust life? Who can rely
  On the sight that meets the eye?
Gone from human view,[3] thou must
  To thy base return as dust.
Evil manners, ways well tried
  In this world, will no more hide
Moral faults than God-spun mesh,
  Made from light, hid Adam's flesh.[4]
Think again, and whilst thy skin

Holds all that thou art within,
  Recognize thy Maker – He
    Shews the path of life to thee.
All that live, once full their lot
  Of years, are planted in death's plot,
Nor know why He did appoint
  Time and place to be conjoint
That, forthwith from birth, will set
  All inside a fishing-net,[5]
After death their clan to greet
  In the shades, where each must meet
Such reward as justifies
  What he made his merchandise,
Eating from his haversack
  Fare that he himself did pack,
Placed in rank as fits the worth
  Of what he achieved on earth.
Angels, rainbow-hued,[6] dilate,
  Praising wonders passing great
Wrought by Him who gives, or takes,
  What one rich, and one poor makes;
Health, disease, He likewise sends,
  Anything He starts, He ends.
All foreseeing, what He wills
  He keeps hid from human skills.
Heaven's choirs surrounding raise
  Swelling waves of song-borne praise:
Yet, with all their homage, they
  Who extol Him can but say:
'Who is He, whose very place
  Lies beyond our ken to trace?'[7]

f. 38b

---

[1] A poem inserted into the morning thanksgiving for the creation of light. 'Ophan is a type of angel, referred to in *Ez.* 1, 16 and 19 f, and seen praising God in *Ez.* 3, 13. For a description of the liturgical setting, see p. 18. [2] *Mishnah, 'Aboth* III, 1 ('From a fetid drop to a place of dust and worms'). [3] *Mey 'ayin* (end of line 3) is to be corrected to read *me-'ayin*. [4] The coats of 'skin' ('*or*) made by God for Adam and Eve (*Gen.* 3, 21) were represented in rabbinic lore as being of a quasi-mystic quality, and made from 'light' ('*or*) – according to one view of as fine a texture as the transparent fabric made at Beth Shean: *Midrash Gen. Rabbah* 20, 12. L. Ginzberg (*The Legends of the Jews*, V, p. 198, n. 79) lists the sources that detail the subsequent history of these garments, which passed through Cain to Nimrod, etc. Cain is mentioned here rather than Adam because of the exigencies of the rhyme. [5] Literally: 'netted antelope': *Is.* 51, 20. [6] *Hashmal*, mentioned in *Ez.* 1, 4 and 27, is of uncertain meaning (the *New English Bible* renders, from the context, 'radiance'). Like 'ophan, it became identified in tradition with a type of angel, because of its contextual setting. The 'rainbow' is suggested by vv. 13, 15. [7] This interpretation of the supposed implications of the last words in *Ez.* 3, 12 occurs in *Pirqey de-rabbi Eliezer*, 4, end, whence it was taken up into several of the liturgical embellishments of the *Trishagion* ('holy, holy, holy', *Is.* 6, 3).

---

## 10 Me'orah[1]

[By Isaac Ibn Ghayyat. The acrostic reads: יצחק, 'Isaac'.]

Thou garden-dwelling maid,[2] put forth thy green,
Thy blossom don, fruits of choice hue display,
Let spiceman's scents, breath-wafted, mark thy train,
And thine own light, thy rising sun, be seen.
With brilliance flood the east: the nations' way
Let thy light point, kings by thy brightness reign.[3]

Blow, north wind, blow! Thou, gentle south,[4] restore
Her exiles spurned, their far-flung horde's complaint.
From dust shake thyself free[5] – despair is vain;

As I live, I forget thee not. Thy gore
I rinse, from filth I cleanse away thy taint:
Rise from engulfing hell,[6] thy rest regain.[7]

The host of them that harry thee, and press,[8]
Shall lick the dust beneath thy feet;[9] to thee
Tribute they render, in thine own domain.
Lay weeds aside, wear jewels, not mourner's[10] dress;
See, fresh I make thee sprout: relit by Me[11]
Messiah's candle shall undimmed remain.

Ascending savours of thine offering
Shall, from thine altar with God's good will meet.[12]
Thy priests shall guard the shrine,[13] and stand again
To bless thee: new hymns on thy Sabbath sing,
New songs of praise, Passover-tide to greet:
Thy sun shall no more set, nor thy moon wane.[14]

    As it is written: 'And the nations shall walk by thy light,
and kings by the brightness of thy rising';[15] and it is
said: 'Thy sun shall no more go down; neither shall
thy moon withdraw itself',[14] etc.

---

[1] A poem to be inserted before the closing words of the morning thanksgiving: 'Blessed art Thou, O Lord, Creator of light'. It literally means: 'Light [poem]'. For a description of its liturgical setting, see p. 18. [2] S. of S. 8, 13. See poem 2, introductory note. [3] Is. 60, 3. [4] S. of S. 4, 16; Is. 43, 6. [5] Is. 52, 2. [6] In the 5th line, in place of [qumi we-he'ali] mi-nuḥekh, read mi-goḥekh, 'from that which bursts forth [around]', or possibly 'which belches out'; cf. Ez. 32, 2. [7] Ps. 116, 7. [8] In the 6th line, for the 4th word mishḥekh, presumably read moshekhekh, 'the one who drags thee away'; cf. Ez. 32, 20. [9] Is. 49, 23. [10] In the 7th line, for mizraḥekh, 'east', read marzaḥekh, 'mourning', cf. Jer. 16, 5. [11] Ps. 132, 17. [12] Is. 56, 7. [13] In the 8th line, the 4th word from the end, missaḥekh, should read mesakkekh, 'screen' or 'veil [of the tabernacle or holy of holies]'; Ex. 26, 36; 35, 12. [14] Is. 60, 20. [15] Is. 60, 3.

---

## 11 Me'orah[1]

[By Judah Hallevi. The acrostic reads: יהודה, 'Judah'.]

Orphaned, hope's prisoner[2] in Thee shall find
Mercy:[3] his heart, by fires of suffering burned,
Hopes on, from constant moving sick in mind,
And dreams thy captive hosts by Thee returned,
As prisoners dream of ransom from their plight.

My mercies' surge this younger son holds dear:
Or e'er he thinks on Me, my love is stirred.[4]
Is that my son's voice?[5] Esau's spawn I hear:
A wraith's voice thine, my son, from Hades heard;
Thy rival's roar sounds with the lion's might.[6]

But when requital's day shall come, beside
Rainstorms that shower vengeance, I shall send
My mercy's dew:[7] thee shall my plans divide
From them; thy dew[8] with blessing shall descend,
Which on the nations shall with wrath alight.

Faithful to thee my changeless Word; what they,
Devious, demolish, is rebuilt by Me.[9]
Dost cry? Clear shall the watchman's answer say,
'O prisoner of my foe, arise, and see,
God is thy shade:[10] theirs is departed quite'.[11]

Why say ''tis hopeless',[12] whilst God's help is thine?
Why grieve for wounds from which thy hopes must spring?
In but a trice thy lamp thou shalt see shine
Which to thy mourning-days their term shall bring,
And God, world without end, shall be thy light.[13]

---

[1] See poem 10, n. 1. [2] Zech. 9, 12. [3] Hos. 14, 4(3). [4] S. of S. 2, 7. [5] Gen. 27, 18 and 22. [6] Zech. 11, 3. [7] These references to dew glance forward to the major theme of the additional service of the day; see poem 15, introductory note. [8] Hos. 14, 6(5). For the notion that dew may sometimes be noxious, see Midrash Lev. Rabbah 28, 3 and 5, on Lev. 23, 10. [9] Mal. 1, 4 (ironical inversion). [10] Ps. 121, 5. [11] Num. 14, 9. [12] Jer. 2, 25. [13] Is. 60, 20.

---

## 12 'Ahabah[1]

[By Joseph. The author's name appears in an acrostic: (sic) יושף, 'Joseph'.]

My dove,[2] grown wan – thou longest for rest;
Daughter, thy sighs for freedom yearn:
How long as a captive, scorned, depressed,
Must dwell, must cry: 'how can I learn,
Alone, to bear confinement's part,
With surging through my lonely heart
Pangs of my bonds, so tightly tied
By foes – the thorns that prick my side?'[3]

f. 39a

I look, O Lord, for thy saving dew:[4]
My lovesick heart when wilt Thou mend?
Cast down mine enemies, aye, pursue
Their scouts; on those perdition send
Who root and branch would axe. I moan,
Bitter that all my life, alone
I roam where hills and mountains keep
Repeating echoes whilst I weep.

Rejoice and sing,[5] my beauteous hind,[6]
Oppressors thou shalt yet oppress.
My daughter, repair the paths, and find
Thy way to courts of holiness,
My best-loved spot; let music's choir
Rejoice thee there, in rich attire
Clothe thee, in silks and rich brocade
With jewels set off, and pearls inlaid.

Captivity's chains I loose for thee:[7]
Dawn breaks o'er exile; thy sun's ray
Bids thee come home, that now art free.
No more my bond I take away[8]
From people crushed, my faith, my truth:
Mindful of love that marked thy youth[9]
My slave I place where henceforth springs
From him a noble line of kings.[10]

---

[1] A poem to be inserted before the closing words of the thanksgiving beginning: 'With everlasting love Thou hast loved us'. It literally means: 'Love'. For a description of its liturgical setting, see p. 18. [2] S. of S. 2, 14. See poem 2, preliminary note. [3] Num. 33, 55. [4] See poem 15, introductory note. [5] Zech. 2, 14(10). [6] Prov. 5, 19. [7] Ps. 116, 16. [8] Is. 54, 10. [9] Jer. 2, 2. [10] Gen. 35, 11.

---

## 13 Zulath[1] [Author unknown. Alphabetical acrostic.]

In ancient times Thou didst reveal thy face
To Moses, meekest of the human race.[2]
Speaking him fair: 'I will exalt thy name,[3]
A memory down endless years the same:
A saint remembered ripples blessings through his fame.[4]

    My ways I show thee,[5] raising thy degree
    Beyond what any prophet else shall see.[6]
    Go, land the Dragon,[7] caught in thy net's twine.
    From prison lead this folk – both mine and thine[8] –

Thus I exalt thy name: of blessing be the sign.[9]
Quoth Moses: 'Lord, my Maker, pointing straight
The road, Thou dost my heart invigorate.
Yet fear of Pharaoh[10] grips me; my soul quakes
Lest, all my message heard, my bones he breaks,
No blessing then – rather a curse – my mention makes.'[11]

    'Nay', God replied, 'thy stirling worth I know,[12]
    Thy brother Aaron too, and shall bestow
    Glory on both, all people will behold:
    Go in my Name, and see this staff you hold,[13]
    That with my blessing shall you both this day enfold.'[14]

Well-chosen words before the king[10] they spoke:
'Those God primevally[15] chose for his folk,
This noble race,[16] let go; no more impress
Their labour, winning profit to excess;
Their load removed, earn thanks from those who then shall bless.'[17]

    The Dragon, breathing fire, his answer roared:
    'What rank is his', he snarled, 'whom you style "lord"?'[18]
    What can he do? Be gone![19] I will not lend
    My ears; his staff – of wood – I hold contemned.'
    Pharaoh recked nought of blessing that the Lord might send.[20]

God struck the tyrant down: his holy power
Smote, wondrous, all firstborn on midnight's hour.[21]
Redemption those redeemed new songs did teach[22]
To praise Him who by deeds fulfilled his speech,
Whom mankind's praise and blessing cannot ever reach.[23]

---

[1] A poem inserted between the declaration of God's uniqueness ending: 'There is no God except for Thee', and a recital of Israel's providential history, including the exodus. The name itself means: 'Except [for]'. For more on the liturgical setting, see p. 18. [2] *Num.* 12, 3. [3] *Ex.* 32, 10. [4] *Prov.* 10, 17. [5] *Ex.* 33, 13. [6] *Deut.* 34, 10. [7] I.e. Pharaoh; *Ez.* 29, 3. [8] *Ex.* 3, 10; 32, 7; 33, 13. [9] *Gen.* 12, 2. [10] Ḥophra (Greek *Apries*, 26th Dynasty) ruled Egypt 589–64, in the time of Jeremiah (*Jer.* 44, 30); Necho II (*II Kings* 23, 29), slightly earlier, was a contemporary of King Josiah. Jewish time-concepts take such anachronisms in their stride. [11] *Gen.* 27, 12. [12] *Ex.* 33, 12. [13] *Ex.* 4, 17. [14] *Ex.* 32, 19. [15] *Deut.* 33, 27. [16] *Ps.* 47, 10(9). [17] *Il Kings* 5, 15. [18] *Ex.* 5, 2. [19] *Ex.* 10, 28. [20] *Ps.* 109, 17. [21] *Ps.* 78, 51; *Ex.* 12, 29. [22] See n. 1. [23] *Neh.* 9, 5.

## 14 Ge'ullah[1]

[By Joseph. The author's name appears in an acrostic: יוסף, 'Joseph'.]

Those who ask me to name my ransom's date
    Fill me with pain;
'From my Redeemer's love estranged I rate',
    Hushed, I complain.
Spoilers, intent to grieve, round me their hate
    Like firebrands rain.
Enthroned on high, give ear: regard, I pray,
    My passioned plea;
Thine heritage[2] with wondrous mercies stay,[3]
    My saviour be.[4]

Let thy son glimpse thy glory, his trust based
    On thy Name, sure,
Whose joy in Thee gives thy law honeyed taste,
    As manna pure;
He cries: couldst Thou forget him, Father, placed
    Captive, obscure?
Thy saving dews,[5] thy mercies' dews direct
    My praise to Thee:
Answer me: in thy shade, thy splendour decked,
    Lord, bandage me.

Don zeal, might's armour, anger gird; nor close
    Thine ear to tears
Of one afflicted, who no raiment knows
    But his own fears,
Weak from deceits invented by his foes
    And from their jeers.
I meet Thee, languishing, to beg thine aid,
    Pray grant it me;
Hear on this day my words before Thee laid
    To call on Thee.

My limping gait fills rough men[6] with delight,[7]
    They sneer,[8] hard-faced;
My days of glory gone – a shadow's flight –
    I stray, displaced.
Malignant forces[9] talk, my folk to spite,
    My pride disgraced.
Steady me: on my road thy flag display
    Raised over me,
My captive years, Redeemer mine, repay,[10]
    Redeem for Thee.[11]

f. 39b

---

[1] A poem inserted before the closing words of the thanksgiving for redemption, ending: 'Blessed art Thou, O Lord, who didst redeem Israel'. The word means 'Redemption'. For a discussion of the liturgical setting, see p. 18. [2] *Deut.* 32, 9. [3] *Ps.* 17, 7. [4] *Ps.* 89, 27 (26). [5] See poem 15, introductory note. [6] *Judg.* 9, 4. [7] *Ps.* 35, 15. [8] *Ps.* 35, 21. [9] *Rahab*, 'arrogance' or 'boisterousness', identified with the primeval sea-monster, and thus also with sinister forces and the enemy; *Job* 9, 13. [10] *Zeph.* 3, 20. [11] *Ruth* 4, 6.

[The Additional Service

Beginning from the Additional Service on the first day of Passover, the reference to God 'who causes the wind to blow and the rain to descend', that is included in all the statutory services during the autumn and winter months, is replaced for the duration of the summer by the words: 'who causes the dew to descend'. The change is marked by liturgical ceremoniousness, hymns being inserted before the climax of the benedictions leading up to the point where the rain/dew reference stands.]

## 15 Magen[1]

By Rabbi Solomon Ibn Gabirol, of blessed memory
[The acrostic reads: שלמה, 'Solomon'.]

Crushed was thy folk, whom Egypt's sun[2] did burn,
    And now by roaming wearied: grant them rest
With thy dew freshened, let their sap return;
    Thou, God, dost answer those who are oppressed,
When comes the time[3] that thy grace is revealed
    To them that trust Thee Thou dost prove a shield.[4]

---

[1] The 1st benediction of the *'Amidah* (the main prayer sequence in every service) focusses on the patriarchs and ends: 'Blessed art Thou, O Lord, the shield of Abraham'. The term *Magen* means 'shield'. For more on the liturgical setting, see p. 18. [2] *S. of S.* 1, 6. See poem 2, introductory note. [3] *Ps.* 69, 14(13). [4] *Ps.* 18, 31(30).

## 16 Meḥayyeh[1]

[By Solomon Ibn Gabirol. The acrostic reads: שלמה, 'Solomon'.]

Thy spirit send:[2] our corpse to life recall,
Our fairest land[3] to pristine youth restore;
From Thee our fruit stems, that art good to all:[4]
Surely Thou wilt revive us, as of yore.[5]

---

[1] The 2nd benediction of the *'Amidah* is concerned with the resurrection, and ends: 'Blessed are Thou, O Lord, who dost revive the dead'. *Meḥayyeh* means: 'Reviving'. For more on the liturgical setting, see p. 18. [2] *Ps.* 104, 30. [3] *Jer.* 3, 19. [4] *Ps.* 145, 9. [5] *Ps.* 85, 7(6).

## 17 Preamble to the Prayer for Dew

[By Solomon Ibn Gabirol. It contains the first portion (א-ה) of a quadruple alphabetical acrostic.]

With dew stored up by Thee, the earth to purify,
Invigorate those heaped to rot, like straw once threshed.[1]
For Abraham's sake, who Thee his son did not deny,
Make Reuben, under *Aries* his sign, refreshed.

With dew of blessing make to tinkle mountain rills,
Down slopes covered in produce sweet, by light caressed;
In April bless a people fainting from their ills,
And to thy promise look, which said they should be blessed.

> As it is written: 'Therefore God give thee of the dew
> of heaven, and of the fatness of the earth, and plenty
> of corn and wine.'[2]

With dew, Thou whom men turn towards, thy might to lend,
Wake those redeemed from dungeons dragons did surround;
As *Taurus* rises, Simeon's tribe do Thou defend,
For Isaac, who upon thy temple's rock was bound.

With dew make fertile sun-baked soil, hoe out its weeds;
Those travel has made poor, enrich from thine own stock,
At May's approach think on those lost: provide their needs
Who yearn to hear upon the door their Lover's knock.

> As it is written: 'I sleep, but my heart waketh: it is
> the voice of my beloved that knocketh, saying, open
> to me, my sister, my love, my dove, my undefiled;
> for my head is filled with dew, and my locks with
> the drops of the night.'[3]

With dew supply my cottage homes and rolling park,
In time of my prosperity, Lord, give me rest,
For Jacob, on thy throne engraved[4] to be my mark,
Let *Gemini*'s sign Levites see in splendour dressed.

With dew that meets rough ground and lowland, send thy boon
On land wind-swept like bones,[5] where no decay can thrive;
The season's rhythm fix, vision to bring with June,[6]
For all of Jacob's scattered folk who may survive.

> As it is written: 'And the remnant of Jacob shall be in
> the midst of many people as dew from the Lord, as
> the showers upon the grass, that tarrieth not for man, nor
> waiteth for the sons of men.'[7]

With dew that overflows drench Zion's base[8] unmoved:
Thy dove, trapped in the rocks, send forth on soaring wing,[9]
For Moses, by Torah, his witness, spotless proved,
Let Judah's lion out from *Cancer*'s covert spring.[10]

With dew, in heaven's vaults to foster growth assigned,
Cleanse those that trust in Thee, as jasper clear to shine:
When comes July, the prophet's words keep Thou in mind
Who spoke of peace, sown for all time, a fruitful vine.

> As it is written: 'For the seed shall be peace; the vine
> shall give her fruit, and the ground shall give her increase,
> and the heavens shall give their dew; and I will cause the
> remnant of this people to possess all these things.'[11]

[1] *Is.* 25, 10. [2] *Gen.* 27, 28. [3] *S. of S.* 5, 2; see poem 2, introductory note. [4] Rabbinic tradition asserts that the human figure on the divine chariot-throne (*Ez.* 1, 10) displays the features of Jacob: *Babylonian Talmud, Ḥullin* 91b. [5] *Job* 33, 21. [6] The reference is probably to the feast of *Shavu'oth* (Pentecost) on 6 *Sivan* (May–June), that commemorates the giving of the Torah. [7] *Micah* 5, 6(7). [8] *Ps.* 87, 1. [9] *S. of S.* 2, 14. [10] *Gen.* 49, 9; *Deut.* 33, 22. [11] *Zech.* 8, 12.

f. 40a

## 18 Hymn   [Possibly by Solomon Ibn Gabirol.]

Thou whom all creatures trust, their refuge and their shade,
That givest all their prey, their sustenance as due,
Crown this our year, by winter's clouds near perfect made
Bearing late rains; now let the heavens give their dew.

The standing corn with dew-drops bless, health-giving bread,
That they who con thy royal law like stars may gleam:
Girdle with joy leas shimmering in moisture shed,
That garlanded in blooms[1] a bridal train may seem.

Thy bounties manifold, as if in words, they praise,
Lord of surpassing might, thy Name raised high above:
When we ask, guide us like a lamb that long-lost strays:[2]
Gentle as dew, give Abraham truth, give Jacob love.[3]

Seek Thou this lost sheep, so long slaughtered for thy sake,
Jacob's survivors, midst the nations, near unknown;
Let their root flourish like the rose,[4] young shoots to make,
Their lords' discarded slaves, now on the dunghill thrown.

Do Thou have someone raise him from the dust: with dew
Streaming like cloudbursts bring him back to life again,
To lead him,[5] as Thou didst long since, with cords that drew
Him gently harnessed, checked but by love's guiding rein.

On plain and mountain, plenty for God's noble trees:[6]
Let granges burst with corn, each press with wine and oil,
May sounds of joy across the land each hamlet seize
That dwells contented, built upon ancestral soil.

Lord God, how splendid, the world over, sounds thy Name,[7]
The flag that to thy company their meaning gave!
Thy folk for consolation bring to Thee their claim,
To Israel give that blessing all so eager crave.

Exulting at the limpid dew, the peasant sings
To see the leafy vale and grassland freshly green:
For Aaron, designate to bring thine offerings,
Do Thou, when *Leo* reigns, lend Issachar thy screen.

With saving dew have this folk henceforth nobly ranged
Whom murder overtook;[8] let them now bloom anew,
In August to rejoice, no more a folk estranged;
Restored, as when the manna came fresh with the dew.

> As it is written: 'And when the dew that lay was gone up,
> behold, upon the face of the wilderness there lay a small
> round thing, as small as hoarfrost on the ground.'[9]

With dew let hills rejoice, and meadows in the plain,
Where trees and grass look for its fall. Once, in the field
Joshua stood to arms all night:[10] for him, sustain
Zebulun, who displays *Virgo* upon his shield.

With dew, mindful of mercies Thou of old didst show
To Israel whom, maid-like, as fair-browed[11] Thou addressed,
Cool for thy dove September's heat, as if with snow
From Salmon's peak, or icy dew from Hermon's crest.

> As it is written: 'As the dew of Hermon that descended upon
> the mountains of Zion: for there the Lord commanded the
> blessing, even life for evermore.'[12]

[1] *I Kings* 6, 18. [2] *Jer.* 50, 17. [3] *Mic.* 7, 20. [4] *Hos.* 14, 6(5). [5] *Hos.* 11, 4. [6] *Ps.* 104, 16. [7] *Ps.* 8, 2(1). [8] Hinting at the destruction of the Temple, commemorated by the fast of 9 *'Ab* (July–August). [9] *Ex.* 16, 4. For *be-yom* (12th line, 1st word), read *ke-yom*. [10] *Josh.* 8, 9. [11] *S. of S.* 6, 7. See poem 2, introductory note. [12] *Ps.* 68, 15(14); 133, 3.

## 19 Hymn

[By Isaac. The author's name appears in an acrostic:
יצחק , 'Isaac', followed by a quadruple alphabetical
acrostic, letters מ-ע.]

Pray, from above thy blessing pour[1]
On pasture-lands, and on the few
Yards the smallholder tills, with more
Than they shall need, of heaven's dew.[2]

Pray, those dispersed across the east[3]
Give cause in song to raise their voice,
Seeing their land's produce increased
As heaven's dew[4] makes them rejoice.

Pray, how long must hell's belly pen
This cadet branch, whose fate is set
To roam, an outcast slave? And when
Shall dew in him new life beget?[5]

Pray, bind his wounds, relieve his pain
Who, like some grape that ungleaned stays,[6]
Waits one to tend, welcome as rain,
Or dew 'neath summer's torrid blaze.[7]

Pray, raise one languishing, aquake
Through fear, whom chasers hot pursue;
Save him: thy dew's salvation make
Descend on him like Hermon's dew.[8]

With dew that keeps fresh summer days
Through hope down years that still must roll,[9]
Deliver Dan, whom *Libra* weighs,
For Samuel and his lamb burnt whole.[10]

With dew thy gently nurtured race
Moisten, that now in dungeons lies,[11]
Erect, their autumn route to pace –
The season when their dead shall rise.

　　As it is written: 'Thy dead men
　　shall live, together with my dead
　　shall they arise; awake and sing,
　　ye that dwell in dust: for thy dew
　　is as the dew of herbs, and the
　　earth shall cast out the dead.'[12]

With dew, O Lord of heaven, tend
My self-grown shoots;[13] fence them, to grow,
For David's psalms: support extend
To Naphtali in *Scorpio*.

With dew from clouds in heaven's hall
Give those who hope a sign that cheers;
Pledge them that in November call:
'Thy folk shall march, all volunteers'.

f.40b　　As it is written: 'Thy people
　　shall be willing in the day of thy
　　power, in the beauties of holiness
　　from the womb of the morning:
　　thou hast the dew of thy youth.'[14]

---

[1] *Mal.* 3, 10: for *'al* (4th word) read *'ad*. [2] *Gen.* 27, 39.
[3] *Is.* 11, 11. [4] *Zech.* 8, 12. [5] *Job* 38, 28. [6] *Mic.* 7, 1.
[7] *Is.* 18, 14. [8] *Ps.* 133, 3. [9] *Dan.* 7, 25. [10] *I Sam.* 7, 9.
[11] *Job* 40, 13. [12] *Is.* 26, 19. [13] *Is.* 37, 30. [14] *Ps.* 110, 3.

## 20 Hymn

[By Isaac. The author's name appears
in a mutilated acrostic: יו[צח]ק, 'Isaac'.[1]]

The Lord ordain
　　Thy latter end
Shall thy beginning
　　Far transcend,
And as in days
　　That thy youth knew
Shall have once more
　　Thy childhood's dew.[2]

Like years gone by[3]
　　Renew our days,
That age may vie
　　With youth's brief phase;
Midst crowds that hurt
　　Me, Lord, contrive,
Like dew from Thee[4]
　　We shall survive.

In debt, we gasp
　　For breath, for shade,
Hoping that Thou
　　Wilt send us aid,
When hills sweet wine,[5]
　　Leas fat exude,[6]
By clemency
　　From Thee bedewed.

Thy words fulfil,
　　Let vision drive
Years, till we see
　　Thy works revive;[7]
For folk near Thee,
　　Or joining, bright
Shed over them
　　Thy dew of light.[8]

---

[1] In the text in the Sarajevo *Haggadah* (f. 61b),
*yeḥaddesh* is preceded by *ṣur*, 'Rock'. [2] *Ps.* 110, 3.
[3] *Lam.* 5, 21. [4] The Sarajevo *Haggadah* includes,
before *yiheyeh she'erithekha* (end of 2nd line), *ke-ṭal
me-'eth 'adonai* (*Mic.* 6, 6[7]). Since this is obviously
the original text, it has been included in the translation.
[5] *Amos* 9, 13. [6] *Ps.* 65, 13. [7] *Hab.* 3, 2. [8] *Is.* 26, 9.

## 21

[By Solomon Ibn Gabirol. There is a quadruple alphabetical acrostic – including the letters פ-ת –
thereafter: שלמה הקטן[?], 'Solomon the minor'.]

With dew let garden watercourses brimming flow[1]
Past shrubs well-shaped, fruit-laden trees to charm the sight;
For Solomon, who, palms outspread, once prayed, bowed low,[2]
When *Sagittarius* takes aim, give Dan delight.

With dew of righteousness shine forth; look how they fare,
This wizened folk; renew their sap, fresh as the pine.
When come December snows, their host resettle, where
At first they lived, in that fair land of corn and wine.

　　As it is written: 'Israel then shall dwell in safety alone: the
　　fountain of Jacob shall be upon a land of corn and wine;
　　also his heavens shall drop down dew.'[3]

With dew in far-off stores treasured away, distil
Richness on them that hope in Thee: for zeal
Elijah showed, directing sinners to thy will,
When *Caper* rules, Asher in ornaments reveal.

With dew make verdure wet in spring upon the leas,
And swell the summer's fruits, make vintage grow mature,[4]
To trickle, still unchecked, through January's freeze,
Welcome as dew when we midsummer must endure.

As it is written: 'For so the Lord said unto me, I will take my
rest, and I will consider in my dwelling place like a clear heat
upon herbs, and like a cloud of dew in the heat of harvest.'[5]

With dew of plenty check siroccos' broiling air:
Oppressors, foes, hack down, minding Elisha's haste
To ask Elijah's spirit in a twofold share;
Pleasure beneath *Aquarius'* spouts let Joseph taste.

With dew thine answer give to one, in suppliant mien,
That stands before Thee; mercy unto him renew:
Be pleased, in Zion a redeemer shall be seen
In February, be to Israel as the dew.

As it is written: 'I will be as the dew unto Israel: he shall
grow as the lily, and cast forth his roots as Lebanon.'[6]

With dew spread north, south, east and west, thine oath fulfil,
For Obadiah: hasten on the march of time;
As he prophets concealed, whom tyrants sought to kill,
Let *Pisces* bring to Benjamin glory sublime.

With dew ransom my root, to bloom at life's return;
On Passover, accept my cry: in March, sustain
Thy folk with kindness, whom their foes as refuse spurn;
The doctrine I should hear, let fall like gentle rain.

As it is written: 'My doctrine shall drop as the rain, my
speech shall distil as the dew, as the small rain upon the
tender herb, and as the showers upon the grass.'[7]

[1] *Ps.* 65, 10(9). [2] *I Kings* 8, 54. [3] *Deut.* 33, 28. [4] *Mic.* 7, 1. [5] *Is.* 18, 4. [6] *Hos.* 14, 6(5).
[7] *Deut.* 32, 2.

## 22 Hymn

[By Isaac ben Zeraḥyah. The acrostic reads: יצחק, 'Isaac'.]

This day make I petition to my Rock,
Him whom I praise, for dew: that He may please
To bless my land with produce that shall stock
My barns, to bless the fruit upon my trees:

'For his goodwill may this prayer prove the cue,
And may my words fall gentle as the dew'.[1]

This day for sustenance I seek: so much
As my house needs, for bread. My soul, present
For offering, these words; Lord, with thy touch
My prayer accept which as my gift is meant.

Thy dew I ask, that herb-beds may retain
Their green: pour blessings on me, till I shout
With lips and heart: 'Enough!' Bid health sustain
My body strong, until the year is out.

My weeks of labour watch, times on the farm
To reap and plough: each day's hopes make complete,

All my tomorrows blithe, in winter warm
Keep me, and keep me cool in summer's heat.

Reveal that date my exiled tribes desire,
Brought home: restore the Temple's cornerstone,
Priests to their altar, Levites in the choir,
And David's scion on his royal throne.

f. 41a

Our God, and God of our fathers:
With dew of scintillating light[2]
    lend royal splendour to the land,
With dew that blessing brings
    give blessing to the land,
With dew inspiring joy
    bring greatness to the land,
With dew on young grass sparkling
    bring richness to the land,
With dew that brings crowds thronging
    give glory to the land,
With dew that comes unfailing
    be seen to meet the land,
With dew that gives vitality
    show grace unto the land,
With dew that heralds goodness
    do Thou purify the land,
With dew that brings deliverance
    direct aright the land.

For in very truth it is Thou, O Lord, our God and God
of our fathers, who dost cause the dew to descend: prithee
make its descent be to us for light; for good; for blessing;
for life; and for plenty. Thou dost sustain the living, etc.[3]

[1] *Deut.* 32, 2. [2] Alphabetical acrostic, *'aleph-yod*. [3] The text of the statutory form
of the additional service is here resumed (see poem 15, introductory note), the prayer
continuing: 'Thou dost sustain the living in mercy and quicken the dead in abundant
lovingkindness . . . blessed art Thou, O Lord, who dost quicken the dead'.

[Hymns for the Second Day]

## 23 Introduction [to Nishmath][1] for the Second Day of Passover

[By Isaac Ibn Ghayyat. The acrostic reads: יצחק, 'Isaac'.]

Thy Name I know – majestic, passing great:
Mine eye descries Thee not, save through thy deeds,
To know whom wears the wise, till each concedes
Thy mystery too high to contemplate.
In these, my daring thoughts, I correlate
My search for Thee: the inward eye succeeds,
And, what it seeks achieved, my vision leads
To view the soul, bound to thy throne of state.

Thou didst Thyself breath into man his soul,
Though what she must inhabit is but slight,
Mere feeble flesh, a frame to dust returned.
Can what is visible survey the whole,
And man, myopic, claim to hold in sight
What holds, invisible, all else discerned?

[1] See poem 6, n. 1.

## 24 Introduction

[By Solomon Ibn Gabirol. The acrostic reads:
שלמה , Solomon'.]

'That[1] gate long closed, unchain,
    And through it send to me
My hart,[2] come back again,
    That long ago did flee,[3]
Returned to my embrace,
    My bedfellow to be,[4]
And leave, for me to trace,
    Entranced, the scent of Thee.'

'Fair bride, who is this swain
    Thou wouldst I send to thee?'[5]
'Fresh-skinned, to Him pertain
    Features a joy to see.
He is the One whose face
    I draw, my Lover He,
And Friend,[6] mine by his grace:
    Anoint Him, King to be!'

---

[1] This poem is based on the exegesis (traceable, in its germ, to late antiquity) of *S. of S.* 5, 9–16, which construes the physical description of the lover's features as a mystical statement regarding the divine 'physiognomy' (see the article by G. Scholem on *Shi'ur Komah, Encyclopaedia Judaica*, 14, 1417). The poem takes the form of a dialogue between Israel and God, conceived of both as the Lover and as simultaneously distinct from Him, in terms of sublimated eroticism. At the end, the divine figure becomes fused with the Messiah, and the address of the beloved is tacitly switched from Him to the 'daughters of Jerusalem' (5, 16) – simultaneously, perhaps, both the curious Gentile world and the angels of God's heavenly retinue. [2] *S. of S.* 2, 9. [3] *S. of S.* 5, 6; 8, 14. [4] *S. of S.* 1, 13. [5] *S. of S.* 5, 9. [6] *S. of S.* 5, 10f and 16.

## 25 Nishmath[1]

[Authorship uncertain. There is an apparently mutilated acrostic: שלמ , 'Solom . . .'.]

The breath of those who, God-bidden, this Passover feast keep
Extols his might, who saved their clans but drowned their foemen deep:
    'God's mercies I recall, on Him my praises heap'.[2]

The breath of those gasping from fear of traps the Dragon[3] laid
Praises their Rock, who Memphis' sons did punish with his blade;
    'Moses He sent, and Aaron, whom his choice He made'.[4]

The breath of those delivered from the thorns their sides did rend
Acclaims Him who works miracles, his mercies without end:[5]
    'Egypt's firstborn He smote; his mercies e'er extend'.[6]

The breath of those afflicted,[7] who from force did gain relief,
Crowns Him on high who, where is pain, brings ease in place of grief:
    'Captives He frees: backsliders, parched, must hug their reef'.[8]

The breath of those redeemed by Thee from their enslaver's might
Glorifies Thee, whose deeds, wrought in their days, they shall indite,
    'Done for those trusting Thee, before all mankind's sight'.[9]

f. 41b   The breath of those whose whole desire it is thy will to please
Exalts Thee, who the Ocean's crashing battle dost appease,
    Saying: 'Could only our mouth sing loud as the seas!'[10]

---

[1] See poem 8, n. 1. [2] *Is.* 63, 7. [3] I.e. Pharaoh: *Ez.* 29, 3. [4] *Ps.* 105, 26. [5] *Ps.* 136, 4. [6] *Ps.* 136, 10. [7] For *me'unneh*, read *me'unney*. [8] *Ps.* 68, 7(6). [9] *Ps.* 31, 20 (19). [10] See poem 8, n. 13.

## 26 'Ophan[1]

[By Isaac Ibn Ghayyat. The acrostic reads:
יצחק, 'Isaac'.]

Thy praises, Lord,
    Men love to tell.
Yet thy deeds' might
    Not one can spell,
Or wonders show
    Which, night and day,
Thine intellect
    Brings into play.
Thou, through thy Word,
    Didst bring to birth
Each single thing
    Upon this earth.
No other's deeds
    Thy greatness share,
O Lord, my God
    Beyond compare.[2]

All-seeing, Thou
    No eye dost need
Nor hand must use
    To do thy deed,
Nor mouth to speak:
    Thou livest on,
Unlike to man
    Tomorrow gone.
Since days of yore
    Full well men know
If Thou dost smite[3]
    'Tis Thou also
Dost heal; both ill
    And good dost Thou
Effect:[4] to both,
    As fair, we bow,
Since not by eye
    But in the mind
Canst Thou be seen
    By human kind.
Witness thy deeds
    That Thou art there;
O Lord, my God
    Beyond compare.

Wisdom in Thee
    Transcends[5] the wise,
Knowledge so vast
    It mystifies
Our little minds,
    Far, far beyond
What learned men
    Have ever conned.
The things that Thou
    Left incomplete,
To start, to end,
    Who shall compete?
Though from men's eyes
    Thou art concealed,

Through miracles
    Art Thou revealed.
No point assigns
    Thy height a place,
Yet Thou dost fill
    The whole world's space,
That bears not Thee:
    Thou dost it bear,
O Lord, my God,
    Beyond compare.

Holy thy Name
    Is called: the band
Of angels, too,
    That round Thee stand,
Made of the stuff
    Of purest light
Sapphire refracts,
    A mystic sight
Unlike in form
    To men, lest they
By any sense
    Be led astray.
Four regiments,
    Each one distinct,
Advance, in praise
    As one choir linked,
Who would to Thee
    Homage express,
Holy beyond
    All holiness.
Within thy courts
    They fill the air:
O Lord, my God
    Beyond compare.

---

[1] See poem 9, n. 1. [2] *Ps.* 40, 6(5). [3] *Deut.* 32, 39. [4] *Is.* 45, 7; *Eccles.* 3, 11. [5] In the 6th line, for the 4th word, *niphle'tha*, probably read *niphleytha* with yod.

# 27 Me'orah[1]

[By Abraham Ibn Ezra. The acrostic reads: אברהם, 'Abraham'.]

With heart and eyes downcast I turn to Thee
Who dost an humble, contrite heart regard:
Look Thou upon mine eye, see what I see –
A groaning folk, by suffering pressed hard.

Captive, thy son must cry: wearied, distraught,
Sated with gall, his temper will not wait
Submissive, checked – they who by grief are caught
May not be checked, but must expostulate.
The son of an estranged wife, preferred
Over the firstborn by a well-loved wife,
Inverts the law we from thine own mouth heard.[2]
Like blazing coals, fury in me is rife:
The Temple – God's own residence He to me gave –
Heritage of that brother meant to be my slave![3]

My sires strayed from thy will, and so, ungraced,

Did bear their punishment; whilst I, that hold
Fast to thy splendid robe, must see laid waste
Fields, precious to us still, we tilled of old.
Father, wouldst Thou in wrath condemn to die
Sons for their fathers' sins?[4] To Thee I cleave,
As cleave I must, for, shouldst Thou kill me, I
Yet hoping on Thee,[5] could not ever leave.
Should I, the One forgot, a second by him range,
Then forget Thou – my folk for uncouth folk exchange!

On Thee dependent, full of trust am I,
For, other is there none who carries out
His very word. To whom else should I cry?
Did I before a wooden image shout,
Would it, by any action, answer me?
Should I in front of alabaster crave
Some saint's assistance, would he hear my plea?
Lord, take me, who am thine exclusive slave.
Fetter my captive neck:[6] harsh irons let me bear,
Or pierce my ear[7] – the slave's mark as my jewel I wear.

Another's captive, I must bear the yoke
Of wandering. My Rock, upon my sore
Lay balm; crops withered before harvest, soak
With dew,[8] thy mercy let the fruit restore.
Bring back the ancient days,[9] once more renew
That youthful love which once did us enfold:
Dismiss from near Thee this rebellious crew,
As when God guarded me in days of old.[10]
Open thy gates to save me! Calling, let me hear
Thine answer: with thy truth[11] light[12] me the course to steer.

---

[1] See poem 10, n. 1. [2] *Deut.* 21, 15–17. [3] *Gen.* 27, 29. Esau/Edom is, in rabbinic convention, the archetypal figure of Rome, and thus also of Christendom. Jerusalem was captured by the Franks in 1099, when Abraham Ibn Ezra was ten years old. [4] *Deut.* 24, 16. [5] *Job* 13, 15. [6] *Is.* 37, 29. [7] *Ex.* 21, 6. [8] See poem 15. [9] *Lam.* 5, 21. [10] *Job* 29, 2. [11] *Ps.* 43, 3. [12] See n. 1.

f. 42a

# 28 Me'orah[1]

[By Joseph. The author's name appears in an acrostic: יוסף, 'Joseph'.]

Fair hind,[2] exult, beloved mine:
Yet shall thy throngs, at ease, take rest;
Folk that now groan shall, at my shrine,
My footstool,[3] be by joy possessed.

The hart that from his temple fled[4]
Shall come back home, to his repose,
And ease those outcast, who now dread
The hatred shown them by their foes.
Messiah's throne firm on its stead,
From sea to sea his kingdom grows,[5]
Their cry ascends, to mine ear sped
By twinned taskmaster's[6] unkind blows.
At ease, my city's crowds[7] shall play
Like one who, trapped, got clean away.

Harsh exile's memory shall fade
When I bring home all those outcast
In princely crowns and jewels arrayed;
I search out each, an army vast,

45

Nor think of sins sedition made,
Mutinous arms that I did blast:
Their haltered foes shall I degrade
That ate my flock's toil in years past.
My glory shall my hind survey,
Herself graced by her jewels' display.

Come hither, Lord, come, view the bride
Who life-long yearns to be called thine;
Set but her heart thy road to stride,
Then she all others will decline.
Let Zion's praise become their pride
Who, intimate, may share thy shrine;
Mid gardens cool that streams divide
My honey taste, and quaff my wine,[8]
Savour mine incense, hear my lay,
Song which thy mystic charms[9] essay.

Thy glory to this world restore,
Lord, who from age to age dost reign,
Exalted, hidden, evermore
Feared – thy fear must our law remain.
For those oppressed, ashamed and poor,
Lighten their darkness; do Thou train
My will unto thine own; outpour
Light which, from Thee, mine eye may gain,
Whilst I, with bell-like voice, shall say,
'Rise, forward! Dawn lights up my day'.

---

[1] See poem 10, n. 1.  [2] *Prov.* 5, 19.  [3] *Is.* 66, 1.  [4] *S. of S.* 2, 9; 5, 14.
[5] *Ps.* 72, 8.  [6] I.e. Esau-Edom-Christendom; see poem 27, n. 3.
[7] Ozni and Eri, sub-clans of Dan listed in *Num.* 26, 18, here stand
for the common populace of Israel.  [8] *S. of S.* 4, 16; 5, 1.
[9] *S. of S.* 5, 10; see poem 24, n. 1.

---

## 29 Me'orah[1]

[By Joseph. The author's name appears
in an acrostic: יוסף, 'Joseph'.]

My daughter, hear,[2]
    See, have a care:
View not exile
    With gaunt despair.
Hear thou, my dove,[3]
    Mid foemen's ring:
Rumour precedes
    Salvation's spring;
Long hast thou hoped
    To see its rise,
Look well – for now
    Before thine eyes
My secret love
    Shall be revealed.
For but a trice
    Must thou be steeled
To bear the yoke
    All captives wear:
Nor, by the foe
    Wearied, despair.
Wait: all thy hopes

Redemption make.
For I recall
    'Twas for thy sake
A covenant
    Had I designed;
Nor lightly, but
    With thee in mind,
My might compelled
    Captors' respect.
Frail was that lamb
    I did protect
Guarding her safe
    From lion's jaws;
'Tis fragments now
    From foemen's claws
I clutch, distraught,
    Rich but in pain,
Yet out all lands
    Brought home again.
See, daughter, scan
    The skyline; build
A stately home
    With beauty filled;
Back to my shrine
    Glide, on thy wings,
As swallows' flight
    Each homeward brings.
Do I not call
    Thee, 'come, my bride.
From Lebanon
    Come, at my side?[4]
My throne I set
    All jewelled for thee,
Come, come, my love,
    Sit there with Me.'
If saving signs
    So long delay,
Whilst evil men
    Must hold their sway,
My people's fault,
    Their sin, is cause:
Those whom I called
    Forgot my laws.
Afflicted, bound,
    Yet, my son's guile
Compounding sin
    Made him more vile.
If sire am I,
    Where is that fear
A son should show?[5]
    And yet, I clear
Zion's approach;
    Towards her hill
They march, and I
    With pleasure thrill.
Courage! Let all
    Keep hope alive,
Let rescue's hope
    Your hearts revive

That now do weep,
    By troubles bowed:
Soon, soon shall I
    Requite the proud.
Thou, over foes
    Shalt triumph see
When comes the hour
    That sets thee free,
Making the pit
    So long dark, bright,
And thou shalt step
    Forth into light.

---

[1] See poem 10, n. 1. [2] Ps. 45, 11(10).
[3] S. of S. 1, 14; see poem 2. [4] S. of S. 4,
8. [5] Mal. 1, 6.

---

## 30 'Ahabah[1]

[By Solomon Ibn Gabirol. The acrostic reads: שלמה, 'Solomon'.]

To his closet let Him bring me.[2] This, my swain,
Most exalted He, most handsome. 'Tis a maid
That, recalling Him, is love-sick: I would fain
Lose my passion's fire, to dwell but in his shade.[3]
He my hero is, my love, whose banner's train[4]
I did follow, long ago, and his parade
Lit my darkness,[5] with me only did remain,
And my soul his own, all rivals spurned, I made.

My words rave,[6] for He is gone, who did escort
My youth's time, and gave his love to me. I own
That the fault is mine, whose steps did stray, and brought
Sin's entanglement about me – mine alone.
Yet because of Him, alack! my soul is caught
By a torrent of remorse; from me is flown
All my good; He eyes me, leaving me distraught,
And the wounds I bear, sick wounds, to all are shown.

Lord, Thou fortress where the poor for refuge hide,
Thou wilt not disdain me, though my language fail,
Nor look on whilst Jacob's host is terrified
Amid straits, yet neither strives, nor would assail
Thee that formed him, yet Thou hast near nullified
Thine own covenant, hast cursed him, made him quail
Self-despised: and yet, his steps turn not aside
From thy way, nor thinks he at his Lord to rail.[7]

Waken love, aroused as my espousals' day,[8]
Love which, wakened, with but pure refinement glows,
To make thy saving grace gleam white, far away:
Then sing I, as long since, song my mouth still knows,
Of love. For yet his Word good news shall convey
To folk that He – none else – freed from Memphis; those
Born of Jacob, ever mindful when they pray
That it was God Himself their forefather chose.[9]

f. 42b

---

[1] See poem 12, n. 1. [2] S. of S. 2, 4; 3, 4; see poem 2, introductory note. [3] S. of S. 2, 3.
[4] S. of S. 2, 4. [5] Job 29, 3. [6] Job 6, 3. [7] Job 1, 22. [8] Jer. 2, 2. [9] Is. 41, 8.

---

## 31 Zulath[1]

[By Abraham Ibn Ezra. The acrostic reads: אברם, 'Abram'.]

I bid the north wind[2] bear my hosts, the south my children send,
To dwell in courts whose walls the Lord's right hand itself shall mend;
Humble shall come Messiah, on an ass,[3] whilst I attend
    God's shrine, there as a singer in his choir
      To tune my psalmody unto the lyre,
        Such service He me bade.

Days of joy are here, no more to cease; grief-laden days
Pass, as though they had never been, for God his tent shall raise
Where pitched of old: our new age to be born no more delays,
    Its words reflecting manna that it eats,
      Wonders it works shall rival David's feats,
        Against Elijah's weighed.

Beloved, from captivity come forth, in beauty crowned;
Glory restored to thee once more, as in thy youth, comes round,
Dispersed, homeward to God's fair land spring, hart-like, at a bound:
    The end is glory; arms will He display,[4]
      His covenant's avenger: I shall pray
        As I have ever prayed:

Lord, my protection, heal my wounds, send cures to ease my pain;
Remove oppressors' ire, and grant my friends may substance gain,[5]
Till come redemption's times foretold[6] will I my hope sustain.
    I call Thee, answer: sheep by Thee sold, buy;
      Mend walls by Thee breached; in thine old lodge lie,
        Haste Thou, to bring me aid.

Thou wast our fathers' help, etc.[7]

---

[1] See poem 13, n. 1. [2] Is. 43, 6. [3] Zech. 9, 9. [4] Num. 25, 7; Phineas is often identified with Elijah,
traditionally the harbinger of the Messiah. Here (as occasionally elsewhere) the Deity and the
messianic figure are functionally blurred. [5] Prov. 8, 21. [6] Dan. 12, 7. [7] The catchword of the
continuation of the statutory prayer; see poem 13, n. 1.

---

## 32 Ge'ullah[1]

[By Isaac Ibn Ghayyat. The acrostic reads: יצחק, 'Isaac'.]

Down the years my sentence drags[2] I look to see thy sweet rewards
When I cheer, midst those released with me, thy regiment of wards.

My careworn heart by those through comfort confident, is scared:
At my tears they sing for joy; yet I to hope, afflicted, cling,
Vanquished, in my cell I think me on thy walls, my triumph aired;
I shall yet rule o'er my foes, do Thou but squeeze them in thy ring.

In my fancy's happy flutter I consider the world's end:
By those that cast me down for years unending though confined,
I shall build[3] my holy precincts; on those envious, descend
Chagrin's gripes when I, in but a trice, their chains shall leave behind.

Lord, who savest me, reveal thy sword which shall thy foemen smite,
Let my sin no rod provide, wherewith to chastize thine elect;
In thy glory re-establish on my hill streams of delight,[4]
And, my thirst slaked, let me witness in my shrine thy deeds' effect.

Though redemption lingers, trusting in thy covenant midst straits,
I my stronghold shall discover to endure thy wrath, and see
If my praise may give Thee pleasure as I, eager, watch thy gates,[5]
Till towards my throne my people shall march in, redeemed by Thee.

[1] See poem 14, n. 1. [2] *Job* 14, 14. This poem relies substantially for its effect on the use of homonyms, or of two senses of the same word: 1st line *șeba'i*, 3rd line *ḥeyl*, *'așor*, 5th line *ḥabaleykha*. [3] In the 5th line the 1st word, *'ebkeh*, must be corrected to *'ebneh*. [4] *Ps.* 36, 9(8). [5] *Prov.* 8, 34.

[Hymns for the Intermediate Sabbath]

## 33 Introduction [to Nishmath][1] for the Intermediate Sabbath of Passover

[By Judah Hallevi.]

If spheres of heaven glimpsed Thee and did fear,
And sudden silence stilled the Ocean's roll
Cut off by thine advance, how shall the soul
Think to thy conclave that she may draw near,
Source of that fire whose heat the rocks must sear[2]
Till they ignite? Nay, but she shall control
Her dread, and with thy help make for her goal,
Knowing 'tis Thou that dost her courage cheer.

Thus has she title to associate
With angels that have right of audience
And, ministering, on thy glory gaze:
And since to Thee it is appropriate[3]
To bring the worship of obedience,
Therefore to Thee each soul shall offer praise.

[1] See poem 6, n. 1. [2] In the 2nd line, for *melahaṭoth, we-nișmathu*, read *melaheṭeth, we-nișșathu*, with the Sarajevo *Haggadah*, f. 71a. [3] *Ps.* 33, 1.

## 34 Introduction

[By Solomon Ibn Gabirol. The acrostic reads: שלמה, 'Solomon'.]

'Greetings I bear my Friend,[1]
   My Friend, so lithe and fair,[2]
Greetings from her whose brow
   Breathes the fruit-garden's air.[3]
Come, with thy saving grace,
   Come forth, thy sister[4] greet,
Gallant as Jesse's son
   When he his foes did meet.'[5]

'My fairest, what is cause
   Passion to stir so fast,
With tinkling voice, like bells
   Heard when robed priests go past?[6]
When love herself shall judge[7]
   'Tis time, then, at her cue,
I haste Me to thy side
   Gentle as Hermon's dew.'[8]

[1] In place of *ben*, 'son of [my friend]', the reading *lekha*, 'to Thee', found in a number of texts, is here adopted (see I. Davidson, *'Oșar ha-shir we-ha-piyyuṭ*, iii, p. 463, no. 1224). *Ben* is appropriate if the piece is used as a wedding poem. [2] *S. of S.* 5, 10. [3] *S. of S.* 4, 3. [4] *S. of S.* 5, 1. [5] II *Sam.* 12, 26f. [6] *Ex.* 28, 35. [7] *S. of S.* 2, 7. [8] *Ps.* 133, 3.

## 35 Introduction [to Nishmath][1]

[By Solomon Ibn Gabirol. The acrostic reads: שלמה, 'Solomon'.]

My spirit's genuflexions match my knee
As I approach Thee, fearful and prostrate,
Well knowing that in thy sight I may be
Reckoned no more than some invertebrate.
Thou fillest the whole world: can those like me
Find means to praise Thee, infinitely great?
Thy glory heaven's angels do not see,
Comparison with whom I cannot rate.
Yet, for that goodness Thou dost shew, to Thee
My soul would fain her gratitude equate.

[1] See poem 6, n. 1.

## 36 Muḥarrakh[1]

[By David ben Eliezer. The acrostic reads: דויד, 'David'.]

Concealment is thy palanquin;
   Renew our songs of cheer,
Ransom thy folk, O Lord, whose might
   Transcends the stratosphere.

Deliver them, to dwell serene,
   Their city filled with noise
Of wedding praises, lads and maids
   Singing of wedding joys.

Let those that trust in Thee have ease,
   To them contentment send,
Gladness of heart from heaven speed,
   Joy that shall know no end.

Protected thus, thy throngs rejoice
   Reflecting light divine:
So Israel, guarded by the Lord,
   Like holy lamps[2] shall shine.

Fair bridegroom, may God grant thee life
   Midst friends, thy sons to see:
He that knows all, so will thy joys
   That blessèd they shall be.

So, too, may all our kin be blessed
   With life and endless peace,
Whilst, prospering, thou shalt observe
   Thy handiwork's increase.

All thou wouldst have, unmarred by grief
   Joy in thy house abide:
Flourish, with eyes turned upward, go
   Forward, with thy fair bride.

[1] See poem 7, n. 1. This poem, intended for the celebration of weddings, has no connection with Passover. [2] *Zech.* 4, 2.

## 37 Nishmath[1]

[Author unknown.]

The breath of friends, our groom's escort that speed him on his way,
Risen betimes, proclaims thy rule upright, who all dost sway:

'His heart is full of joy against his bridal-day'.[2]

The breath of love's own bride, this maid of form and stature fair,
Praises Thee: wisdom's merchandise knows none that may compare:[3]
   'A noble wife more than all jewels is treasure rare'.[4]

f. 43b
The breath of this our groom, his locks with wreaths of glory bound,
Acclaims thy grace; companions, all eyes on him, stand round,
   'With chaplet garlanded, by his own mother crowned'.[2]

The breath of this our bride, so fair she beauty's crown must daze,
Hymns Thee, her gratitude for love with psalms before Thee lays;
   'Beauty is vain: she that fears God deserves all praise'.[5]

The breath of those assembled in the house where they would be,
Fathers and sons, in holiness as Holy worship Thee,
   Saying: 'did praise but fill our mouths wide as the sea'.[6]

---

[1] See poem 8, n. 1. This link-poem, which has no connection with Passover, is intended for use on the Sabbath preceding a wedding. [2] S. of S. 3, 11. [3] Prov. 3, 14. [4] Prov. 31, 10. [5] Prov. 31, 30. [6] See poem 8, n. 13.

## 38 Nishmath[1]

[By Joseph. The author's name appears in an acrostic: (sic) יושף, 'Joseph'.]

The breath of Israel, joyful, by their day of rest restored,
Declaring Thee unique, both young and old in praise accord,
   'Let them be glad, exult in joy before the Lord'.[2]

The breath of those that praise with voice, conjoined with music's art
Addresses Thee, whilst sages with their learning play their part,
   'The joy that in the Lord they find shall fill their heart'.[3]

The breath of those survivors who to con thy laws delight
Exalts Thee on this Sabbath, in Passover yet more bright,
   'Exult ye, in the Lord rejoice, all ye upright'.[4]

The breath of those, a remnant, who thy laws entailed confess,
To Thee, O God of Jeshurun, their thanks renewed address,
   'Open the gates, that I may come in thankfulness'.[5]

The breath of those dispersed, that so they may be purified,
Blesses Thee, who dost let them hear, though scattered far and wide,
   'Voices of happiness, as bridegroom calls to bride'.[6]

The breath of those that link their hymns to Scriptures read this day
Sanctifies Thee, with joyful sounds of those who bid us pray,
   'Before the Lord of Hosts our thankful words to lay'.[6]

The breath of those that do thy will with all their heart, to Thee
Sings praises, Lord of saving acts, who wast, art, and wilt be,
   Saying: 'Did praise but fill our mouths wide as the sea'.[7]

---

[1] See poem 8, n. 1. [2] Ps. 68, 4(3). [3] Cf. Zech. 10, 7. [4] Ps. 32, 11. [5] Ps. 118, 19. [6] Jer. 33, 11. [7] See poem 8, n. 13.

## 39 [Introduction to] Kaddeesh[1]

[By Isaac. The author's name appears in an acrostic: יצחק, 'Isaac'.]

God's awe precludes attempt
   His greatness to relate,
Beside whose glory, pomp
   Of kings as cheap must rate.

Man's little life affords
   Him chance on Thee to wait:
How wait on One, Himself
   From creatures[2] separate?
Vocation to his house
   Is man's; God's praise narrate,
His glory, on thy lips
   Drawn[3] from its spring, dilate.
Thy splendour, Lord, but glimpsed,
   Must my speech dislocate,
That would declare thy Name
   Holy, supremely great.

---

[1] See p. 17. [2] In the 2nd line, the words *mi ṣur* are to be corrected to read *miy[e]ṣur*. [3] In the 3rd line, the last word (ignoring the refrain), *dal*, is the imperative of the verb *dlh*, 'draw water'.

## 40 'Ophan[1]

[By Judah Hallevi. The acrostic reads: יהודה, 'Judah'.]

In what He made[2] the Maker hides his face:
Yet distance must Creator separate
From creatures, though his glory permeate
The earth,[3] itself too narrow for his place.

Intelligences, all incorporate
As angels, from his spirit He derived,
In courses set, each potency contrived,
All from his holy light to emanate.
Functions, to their degrees appropriate,
Assigned authority they all fulfil;
Each to the next communicates his Will
Whose fount pours light, through them to radiate,
And all desire their Maker's ways to emulate.

Through skies his breath sweeps clear, each marches straight,[4]
Or, like stiff metal, motionless is held
Through awe, with which the hearts of all are spelled.
f. 44a
The very course they run makes operate –
Vessels to draw, and pour, and make gyrate
The spheres, by power divine; though round their poles[5]
They swing, their dispositions He controls
Who all that they perform must approbate,
And in his Will's entire construction integrate.

All things – the minerals inanimate,
Plant-life, and what has sense, are classified
In families, from clods to lions' pride,
Stamped as his seals' impressions regulate.
The same four elements will generate
Pebbles and coral, crystal, from his light
Nourished; his grace sustains them for our sight:
Of all with which He earth did populate
To found a species, his right hand decides its fate.

One genus did He make articulate,
By reason raised aloft: and of that kind
He gave to one group a more powerful mind –
The people chosen for his own estate.[6]
Who, when they sing *Trishagion*,[7] equate
Themselves with Seraphim, and heaven's host

Of choirs that He antiphonal did post
For his own sake, like all He did create,[8]
To crown with praise his majesty made consecrate.

[1] See poem 9, n. 1. [2] The 3rd word is to be read *be-yŏṣro* (not *be-yōṣero*).
[3] *Is.* 6, 3. [4] *Ez.* 1, 9. [5] On f. 44a, in the 1st line, the 4th word from the end (*be-ṣiddo*) is to be corrected to *be-ṣiro*. [6] *Ps.* 33, 12. [7] *Is.* 6, 3. [8] *Prov.* 16, 4.

## 41 Me'orah[1]

[By Judah Hallevi. The acrostic reads: יהודה, 'Judah'.]

Dozing on exile's wings, apart
    In far-off prisons must I sleep;
    Of dignity bereft, I keep
Silent, disconsolate at heart.

Lord, Thou my Friend, my heart replace
    In me, and me in my fair Land:[2]
    So long my parts by earth's globe stand
Riven, I seek no worldly grace;

As purchase on God's throne they hang,
    And so I need nor friend nor kin
    Nor royal wealth. Who for his skin
Has drugs, fears not the viper's fang.

He need not shiver at the bleat
    Of sheep, who potentates has downed:[3]
    Shade in my Maker's glory found
Affords me stance, and shy retreat.

My inmost thoughts who claims to read,
    Or bid my musings that my King
    They must debar from entering,
That I things most sublime may heed?

My love in Him, my Friend, I vest;
    Though He in prison did me bind,
    In Him my thoughts their centre find,
Walk I abroad, or should I rest.

Cause of results, by Him are weighed
    Our actions,[4] whether to redeem
    Or keep confined: myself I deem
A free man, though I slave am made.

I mock the foe who dared erect
    My prison; crabbed, though I may see
    The pomp of kings, from envy free
I lack nor grace, nor self-respect.

Pining, I yearn to be the least
    Of ministers within thy shrine,
    Nor crave like prelates rich to dine
Nor seek the rank of princely priest,[5]

To serve, an humble acolyte,
    Him from whom saving comes and aid,
    The Base whereon each base is laid,
Fount of all honour[6] and of light.

[1] See poem 10, n. 1. [2] *Ez.* 20, 6. [3] *Judg.* 5, 13. [4] *I Sam.* 2, 3.
[5] *Dan.* 11, 22. [6] Cf. *I Chron.* 29, 14.

## 42 'Ahabah[1]

[By Moses. The author's name appears in an acrostic: משה, 'Moses'.]

I long to see God's goodwill day,
Redemption's year, home rule restored:
Of ransom's date ne'er shall I say
'No hope', by new hopes ever shored.

My heart must surge, yearning made yet more keen,
When wrong hands hold those objects I respect:
The base don robes of state, themselves to preen
In my despite – of peoples, God's elect.

A captive may wear triumph's dress,
Exiles may garb them might to wield:
My heart, steadfast in faithfulness,
Is quickly by its own faith healed.

My sheltered youth had for its glory's sign
God's house, by roaming[2] whence I am denied
Oracles ephod-wearing[3] priests divine,
By no prophetic vision fortified,
Since ever I began to wander far and wide.

My Friend is from my precincts fled,
Where He once greatness did confer;
Is He to new companions sped,[4]
f. 44b    Revealed, new peoples to prefer?[5]

Harried by troubles I so long have met
With goodwill, increased suffering's new weight
I scarce feel on my shoulders, whilst I set
My heart that wondrous time[6] to contemplate,
Of glory, kept for me against the destined date.

Fleeing to Thee, that aid I pray
Thou for love givest, not reward:
Vanquished, I cling to hymns I lay
Before Thee – prayers are now my sword.

I face the homeward road: in mine own land
Renew thy rule, where I my King aspire
To see with the King's Herald[7] when, as planned,
My sweetest fruit,[8] hopes long deferred,[9] transpire –
The bond and covenant,[10] as set forth to my sire,

And my ears hear good news: 'I speed
Awakened love, to pity sons
Of Abraham, my loved friend's seed:[11]
Ye shall be yet my treasured ones'.[12]

[1] See poem 12, n. 1. [2] MS *nadarti*, perhaps already corrected to *nadadti*.
[3] *I Sam.* 23, 6f. [4] On f. 44a, penultimate line, *baraḥ* (6th word from end) is corrected to *'araḥ* by M. Wallenstein; *Job* 34, 8. [5] The last line of f. 44a is by error repeated on f. 44b. [6] *Dan.* 12, 6. [7] *Is.* 52, 7. [8] *S. of S.* 2, 3.
[9] *Prov.* 13, 12. [10] *Ez.* 20, 37. [11] *Is.* 41, 8. [12] *Ex.* 19, 5.

## 43 'Ahabah[1]

[By Judah Hallevi. The acrostic reads: יהודה, 'Judah'.]

Lord, raise thine arm for those (amongst them me)
Who wait in hope, yet question: on the breast
Of hardship raised, the feebleness they see
Self-styled redeemers show; doubt nags them, lest
Thine hand, too, impotent should prove, like all the rest.

So before God my path, I pray,
Keeps steady:[2] He, by pity moved,
Perchance will note how feeble they
Who wave redemption's flag have proved.

Enslaved that son Thou didst the master name,[3]
His home, that was thy shrine, foes occupy
In turn: when shall I hear the horn proclaim[4]
To my small remnant that the time is nigh
Of freedom's year, what Moses wrote to justify,

When shall the dead of dew[5] hear tell
Whose light in them shall life inspire,
When shall I hear their voices swell
That in thy Temple serve in choir?

Wearied, I see my history pursued
And caught by tragedies: hate drives each foe
Resentful still, with my handful to feud,
Survivors; wonders that thy hand did show
To me, renew, sign of the good Thou wilt bestow.[6]

Keep of those blessings my youth knew
Something to bless my eventide,
Vengeance to wreak on Esau's crew[7]
And other enemies beside.

My love for Him that loves me stored away
I hold – how long, how long till comes the date
When, merciful, Thou turnest, on the day
I give it Thee; that day my watchmen[8] wait,
To voice in thy behalf words they in faith translate:

'Come, all my lost ones, bring ye near
All them that faith keep with me[9] still;
With Jesse's shoot[10] come, meet me here,
The place where I my Word fulfil:

My chariot is late, its footbeats slowed;
But to its depths is my compassion stirred,
For you in greatest measure has it flowed.
Awaken, then, your love: I have averred
That recompense for deeds on all shall be conferred,

Grace for those who my love sustain,
On them who left Me, vengeance poured:
For foes I enmity retain,
For those that love Me, kindness stored.'[11]

---

[1] See poem 12, n. 1. [2] Ps. 119, 5. [3] Gen. 27, 29. [4] Lev. 25, 9f. [5] Is. 26, 19. [6] Ps. 86, 17. [7] Gen. 36, 21. [8] Is. 52, 8. [9] Ps. 50, 5. [10] Is. 11, 1. [11] Ex. 20, 34; 20, 7(6).

## 44 'Ahabah[1]

[By Judah Hallevi. The acrostic reads: יהודה, 'Judah'.]

Return, my Hart,[2] thine own room waits,
Return, sit on thy throne of state:
Too long the stranger desecrates
My court, stampeding[3] past the gate.

Why at this hour dost Thou with succour stay
My foes, to flaunt the sceptres of their pride?
When to my Rock of strength for help I pray;
His mercies He should rouse, and let those wide
Dispersed in distant isles know they are not denied

By grief, on Goodwill day, my wall
To build with precious stones,[4] to shine
Where king and prince alike shall fall
Worshipping God before my shrine.

But those who, when thy love's blows did chastize,
Thought void the covenant, terrors shall wrap
On Vengeance day:[5] a flash-stream from their eyes,
Their tears course down, as they quick meet the trap
Prepared by fate;[6] the future shall my merits cap.[7]

Hasten my Freedom day, to hear
Through holy courts the trumpet ring,
The hills where I once lived to cheer
With sound of music where men sing.

My King's highway, firm founded, those shall lead
Who march redeemed, the steep peaks all made plain,[8]
The waters dried: a voice calls them, now freed;
The Red Sea's margin bounds my land again,
Her border through the Philistines runs, by the main.[9]

Glory marks out my turbaned head,
Rich tired, because no prison made
By foemen ever shook my tread;
My steps I kept firm, undismayed.[10]

Prepared for thee, Messiah, waits a throne:[11]
Sit thou thereon for ever; not by might
Shalt thou the peoples govern, but alone
My spirit.[12] Thou my flock shalt lead aright
To rest in my house, saved from lions thou shalt smite.

Return they will, my chosen few,
Jacob's survivors;[13] for I bear
In mind the love so long I knew,[14]
Freedom from prison I declare.[15]

---

[1] See poem 12, n. 1. [2] S. of S. 2, 9; 3, 4; see poem 2, introductory note. [3] Is. 1, 12. [4] Is. 54, 12; Esther 1, 6. [5] Is. 34, 8. [6] Deut. 32, 35. [7] Jer. 31, 15–16 (16–17); the 4th word on the penultimate line of f. 44b is to be read u-le-phō'ōli. [8] Is. 51, 10; 40, 4; 11, 15. [9] Ex. 23, 31. [10] Dan. 11, 1; Ps. 18, 37 (36). [11] Is. 16, 5. [12] Zech. 4, 6. [13] Is. 10, 21. [14] Jer. 31, 2 (3). [15] Is. 61, 1.

## 45 'Ahabah[1]

[By Joseph. The author's name appears in an acrostic: יוסף, 'Joseph'.]

The fairest hind yearns for that fairest Land:[2]
Lord, bring her, outcast, home, from far recess
Of her captivity, raise high thy hand,
With bared arm thrash mine enemies. Her dress
Of exile, take away: in dust she lies,
A fawn forlorn, yet, from the pit, she tries
Through her best singing, much-sought love to realize.[3]

For Zion's hill she longs, for freedom's mound,
Where stands God's shrine, as though some marriage-bower:[4]
She comes, in perfumed robes swathed all around,
For God Most High. Proclaim, O Lord, the hour
That frees oppression's prisoner. Mine eyes
Make light, through words the prophet wrote advise
Thy remnant Thou wilt guide them yet, with cords love ties.[5]

All books thy prophets wrote the truth foretold:
More than all people's soothsayers, those claimed

f. 45a

To witness[6] for Thee, wonders did behold,
And, shown thy might, as thine own seers were named.
Deign, then, her from thy heights to recognize
Who plights her words with sweet voice,[7] noble-wise,
'My love his banner lift,[8] of love o'er me to rise'.

My daughter, raise thy voice in song and cheers:[9]
Yet shalt thou see, restored as cornerstone,[10]
A heritage of glory. Wherefore tears
And lamentation, why dost thou disown
Thy finery? Be calm, nor weep. Time flies,
And respite hastes: I lead thee, in the guise
Of mercy:[11] strong as death, nought love denies.[12]

---

[1] See poem 12, n. 1. [2] Prov. 5, 9; Ez. 20, 6. [3] S. of S. 3, 1. [4] S. of S. 3, 9.
[5] Hos. 11, 4. [6] The 6th word in the 7th line, 'eyrey (?), should probably be
corrected to read ṣirey. The possessive suffixes in this stanza, vocalized as feminine
(-ayikh), are to be corrected as masculine (-eykha). [7] S. of S. 2, 14. [8] S. of S.
2, 4. [9] Is. 54, 1. [10] Ps. 118, 22. [11] Jer. 31, 2(3). [12] S. of S. 8, 6.

---

## 46 'Ahabah[1]

[By (probably Abraham) Ḥarizi. The acrostic reads: חריזי, 'Ḥarizi'.]

'My lovesick maid,[2] come, say
     Why, like a boiling sea,
Thy heartbeat runs away.'
     'My fire it is, in me
Blazing, so long I stray,
     My heart must broken be;
Sleepless,[3] though slumber weigh
     My lids, my heart in fee
To wakefulness, I stay
     Like some poor man at plea,
Whilst on my Friend I lay
     Both eyes – my husband He.

God's foes, so multiplied,
     My sickness aggravate;
Cairo upon one side
     And Baghdad at my gate
Have ended beauty's pride.
     Christian and Arab[4] hate
My ornaments divide,
     One in my gown, ornate,
The other glorified
     In scarlet robes[5] of state.

Oppressor's yoke I bear,
     And daily raise mine eyes
To Thee, and ask, whence, where
     That aid I crave shall rise?[6]
Take me, thy wine[7] to share
     As each the other plies.
And if, sick from despair,
     The spirit in me dies,
To taste a draught so rare
     New life forthwith supplies.'

'My soul-mate, moved by zeal
     And ire I come, post-haste,
With wayward ones to deal
     I go, no time I waste,

In might Myself reveal,
     To crush all tyrants braced:
No more the stranger's heel
     Dread, nor his hordes, hard-faced,
Who claim that I repeal,
     Turned foe, thy love disgraced.

My dove,[8] I snap the snare
     The fowler set,[9] go free:
To thy grim foe declare
     "Now comes my time of glee.
The bond my Friend did swear
     Forgotten[10] shall not be,
His covenant, his care,
     The love He bears for me".'

---

[1] See poem 12, n. 1. Elsewhere this hymn is assigned to
Simḥath Torah (the last day of [extended] Tabernacles).
[2] S. of S. 2, 5. [3] S. of S. 5, 2. [4] Ishmael regularly stands
for the Islamic world in rabbinic convention; for Edom
as Christendom, see poem 27, n. 3. [5] Alluding probably
to the college of cardinals. [6] Ps. 121, 1. [7] S. of S. 2, 4.
[8] S. of S. 2, 14. [9] Ps. 124, 7. [10] The last word of the
penultimate line, 'eshkaḥ, should be corrected to yishkaḥ.

---

f. 45b

## 47 'Ahabah[1]

[By Abraham Ibn Ezra. The acrostic reads: אברהם, 'Abraham'.]

Long is my time – for how long cursed,
     My glory gone, my sun long set?
Parched, for those promises I thirst
     Scripture foretold would prove true yet.

A captive, I must wait,[2] all respite foiled,
Down years I cringe; pain and fear make me gaunt:
Delights once mine are by tormentors[3] spoiled,
Within my shrine foemen their armies flaunt
At God's sons: 'Who is this, that you name "Rock"', they taunt.[4]

     'Your minds beguiled, the seer did go;
     No God-led host has terrified
     Nor handmaid's[5] sons, nor brother's.[6] Know,
     False was the word he prophesied.'

Captive, her answer shows her noble mind:
'Uncouth men slander me. Exile deprived
My sons – my Temple fair they left behind,
And beauteous Land,[7] which your saints[8] then contrived
To grab, and tell me judgement-day has now arrived.'

     Have mercy, Lord: awesome was she,
     A byeword now, and shrunk; by pains
     And hardship tested, calumny
     She bears, and all alone remains.[9]

Lady, protest not so: loud in mine ear
Thy cry sounds. Yet that vision shall transpire
Which Scripture tells. The Lord whom thou dost fear
Judges[10] thy cause. I raise my hand yet higher,
Hasting to pour on thine oppressor all mine ire.

     Vengeance in majesty to wreak
     On sons[11] of luxury I wait:
     With music's tones my Name bespeak,
     The time is nigh – thy wedding-date.

Compound for thy cosmetics unguents choice:[12]
Forthwith the shadows flee,[13] and He shall pay
Thy ransom who thy Master is. Rejoice
With Him thou shalt; but loutish hordes, who say
Thou art defiled, the King's sword shall like refuse lay,

> When I, for foes, my wrath record,
> My old affection for my dove,[14]
> To glory all her throng restored,
> I say, 'How fair, how pleasant love!'[15]

---

[1] See poem 12, n. 1.  [2] *Job* 13, 15.  [3] The last word in the 3rd line, *me'annim*, should be corrected to *me'anni* (or *-neh*, Wallenstein).  [4] In the 4th line, the 8th word should read *yo'mar* (without copula: Wallenstein).  [5] Ishmaelites (descended from Hagar), here signify Arabs; see poem 46, n. 4.  [6] Edomites here signify Christians (Franks); see poem 27, n. 3.  [7] *Ez.* 20, 6.  [8] *Qedeshim* (7th line, 4th word) pejoratively and sarcastically for *qedoshim*; the reference is to Crusaders.  [9] *Lam.* 1, 1.  [10] *Is.* 33, 22.  [11] In the 11th line, the 1st word, *be-bikhyi*, is to be corrected to *bi-beney* (Wallenstein).  [12] *S. of S.* 4, 14.  [13] *S. of S.* 1, 17.  [14] *S. of S.* 2, 14.  [15] *S. of S.* 7, 7(6).

## 48 Zulath[1]

[By Abraham Ibn Ezra. The acrostic reads: אברם, 'Abram'.]

Thou Rock, styled Israel's Rock, we cry,
Arise, nor Israel aid deny.

Of yore, O Lord, thy right hand Thou didst raise:
See now thy son, a slave – thine own firstborn[2]
Sold to the race his sire's handmaid[3] did spawn;
Yet thy Law states he is thy slave, always.[4]

Resentment burns: in Esau's[5] gate confined,
Enslaved! God's word reversed – that elder son
Should serve the younger.[6] Shall God's holy one
Cry out, yet from fouled hands no saviour find?

Wounded and weak, who giants slew, I say
No word to them that taunt; my tongue is still,
For Israel sleeps – what else to do, until
Michael the Prince stands up,[7] on time's last day?

Since my House was destroyed, expatriate
My love roams. To no stranger's place I go;
But when thou comest home to God's Mount, know
In thy midst Israel's Holy One is great.[8]

---

[1] See poem 13, n. 1. Elsewhere, this poem is assigned to *Shabbath Bereshith*, when *Gen.* 1 is read.  [2] *Ex.* 4, 22.  [3] The Arabs, supposedly descended, through Ishmael, from Hagar.  [4] *Lev.* 25, 55.  [5] *Gen.* 27, 12; for Esau/Edom/Rome/Christendom, see poem 27, n. 3.  [6] *Gen.* 25, 23.  [7] *Dan.* 12, 1.  [8] *Is.* 12, 6.

## 49 Ge'ullah[1]

[By Joseph. The author's name appears in an acrostic: יוסף, 'Joseph'.]

I know that my Redeemer lives;[2] his rite
And right it is to ransom. As of yore
My Maker shall, as Husband,[3] his troth plight
To me, his bride, and He will build once more
My Temple and my city where they stood before.[4]

> But Zion now, forlorn and maimed,
> Not one with her distress affects;[5]
> All but forgotten, she is named
> The city that the world rejects.

Though time drags slow, the promised end delays,
My hope in Him remains intact,[6] for He
In mercy to all those whom He shall raise
Out of the dust to immortality
Will rebuild ramparts, stirring up his charity.

> The exiles' remnant[7] He will homeward lead,
> Gathered in ones and twos, till they march forth
> From cities, villages[8] – a host indeed,
> From east and west, from south and north.

And then, from distant lands, whilst I look round,
My sons shall come,[9] and I requital deal
Condign, upon my neighbours to redound;
Each fresh thought my new gladness shall reveal,
My mouth shall fill with song, laughter unchecked shall peal.[10]

> I lift my head above my foes,[11]
> My soul rejoices, finding peace,
> That languished long, for now she knows
> The time has come for her release.[12]

Burst into song,[13] my daughter: you, as well,
Upright in heart, together with her sing,[14]
As head and cornerstone you now shall dwell
Brought home; that you may faith and reason bring,
An angel clears the way: see to your victualling.

> Not like some rabble shall you fly[15]
> Confused, but dignified your poise;
> Not sorrow-laden, with a sigh
> Come you forth, but replete with joys.[16]

---

[1] See poem 14, n. 1.  [2] *Job* 19, 25.  [3] *Is.* 54, 5.  [4] *Jer.* 30, 18.  [5] *Jer.* 30, 17.  [6] *Job* 13, 15.  [7] *Obad.* 20.  [8] *Jer.* 3, 14.  [9] *Is.* 43, 6.  [10] *Ps.* 126, 2.  [11] *Ps.* 27, 6.  [12] *Ex.* 8, 11(15).  [13] *Is.* 54, 1.  [14] *Ps.* 32, 11.  [15] *Is.* 52, 12; 35, 10.  [16] *Is.* 55, 12.

## 50 Ge'ullah[1]

[By Nahum ben Jacob. The acrostic reads: נחום, 'Nahum'.]

My garden shooting spikenard shows
  Crocus too: nettles, chopped away,
Dry off, but by the stream the rows
  Of myrtle buds begin to splay.

Each tree strips off its widow's weeds
  And burgeons, garbed in robes whose sheen
Reflects a light, wherein love breeds
  Joy, triumphing[2] with nature's green.

Swallows and turtle-doves, each bill
  By singing stretched, set forth[3] his praise
That made us all: their chirpings thrill
  And twitter, where the shadow plays.

They flit through willows chirruping;
  Rose-beds their deep red mantles link,
And round the pomegranate veils cling
  To each branch – white lawn, tinged with pink.

Those scents the garden-flowers waft,
  Asleep, awake, our sense imbue;
The north wind,[4] with a gentler draught[5]
  Upon the spice-plot sprinkles dew,[6]

Dew that toil's memory dispels,
    The poor from all their cares released.
Mine eye has glimpsed a ray, that tells
    The sun is rising in the east.

The trees that in my garden grow
    Have let a lusty sapling[7] shoot:
A voice in my ear murmurs: 'so
    A sprig blossoms, from Jesse's root'.[8]

God pities his old dwelling-place,
    Freedom in this year's date has gleamed;[9]
My true love looks me in the face,[10]
    Captives may hope to be redeemed.

---

[1] See poem 14, n. 1. [2] In line 2, the 3rd word from the end should probably be *'alezu* (with *zayin*). [3] *Judg.* 5, 11. [4] *S. of S.* 4, 16. [5] In the 6th line, the 9th word should read *ruaḥ*. [6] See poem 15, introductory note. [7] *Ps.* 37, 35. [8] Cf. *Is.* 11, 1. [9] *Is.* 63, 4. [10] *Is.* 52, 8. But David's reading *be-'oni* for MS *be'eyni* is probably original.

## 51 Ge'ullah[1]

[By Judah Hallevi. The acrostic reads: יהודה. 'Judah'.]

For my pain I have a salve, for my disease there is a cure!
There come thoughts
    to give me strength, that do my confidence assure.

Time, revolving, changes purpose: new each morning, vacillates,
Opens windows here
    and shuts them there, slams shut or unlocks gates.
His inconstancy abides, to prove our guesses wrong; I know
I shall yet go home,
    and build my nest once more where myrtles grow.
Once again my arm, uplifted, shall reveal my strength, and drive
Headlong those whose hatred led them with me bitterly to strive.

Nature's law, that we must serve until released,[2] is known to all;
But a little, and the time is come for our return[3] to call,
Time to raise some up, bring others low;[4] the sentinel[5] to post,
O our Rock, who to the glory of thy Land[6] shall guide thy host.
Time is come, O my Beloved, that to me Thou shouldst renew
All the love Thou
    dost remember, that same love which our youth knew.[7]

See, the planets in their orbits are come round, and once again
In their constellations reappear disposed, once more to reign
In the mansion of *Aquarius*,[8] as then. God did decide
It was they who, at redemption's hour should, dominant, preside;
They were hung in heaven's vault, and authorized to make proceed
Each occurrence of creation in the way that God decreed.

f. 46b   Seafarers all and traders,[9] you with caravans so bold
To range west and south through deserts, just to trick a man for gold,
Turn your eyes aloft: mark well how God, in all ways perfect,[10] signs
By a beacon[11] – see, his Mount, so fair, is raised up clear, and shines
Calling priest and prophet: Freedom He to those in fetters gives,
For the One I know to be both Father and Redeemer lives.[12]

---

[1] See poem 14, n. 1. Elsewhere this poem is assigned to the Feast of Tabernacles. [2] *Job* 14, 14. [3] *Is.* 30, 15. [4] Cf. *Eccles.* 3, 1f. [5] In the 6th line, the 8th word is *ha-meṣappeh* (the *he* is almost obliterated). [6] *Ez.* 20, 6. [7] *Jer.* 2, 2. [8] The reference is obscure. Aquarius is linked to the month of *Shevaṭ*, on 15th of which the agricultural new year marks the beginning of spring; but this scarcely seems to explain the allusion. [9] The connection in thought is effected by the dependence of ships and desert travellers on the stars for navigation. [10] *Ps.* 37, 37; *Deut.* 32, 4. [11] *Ps.* 60, 6(4). [12] *Job* 19, 25.

## 52 Ge'ullah[1]

[By Abraham Ibn Ezra. The acrostic reads: אברם. 'Abram'.]

My heart is sad, my flesh grows weak and wan:
My angel sped, and my Redeemer gone.
My voice is weak, and ghostly shrill,
For I am ill.

In my captivity long years I waste,
For few days in that fairest city based,
Ere to the foe's hands my estate was passed,
And fired – my date-palms victims of his blast.
My tears' stream, rivers inundate,
My Nile,[2] in spate.

Brutish men laud their gods of stone and wood,
Burn fires before them – fools! – all to no good;
Lord, trounce them, tumbled to catastrophe,
Who like a lion roar, enraged with me
For praising Thee. At me they rail,
Held in their gaol.

Blot out their wicked triumph in a cloud,
Like chaff sweep out all evil-doers, cowed.
Lead gently those who, straggling, roam distressed;
Yet shall I sing, on my Beloved's breast,
Forget, in my tent, restless days,
Once music plays.

Thy treasured people's camps[3] acquire again,
The titles to redeem them – these regain.
Father, my Maker, send the Seer, to guide,
Thy Messenger speed. In my room reside
Once more. Arise, my helper be,
Redeeming me.

---

[1] See poem 14, n. 1. [2] *Ez.* 29, 3. [3] After the 1st word in the 8th line, the words *tehillah ke-'az beneh* have been omitted by the scribe.

## 53 Ge'ullah[1]

[By Abraham Ibn Ezra. The acrostic reads: אברהם. 'Abraham'.]

I yearn – nor know in what retreat
That noble Hart[2] lies; can none trace
For me the print left by his feet,
Or point me to his footstool's[3] place?

Within my ribs my passion's rage
Burns like a furnace; from mine eyes
Tears' flash-floods down my cheeks rampage.
I ask those who can recognize
One lovesick:[4] 'Greet this Personage,
Though his hard heart greetings denies
The sender, who, through roaming sore
Wearied, can bear his load no more.'

My chiders' harsh words on my ear
Fall sweet, though I, a captive, see
Much hardship, and the scorn must bear
Of youths:[5] soon, soon, for my sake, He,
The love for those He now holds dear
Checked, will from roaming summon me

To serve Him,[6] at his rebuilt throne
Made of rare skins[7] and costly stone.

That people Thou didst take, and name
Thy heritage[8] and thy firstborn,[9]
Mockers now for their subjects claim:
Sated with bitter words of scorn,
Sick, faint, they cry, 'Father, thy fame
Recall, thy mercies!'[10] Lord, those worn
Remember, pure in heart; nor yet
Traitorous Edom's[11] sin forget.[12]

A captive, I am schooled to bear
Insults the Arab peoples[13] fling,
Nor for rich recompense I care;
For love of Thee I patience bring.
Thy[14] service is my only prayer;
Who serve false gods, to ruin cling.[15]

To thy son, sold by Thee, reveal
The vision's date, what means the dream;[16]
47a But, if Thou wouldst the date conceal,[17]
No matter: since Thou wilt redeem.

---

[1] See poem 14, n. 1.  [2] S. of S. 2, 9.  [3] Lam. 2, 1.
[4] The 4th word in the 4th line should read neḥeleh.
[5] Job 30, 1.  [6] The last 4 words of the 7th line
should read nad la'abod ṣur pō'alo.  [7] Ez. 16, 10.
[8] Ps. 33, 12.  [9] Ex. 4, 22.  [10] Ps. 25, 6.  [11] See
poem 27, n. 3.  [12] Ps. 137, 7.  [13] Gen. 22, 21; 25, 3.
[14] In the penultimate line on f. 46b, before the last
word, rab has been omitted.  [15] Ex. 22, 19(20).
[16] Dan. 7, 1f; 8, 1f.  [17] Dan. 12, 4.

---

[Hymns for the Seventh Day]

## 54 Introduction [to Nishmath][1] for the Seventh Day, being the Day when the Song [of Moses][2] is read, by Rabbi Judah Hallevi, of blessed memory

[The acrostic reads: יהודה, 'Judah'.]

Beloved of me thy praise –
    My heart it floods with joy.
O Rock! would I to Thee
    A sea of hymns deploy,
No fraction of praise due
    Could any tongue declare:
Wearied, with my Stronghold
    They find nought to compare.
Thy greatness, as I may,
    In part I fain would tell,
Whose measure in the full
    I lack the strength to spell.
Clasp Thou to Thee my heart:
    Then richest joy I gain,
My Rock, and so in Thee
    Do I forget my pain.

Deign to accept my song
    This day, and all the days
That there is still in me
    Breath to shew forth thy praise.[3]

---

[1] See poem 6, n. 1.  [2] Ex. 15, 1f.  [3] Job 27, 3.

---

## 55 Introduction[1]

[By Levi ben Jacob Ibn Altabban. The acrostic reads:
ללוי, 'by Levi'.]

How long, thou mighty arm
    Of God, must I be torn
By fear of man; one side
    Scarred by the Christian's[2] thorn,[3]
One by the Arab's?[4] Thou
    Rejectest me, distressed,
To mourn, my head in dust,[5]
    My flesh in sackcloth dressed.[6]
'Twas Thou, before thy folk
    Redeemed didst dry the main;
Put on thy strength,[7] be decked
    In splendid might again:
Until o'er kings I rule,
    My heart from Thee must crave
This comfort – see me here,
    Of mine own slaves the slave.[8]

---

[1] See p. 17.  [2] See poem 27, n. 3.  [3] Num. 33, 55.
[4] See poem 46, n. 4.  [5] Lam. 2, 10.  [6] Job 16, 15.
[7] Is. 51, 9-10.  [8] Gen. 27, 29.

---

## 56 Muḥarrakh[1]

[Introduction to Nishmath[2]]

By Ḥiyya Ibn Al-Da'udi.]

All that hath breath, praise God,[3] whose hand
Made earth firm in her borders stand.

The heavenly realms sing to his name
Whilst men below tell forth his fame,
Each bird, each beast his eye must bend
On Him for food, who did suspend[4]
The world, a balanced cluster, planned
Within earth's borders firm to stand.

Deeds unforgettable I praise,
Recalling how He once did raise
A noble stock, snatched from the sea,
Marshalled by Moses, soon to be
Beflagged, his own awe-circled[5] band
Who made earth in her borders stand.

God, present in his world, declares
Heaven his throne, and to it pairs
Earth for his footstool:[6] may He speed
His word, the promise He decreed,
f. 47b Who breath to all, in every land
Gave,[7] when He caused earth firm to stand.

[1] See poem 7, n. 1.  [2] See poem 6, n. 1.  [3] Ps. 150, 6.  [4] Job 26, 7.  [5] S. of S. 6, 4.  [6] Is. 66, 1.  [7] Is. 42, 5; see poem 6, n. 4.

## 57 Muḥarrakh[1]

[Probably not by Abraham Ibn Ezra; the acrostic reads: אברם, 'Abram'.]

God's Name, wherewith nought can compare,[2]
Be blessed by all that breathes the air.[3]

Transcending all, Thou art Unique,
High, wondrous high, from all concealed;
Yet in thy miracles we seek
To glimpse thy mystery revealed.
Thou didst set princes' hearts aquake
When Thou through seas a path didst make.

Through us thy deeds were known worldwide,
That cleft through rock a riverbed,[4]
When we from thirst had almost died,
By Thee on honeyed manna fed,
And all of those who envied me
Their homage[5] paid, on bended knee.

Defending us, Thou didst gainsay
All arguments our foes could raise;
Requite them: send[6] him not away
Empty, that with his whole heart prays.
Who call on Thee, thy Name confessed,
Blessing that Name, themselves are blessed.

Fair hind, why dost thou stand and moan
Like some lost dove,[7] far from her nest,
Trembles to find herself alone?
Forbear: be thou no more distressed.
Enduring so long exile's night;
Arise and see, there comes thy light.[8]

[1] See poem 7, n. 1. This poem is elsewhere assigned to the Feast of Tabernacles. As its conclusion indicates, it is a Me'orah (see poem 10, n. 1).  [2] Ps. 40, 6(5).  [3] Ps. 150, 6.  [4] Ps. 78, 15.  [5] Gen. 41, 43.  [6] In the 6th line, the 2nd and 4th words from the end should read tasheb, tashib.  [7] Ez. 7, 16.  [8] Is. 60, 1.

## 58 Nishmath[1]

[By Isaac. The author's name appears in an acrostic: (sic) יסחק, 'Isḥaq'.]

The breath of those from dark to light gone free
Declares past blessings' reach[2] thy unity;
'Kingdoms God shook, laying his hand upon the sea'.[3]

Their breath – a remnant, with all to them dear
Led by Thee, singing praise, from Memphis clear –
Extols Thee: 'Glad was Egypt, to be free of fear'.[4]

The breath of those who, feasting, praise indite,
Sings of thy mercies, shewn in Egypt's sight,
'Thy raging fury, sending angels to cause blight'.[5]

The breath of those that call on Thee in straits[6]
Sanctifies Him who from bonds extricates,[7]
Jacob's might-girdled Lord;[8] his praise relates,
'Who bares the forest, hinds' travail accelerates'.[9]

Their breath whose sires served Thee, in Hebron laid,
Tells future ages awesome deeds displayed,
'Leading thy folk, Moses and Aaron shepherds made'.[10]

The breath of Israel, exiled wheresoe'er,
In north or west, thy people all declare:
'Though like the sea our mouths song-filled, our praise too spare'.

[1] See poem 8, n. 1. Elsewhere this poem is assigned to the Intermediate Sabbath in Passover.  [2] Neh. 9, 5.  [3] Is. 23, 11.  [4] Ps. 105, 38.  [5] Ps. 78, 49.  [6] Ps. 120, 1.  [7] Ps. 68, 7(6).  [8] Ps. 65, 7(6).  [9] Ps. 29, 9.  [10] Ps. 77, 21(20).

## 59 [Introduction to] Kaddeesh[1]

[By Jacob ben Me'ir (Tam). There is an alphabetical acrostic.]

New songs be in the Temple multiplied,
That place to God's most holy name allied,
        'Magnified He, and sanctified'.

God, the first uncaused Cause, no limit knows,
Supremely great: tent-like, the heaven's frame
He stretched,[2] that round its pole revolving goes.
He formed and set alight a lamp, whose flame
Unquenched with mystic irridescence glows.
Do you, then, in great love, his might acclaim,
        'Sanctified his most awesome Name'.

Dwelling on high, God's vision, crystal clear,[3]
A splendid palace did on earth decree,
That there his glory might straightway inhere.
To meet Him, I affirm my faith that He,
As Sovereign, his courts will once more tier
Around his inmost sacred shrine to be
        Restored: 'May you, yet living, see'.

Beyond the outmost stratosphere He dwells
On high, in very truth beyond all rate
His wonders' scale. His ordinance compels
All men, none failing, praise to concentrate,
That his Name's majesty for ever spells.
Let every mouth his rule concelebrate:
        'Glorified He, supremely great'.

[1] See p. 17.  [2] Is. 40, 22.  [3] Hab. 1, 13.

## 60 'Ophan[1]

[Possibly by Yaḥyun.]

Unique in majesty, He calms the crash
Of waves[2] in mercy; heavens, tent-like He
Stretched out unaided,[3] and above the lash
Of hurricanes He strides across the sea.[4]

Thy majesty no tongue can tell – the tale
Exceeds recount.[5] No action can occur,
Whether to smite, or healing those that quail
In pain,[6] unless thy Will therein concur.
All life looks to thy goodness not to fail,
When Thou surveyest all that is astir.[7]
Thy Name a refuge is, beyond compare,

Like Thee exists no stronghold anywhere.
The mountains quake, stricken by fear of Thee,
Whose mere rebuke can render dry the sea.[8]

Observe all this: the prophet's vision heed,
To know who ordered this whole scheme of things;
Let not astrologers' false art mislead,
Nor he whose twisting hands[9] read happenings
In clouds. All is from God: no single deed
From chance, but from divine intention springs.
He it was stablished this our globe in place,
And set round it the mighty spheres in space;
He makes day night, and then makes night day flee,
And his dominion runs from sea to sea.[10]

Who set the laws within each element
To act, each by its nature? Who designed
The spheres, and on their orbits spinning sent,
Which same, as angel hosts their mission find,
Some with stretched wings, others to wheels' shape bent,
To serve, each as arranged by rank and kind?
Who is it, swathed in mystery, their height,
Measures, and width, each for his purpose right?
His glory lights the world; that it should be
Firm, by his Word He holds in bounds the sea.[11]

To Thee I spread my palms, who hearkenest[12]
To prayer: I come, within my heart the ways[13]
Of thy powers set – those powers, by me confessed
When I am worshipping, inform each phrase.
Yet, how shall adoration be expressed
In words to Thee, to whom is silence praise?[14]
God's hand each living soul holds;[15] free from strife
Through laws He made, all shall be kept in life.
His glory guard us from adversity
Who gave us courage mid the raging sea.

---

[1] See poem 9, n. 1. [2] *Ps.* 65, 8(7). [3] *Is.* 44, 24. [4] *Job* 9, 8. [5] *Ps.* 40, 6(5). [6] *Deut.* 32, 39. [7] *Deut.* 26, 15. [8] *Is.* 50, 2. [9] *Gen.* 48, 14. [10] *Zech.* 9, 10. [11] *Ps.* 104, 9. [12] *Ps.* 65, 3(2). [13] *Ps.* 84, 6(5). [14] *Ps.* 65, 2(1). [15] *Job* 12, 10.

f. 48b
(f. 51b;
copied
twice)

## 61 Me'orah[1]

[By Judah Hallevi. The acrostic reads: יהודה, 'Judah'.]

Thy wonders are recalled by heaven's force,
A mighty host, that on their orbits swing
Round from the south, to follow through their course
Along their bounds, whilst earth shall cause to spring
Her produce, rising to thy law's just summoning.

> Those awesome powers recount, each day,
> His hand wields: let thy work complete
> Their mission. Age to age shall say,
> 'That law will ne'er become effete'.[2]

Setting them moving through vast heaven's tract,
Thou badest them their light on earth bestow,
Nor they, nor we perform a single act
Save as thy Will directs, to bring them low
Or raising them: as Thou commandest, they do so.

> When Thou dost bid thy host eclipse
> Darker than black they turn, to spill

---

Thy folk, which in the dungeon sips
Of bitter draught more than its fill.[3]

If Thou art my redeemer, must I lie
So long between foes blazing hate[4] at me,
Arab[5] and Christian[6] – judging me, and I,
Their senior in age, must ever flee,
A wanderer, whilst they have ease, from trouble free?

> Thy siege invest them close, like Tyre,[7]
> Like Hazor[8] raze their public court;
> Protect thine own, safe to retire
> Within thy shrine, as though a fort.

Console with gentle words them who repose
Their hope in Thee, and help them to forget
Revilers' insults which the curser throws
In poor men's teeth, who upon Thee have set
Their eyes, redemption's fateful year[9] awaiting yet,

> And prophets' promises combine
> With heralds' news, to end their quest
> For freedom's year – how, in thy shrine
> The swallow has rebuilt her nest.[10]

(f. 52a) Redeem Thou canst – thy hand lacks not the power[11]
Thy folk to ransom; if my sins delay
My ransom, Thou hast plenty[12] for the hour.
But where are gone those deeds Thou didst display,
The strength thy name can boast, thy glory's mighty way?

> If thy strong arm to help[13] us wakes,
> No[14] obstacle shall block our flight:
> Paths that were twisted, thy word makes
> Straight, and the darkness turns to light.[15]

---

[1] See poem 10, n. 1. Elsewhere this poem is assigned to *Shabbath Ha-ḥodesh*, the one preceding, or on, 1 *Nisan*, and so two weeks or more before Passover. [2] *Ps.* 148, 6. [3] *Lam.* 3, 15. [4] *Ps.* 57, 5(4). [5] See poem 46, n. 4. [6] See poem 27, n. 3. [7] Doubtless Judah Hallevi superimposed the Crusaders' capture of Tyre in his own lifetime (1124) on the biblical reference (*Ez.* 29, 18) to Nebuchadnezzar's abortive siege. [8] *Josh.* 11, 10f. [9] *Is.* 63, 4. [10] *Ps.* 84, 4(3). [11] *Is.* 50, 2. [12] *Ps.* 130, 7. [13] The 6th word from the end of the penultimate line of the poem on f. 48b (also f. 52a, line 2) is to be vocalized *le-ʿōzri*. [14] The reading *'eyn* (f. 52a, 2nd line, antepenultimate word) is slightly easier than *'ey* (f. 48b, penultimate line). [15] *Is.* 42, 16.

## 62 'Ahabah[1]

[By Isaac Ibn Ghayyat. The acrostic reads: יצחק, 'Isaac'.]

Fair crown of Zion's hill,[2] beneath the heel
Of Memphis' mighty host, thou mangled prey
Of lions, fearful, hoping for the day
When thy Redeemer comes, to make appeal
That He restore thy fane: know, I shall heal
The wounds and pains distress on thee did lay,
'Making thy days long: I save him that kept my way'.[3]

A folk whose beauty exile dulls, distressed,
In a strange nation's dungeon close confined –
Their very merchandise – looks where to find
Cure and some recompense, so long oppressed.
The covenant recall, and let them rest.
Visions fulfilled of leas in sheepfolds dressed,[4]
All gifts: 'My firstborn him I make',[5] like new fruit blessed.

Fie, Heliopolis![6] Thou, the most mean,
Despised of peoples,[7] soon ransacked: for lo!

With raving war-cries soon there comes a foe
Shall search out all – fat priests, soothsayers lean!
My people have nor priest nor prophet seen,
Though undivorced by Me;[8] kept safe,[9] they know
Secrets, as Moses sang: 'To God, my best I show'.[10]

I speed to snatch those locked away; my fane
With choice woods I rebuild, in glory dress
Anointed priests.[11] With their spoils who oppress
I dower my bride,[12] when he shall come – my thane,
Advancing to ascend my Mount again,
Armed camps[13] I rout, and save him. Ampleness,
Peace, like a stream,[14] I bring, to those yet in duress.

Egypt's[15] flames sear my folk; taskmasters cry
'Give! Give!' Leech-like[16] they eat their flesh, intent
To crush her. She hopes yet, with eyes still bent
A flame upon my altar to descry,
My shrine on gold foundations built:[17] for I
Love those that love Me,[18] with a sire's love, spent
On sons – in Israel's youth, my love to Egypt sent.[19]

f. 49a

---

[1] See poem 12, n. 1.  [2] Ps. 48, 3(2).  [3] Ps. 91, 14, 16.  [4] Ps. 65, 14(13).  [5] Ps. 89, 28(27).
[6] Gen. 41, 50.  [7] Ez. 29, 14.  [8] Is. 50, 1.  [9] Ex. 14, 20.  [10] Ex. 15, 2.  [11] Zech. 4, 14.
[12] I Sam. 18, 25.  [13] Ps. 27, 3.  [14] Is. 66, 12.  [15] Job 9, 13; Is. 30, 7.  [16] Prov. 30, 15.
[17] Is. 54, 11.  [18] Prov. 8, 17.  [19] Hos. 9, 1.

## 63 'Ahabah[1]

[By Abraham Ibn Ezra. The acrostic reads: אברם, 'Abram'.]

O for the days when God enjoyed
     My fellowship,[2] and talk went round![3]
     But now, on me my Friend has frowned
Disgrace, rejection, his soul cloyed.[4]

From Memphis freed, with cloud[5] and fire,
     Me to his holy Mount He brought
     Gently, that by his Envoy taught
He might with holiness inspire.[6]

Led to my heritage, I spied
     In that pure Land all that is fair:[7]
     I built for God a temple[8] there,
Tranquil to have Him at my side.

Sin shattered me, nor leaves me free;
     My Rock forgot me not before,
     Yet now forgets;[9] I feel no more
My Shepherd's arm to gather me.

Disdaining down unending years
     Zion his city, thence He sent
     Those who keep faith with him,[10] now pent
In hands of idol-worshippers.

Let Him search me: I could not seem
     To serve some second god.[11] If so,
     Why spurned He me, so long ago,
And even now will not redeem?

God's love and justice my theme-song[12]
     Has ever been. I shall forget
     Hardship: outside my heart I set
Thoughts that my exile still drags long.

My youth's bond[13] I recall, above
     All else my guard from foes, who roar
     To swallow me: that bond, once more,
Will bring me back my husband's love.[14]

---

[1] See poem 12, n. 1.  [2] Job 29, 2.  [3] Is. 58, 9.  [4] Jer. 14, 19. In the 2nd
line, the 5th word should read ga'alah.  [5] In the 2nd line, the 10th word
should read u-ba-'anano.  [6] Ex. 19, 6.  [7] Job 28, 10.  [8] I Kings 8, 13.
[9] Is. 44, 21.  [10] Is. 26, 2.  [11] Ps. 44, 21–2 (20–1).  [12] Ps. 101, 1.  [13] Jer. 2,
2.  [14] Gen. 29, 32; Hos. 2, 18(16).

## 64 Zulath[1]

[By Judah Hallevi. The acrostic reads: יהודה הלוי, 'Judah Hallevi'.]

It was upon a wondrous day
     That Moses, Amram's son,
Became distinguished by the way
     He God's approval won.
God caused a vision to appear
     That in the bush he spied.
Clothed by God's spirit, he drew near
     And forthwith prophesied.
As Bridegroom's[2] groomsman Moses sped
     His love-letter to send:
The lovesick maiden,[3] as she read,
     Quoth: 'Hark, here comes my Friend'.[4]
The youthful Husband through the waste
     His saving chariots[5] sent;
The Holy Spirit bade them haste,
     Bearing his words they went.
God's voice went forth direct:[6] it wings
     To Moses' ear, and thrills:
'My Love is like a hind, that springs
     O'er mountains, through the hills'.[7]
Early and late He takes my part,
     Rebuking Pharaoh's pride,
Or sometimes courage to impart
     When scholars He would guide.
Plague upon plague He sends, designed
     To save us from their throng,
'Through windows peeping, from behind
     The lattice, watching long'.[8]
O'er thee my standard floats:[9] I rule
     Alone. This Pharaoh said
Vainglory makes him god – poor fool,
     He soon shall lose his head.
Arise beloved, come, fair maid.
     Gone rains and winter's blast:[10]
Slavery's time is fully paid,
     Oppression's hour is past.
Nightingales, turtles sing,[11] our strength
     God wakes and will renew.
For Abraham's vision[12] will at length
     Transpire – the date is due.
Light I laid by for Israel springs
     To shine, bright as the day,
Glory to find, as priests and kings
     Whilst sun and moon shall stay.

f. 49b

I planted vines, and kept each root
    (All muscats)[13] guarded well:
They bloom, and from each tender shoot
    There wafts a fragrant smell.[14]

I snapped thy yoke, and placed instead
    On thee a fair-wrought chain:
Thy foes I drowned, but thy host led
    Dryshod across the main.

Noble princess,[15] let thy lips grace
    Some song – made through thy choice
Yet sweeter: Shew me, pray, thy face
    And let me hear thy voice.[16]

Thy song I hear, thy noble word,
    How thou dost undertake
To keep God's law, as yet unheard
    By thee, till Moses spake.[17]

I long therefore to have thee near,
    My temple home to share;
Thy voice sounds sweetly in my ear,
    Thy face is wondrous fair.[18]

I gave thee tablets, sapphire-decked,
    To set forth my laws' sense:
Foxes that day my vineyard wrecked,
    When they broke through its fence.

And so a golden calf they fake,
    For glory changed:[19] among
The vineyards foxes havoc make,
    And all the vines are young.[20]

For all that, I will yet restore
    Thy host, its might will mend;
I will turn back, and, as before,
    Their talk, their voice attend.

Though enemies sell thee for gold,
    Or foes should swallow thee,
The law states: 'Though one has been sold
    Redemption he may see'.[21]

O Lord Eternal, see how hard
    We suffer; so this day
We ask Thee, hearken, to regard
    Thy people when they pray.

Conduct them home, both small and great,
    To their Land, as they prayed
To Thee, so long expatriate,
    Ever our fathers' aid.

---

[1] See poem 13, n. 1. [2] See poem 2, introductory note. [3] S. of S. 2, 5.
[4] S. of S. 2, 8. [5] Hab. 3, 8. [6] S. of S. 7, 9. [7] S. of S. 1, 8–9. [8] S. of S.
2, 9. [9] S. of S. 2, 4. [10] S. of S. 2, 13; 11. [11] S. of S. 1, 12. [12] Gen. 15,
9; 13. [13] Jer. 2, 21. [14] S. of S. 1, 13. [15] Ps. 45, 14(13). [16] S. of S. 1, 14.
[17] Ex. 24, 7. [18] S. of S. 1, 14. [19] Ps. 106, 20. [20] S. of S. 2, 15.
[21] Lev. 25, 48.

---

# 65 Ge'ullah[1]

[By Isaac Ibn Ghayyat. The acrostic reads: יצחק, 'Isaac'.]

Through months by hundreds, days past numbering,
I nurture hope, but tribulations bring

Sheer disappointment. Yet, I know, time flies,
Winging God's saving acts, as o'er the skies
The eagle soars, fleet as across the sand
Courses the antelope: while, on thy band,
Thy chosen lot,[2] misfortunes ever fall.
On backwoods and on townsfolk, one and all.
Thou lookest on. Where, now, those wonders shown
Of old, thine awesome deeds of justice, known
To those who, for Redeemer, none but God will own?

Too short my stride[3] for history's grim trail
Of woes; would I keep pace, my strength must fail.
Trouble's torch-bearing troops invest my reins
As though, while sleeps my joy, my grief remains
Awake. Each day hardship lays bare, and straits:
In captors' hands my flock, surrendered, waits.
My ransom's gate is shut: for how long more
May no one come within, redeemed? Wherefore
Lingers that destiny prophets foretold of yore?

Alas! Too often visions of my seers
Proved a mirage, that floats and disappears
Over deceptive waters: to extend
Credence, spelled disillusion in the end,[4]
When presaged joys for cruel facts were changed:
With gall they mixed my honey, and arranged
Things so, that I must needs eat what I cooked.
And yet – recall her love, on whom all looked
As beauty's consummation:[5] for her sake
Vision of wonders still to come awake.

Bring close those whom thine anger distanced; tend
With gentleness the flock Thou didst intend
To mark for butchery.[6] Break off the yoke
Which scoffing foes have laid upon thy folk,
As, long since, Thou didst break. Establish those
That stood within thy courts, till Thou didst close
Thy door behind them. Just art Thou indeed,
From first to last, in all Thou hast decreed.[7]
Thy law, ordained beforehand, did provide:
'See not thy neighbour's sheep astray, and hide'.[8]
Fulfil thy law, for sheep Thou didst expel
Thyself, and to the House where Thou didst dwell
Make good thy pledge, as Thou didst undertake
When in a compact Thou our hand didst shake.[9]

---

[1] See poem 14, n. 1. [2] Deut. 32, 9. [3] Job 18, 7. [4] The last word on the 8th line reads
le-sophi or le-suphi (with sin); possibly le-sophi (with samekh) was intended. [5] Lam. 3,
15. [6] Jer. 12, 3. [7] Ps. 51, 6(4). [8] Deut. 22, 1–3. [9] Prov. 22, 26.

[Hymns for the Last Day]

f.50a

# 66 Introduction[1]
# for the Last Day of Passover

[By Solomon Ibn Gabirol. The acrostic reads: שלמה, 'Solomon'.]

How long wilt thou lie in the tomb,
    Thou sprig of Jesse's root?[2]
Winter is past:[3] arise and bloom,
    With buds that promise fruit.

Why should a slave rule princes' seed,
  And Christian Edom[4] win
A royal throne, that was decreed
  For his own younger twin?[5]

I have a thousand years incurred
  Of servitude, disgraced
In exile, like some lonely bird
  That haunts the empty waste.[6]

No white-robed angel[7] might I find
  That could the date reveal
When comes the end: God bade one bind
  It hidden, under seal.[8]

---

[1] The concluding day of Passover, on which *Is.* 11–12 is read, is particularly associated in tradition with messianic aspirations regarding the 'future Passover' (*pesaḥ shel 'athid*). That perhaps accounts for the assignment of this poem, with its initial glance at the prophetic reading and its whimsical rejection of eschatological calculations, to the liturgy of the day. Elsewhere it is assigned to the intermediate Sabbath.  [2] *Is.* 11, 1.  [3] *S. of S.* 2, 11.  [4] See poem 27, n. 3.  [5] *Gen.* 27, 29.  [6] *Ps.* 102, 7(6).  [7] *Dan.* 12, 6–7.  [8] *Dan.* 12, 4.

## 67 Introduction

[By Isaac Ibn Ghayyat. The acrostic reads: יצחק, 'Isaac'.]

Why from my tree dry branches snap
  My virtues' drought explains:
The Christian's[1] tree grows, full of sap,
  By streams where my sin drains.

To be their shoe, whose land once my
  Shoe trod, is hard to bear,
Or wash that nation's feet, whom I
  My washpot did declare.[2]

And Esau's hair – that shaggy mop –
  Smothers my clean neck's sides,[3]
Since I nor razor find, nor strop,
  And barber none provides.

Glib talk the eschatologists[4]
  And say, the wandering Jew
Goes home, in peace – each one insists –
  His latter days to view.

Ask rather Him, who veils[5] a date
  He might reveal; 'tis He
Hope's prisoner[6] can extricate
  And send the captive free.

---

[1] *Gen.* 36, 28; see poem 27, n. 3.  [2] *Ps.* 60, 10(8).  [3] *Gen.* 27, 11; 16.  [4] Prognostications regarding messianic chronology are discouraged in rabbinic Judaism, as fostering an artificially prolonged crisis mentality; see Babylonian Talmud, *Sanhedrin* 97b.  [5] *Dan.* 12, 9.  [6] *Zech.* 9, 12.

## 68 Muḥarrakh[1] [Author unknown.]

For God, my Rock, my being yearns:
  When from his works, to contemplate
His mystic glory my eye turns,
  My mind is balked, inadequate.

My thoughts range, plotting means whereby to know
Thee, who in the empyrean dost dwell,
Although thy work is seen on earth below.
Who, save Thou, fashioned me, that didst compel
My dust, compact? I flounder,[2] when I fain would tell

  Who is First Agent of my deeds.
  Days now gone by his might recount,
  Evinced in thinking that proceeds
  Through wise men's minds,[3] but from thy fount.

But stronger grows my step, when I essay
My Maker[4] (mindful of his works) to praise:
My toils through Him forgotten, while I play
My pipe exalting Him in all his ways.
Each living soul would fain remember Thee, and gaze

  Upon thy beauty, and would cling
  Hard to thy glory's shrine.[5] Untie
  My bonds: death's firstborn,[6] trespassing,
  My lost ones[7] seeks to multiply.

f. 50b

Meanwhile a foolish shepherd[8] multiplies
My loutish thoughts and vain meanderings.
My Maker I entreat. Though He applies
Sickness, and, for my fault, with pain He stings,
A cure for every malady his mercy brings:

  Whom He protects, He will restore[9]
  Made great behind my battlement,
  My fringed sign recognized[10] once more,
  As sign of love hard by his tent.[11]

---

[1] See poem 7, n. 1.  [2] In the 5th line, the penultimate word is to be vocalized *be-shalli* (Wallenstein).  [3] *Job* 5, 12.  [4] In the 7th line, the 3rd word is to be vocalized *mē-'osi* (or *-say*, Wallenstein).  [5] The last word of the penultimate line of f. 50a should be *debirekha* (without *be-*).  [6] *Job* 18, 13.  [7] The 5th word in the last line of f. 50a is to be vocalized *shakhli*, 'my bereavement' (Wallenstein).  [8] *Zech.* 11, 15.  [9] *Is.* 49, 6; the 2nd word of the 3rd line on f. 50b should read *yashib*.  [10] *Gen.* 38, 25.  [11] The final word should have *be-* prefixed (*be-'ŏhŏlo*).

## 69 Muḥarrakh[1]

[By Abraham Ibn Ezra. The acrostic reads: אבר[ה]ם, 'Abra[ha]m'.]

  My Maker I[2] would justify:
  Ye angels,[3] tell me how. If I
  In very truth belong with you,
  Have I with mortals ought to do?

'Know, denizen, of truth, the world is vain,
And those therein; its prizes are a snare
For worldly men. Yearnest thou to attain
A place near God, his renegades to forswear?
Cling, then, to wisdom's ladder – mount the angels' stair.[4]

  Wisdom from deep inside thee springs,
  Within thyself the well that brings
  Thee understanding: do not fail
  To draw it up, with ne'er a pail.

Thy Rock is thy foundation. In desire
To act, thou findest pleasure. Give thou heed:
Each purpose[5] will its instrument require –
The body's parts. Take, then, the road to lead
To the domain of truth, where forms no matter need,

No implements their actions move;
Indeed,[6] the wise have thought to prove
That substances in that domain
Imperishable must remain.

[Thou[7] soul integral, gird thyself to tend
Thy pleasure-garden:[8] therein feast thine eyes
Upon God's glory. Bodies in the end
Into the pit are thrown; thou shouldst despise
The flesh that will but turn to worms, so soon it dies:

To cherish it were labour lost.
If never sinful notions crossed
Thy branching thoughts, then hast thou ground
In exaltation to abound.']

God, our eternal home,[9] within whose hand
My spirit rests[10] – to Him[11] I look, to test
Thoughts which, unuttered, He will understand.
For my part, all my strength will I invest
To rouse my soul, my chiefest glory,[12] to her best:

So long to wisdom's path I hold
My tent knows peace;[13] God will enfold
My firmness in his dignity,
My Rock and my Redeemer He.[14]

---

[1] See poem 7, n. 1. The manuscript exhibits substantial variants (some unrecorded) from
I. Levin's critical text of this poem in *Shirey Ha-qodesh shel 'Abraham Ibn 'Ezra* (1976) i,
pp. 244f. [2] The first speaker in the dialogue is the soul. [3] *Job* 1, 6. [4] *Gen.* 28, 12.
[5] In the 6th line, the 4th word from the end is *sorekh*. [6] For the 1st word of the 8th line the
better reading is *'ulam*. [7] The Hebrew text of the stanza omitted is as follows:

התאזרי, כלולה, כלך לשמר ולעבד
גן תענוג אשר נתן לך: בו תחזי כבוד
האל! ומאסי גו ישלך בבור. ובאבד
עצמו ושב בשרו רמה – הבל תכלכלי!
אם אין ביד סעיפך אשמה – רני וצהלי!

[8] *Gen.* 2, 15. [9] *Ps.* 90, 1. [10] *Job* 12, 10. [11] In the 9th line, the 5th word should be
corrected to *'elaw*. [12] *Ps.* 57, 9(8). [13] *Job* 5, 24. [14] *Ps.* 19, 15(14).

---

# 70 Nishmath[1]

[By Isaac ben Judah of 'Senir' (Mont Ventoux, Provence). The acrostic reads: השניר , 'Of Senir'.]

The breath of those whom heathen harrass for their sport
When synagogue they seek, but are to prison brought,
In dungeons hidden,[2] glorify Thee thence, as they were taught.

Their breath – a trembling remnant who went forth this day
To supplicate for life,[3] exalts Thee, as they pray
From out the crannies where they hide themselves away.[4]

The breath of those who, fearful, cry from burdening
Of cruel lords, yet to thy Name contrives to sing,
Whilst persecutors round their doors shout: 'Time now stones to fling'.[5]

Their breath – a lonely few – proclaims Thee as Unique,
Midst people who – rough-tongued, obtuse[6] – occasion seek,
Taunting: 'You snared our idol; for his blood we vengeance wreak'.[7]

The breath of those who shattered, crushed, must bear the weight
Of the foe's burning ire, hymns Thee; whilst yet there wait
Stone-slingers, all with deadly aim,[8] ready to rush the gate.[9]

f. 51a

---

[1] See poem 8, n. 1. This poem refers to the confinement of Jews during the Christian Holy Week.
Elsewhere it is assigned for recitation on the intermediate Sabbath of Passover in those years when it
coincided with Easter Saturday. [2] *Is.* 42, 22. [3] *Esther* 7, 7. [4] *I Sam.* 14, 11. [5] *Eccles.* 3, 5; the
allusion is to the stoning of the Jewish quarters at Eastertide. [6] *Deut.* 32, 21. [7] *Ez.* 3, 20 (glancing at
the charge of deicide). [8] *Judg.* 20, 16. [9] *Is.* 22, 7.

---

# 71 [Introduction to] Kaddeesh[1]

[Author unknown.]

Lord, wilt Thou for all time forget
I built for Thee a fane,
And increase might to those who yet
Revilement on Thee rain?
Does my bald arrogance not let
Me see thy face again?

Raise me from my captivity
As from the pit, and smite,
O Rock, those who, thine enemy,
Against me wage their fight:
Reck not of mine iniquity,
Speed me thy mercy's flight.[2]

Must Thou still make my time extend
In exile? Bid be tied
Thine ire;[3] not for me mercy send,
But for thy sake,[4] to guide
All men in awe of Thee to bend:
Thy Name be sanctified.

---

[1] See p. 17. [2] *Ps.* 79, 8. [3] In the last line, the 7th word should be
vocalized *za'ame[y]kha*. [4] *Is.* 43, 5; *Ez.* 26, 22.

---

# 72 'Ophan[1]

[By Moses Ibn Ezra. The acrostic reads: אני מש[ה , 'I am Moses'.]

Thy Presence, Lord, midst mankind stalks,
Thy Truth midst thronging angels walks.[2]

Angels of mystery
Those in the height,
Holy consistory,
Star hosts in flight,
Ask where his place is
Whose throne is the skies,
Earth, a mere basis,
His footstool supplies.[3]
Awestruck, the whole conclave
Call holy the Name,
His holiness God gave,
With mighty acclaim.[4]

And earth's matching college
Of faithful, in fear
Enveloped, acknowledge
Him all must revere;
The sages, detecting
His Law's every breach,
And scholars, protecting
The trust they must teach:
All these likewise render
Their homage, their praise,
With gratitude, tender
Each awe-spoken phrase;
Their worship's prostration
In reverence planned,
The whole congregation

---

In one holy band.[5]

The Heavens, created,
    Flashed[6] light straightaway
When earth He located,
    Suspended to stay.[7]
His angels, enjoying
    Superior reach
Of mind for deploying
    He fashioned: to each
His function explaining,
    And bidding him fix
His purpose, disdaining
    With mankind to mix.[8]

[Then you, brothers, ever
    Were called, Him to serve,
So long you endeavour
    His laws to observe,
Subduing your own will
    To his,[9] whose whole Law
You gained, and you see still
    The same you then saw,
When bidden, 'be holy:
    If each so shall try,
Know I this folk wholly
    Mine own sanctify'.[10]]

Thrust out sighs and grieving
    From all who are sad,
Who, new life receiving,
    Henceforth shall be glad.
Gates long disappointed,
    In mourning, shall sing,
And priests new anointed
    Their sacrifice bring;
And then we all, meeting
    At our shrine, in pride,
Will bring lambs for eating
    Each Passover-tide.[11]

---

[1] See poem 9, n. 1. [2] Ps. 89, 6(5). [3] Is. 66, 1. [4] Ps. 89, 8(7).
[5] Num. 16, 3. [6] For *yahellu*, Bernstein's text reads *yah lo*, 'Lord,
by no [physical] act', and implying: 'but by thy mere word'.
[7] Job 26, 7. [8] Num. 16, 26. After this stanza the following one,
which is required to complete the acrostic signature (*mem shin*),
has been omitted, but is printed here from Bernstein's text:

מְשָׁרְתָיו אָז הֱיִיתֶם     בְּמוֹצָא פִיו חֲיִיתֶם
זְמָן חֻקָּיו עֲשִׂיתֶם     וּבִרְצוֹנוֹ רְצִיתֶם
וְאֶת דָּתוֹ קְנִיתֶם     הַיּוֹם אֲשֶׁר רְאִיתֶם
וְהִתְקַדַּשְׁתֶּם     וִהְיִיתֶם קְדֹשִׁים:

[9] Mishnah, *Pirqey 'Aboth* II, 4. [10] Lev. 11, 44. [11] Compare the
culminating benediction of the *Haggadah*, f. 33a (p. 35).

---

# 73 Me'orah[1]

[By Nahum. The author's name appears in an acrostic: נחום , 'Nahum'.]

Lo, the winter is gone[2] – gone with it too, my pains:
With the fruit-trees in bloom, blooms my heart – there joy reigns.

The spice-beds waft perfume, and the orchard's a sight
Of blossom, God's loved ones to fill with delight.
Thou noble Hart,[3] chased till Thou fleddest my shrine,
Come Thee back, to drink milk, yea, to drink my spiced wine.[4]

---

Routing sadness, flower-beds round trim[5] myrtles sprout,
Woven fabric-wise, repeating, driving sorrows out.
Myrrh scatters round me from the physic-garden's[6] bed,
And by my seat the nut-tree's[7] fronds like buckets spread.

Gratitude's leaf twixt plants through shadows twists and turns;
Within a golden[8] goblet set with jewels there burns
f. 51b    A ruby vintage, shall my foemen's gall off-set,
The sorrows buried in my heart make me forget.

My Friend[9] has left the city's grazing deer, to rest
In forest glades: turn back, seek thy beloved's breast,
Swathe her in song,[10] my even with thy lamp make bright:
Through Thee shall my anointed cherub[11] show me light.

---

[1] See poem 10, n. 1. Some of the imagery in this poem is obscure, and needs further elucidation.
[2] S. of S. 1, 11; see poem 2, introductory note. [3] S. of S. 2, 9. [4] S. of S. 8, 2. [5] S. of S. 7, 3(2).
[6] S. of S. 5, 13. [7] S. of S. 6, 11. [8] S. of S. 5, 14. [9] S. of S. 5, 10. The 2nd word in the 2nd and
3rd lines on f. 51b must be corrected to (*le-*)*dod* (not *dor*). [10] The word *be-shirim* has been
added in minuscule, in the left-hand margin (f. 51b, 2nd line). [11] Ez. 28, 14.

---

# 74 Me'orah[1]

[By Isaac Ibn Ghayyat. The acrostic reads: יצחק , 'Isaac'.]

Haste, soon be seen that longed-for day
    When Thou wilt robe me, Lord, in pride,
    And those who warped[2] reliance lay
    On idols, shall in shame abide,
When long-term captives, from their pit released,
On light of thy face, Lord, their eyes shall feast.[3]

    Those thy possession[4] called at first
    Repurchase; pilgrims[5] show thy smile,
    Who for thy saving fountains[6] thirst,
    And all through their age-long exile
Have clung to thy Name faithful, nor did care
From the contempt they earned their face to spare.[7]

    Strengthen the hearts of those who quail
    From foemen's shout that God defies,
    And those who crush the poor, assail,[8]
    Whipping them scattered. Terrorize
Strangers, who aim at us their arrows' flight:
Drag them where they shall die from vipers' bite.

    Thou Holy God, who didst of old
    Know well thy sheep, tend them and lead
    Thy flock to meads by Thee foretold.
    View me this day, my voice to heed;
From thy mouth blessed, thy firstborn's[9] progeny
Make speed, redeem, that they may go forth free.

---

[1] See poem 10, n. 1. [2] 1 Sam. 20, 30. [3] Ps. 89, 16(15). [4] Ex. 15, 16. [5] Ex. 23, 15.
[6] Is. 12, 3. [7] Is. 50, 6. [8] Amos 2, 7. [9] Ex. 4, 22.

Poem No. 61, beginning *Yizkeru pil'akha
ṣeba' marom*, 'Thy wonders are recalled
by heaven's force', was repeated by the
scribe in error; it appears on f. 48b, and
has been translated in sequence.

f. 52a

## 75 Me'orah[1]

[By Isaac Ibn Ghayyat. The acrostic reads: יצחק, 'Isaac'.]

God saved us: on his glory's vision feast thy sight;[2]
Responding, his great bounties unto us[3] recite.

Let one now sick, despondent that the moon[4]
So long rides high, consider – there comes soon
Daybreak, to mark night's end, and morning mist[5]
Seeks yester-eve's gloom out, by light dismissed.
Curse not, cramped by tomorrow's ills: reflect,
Observe that shade which shall us all protect;[6]
For know, should that one day decline, then we
Forthwith by foemen near consumed must be.
My dove, long silent,[7] see, thy Maker's power
Triumphant sends disaster, making cower
The armies of the Cross,[8] the strangers' rout
Confused as dreamers' thoughts all lead to doubt.
His sudden vengeance falls upon the breast
Of one whose crashing boot[9] so long oppressed,
And mourning[10] brought, with hunger's lash;[11] rich fare
God feeds us, whilst the tyrant's sons despair.
Who lives unwearied[12] till the future age –
Shall wonders wrought by God for us engage
His mind? Nay, such will to oblivion drive[13]
That greater day which shall the dead revive:
A sign to those who roam – rest shall they know,
And see Him, pointing each a hand, to show
'This[14] is our Friend,[15] who raised us out of hell,
Cleansed of the dust of death where we did dwell'.

Therefore with silent mouth endure the days
Of pain, look to return; for nothing stays
Past its allotted time. Suppress thine ire,[16]
Though grief resentment in thy heart[17] inspire.
God, why art Thou inactive? Brace Thee, stand
Against the nightfall's perils. View thy band,
The people who in darkness lodge[18] all night;
At morning, turn, and God shall prove our light.[19]

---

[1] See poem 10, n. 1. [2] In keeping, perhaps, with the eschatological motif of the last day of the Festival (the 'Passover of the Future', see poem 66, n. 1,) this poem glances at the beatific vision of the righteous in the world to come. See below, n. 14. [3] *Is.* 64, 7. [4] In the 2nd line, the 5th word should be *sahar* (with *he*). [5] *Gen.* 2, 6. [6] *Ps.* 91, 4. [7] *Ps.* 56, 1. [8] Isaac Ibn Ghayyat's dates (1038–89) admit of the possibility that he here had in mind the defeat of Alfonso VI by the Almoravid Yusuf ibn Tashfin at Zalaca, near Badajoz, in 1086. [9] *Is.* 9, 4(5). [10] In the 5th line, the 9th word should be corrected to read *he'ebilanu*. [11] *Deut.* 32, 24. [12] In the 6th line, the 3rd word should be vocalized *le'uth*. [13] *Is.* 43, 18f. [14] *Is.* 25, 9; in the *Babylonian Talmud* (Ta'anith, end f. 31a), Rabbi Eleazar stresses the deictic demonstrative, *zeh*, picturing the future dance of the righteous around God, while they pay homage with manual gesture. [15] In the 7th line, the 8th word should be *dod* (possibly corrected in the MS). [16] *Prov.* 21, 14. [17] In the penultimate line, before the last word, *leb* (erroneously repeated) has been erased. [18] In the last line, over the 5th word from the end, *lanu* has been inserted, cf. *Is.* 9, 1(2). [19] *Ps.* 118, 27.

## 76 'Ahabah[1]

[By Isaac Ibn Ghayyat. The acrostic reads: יצחק, 'Isaac'.]

My Hart[2] has fled my lodging, friends:
    Know you when He comes back, to dwell
With me? See that He answer sends
    To you – my angel-love – to tell.

He bore away my other heart,
    And how shall I my grieving bear?

With all my joy did He depart,
    Nor knew on whom He thrust my care.
Hard, hard it is to be bereft
    Of glory that his presence lent;
He roams afar, and I am left
    Without his splendour's ornament.
Where are those days when, close beside
    My neck,[3] his bent, when, with his lip
So tightly to my own applied,
    Upon my tongue did honey drip?[4]
Though He forget He did respect
    My deeds of grace,[5] how can He all
Our friendship's pleasures now reject
    When I was held in Egypt's thrall,
When He upon my gaoler laid
    In Thebes[6] his signs, my throng to prise
Free from his hold, and then displayed
    The Red Sea split before mine eyes?
His glory He made manifest
    To me: words in my ear He spoke
His whispered love for me expressed,
    Kindled[7] my flame, my love awoke.
He viewed my tinkling robes, the scent
    Of incense.[8] But since Thou art fled
I have endured much harrassment
    Because thy glory from me sped.
For all that, I would rather be
    Thy slave (as though my ear were bored)
For life; nor would I go forth free
    From thy domain – I love my Lord.[9]

---

[1] See poem 12, n. 1. [2] *S. of S.* 2, 9; 5, 6; 6, 1; see poem 2, introductory note. [3] *S. of S.* 4, 9. [4] *S. of S.* 4, 11. [5] *Ps.* 77, 10(9). [6] *Jer.* 46, 25. [7] The 1st word of the 3rd line from the end should be *u-le-harer* (possibly corrected from *u-le-hared*; MS British Library Or. 1404, f. 48a, reads *u-le-heder*). [8] *Ex.* 28, 34; 30, 7. [9] *Ex.* 21, 5–6.

f. 52b

## 77 'Ahabah[1]

[By Nahum ben Jacob. The acrostic reads: נחום, 'Nahum'.]

Fair one, a belt of valour place
    Around thy waist:[2] soon help brings calm;
If tension makes thy heart to race,
    To Gilead go,[3] and get thee balm.[4]

Though sorrow's torrent piles its waters high
To stand in heaps,[5] God will his wind direct[6]
In but a trice, and they shall straight be dry;
Hades shall not, with closed well-mouth,[7] hold checked
The folk who lie within he did so long subject.

    Why from thy stocks[8] press to escape,
    Or lions for thy host prefer?
    Nay, from the lion's carcase scrape
    Thy honey:[9] go, pluck thee thy myrrh.[10]

He that in might dried the Red Sea, and laid
A path between its waves, a blow shall deal
To grieve the lion's heart. Those whom He made
His seedling, on their head He will reveal

A garland: though He pain me now, no pain I feel,
 My heart no pang: I chose the fate
That leaves me by my Friend's ire chased:
 Be I a victim consecrate,
 Then come I to his altar chaste.

In Thee alone I trust, my King, whose store
Of glory fills the earth;[11] thy hand did press
The heavens flat.[12] When heavens are no more,
Still shall that soul exult, whose happiness
Is in thy law; send us the balm, our wounds to dress,
 Choice fruit of Gilead,[4] refined
 As balm – first aid against the hour
 When foes press hard: that I may find
 My Helper's strength shall prove my tower.[13]

[And I – all eagerness to answer thee,
Calling in anguish – through the lattice spy;
Arise, from hardship's house get thee out, free.
To Zion up, where once the Hart lay, lie;
There those afflicted that did call, shall hear reply.
 Roaming's bars hold thee pent, distressed
 To lie; bestir thyself, haste, go,
 The mount ascend: towards the crest
 Of good, of God's light, strive to flow.]

---

[1] See poem 12, n. 1; but the conclusion of the last stanza (missing in this MS, see below, n. 13) shows that this poem is in fact intended as a *me'orah* (see poem 10, n. 1). [2] *Ps.* 93, 1. [3] In the 2nd line, the 3rd word from the end must be vocalized *'ali*. [4] *Jer.* 8, 22. [5] *Ex.* 15, 8. [6] *Gen.* 8, 1. [7] *Ps.* 69, 16(15). [8] In the 4th line, the 11th word, *be-sodekh*, 'in thy secret conclave', yields no apparent sense. The emendation *be-saddekh*, 'in thy stocks', adopted *faute de mieux* in the translation, suggested itself before I found that David's text reads *be-dodekh*, 'against thy Friend', and cites no variants. [9] *Judg.* 14, 9. [10] *S. of S.* 5, 1. [11] *Is.* 6, 3. [12] *Is.* 48, 13. [13] *Ps.* 61, 4(3). In David's text this stanza begins not *malki*, but *wa-'ani*, and the acrostic is completed by the following stanza, included in the translation above:

וּבְצַעֲקָתֵךְ אֶעֱנֶה    מֵצִיץ בְּעַד חַרָךְ אֲנִי
צִיּוֹן עֲלִי אֵל מִשְׁכָּנִי    קוּמִי, צְאִי מִבֵּית עֳנִי
אָז נַעֲנֶה כָּל נַעֲנֶה;    עָפָר, בְּתַחֲנוּנוֹ חָנִי

חַ הַנּוֹדֵד, הִתְעוֹרְרִי    הַשּׁוֹכְבָה תַּחַת בְּרִי –
וּלְטוֹב אֲדֹנָי נַהֲרִי    לַעֲלוֹת לְהַר אֵל מַהֲרִי

---

# 78 Zulath[1]

[Author unknown. There is a fragmentary alphabetical acrostic: ט-א.]

The foreigner[2] came fast – too soon:
 Ten marches[3] he had made
The day his sun went down at noon[4] –
 Judgement on him was laid;

Judgement on high, when he had planned
 *Halting at Nob*, to waste
Ephraim and Judah, *with raised hand*
 As Zion's mount[5] he faced.

His road shrank, as before our sire
 The road foreshortened[6] (he
Went from Beer Sheba, from the ire
 Of Esau forced to flee.

Good man or bad, his way each wends,
 But God the wicked stops:
*The Lord of Hosts* upon him sends
 *Crashing the trees He lops*).[7]

'My warriors are gathering',
 (Quoth He), 'my wrath shall see
Vengeance on foes, and kings shall bring
 Their tribute unto Me.[8]
To sacrifice goodwill I show,
 Bread offered at my shrine
By fire shall please Me.[9] *There shall grow*
 *A shoot from Jesse's line.*'[10]

His promise God will implement
 Who dwells on high, *and teach*
*Him, through the fear of God, to scent*[11]
 Those whom his sting must reach,

*That he so judge the poor, to serve*
 *The right* in kingdoms twain,[12]
*And when the meek rebuke deserve*
 *In equity restrain.*[13]

His bolts death to the foeman send
 By scores: should he repair
The wall, none breach it; but to mend
 What he has breached, none dare.

*His loins are girt in righteousness,*
 *His belt is faith:* a child
From Bethlehem *shall safely play*
 *Round asps' holes,*[14] in the wild

Where lions stalk, where waiting *lay*[15]
 *The cockatrice* to sting,
*The weanling shall in future play,*
 Nor suffer anything.

My God is He: I glorify
 Him,[16] when his deeds I see,
Wonders that wasteland beautify
 With many a fair tree.[17]

f. 53a  *As when we came from Egypt, so*
  *The remnant shall be led*
*Forth from Assyria to go,*
 *A firm highway to tread.*[18]

As then, thy mercies send, thy love,
 Lord, to encounter me:
When Thou exaltest me above
 Nations, I exalt Thee.

*I give Thee thanks: thine anger's blaze*
 *Turn back, and comfort me;*[19]
'Tis good to render thanks,[20] to praise
 For what mine own eyes see,

And what by ear I learn from sire
 And grandsire,[21] deeds from long
Ago, that gratitude inspire:
 *God is my strength and song.*[22]

And so I, singing, thankful, tell
 Wonders He wrought;[23] the tale
Recount among the nations, spell
 His glory;[24] nor shall fail

The story till most distant time,[25]
 His awsome strength to show,
*His mighty acts* in every clime
 *Let all the peoples know.*[26]

*He acts in triumph*, when besought
   Responds to all who seek:
*Through all the world let there be brought*
     *Knowledge,*[27] He is Unique,

Jeshurun's God:[28] *sing*, jubilate,
   *Zion,*[29] with joy outpoured,
*Exult, within thy midst is great*
     *Israel's own Holy Lord.*[30]

Eternal God, our suffering
   See, hear what we have prayed
This day: do Thou all homeward bring,
   Who wast our fathers' aid.

---

[1] See poem 13, n. 1. This poem elaborates the text, appearing here in italics, of the prophetic reading for the day (*Is.* 10, 32–12, 6). [2] I.e. Sennacherib; *Is.* 36, 1f. [3] In the *Babylonian Talmud* (*Sanhedrin* 94b, *infra*), Rab Huna infers this from the places listed in *Is.* 10, 28–30. [4] *Amos* 8, 9. [5] *Is.* 10, 32. [6] *Sanhedrin* 95b; *Gen.* 28, 10. [7] *Is.* 10, 33. [8] *Ps.* 68, 30(29). [9] *Is.* 56, 7. [10] *Is.* 11, 1. [11] *Is.* 11, 3. [12] I.e. Ephraim (signifying Joseph) and Judah; *Ruth* 4, 18. [13] *Is.* 11, 4. [14] *Is.* 11, 5 and 8. [15] *Is.* 11, 8. [16] *Ex.* 15, 2. [17] *Is.* 41, 19. [18] *Is.* 11, 16. [19] *Is.* 12, 1. [20] *Ps.* 92, 2(1). [21] *Deut.* 32, 7. [22] *Is.* 12, 2; *Ex.* 15, 2. [23] *Ps.* 111, 4. [24] *Ps.* 96, 3. [25] *Ps.* 78, 6. [26] *Is.* 12, 4. [27] *Is.* 12, 5. [28] *Deut.* 33, 26. [29] *Is.* 29, 1. [30] *Is.* 12, 6.

## 79 Ge'ullah[1]

[By (Moses?) ben Shesheth. The acrostic reads: בן שׁשׁת, 'ben Shesheth'.]

His love, who is my Friend, I see,
His all-embracing majesty –
     Humble I feel, and small.

The Rock my heart rests on is He,
My King, to seek whose charity
     Like some poor man, I call.

Raise Thyself, my Redeemer, lest, misled,
My foes triumphant see my glory sped
     And, gloating at my fall,

Claim for their idol victory:
Nay, shall one held aloof by Thee
Lord it o'er my inconstancy?
Prophet let him not claim to be,
     Most reprobate of all.

My soul is in the lions' den; struck dumb
By sickness, must I lie. Still my foes come,
     Wild beasts, to harry me:

How answer pagan fools, who say
To sons befouled by sin, 'Away!
     Crass folly all can see'?

I come prepared to answer it:
Thy words stand clear in holy writ,
     Content with that are we.

Who deals in falsehood, wry is he, abhorred,
Though he may flourish like the bay-tree: Lord,
     Rise, lay his secrets bare:

Advance in glory, clear the ways;
If Thou the trail of truth shalt blaze,
     Our standards will we bear,

Beacon-like, may my flame ne'er fail,
Righteousness that Thou dost unveil
     Shall we for banners wear.

Dismissing what is vain, from on high send,
Ban those that scoff at truth; my sapling tend
     To root, by Thee bedewed;

Why should my foes uproot thy stem?
Must I misfortune hear of them,
     My fruit, by locusts chewed?

They once a barley-cake[2] did seem,
Flattening tents, in Midian's dream,
     Midst cymbals' clash renewed.

Gone is my champion from me,
With cherubs keeping company
     In song's beatitude.

One whose path strays, along thine own path guide:[3]
Thy might redeem him, who to Thee has cried.
     Sorely rebuked, he wails;

To those who must weep for their kin
Thy spirit grant, courage to win,
     In every one that quails.

Arise, my people, leave your grief,
Harried no more: joy brings relief,
     And merrymaking hails.

Come, dry your ocean-depths of tears,
You that have sighed down countless years
     Sing loud, now trouble fails.

The sun-broiled servant gasps, his Master's place
In shade to reach; do Thou, of thy rich grace,
     Let him dwell in thy shade;

Whom thy great heart from sin has freed,
To his oppressors sold, make speed,
     Redeem, thine once more made:

In evil-doers' hands must he
Cry out, from hell's profundity,
     This day is he afraid.

'Redeem Thou him that is thy slave,
From wolves, from lions' fury save',
     He prays, and ever prayed.

---

[1] See poem 14, n. 1. This elaborate echo-poem (which has no clear link with Passover, and is elsewhere assigned for use on the Feast of Tabernacles) relies for its effect on homonyms and multiple meanings of the same word. Many of these have defied penetration, and the loose rendering given here makes no claim to offering a full interpretation. [2] *Judg.* 7, 13f. [3] The 4th word of the penultimate line on f. 53a must be vocalized *hadrekh*.

## 80 Ge'ullah[1]

[By Jacob. The author's name appears in an acrostic: יעקב, 'Jacob'.]

Arise, O Lord: reveal what Thou didst hide[2]
Against my destined date, when shall be dew[3]
Of glory on my garden. Mine eyes' tide
Of tears runs down to Thee; turn back, renew
That base where firm I stood. Thy word fulfil;
Balm shall it be upon my heart, to thrill
With life restored, and Thou wilt then distil
Oil on my head, my cup through fulness spill.[4]

A captive, on my shoulder I must bear
That yoke which sons of foolishness[5] deride

f. 53b

65

As but my veil:[6] to answer I forbear,
Silent, and in captivity abide,
And to mine adversary's taunts I make
No answer save on this my case to stake,
That I, O Lord, am captive for thy sake;
In place of armaments[7] thy Name I take.

Lord, smothered beneath thorns thy vineyard lies:
Tend it, and weed therefrom each single tare;
Thy folk as sovereign let all recognize,
And make them sing, restored to what they were,
Thy folk, none other's; prithee, exchange no more:
With hand raised, these a second time restore,[8]
With desolation smite those who, before
Proved as allies, a useless arm in war.[9]

Towards thine own betrothed[10] turn Thou thine eye,
That precious people which, as merchandise
Was sold, yet for no price:[11] for Thyself buy
This lost sheep.[12] All those rights that are the prize
Of married bliss,[13] make hers. Let not thy fawn
Be left as prey, by hungry lions torn:
From where she lies in fetters, all forlorn,
Redeem her, back from land of Lethe[14] drawn.

[1] See poem 14, n. 1. [2] Ps. 31, 20(19). [3] See poem 15, introductory note. [4] Ps. 23, 5. [5] In the 3rd line the 8th word must be vocalized *tŏhŏlah*. [6] Clearly alluding to the representation in Western Christian art of the Synagogue blindfold, opposite the Church. [7] Job 41, 18(26). [8] Is. 11, 11. [9] Ps. 78, 57. [10] Hos. 2, 21(19). [11] Is. 52, 3. [12] Jer. 50, 7. [13] Ex. 21, 10. [14] Ps. 88, 13(12).

## 81 Ge'ullah[1]

[By Nahum ben Jacob. The acrostic reads: נחום, 'Nahum'.]

Thy strong arm and thy mercies – where, O where?
Must we of thy hand's ransoming despair?[2]

Wild boars through thy once pleasant arbours root,[3]
To mountain ash[4] abandoned rank it grows;
Its spring dried out, gone all its fair-trained fruit,
No taste, no perfume from its orchard blows:
Clouds that can save, send scudding, to repair
Thy plot, by dew made fresh borne on the air.

Thy chosen one in favour didst Thou style
Firstborn,[5] and in thy crucible refined,
Then tossed into the pit for this long while,
For Christian sons of Esau[6] there to bind;
To hold him slave, how shall this Edom dare,
Him that to be thy slave Thou didst declare?[7]

'My son, what matter, though the Edomite[8]
Holds thee his slave? Wait but a trice, and He
Destruction meets, and thou shalt find delight –
The wealth of kings, richness of Araby
To suck: I give thee ornaments to wear,
Thou shalt rule Edom, no more his rule bear.'

Thou herald of deliverance,[9] take wing,
Soar like the eagle, come, with ringing sound
Of cymbals, horns, and voice of thanksgiving:
Strengthen the heart of one whom sickness found,
Haste him from exile home. Thy Rock shall care,
As thy Redeemer, ransom to prepare.

[1] See poem 14, n. 1. [2] Is. 50, 2. [3] Ps. 80, 14(13): the boar, regarded in early-rabbinic times as the symbol of pagan Rome, merges, with Rome itself, into a symbol of Christendom. [4] Ez. 17, 5; Babylonian Talmud, Sukkah 34a. [5] Ex. 4, 22. [6] Gen. 25, 13; Esau/Edom regularly stands for Rome/Christendom in rabbinic convention. [7] Lev. 25, 55. [8] Gen. 36, 4. [9] Is. 52, 7.

f. 54a

## Grace after the Meal

[The Grace, added to the MS at a later date, is to be read before the main text on f. 33b.]

If three or more, but fewer than ten [adult men], are in the company, one takes the lead in reciting grace for all, beginning with the following request for attention: 'Let us bless Him from whose store we have eaten'; to which the remainder respond: 'Blessed be He from whose store we have eaten, and thanks to whose goodness we continue in life'. If ten or more are of the company, the formula is: 'Let us bless our God from whose store we have eaten, and thanks to whose goodness we continue in life', the response being similar. In the presence of a bridegroom the formula is: 'Blessed be our God, in whose dwelling-place there is joy, from whose store we have eaten'. A single individual should begin as follows:

Blessed be He that satisfies the hungry; blessed be He that gives drink to those athirst: blessed be He, blessed be his Name, blessed be his gift for ever and ever.

BLESSED art thou, O Lord, our God, king of the cosmos: who feedest the whole world with goodness, grace, loving kindness and mercy, giving bread to all flesh, for his mercy endureth for ever.[1] His great goodness[2] is with us perpetually: He has not, nor ever will cause us lack of food, for all time, for the sake of his great Name. For He feeds and sustains all, doing good to all, and providing food for all his creatures whom He has created; as it is said: 'Thou openest thy hand, and satisfiest every living creature with good will'.[3] Blessed art Thou, O Lord, who feedest all.

For our Land and our heritage:

f. 54b

WE GIVE THANKS to Thee, O Lord, our God, for that Thou didst cause our fathers to inherit a Land desirable, goodly and broad; the covenant and Torah; life and sustenance; for that Thou didst bring us forth, O Lord, our God, from the land of Egypt, and didst redeem us from the house of bondage; for thy covenant, which Thou hast sealed in our flesh, and for thy Torah, which Thou hast taught [us];[4] for the statutes, deriving from thy divine will, which Thou has made known unto us: and for the food we eat, with which Thou dost feed us, making provision for us every day, every hour, every moment and on every occasion.

FOR all of which, O Lord, our God, we give Thee thanks and bless thy Name; may thy Name be blessed by the mouth of every living being, constantly and for ever and ever. As it is said: 'And thou shalt eat, and be satisfied, and shalt bless the Lord thy God for the goodly Land which He hath given Thee.'[5] Blessed art Thou, O Lord: for the Land, and for the food.

SEND US CONSOLATION, O Lord, our God, in regard to Zion, thy city, and cause us joy, O our King, in the building of the House of thy choosing; speedily mayest Thou restore it to its site. Be pleased, O Lord, our God, to grant us vigour through the observance of thy precepts, and in particular by the
f. 55a
observance of the precept regarding the seventh day, this great and holy Sabbath. For this day is indeed great and holy in thy sight, that we should refrain from work thereon and rest, in love, in accordance with the precept deriving from thy will. And in accordance with thy will, O Lord, our God, grant us rest, that on our day of rest there may be no trouble nor sorrow. And grant that we may witness thy acts of consolation, and in particular the consolation of Jerusalem, thy city: as it is written:

'Like one whom his mother comforteth, so do I comfort you, and through Jerusalem shall you find consolation.'[6] Blessed art Thou, O Lord, who wilt console thy people Israel by the building of Jerusalem. Amen.

HAVE MERCY upon us, O Lord, our God, and upon Israel, thy people; upon Jerusalem, thy city; upon Zion, the dwelling-place of thy glory; upon the sovereignty of the House of David, thine anointed; and upon that great and holy House, called by all thine own. Our God! our Father! our Shepherd! Feed us, make provision for us, and sustain us, and grant us ease, speedily, O Lord, our God, from all our troubles: nor cause us, we pray, O Lord, our God, to stand in need of either the gifts or the loans of our fellow-men, that we may not be embarrassed for ever and ever.

f.55b OUR GOD, and the God of our fathers: may there come before Thee and, on being examined, meet with thy good will, our record and scrutiny; the record of our fathers; the record of our Messiah, the anointed son of David, thy servant; the record of Jerusalem, thy holy city; and the record of all the house of Israel. May the memory of all these come before Thee, to be spared for good, for grace, for lovingkindness, for mercy, for life and for good will, on[7] this feast-day of Unleavened Bread, this goodly day of holy convocation.

REMEMBER US, O Lord, our God, on this day for good: scrutinize us thereon, for a blessing; and deliver us thereon for life. And in regard to deliverance and mercy, do Thou manifest unto us pity, grace, compassion and mercy, delivering us from all trouble and sorrow: and save us, for it is unto Thee that our eyes are turned, as being a king both gracious and merciful.

f. 56a And do Thou build Jerusalem, the holy city, speedily in our days, building her for perpetuity: blessed art Thou, O Lord, who wilt build Jerusalem.

AMEN In our lifetime. Amen. Speedily, in our own days, may the city of Zion be built, and the Temple service be re-established in Jerusalem.

BLESSED art Thou, O Lord, our God, king of the cosmos: for ever God, our Father, our King, our truly majestic Creator, our Redeemer, our Holy One, and the Holy One of Jacob; our Shepherd, and the Shepherd of Israel: who as God and King in thy goodness conferest benefits upon all, inasmuch as on each and every day Thou doest good to us, dealest and hast dealt bountifully with us and so wilt ever deal, with grace and loyal love; with mercy, amplitude, deliverance, prosperity, release from constriction, with peace, blessing and all good.

MAY THE ALL-MERCIFUL be blessed in heaven and on earth: may He be praised and glorified amongst us for ever and ever, extolled amongst us, world without end.

f. 56b MAY THE ALL-MERCIFUL afford us sustenance honourably and not in a manner redounding to our contempt,[8] lawfully, and not by forbidden means.

MAY THE ALL-MERCIFUL exalt our horn ever upwards, and debase all our enemies ever more abjectly.

MAY THE ALL-MERCIFUL deliver us from consignment to Purgatory.

MAY THE ALL-MERCIFUL send manifold blessing upon this house, and upon this board at which we have eaten.

MAY THE ALL-MERCIFUL open unto us the gates of Torah; the gates of light; the gates of penitence; the gates of sustenance and provision; the gates of plenty; the gates of life; the gates of nourishment; and the gates of paradise.

f.57a MAY THE ALL-MERCIFUL bless our host, who is to me master and teacher; himself, his household, all that is his, and all those also who sit at his table, even as our forefathers Abraham, Isaac and Jacob were comprehensively[9] blessed. In like manner may all of us together be vouchsafed a perfect blessing: and let us say, Amen.

ON high may our advocates urge our cause in a way that shall redound, both for our host and for us, to the preservation of our peace, and the receiving of a blessing from the Lord, and justification from the God of his deliverance;[10] and may we find grace, and favourable understanding in the eyes of God and man.[11]

MAY THE ALL-MERCIFUL send us Elijah the Prophet, the good memory of whom ever abides, that he may teach us good doctrine and bring us good tidings. He effects great deliverance for his king and acts in lovingkindness towards his anointed one, even David and his seed for ever.[12] May He who makes peace in his high places[13] make peace for us and all Israel.

FEAR the Lord, ye his holy ones, for they that fear Him suffer no lack; the young lions do raven and suffer hunger, but they that seek the Lord lack no good.[14] The Lord will give strength unto his people: the Lord will bless his people with peace.[15]

f. 57b MAY WHAT we have eaten give us satisfaction, and what we have left be for a blessing: as it is written: 'And he set before them, and they did eat, and left thereof, according to the word of the Lord.'[16] May God be gracious unto us and bless us; may He cause his face to shine upon us, Selah.[17] O give thanks unto the Lord, for He is good; for his mercy endures for ever.[18] Lift up your hands in holiness, and bless the Lord.[19]

Masters, with your concurrence![20] Blessed art Thou, O Lord, our God, king of the cosmos, creator of the fruit of the vine.

[After reciting the Grace after the Meal, one returns to f. 33b of the *Haggadah* to complete the ceremony.]

---

[1] *Ps.* 136, 25. [2] In the 4th line of the 2nd main paragraph the 4th word, *we-ṭubo*, has a superfluous *we-* (erroneously duplicating the last letter of the preceding word). [3] *Ps.* 145, 16. [4] The last word of line 4 carries no abbreviation-symbol: it should be *she-limmadtanu*. [5] *Deut.* 8, 10. [6] *Is.* 66, 13. [7] The 2nd word of the 7th line is incorrectly *'eth* (instead of *be-*) through reminiscence of another context. [8] At the end of the second line, *be-bizzu[i]* lacks its last letter (*yod*). [9] After the 5th word in the 2nd line, *kol* – the normal conclusion – has been accidentally omitted; see *Babylonian Talmud, Baba Bathra* 17a. [10] *Ps.* 24, 5. [11] *Prov.* 3, 4. [12] *Ps.* 18, 51(50). [13] *Job* 25, 2. [14] *Ps.* 34, 10-11(9-10). [15] *Ps.* 29, 11. [16] *II Kings* 4, 44. [17] *Ps.* 67, 2(1). [18] *Ps.* 118, 29. [19] *Ps.* 134, 2. [20] Literally: 'Be considering [i.e. your verdict]'; the formula originated in court procedure, hence the conventional response *ḥayyim*, 'life' (i.e. 'acquittal'). See *Midrash Tanḥuma, Pequdey* 2.

f.5b **82 Laws for the Observance of Passover**

By Judah Hallevi, of blessed memory

[A versified summary, involving an alphabetical acrostic, followed by: אני יהודה הלוי בר שמואל 'I am Judah Hallevi, son of Samuel'. Each section ends with a biblical quotation.]

Licence from God I seek, to summarize
Passover laws, as detailed by the wise,
Whose scholarship with their devotion vies.[1]

This month out from the tyrant's land were led
God's folk, when He struck all their firstborn dead:
Wonders He wrought, and raised their standard high,
As *Nisan*, spring's first month, can testify.[2]
He gently warned their holy stock: 'Take care
Unleavened bread be kept for paschal fare'.
Burn first the leaven, mindful that his Name
You bless, who bids you send it up in flame.[3]
But[4] mark his word,
    beyond gold's worth; search round
Each cranny wherein leaven may be found,
By candlelight, not moonlight or the sun,

f.6a Nor flickering torch – of these God chooses none.[5]
If[6] you go out, and later from your store
You miss a loaf, then you must search once more;
In nooks where mice might gnaw it may be seen

Crumbs, that the sages tell us we must glean.[7]
Or should you find, during the feast, a crust
Of leaven you had deemed disowned like dust
With all you failed to spy, know you stand free
Of all offence – God needs not eyes to see.[8]
Yard-corners,[9] cellars, coops, outhouses, stacks
Where wood is stored, straw, salt, fish, wine or wax,

f.6b All must be searched, save holes too deep or high
Whose dark defies the window of the eye.[10]
Ignore[11] the yard's free space; but walls are due
For checking, if your neighbour is a Jew;
If not, he may imagine that you plan
Some magic in the holes – do what you can.[12]
Beneath[13] collapsed constructions all unchecked
Leaven you may deem void, but must inspect
Where dogs might hide their spoil around the heap
Some handbreadths in – dogs can secrete it deep.[14]
Leaven,[15] disowned on *Nisan's* fourteenth day,

f.7a You may consume till ten o'clock; then stay
An hour, whereafter haste to burn it soon
Lest clouds mislead, and you delay till noon.[16]
If[17] thirty days before the feast remain
And you leave home, first clear from your domain
All leaven; what you carry with you, fling
To sea or desert wind, for scattering.[18]
Leaven[19] you pledge with Gentiles to redeem
After the feast, if kept apart, we deem

Lawful; what Gentiles bring, or chance may leave
f.7b With you, conceal, the remnant to retrieve.[20]
Knead[21] not the dough with honey, wine or oil,
Nor spread the wafer with thin paste you boil;
Steep it for infants: sick and aged folk
Will bless you ere they die, if theirs you soak.[22]
Drinks[23] like Egyptian ale for Jews are banned,
Like practices once rife in Egypt's land;
Knead dough with water stood one night, and shun
Fresh water, tepid from the noonday sun.[24]
My mystic[25] word's import preserve intact:
Scald knives and metal bowls. Forbear to act

f.8a The miser, hoarding earthenware – nay, throw
It out: on damaged crocks no mercy show.[26]
A wooden spoon[27] used through the year, immerse:
Leaven ingrained hot water will disperse.
Hot water rids your kneading-trough of grout –
What it has swallowed, it must needs spue out.[28]
I charge you,[29] by rabbinic rules be bound
For Passover: then you have solid ground
To claim: "Tis good to curb my appetite,
Forswearing dainties wherein I delight'.[30]
Two bowls[31] she needs,
    that kneads: ere dough she nip,
And after, hands in water should she dip.
Lest dough ferment, let no sun on her beat.
f.8b Five cereals Israel use for bread they eat.[32]

---

f.5b אל ילושו בַּיַיִן וְשֶׁמֶן וּדְבַשׁ לֹא יַשְׁלִים אָדָם תַּאֲוָתוֹ **מְפַלֵט** [? צ"ל מלפת] פְּתִים בְּסִיד הַנָּזִיד הִשָּׁמֵר / כְּמִצְוָתוֹ מוּתָּר לְשִׁרְתָן לַנַּעַר וְלַזָּקֵן וְחוֹלֶה בַּחֲלוֹתוֹ בַּעֲבוּר אֲשֶׁר יְבָרְכְךָ לִפְנֵי מוֹתוֹ · **נוֹדַע** שֶׁחֲמוּץ הָאֲדוֹמִי וְזֵתוֹס הַמִּצְרִי כְּמַעֲשֵׂה אֶרֶץ מִצְרַיִם נֶאֱסַר כַּתָּה הַבַּבְלִי וְשֵׁכָר הַמָּדִי לְזֶרַע יְהוּדָה וְאֶפְרַיִם נֶאֱמַר שֶׁלֹּא יָלוֹשׁוּ עִסָּתָם אֶלָּא בְּמַיִם / דְּבָיתֵי פֶּן יֵחַם עֲלֵיהֶם הַצָּהֳרַיִם וְהַשֶּׁמֶשׁ זָרְחָה עַל הַשָּׁמַיִם · **סוֹדִי** שָׁמְרוּ כַּאֲשֶׁר דִּבַּרְתִּי אֲלֵיכֶם סְכִינִין / וְכָל נְחֹשֶׁת וּבַרְזֶל לְהַגְעִיל בְּרוֹתְחִין וְלִמְרֹק כִּי כֵן נִתְחַיֵּיב עֲלֵיכֶם · סוּרוּ מִבְצָע לְהַצְנִיעַ כְּלֵי חֶרֶשׂ

f.8a יְשָׁנִים וּלְהַרְחִיק / מֵאֲהַלֵיכֶם וְעֵינְךָ אַל תָּחוֹס אַל כְּלֵיכֶם □ **עֵץ** פָּרוּר שֶׁנִּשְׁתַּמֵּשׁ בּוֹ אָדָם כָּל הַשָּׁנָה בְּמַגָּעוֹ עָלָיו לְהַשְׁלִיכוֹ/בְּמֵים חַמִּים דָּתוֹ כָּךְ פֹּלְטוֹ כְּבוֹלְעוֹ / עֲרִיסַת הֶחָמֵץ אִם יֵשׁ בּוֹ מַיִם חַמִּים וְחֶלְאָתוֹ תָּתוֹם כַּאֲשֶׁר עָלַיו וְהוֹצֵאתִי אֶת בָּלְעוֹ · **פְּקוּדֵי** חֲכָמִים קַדְמוֹנִים בָּהֶם הִדְבַּק כַּאֲשֶׁר פָּרַשְׁתִּי פֶּסַח בְּלַחְמוֹ עָנִי שָׁמוֹ וְעָשׂוּתָךְ אֲשֶׁר הִזְהַרְתִּי / פִּתְחוֹן פֶּה יִהְיֶה לְךָ לֵאמֹר טוֹב לִי כִּי עֻנֵּיתִי וּמִפִּי מְנֻעָתִי מַטְעַמִּים כַּאֲשֶׁר אָהַבְתִּי **צְרִיכוֹת** / מִצְוֹת חָמֵץ פֶּסַח שְׁנֵי כֵלִים מְצֻנֶּנֶת וּמְקֻטֶּפֶת וּבְיוֹמָם צֻוּוּ שֶׁלֹּא יָלוֹשׁוּ לִשְׁמָן פֶּן יִתְחַמְּצוּ הָעִסָּה בְּחָמָם צֻוּוּי מַצָּה

f.8b מֵחֲמֵשֶׁת הַמִּינִין בְּשׁוּמָם **קָרְאוּ** שֶׁיִּתְעַסְּקוּ אֶת לַחְמָם יִשְׂרָאֵל יֹאכְלוּ בְנֵי בְּעִיסָתָהּ לָשָׁהּ

---

f.6b □ וְהַתַּחְתּוֹנִים שֶׁעָמְקוּ וּלְבָדְקָם אֵינָם קְרוֹבוֹת חֶשְׁכֵי הָרוֹאוֹת בָּאֲרֻבּוֹת **חָצֵר** תּוֹכוֹ אֵין אַתָּה צָרִיךְ לִבְדּוֹק וְהָאֵל / יַגֵן בַּעֲדֶךָ חוֹר שֶׁבֵּינְךָ לָאֲרַמָּאִי שֶׁמָּא בִּכְשָׁפִים יַחֲשֹׁדֶךָ חוֹר שֶׁבֵּינְךָ לְיִשְׂרָאֵל צִוּוּי לְמוּדֵי / חֲסִידֶךָ וְעָשִׂיתָ לוֹ כַּאֲשֶׁר תִּמְצָא יָדֶךָ / **טְהוֹרִים** אָמְרוּ אִם נָפֶלֶת [צ"ל נפל מפלת] עַל חָמֵץ וְכִסּוּ טֶרֶם / נָפְלוּ אִם לֹא בָדְקוֹ יַחֲשֹׁב כְּמוֹצִיא אֲשֶׁר תְּחַפְּשֵׂנּוּ עָמֹק/עָמוֹק מִי יִמְצָאֶנּוּ **יְשָׁרוּ** בָּטוּל חָמֵץ בְּחֹדֶשׁ נִיסָן בְּאַרְבָּעָה עָשָׂר יוֹם / יָפוֹ לֶאֱכוֹל

f.7a כָּל / אַרְבַּע וְלִתְלוֹת כָּל חָמֵשׁ וְלִשְׂרוֹף בִּתְחִלַּת שֵׁשׁ לְהַמְצִיאָם פְּדָיוֹם יְמַהֲרוּ שֶׁמָּא יוֹם מֵעָנָן וִיחַטְּאוּ לְנוֹרָא וְאָיוֹם / וְהִתְמַהְמְהוּ עַד נְטוֹת הַיּוֹם **כְּשֶׁתֵּצֵא** בַּדֶּרֶךְ אִם קוֹדֶם לִשְׁלוֹשִׁים יוֹם וְתִנְעוֹל בֵּיתֶךָ וְתִכְלָאֵם כָּךְ אָמְרוּ □ שֶׁאַתָּה חַיָּיב לְבַעֲרָם [אִם דַּעְתָּךְ לַחֲזוֹר] וַבַהֲלָכוֹת תִּקְרָאֵם כָּל שְׂאוֹר וְכָל חָמֵץ שֶׁבְּיָדְךָ בַּיָּם אוֹ בַּמִּדְבָּר תְּאַבְּדָם וּבִרְשׁוּתְךָ אַל תְּאָרֵם תִּזְרֵם / וְרוּחַ תִּשָּׂאֵם **לֹזֶה** הָאָדָם מַצָּה כְּמִצְוָה נָאֶה / לַעֲשׂוֹת מְחִיצָה בֵּינֵיהֶם [צ"ל לֹוֶה] לְאַחַר הַפֶּסַח מֻתָּר בַּהֲנָאָה אִם הֲרֵינוּ אֶצְלוֹ מְחִיצָה בֵּינוֹ וּבֵין הָאֲרַמִּי] אָמְרוּ לְהַבְדִּילוֹ מַעַן / וְחָטְאָה לְהַג חָמֵץ שֶׁהַכְנִיס גּוֹי אוֹ מָצָא בְּפֶסַח לְכַסּוֹתוֹ בְּעֵת אוֹתוֹ

f.7b רָאָה □ בְּעַד □ הַשְּׁאֵרִית הַנִּמְצָאָה **מַצּוֹת** פֶּסַח

---

f.5b **אזהרות לפסח לר' יהודה הלוי ז'צ'ל**

אֶשְׁאֲלָה רְשִׁיּוֹן שׁוֹכֵן אַפַּדְנֵי מְרוֹמִים    אֲבָאֵר הַיּוֹם הִלְכוֹת פֶּסַח הַנְּעִימִים    אֲשֶׁר בֵּאֲרוּ רַבּוֹתֵינוּ/בְּיֹשֶׁר וְתָמִים    וְהֵמָּה חֲכָמִים מְחֻכָּמִים · **בְּרַח** צֵאת בְּנוֹת אֵל מִדֵּי חוֹמְסָן    בְּהַכֹּתוֹ □ רֵאשִׁית בְּכוֹרֵי אוֹנְסָן    בּוֹ הִפְלִיא עֲלִילוֹת וְיָרֵם קֶרֶן נִסָּן    בַּחֹדֶשׁ הָרִאשׁוֹן הוּא חֹדֶשׁ נִיסָן **גֶּזַע** עַם הַקֹּדֶשׁ בְּנֹעַם אַזְהָרוֹת גִּלָּה / אָזְנָם וַתִּהְיֶינָה מִצְוֹת פֶּסַח שְׁמוּרוֹת    גַּם הַזְהֵר לְבַעֵר עַל בִּעוּר חָמֵץ לְנָאֵזוֹר בִּגְבוּרוֹת    בְּהַעֲלוֹתְךָ אֶת הַנֵּרוֹת **דְּבָרוֹ** שָׁמוֹר בְּכִתָּם לֹא יִסָּלֶה    דָּת בִּעוּר חָמֵץ לְאוֹר הַנֵּר הַגֵּר כַּלָּה    דְּעַ וְהַזְהֵר וּבִלְעֲדֵי אוֹר הַנֵּר וְלֹא לְאוֹר אֲבוּקָה וְלֹא לְאוֹר הַחַמָּה ·

f.6a וּלְבָנָה הֶחָמֵץ/אַל תִּגְלֶה    לֹא בָחַר יְיָ בָּאֵלֶּה · **הֵן** בְּדָרְכֶּךָ חָמֵץ אִם שְׁיָּרְתָ כְּכָרוֹת כִּכָּרוֹת לֶחֶם בְּמִנְיָן אֲצָלוֹת    הוֹרוּ אִם חָסֵר אַחַת מֵהֶם שֶׁמָּא מִפִּיו שֶׁרֶץ/אוֹ אֲכָלוֹת    הֵם אָמְרוּ לִבְדּוֹק שְׁנִית וּמְסַתְּרִים לְגַלּוֹת הָשֵׁב יָדְךָ כְּבוֹצֵר עַל צַלְצַלּוֹת [צ"ל סַלְסִלּוֹת] · **וְאִם** מָצָא פַּת בְּפֶסַח □ חַג מְחוֹלוֹת מֵחָמֵץ וְהוּא שֶׁכְּבָר בִּטֵּל בְּלִבּוֹ אֶת שֶׁלֹּא רָאָה בְּעֵפְעַפַּיִם וְאֵינוֹ נֶעֱנָשׁ כִּי רָאָה תַּמּוּ שׁוֹכֵן שָׁמָיִם כִּי / הָאָדָם יִרְאֶה לַעֵינַיִם · **זָוִיּוֹת** חָצֵר וְאַמְצָעַיִם וְגַג וְיָצִיעַ וְרֶפֶת וְלוּלִין וּמַתְבֵּן וְאוֹצָרוֹת יַיִן וְשֶׁמֶן חֲכָמֵי עַם נְדָבוֹת /זָהֲרוּ לְבָדְקָם וּבָתֵּי עֵצִים וְדָגִים וְדוֹנַג וּמֶלַח וּתְמָרִים תִּבְדֹּק בְּצִוּוּי [תוֹכֵן] לְבָבוֹת זוּלָתִי חוֹרִים הָעֶלְיוֹנִים שֶׁגָּבְהוּ

One kneads,[33] one loads the peels, and one to bake;
No children, deaf-mutes or halfwits may make
The wafers. Pour waste liquid down a drain
Sheer as from mountain slopes descends the rain.[34]
Dough[35] for one kneading should in bulk exceed
Forty and three eggs by one fifth; make speed
To burn the priest's part. Do not masticate
Wheat as a salve for sores that suppurate.[36]
Women,[37] staunch in the part to them assigned,
Ought show, no less than men, they have in mind
f.9a Egyptian servitude, from which released,
To God for all that happened they keep feast.[38]
I bless Him who keeps us alive, to eat
Unleavened bread, the herb with wine to greet
Our memories: three cups,[39] and then I raise
A fourth, as I to Him set forth my praise.[40]
'After the psalms, eat nothing' – so decrees
God's crystal word; yet, if you feel unease,
And must find cure for thirst's tormenting rage,
Cold water will a weary soul assuage.[41]

Thy law of equity I here rehearse,
Eager to spell thy glory in my verse:
My restoration speed, to Thee to sing
At this time, with the year's reviving spring.[42]

---

[1] *Prov.* 30, 44. [2] *Esther* 3, 7. [3] *Num.* 8, 2. [4] *Babylonian Talmud, Pesahim* (henceforth: *BT*) 7b, foot. [5] *I Sam.* 16, 10. [6] *BT* 10b. [7] *Jer.* 6, 9. [8] *I Sam.* 16, 7. [9] *BT* 8a. [10] *Eccles.* 12, 3. [11] *BT* 8a. [12] *Judg.* 9, 33. [13] *Mishnah, Pesahim* (henceforth: *Mishnah*) II, 3. [14] *Eccles.* 7, 24. [15] *BT* 21a. [16] *Judg.* 19, 8. [17] *BT* 6a. [18] *Is.* 41, 16. [19] *BT* 31a. [20] *Is.* 37, 4. [21] *BT* 36a. [22] *Gen.* 27, 10. [23] *Mishnah* III, 1; [24] *BT* 36a. [25] *BT* 30b. [26] *Gen.* 45, 20. [27] *BT* 30b. [28] *Jer.* 51, 2. [29] *BT* 36a. [30] *Gen.* 27, 4. [31] *BT* 42a; *Mishnah* II, 5 (35a). [32] *Ez.* 4, 13. [33] *BT* 42a. [34] *Ez.* 17, 22. [35] *BT* 48b; *Mishnah* II, 7. [36] *Is.* 1, 6. [37] *BT* 108a-b. [38] *Gen.* 42, 29. [39] *Mishnah* X, 1. [40] *Ps.* 116, 13. [41] *Prov.* 25, 25. [42] *II Kings* 4, 16.

---

f.9b ## 83 Hymnic Sequel, by Judah Hallevi

[The acrostic reads: יהודה 'Judah'.]

Awake the seer's vision of captives restored:
Redeemed, let the bride feast her eyes on her Lord.
A folk long rejected to God on high sing,
    Renewed at the season's revival in spring.

לומ' מצה זו מגביה·/מרור זה מגביה
המרור ומתחיל· לומ' הלל עד למעינו מים ואינו
מברך על ההלל מפני שאין קוראין כולו
אלא מדלקין·□ אם תאמר מאי מתחילין·/
לקרותו מפני שנאמר קצת שירה על כוס שני ועוד
מפני·/שיש בו ענין יציאת מצרים וקריעת ים סוף
ומתן תורה □ וכן אין מברכין על ההגדה/שהיא
מצוה שאין לה קצבה ידועה ובדבור
בעלמא שידבר מענין יציאת מצרים יצא ידי
f.23a חובתו [צ"ל – תו] אלא המרבה □ הרי זה
משבח □ ואמ' לפיכך שהוא במקום על הנסים
ואחר/כך מברך אשר גאלנו וכו' ונודה לך שיר
חדש על גאלתנו ועל פדות נפשנו בא"י גאל
ישראל.

□ ואם תאמר הלא צריך לומ' סמוך לחתימה
מענין פתיחה ומעין חתימה □ וכאן אומר סמוך
לחתימה גאולת·/העתיד· יש לומ' כך רצה לומר
ונודה לך שיר חדש על גאלתנו שהיא העתידה
ועל פדות נפשנו זו יציאת מצרים כמו/
/המשיח· מזכירין שנידהם כמו שאמר ימי חייך
העולם הזה כל ימי חייך להביא לימות
f.23b המשיח· ואחר □ כך מברך בורא פרי הגפן

---

Bring back my host's glory, her grief-sickened face,
Thy mercies surround them that look for thy grace;
Roar out on the foe till his fury grows weak.
These words, which recalling thy greatness I speak,
What my tongue may offer as plea for the band –
Those who were once reckoned thy very right hand –
Accept: those rejected let thy favour ring,
    Renewed at the season's revival in spring.

Haste, honour thy promise to take her as bride:
Her rival shall blench, as her own lamp beams wide.
As of yore, on her feast, once more shall she shine;
Take off her black garb, her uncleanness refine,
No longer the weeds of a widow to wear,
Or garments that speak of the captive's despair:
All symbols of mourning away let her fling,
    Renewed at the season's revival in spring.

Thine own exiled daughter grant grace from the skies
f.10a Whom over all peoples as thine Thou didst prize.
As long since, to Zion in mercy return,
That to walk by her light all the nations may learn;
Then princes and peoples her beauty shall daze,
Revealed, like a queen, to their wondering gaze;
All eager, each one to her homage shall bring,
    Renewed at the season's revival in spring.

Thou gavest me Passover precepts; this day
I make them my music, before Thee to lay
As tribute, and hope in thine answer to see
A sign that my musings find favour with Thee;
When I, at this season, my numbers distil
Like raindrops, and seek for thy folk thy good will,
Respond, and accept those whose cause I do sing,
    Renewed at the season's revival in spring.

---

f.20a ## Commentary on the Hallel[1]
by Rabbi Solomon

[PART ONE: PROCEDURAL DIRECTIONS.]

On the first night of Passover one is obliged to drink four cups of wine, symbolically corresponding to the four expressions of redemption in the relevant passage of the Torah: 'I will bring

י"ד בניסן בשבת אין צריך אלא תבשיל אחד
שאין חגיגה דוחה שבת ובכל □ השנים אין צריך
לצלות הביצה כי אם הזרוע לפי שהחגיגה אינה
צריכה להיות צלי· ירושלמי· שלכן לוקחין ביצא
/ודרעא כלו' ביעא רחמנא למפרק יתנא בדרעא
מרממא· והמנהג· לצלות הזרוע על הגחלים
לפי שהפסח אין·/צולין אותו אלא בשפוד של
רמון מפני הטעם שאמרו חכמים ז"ל בפסח שני
[צ"ל + רמון] ואם באנו לחפש אחר שפוד של [צ"ל רמון]
f.22a יהיה טרח גדול· ואחר כך נוטל אחת מן המצות
לפורס לשתים ומשים האחת מהן תחת המפה
לאכול ממנה כזית·/כל אחד ואחד באחרונה
והמנהג לשמה תחת המפה זכר למשארותם
צרורות בשמלותם ומנהג □ לפרוסה קודם
שיאמר ההלל כדי שיאמר עליה הא לחמא עניא·
ומנהג ליטול מן הסל הזרוע והביצה כדי שלא
יבא/להגיזהה·כשיאמר פסח שהיו אבותי· אוכלי'
ונראה כאוכל קדשים בחוץ □ ואחר כך מוזגין
כוס שני ומגביהין·/הסל שיש עליו המצות כדי
f.22b שיראו התינוקות וישאלו· ומנהג להגביה הסל
עד לכתף זכר למשארותם □ צרורות בשמלותם
על שכמם· ומתחיל· לומ' □ הגדה וכשרוצה

---

you out ... deliver you ... redeem you ... take you' [*Ex.* 6, 6]. One must so mix[2] the wine as to make it pleasant to the palate, depending upon quality and individual taste. Each cup, when appropriately mixed, has to measure a quarter *log* [equivalent to the displacement of one-and-a-half eggs]; if one does not finish the whole glass, or even drink the major part, it does not matter.

Since the drinking of each of the four cups constitutes a precept in its own right, the blessing of God as creator of wine is to be recited
f.20b each time. The first cup is linked to the preliminary Sanctification [see f.20a]; the second, to the recital of the *Haggadah* proper [consisting of the central narrative core of the ceremony, beginning on f.22a]; the third, to the Grace after the Meal [beginning on f.54a]; and the fourth, to the completion of *Psalms* 115–118 [on ff.33b–36b].

The customary procedure on the first night is as follows. The company is first asked to be upstanding.[3] Then wine is served to all. [The celebrant] then recites the blessing over the wine and the Sanctification of the feast [see f.20a], and the blessing of God on living to celebrate it [ibid.]. Everyone then drinks, reclining [rather than sitting],[4] in the manner of those used to freedom. Next, a basket, duly arranged, is placed before the celebrant. Upon it there must be three wafers of unleavened bread; some parsley; [another] bitter herb; *haroseth*; the lower leg-bone [of a lamb]; and an egg. He takes the parsley, and having recited over it the blessing of God, creator of what grows in the earth [see f.20b], he dips it in *haroseth* and gives each of the company [not less than] the bulk of an olive of it. The custom of insisting on a foreleg [literally 'arm'] is in reference to God's 'outstretched arm' [*Ex.* 6, 6]. The egg is chosen as being easily digested.[5] Similarly, custom specifies 'parsley' [in Hebrew: *KaRPaS*] because it is an anagram of *PeReKh*, 'hard labour' [*Ex.* 1, 13],
f.21a plus the initial of *Sibloth*, 'burdens' [*Ex.* 6, 7].[6]

כוס לפני כל אחד ומברך בורא פרי הגפן ומקדש
ואומר □ זמן ושותה כל אחד כוסו בהסבה דרך
חירות·ומביא·/סל ערוך ועליו שלש מצות וכרפס
ומרור וחרסת וזרוע וביצה·/ונוטל הכרפס ומברך
פרי האדמה וטובל בחרסת ונותן לכל אחד כזית·
ונהגו בזרוע זכר לזרוע נטויה·ובביצה·/מפני שהיא
קלה להתבשל· ונהגו בכרפס· ולא בירק אחר זכר
פרך סבלות לפי שתמצא בו אותיות פרך· וסמך □
f.21a מסבלות □ ואם אין לו אלא מרור מברך תחלה
שתי ברכות· בורא פרי האדמה· ועל אכילת מרור
ולבסוף אכילה·/בלא ברכה· ולא יברך אחריו
בורא נפשות כוין שדעתו לאכל עוד פעם שנית
ירק כמו שאנו אומרי' שאין □ מברכין על ארב'
כוסות על הגפן אלא בסוף כוין שדעתו לשתות
עוד·וחרסת· זכר לטיט ולתבן זרוע וביצה·/אחד
זכר לחגיגה הבאה עם הפסח כדי שיהא הפסח
נאכל על השבע· שכך היא מצוה שבית המקדש/
קים· בתחלה מביאין הפסח ומברכין מביאין
על אכילת הפסח ואוכל ממנו כל אחד כזית ואח'
f.21b כך מביאין החגיגה ומברכין אשר קדשנו על
אכילת הזבח· וכשגמרו לאכל החגיגה מביאין
הפסח ואוכלין·אתו על השבע· ובזמן שחל להיות

---

If the only herb available is the bitter herb, it should be eaten at this point after reciting both the aforementioned blessing and that regarding the precept of bitter herbs [see f.33a]; and when the appropriate point for the latter is reached, it is to be eaten without [repeating] the blessing. The short grace after eating such items is not to be said, since there is present the intention to eat more greenstuffs later on; in the same way that we say that the grace after drinking wine is not to be recited over each of the four cups, in view of the intention to drink again. The ḥaroseth is to recall the mortar and straw [in Pharaoh's brickyards]. As regards the egg and the leg-bone, [the first] symbolizes the festival sacrifice brought in addition to the paschal sacrifice, which latter was to be consumed after hunger had been fully satisfied. The prescribed procedure in Temple times was that the paschal offering would first be produced, and the benedictional formula recited: 'who hast sanctified us by thy commandments and commanded us to eat the paschal sacrifice'; all the company would then taste one olive's bulk of it. They [f.21b] would then serve the festival sacrifice, and the corresponding benediction ('to eat the sacrificial meat') would be said; only when they had finished it would the paschal sacrifice be properly served, to be eaten when all were replete. In years in which 14 Nisan fell on Saturday, one dish only was requisite, since the slaughter of the festival sacrifice [unlike that of the paschal sacrifice] does not override the Sabbath. There is no need, in any year, to roast the egg as well as the foreleg, since the festival sacrifice could be cooked otherwise than as a roast (Jerusalem Talmud).[7] The reason why the egg [be'a, here in Aramaic] and foreleg are symbolically used [rests on an Aramaic play on words, to show that] 'the All-Merciful one is desirous [ba'e] to redeem us with an out-stretched arm'. The custom of roasting the foreleg on a brazier recalls how, for roasting the

paschal sacrifice, spits made of pomegranate wood were exclusively used because of the taste; (for the Second Passover [observed one month later, by absentees, etc.] the Sages declared[8] that [f.22a] insistence on pomegranate spits would be an imposition).

Next, the celebrant takes one of the unleavened wafers to divide into two, placing one part beneath a napkin for each of the company to eat an olive's bulk of it at the end of the meal. The custom of wrapping it under a napkin records how, at the exodus from Egypt, the people carried 'their kneading-troughs bound up in their garments' [Ex. 12, 34]; and the custom of dividing the wafer prior to reciting the Hallel [here meaning the Haggadah] is in order that one may properly say of it [or its broken pieces]: 'This is poor [man's] bread' [see f.21b]. [When the unleavened wafer is exhibited] it is customary to take from off the basket the foreleg and egg, so as to avoid raising these aloft when one says: 'This paschal offering' etc. [see f.30b] – thereby creating the impression that sacrificial meat is to be consumed outside the Temple.

Thereafter one mixes[9] the second cup: the basket with the unleavened wafers on it is elevated, for the children to see and ask questions. It is usual to raise it shoulder-high, recalling that: 'Their kneading-troughs were [f.22b] [borne] on their shoulders' [Ex. 12, 34].

The celebrant then commences the recitation of the [narrative core of] the Haggadah, elevating the unleavened wafer and the bitter herb at the appropriate points [see f.31a–b]. The first two Hallel-psalms [113–114] are said, but without prefatory benediction, since the full series is not read without intermission. Should one ask why it is begun [but not finished off], the answer is, first, in order that some songs of praise may be recited over the second cup of wine, and second, because [Ps. 114] refers to the exodus, the dividing of the Red Sea and the giving of the Torah. (Similarly, there is no

specific benediction prior to the recitation of the Haggadah itself, since the recounting is a precept without statutory minimum or maximum, and moreover one to be fulfilled by word of mouth only, without action. Provided that one has, to some extent, discussed the exodus, one has [f.23a] fulfilled one's obligation, although it is commendable to do so at length.) One recites the collect: 'Wherefore we are in duty bound to thank Him' [introducing the Hallel], this corresponding to the thanksgiving for the miracles [recited on Ḥanukkah and Purim]; and after [Pss 113–114] one utters the benediction: 'Blessed art Thou ... who didst redeem us ... and then will we sing unto Thee a new song, for our redemption and for thy ransoming of our souls: Blessed art Thou, O Lord, who has redeemed Israel' [see f.32b].

Should one protest [regarding this formulation] that one must include references[10] in the concluding clauses of a benediction both to the substance of its opening and to a summary of its conclusion – whereas here the preamble to the conclusion refers to a future redemption only – it may be rejoined that although the import of the words: 'We will then sing unto Thee a new song for our redemption' does indeed refer to the future, that of: 'and thy ransoming of our souls' refers to the original exodus from Egypt. For in messianic times mention will [still] be made of both, as [rabbinic exegesis] insists,[11] construing the inclusion of the word 'all' in the scriptural injunction to 'remember the day that thou camest out from Egypt all the days of thy life' [Deut. 16, 3] as pointing to the inclusion of the messianic age.

[f.23b] Thereafter the celebrant utters the benediction over the wine, and drinks it, reclining in the manner of those used to freedom. Next, all the company wash their hands, since during the reading of the Hallel [here meaning the Haggadah] they will not have been giving attention to the need to keep them unsoiled. The

---

### Hebrew marginal texts

וַיֵּלְכוּ כָּל יְקוּמִים / לְאוֹר זַרְחָהּ/וְהִלָּהּ
לְהַרְאוֹת הָעַמִּים / וְהַשָּׂרִים אֶת יָפְיָהּ ׀ לַמּוֹעֵד
הַיּוֹם סָדַרְתִּי / מִצְוַת ׀ חַג פִּסְחִי ׀
וּלְשִׁמְךָ שֵׁרַתִּי / בְּנוֹעַם רוֹן פִּצְחִי
וּמֵעִנְגָּךְ סִבַּרְתִּי / לְקַבֵּל אֶת שִׂיחִי /
הֵעַת הִרְעַפְתִּי / כְּמִטְרָךְ לִקְחִי ׀
עֲנֵה כִּי נֶעֱתַרְתִּי / וְשִׂיחָתִי רְצוּיָה ׀ עֲנֵה

**פֵּירוּשׁ הַהַלֵּל לְרַבֵּינוּ שְׁלֹמֹה** [f.20a]

אדם חייב לשתות ארבע כוסות בליל ראשון של פסח □ כנגד ארבע גאלות שכתובות בתורה שהם. והוצאתי והצלתי וגאלתי ולקחתי וצריך למזוג אותן כדי שתהיה השתיה/ערבה הכל לפי היין ולפי דעת השותה וצריך כל כוס וכוס להיות בן רביעי' לוג כשיהיה מזוג מזג הראוי. ואם לא שתה כלו או/רבו יצא'. כל כוס וכוס מארבע כוסות כל אחד נעשה בו מצוה מפני עצמו ומברך על כוס וכוס בורא פרי הגפן וכוס ראשון אומר □

[f.20b] עליו קדוש היום. וכוס שני אומ' עליו ההגדה. כוס שלישי אומ' עליו ברכת המזון. וכוס רביעי גומר עליו את ההלל. וכך/המנהג בליל ראשון של מטרידין כל אחד ואחד [צ"ל + ואחד] כך מביאין

---

אֲשׁוֹרֵר לְשִׁמְךָ רַב הָעֲלִילִיָּה / לַמּוֹעֵד הַזֶּה כָּעֵת חַיָּה ׀ f.9b

**פִּזְמוֹן לוֹ**

יְעוֹרֵר נְאָם חוֹזֶה / לִפְדוֹת הַשְּׁבוּיָה
וְנָעַם צוּר תֶּחֱזֶה / כַּלָּה הַפְּדוּיָה
יְשׁוֹרֵר לְדָר עָלֶיהָ / וְעַם אֶבְיוֹן וְנִבְזֶה
לַמּוֹעֵד/הַזֶּה כַּעֵת חַיָּה גַּם'

הוֹד חֵילִי תְּשׁוֹבֵב / וְשׁוֹד חֲלָיִי תַּרְפֵּא
וְרָב חַסְדְּךָ יְסוֹבֵב / לְעַם יֶשַׁע מְצַפֶּה
וְלִקְרַאת□ צַר תָּיַּב / וַיְחַלֵּם וַיְרַפֵּא*
אֲשֶׁר זְכָרֵךְ אֲנוֹבֵב / בְּעַד יָמִין תִּיפֶּה** ׀ לַמּוֹעֵד
גֶּדֶר הַדַּחֲיָה /
וְכַלָּה לִקְנוּתָהּ / כְּמַאֲמָרְךָ/תְּמַהֵר
וְתָבוֹשׁ אוֹיַבְתָּהּ / וּלְאוֹרָהּ תְּנַהֵר
וּכְיָמִים קַדְמוּתָהּ / בְּהַגָּהּ תִּזָּהֵר
וְתָסִיר קַדְרוּתָהּ / וְטוּמְאָתָהּ/תְּטַהֵר
וּבְגֶדֶר אַלְמְנוּתָהּ / עִם שִׂמְלַת שִׁבְיָהּ ׀ לַמּוֹעֵד
דָּר גִּבְהֵי מְרוֹמִים / חִין עַל בַּת מְגֻלָּה f.10a
אֲשֶׁר□ מִכָּל לְאוּמִּים / לְקַחְתָּהּ לִסְגֻלָּה
וְאֶל צִיּוֹן בְּרַחֲמִים / תָּשׁוּב כְּבַתְּחִלָּה

* צ"ל וירפא ** ? צ"ל תצפה

---

וְעוֹרַכְתְּ וְאוֹפָה בְּיוֹפִי וּמֻכְלָל / קָטָן וְחָרֵשׁ
וְשׁוֹטֶה אַל יְלוּשׁוּ בְּדוֹרוֹן וְחַלּוּל / קִבּוּץ מֵי הָעֲסוֹת
יֵשְׁבוּ בִּמְקוֹם מִדְרוֹן וּמְסֻלּוּל / גָּבוֹהַּ וְתָלוּל □
**רָאוּי** לִהְיוֹת הָעִסָּה מֵאַרְבָּעִים וְשָׁלֹשׁ בֵּיצִים וְחָמֵשׁ בֵּיצָה פְּלִילִיָּה / רֵאשִׁית הָעִיסָה לְהַפְרִישׁ שְׁתֵּי חַלּוֹת תְּרוּמָה / רֶחֶשׁ שֶׁלֹּא יְלָעוֹס אָדָם חִטִּין לָשׂוּם עַל מַכָּתוֹ רְטִיָּה / פֶּצַע וְחַבּוּרָה וּמַכָּה טְרִיָּה ׀ **שִׁמְרוּ** / שֶׁתִּהְיֶינָה הַנָּשִׁים זְהִירוֹת כְּאַנְשִׁים בַּעֲבוֹד[תָּ]ם□ שֶׁעָבְדוּ לִזְכּוֹר כְּשֶׁהָיוּ תַּחַת יַד f.9a מִצְרַיִם וְסָבְלוֹתָם □ שַׁדַּי לְשַׁבֵּחַ וּלְהוֹדוֹת אֶת תְּלָאוֹתָם [צ"ל בְּזָכְרָם אֶת כָּל תְּלָאוֹתָם] וְאֶת כָּל הַקּוֹרוֹת אוֹתָם **תְּבָרֵךְ** לְשׁוֹנִי שֶׁהֶחֱיָנוּ וְקִיְּמָנוּ לְאַיּוֹם וְנוֹרָא תְּמוֹ / לֶאֱכוֹל מַצָּה וּמָרוֹר וְלִשְׁתּוֹת שָׁלֹשׁ כּוֹסוֹת לִזְכִירָה תְּהִלָּה אַעֲרִיךְ בָּרְבִיעִי בַּאֲמִירָה טְהוֹרָה כּוֹס יְשׁוּעוֹת אֶשָּׂא וּבְשֵׁם יְיָ אֶקְרָא **אָסוּר** לֶאֱכוֹל כְּלוּם אַחַר הַלֵּל כְּמִצְוָה צְרוּפָה נִצְרָה [? צ"ל נִרְצָה] לְבָרְאָם [צ"ל לְבָרְכָם] בְּצָמָא לְבַד אִם תִּמָּצֵא [צ"ל תִּמְצָא] תַּצְמָא וְנַפְשְׁךָ לְצַמְאוֹנֵךְ שְׁאוֹפָה יָתֵן לְךָ מַיִם וְתִשְׁתֶּה לְהָפִיק לְצַמְאוֹנֵךְ תְּרוּפָה / מַיִם קָרִים עַל נֶפֶשׁ עֲיֵפָה **יוֹשֶׁר** הֲלִיכוֹת וְצֶדֶק דִּבְרֵי הַתּוּשִׁיָּה הַיּוֹם לְהַגְבִּיר אֱסַפֵּר זְכָרֵךְ בְּנֶפֶשׁ רְצוּיָה שׁוֹבְבֵנִי/מְהֵרָה וְאָז

celebrant takes hold of the two complete wafers, and the broken one, and utters over them the benediction of God 'who produces bread out of the ground', and following on that the benediction: 'Who hast commanded us to eat unleavened bread' [see f.33a]. He breaks pieces of both [the whole wafers] and distributes an olive's bulk to each of the company. He then takes the herb (lettuce), says the benediction: 'who hast commanded us to eat bitter herb'; and then takes unleavened bread and bitter herb together, eating them without any benediction, 'in memory of Hillel in Temple times'. The company then eat and drink whatever they wish.

The meal being now concluded, the celebrant takes the fragmentary wafer that is beneath the napkin, and eats an olive's bulk of f.24a it; after which nothing is to be eaten, as we say [in the *Mishnah*]: 'After the Passover meal they should not disperse to join in revelry'.[12] This applies equally to the final tasting of unleavened bread, that commemorates the paschal sacrifice accompanied by unleavened bread, which was eaten in a state of repleteness after the festival sacrifice, in fulfilment of the scriptural injunction: 'Together with unleavened bread and bitter herbs shall they eat it' [*Ex.* 12, 8]. However, the eating of bitter herbs nowadays [in post-Temple times] being a rabbinical [as opposed to a scriptural] ordinance, the rabbis did not oblige us to eat any of it at the end of the meal, one tasting being sufficient.

They then mix[13] the third cup, over which the celebrant recites the Grace after the Meal [beginning on f.54a]. Thereafter they mix the fourth cup, over which the remaining psalms [115–118] are read. The celebrant then pronounces the blessing on wine [see f.57b], drinks it, and recites the short grace that summarizes three benedictions, beginning: 'Blessed art Thou . . . for the vine and its fruit', etc. Over the other [preceding] cups, however, one has no need to say this short form of grace, seeing that one is f.24b aware[14] of the obligation to say a benediction

subsequent to drinking each several cup, but nevertheless does not do so until reaching the final blessing over wine, following the Grace after the Meal – the point at which it is normal to say first a preliminary benediction over wine and then to drink it. Just so here, with the [third] cup – the one linked to the [completion of] the *Hallel* – waiting to be drunk [after the conclusion of the Grace after the Meal], one says the concluding grace over that cup and in so doing discharges one's obligation over all [four].

All these four cups are to be drunk reclining, after the manner of free men: the unleavened bread must similarly be eaten reclining, but not the bitter herb, this being a reminder of serfdom. Between cups one may drink if one so wishes, except between the third and fourth. The reason for this given in the *Jerusalem Talmud*[15] is lest f.25a one becomes intoxicated, and thus incapable of completing the recitation of the *Hallel*-psalms. But, [it may be remarked,] is one not already in some sense 'inebriated' – meaning, will one not already have drunk quite a lot of wine during the meal? True, but that gives no cause for worry about intoxication since wine taken together with food does not intoxicate, unlike postprandial wine. People are accustomed to refrain from drinking anything after [the four cups] except, if one is dry, one may drink water.

Should one [temporarily] forget to eat the final morsel of unleavened bread and [later] remember, irrespective of whether the *Hallel*-psalms have been said or not, one should wash one's hands (saying the appropriate benediction), say the benediction over bread [again], and eat an olive's bulk of the unleavened bread that has been carefully kept, and then repeat the Grace after the Meal: one will then have left nothing undone, since the order in which the various benedictions are said makes no difference.

If [one doubts the propriety of the foregoing procedure], since one does not [even] drink between the third and the fourth cups, it may be pointed out that in this case the fourth cup takes

the place of the third: a benediction has come to f.25b intervene, and the procedure is improper.

If it is only after the *Hallel* that one becomes aware of the omission [to eat the final morsel of unleavened bread]: since we have no formal knowledge[16] of any fifth cup associated with the recitation of the 'Great *Hallel*' [*Ps.* 136] – the drinking of which is an entirely voluntary matter – it is all the more important that this fourth cup which, as we have explained, is mandatory, [should be dealt with in the procedurally correct way].[17]

Some have raised the question why it is that no benediction of God as creator of the fruit of the ground precedes the eating of the bitter herb. It could be argued that that benediction, already uttered once before the parsley, covers it; to which one might rejoin that the benediction over the wine, said preceding the Sanctification of the feast-day, does not cover the second cup, linked to the narrative core of the *Haggadah*, because the latter itself intervenes, and by analogy the *Haggadah* may be considered to intervene between the consumption of the parsley and the bitter herb. The solution is that the benediction over the bread – 'who bringest forth bread from the ground' – recited before eating the unf.26a leavened bread, covers the bitter herb as well, as we say [in the *Mishnah*]: 'The [benediction over] bread covers all foodstuffs'.[18] And even though some say that the benediction over bread covers such things only as are eaten during the meal [such as condiments], and this cannot be claimed for the bitter herb, nevertheless since its consumption is mandatory it is to be reckoned as a condiment. This might be countered by the contention that although [the benediction over] wine before the meal covers also that taken afterwards, and similarly in regard to pre-prandial and post-prandial consumption of greenstuffs, nevertheless the [benediction over] the cup linked to the Sanctification of the day does not cover the cup linked to the narrative core of the *Haggadah*, which stands in its own

פעמים וזה עושין בשביל התינוקות שישאלו
שזה שנוי מכל הלילות ☐ **עבדים היינו** לפרעה f.28b
במצרים· עתה משיב משאלו ששאלו מה /
נשתנה הלילה הזה מכל הלילות כי עבדים היינו·
ועל כן ☐ אנו אוכלין מצה ומרור כאשר אכלו
הם ולעמוד בהסבה דרך חירות· ואם תאמר אם
/ הם עשו שיצאו אנן מה לנו· ואלו לא הוציא
הקב״ה את אבותינו· ואם תאמר ☐ נאכל מצה
ומרור· ולא נספר בענין **ואפלו** כלנו חכמים מצוה
לספר וכל שכן שיש לנו להודיע למי ☐ [צ״ל + f.29a
שאינם] יודעים כדכתי' ואמרתם זבח פסח הוא
לייי אשר פסח על בתי בני ישראל במצרים
בנגפו את מצרים ואת בתינו [צ״ל בתינו]/הציל
ונאמר והגדת לבנך· ונאמ' כי ישאלך בנך· ויש
לנו לספר כל הענין ☐ מתחיל בגנות ומסיים
בשבח· ובזה יצאנו ידי חובתנו אך כל המספר
ביציאת מצרים אחר אכילתו הרי זה משבח/
**מעשה ברבי אליעזר** ור' יהושע וכו'/וזה/היה
אחר אכילה· דאי קודם אכילתו הוא אמרינן
חוטפין ☐ מצה בלילי הפסח בשביל התינוקות f.29b
שלא יישנו· ואם נזכר ביום כדכתי' למען/תזכר

☐ שיברך אכילת הוי שלא נגמרה המלאכה f.27b
והמנהג המובחר ליטול שתיהן בידו בשעה
שיברך שתי/הברכות ואחר כך יבצע משתיהן·
נשלמו הלכות ד' כוֹסות· ועתה אפרֹש מעט מן
ההגָדה · · · · ·
**הא לחמא** עניא די אכלו אבהתנא בארעא
דמצרים· זו הודעה לתינוקות למה אנו מחלקין
המצה/לשנים כדרכו של עני דלחם עני אכלו
אבותינו במצרים דרך חפזון ומחלקין הפת
לשנים לחביריהם / כאדם שאוכל במרוצה
ובחפזון וכל אחד ואחד אומר לחברו כל דכפין
ייתי ויכול כלומ' מי שלא התקין ☐ הרי אצלי f.28a
מתקן ואל יתמהמה על זה וכן כל מאן דצריך
ייתי ויפסח· השתא הכא לשנה הבאה/בארעא
דישראל כלומר יש לנו לשמוח על זה ולמהר
הענין שאם נאכל בחפזון לשנה הבאה נהיה
בארץ ישראל ☐ ונאכל כרצוננו ואם השתא
עבדי לשנה הבאה בני חורין כל זה מספר
שאמרו רבותינו ועל כן עושין דוגמתן/
**שבכל** הלילות אין אנו מטבלין אפילו פעם
אחת· פירוש קדם אכילה והלילה· / הזה שתי

**הואיל** שבא בשביל עצמו שהוא חובה מעתה f.26b
**המרור** תהיה צריכה ברכה הואיל ושבשביל
עצמה היא באה שהיא חובה· יש לומ'/די לחזרת
שמברכין עליה על אכילת מרור וכבר נכר שבא
בשביל עצמה· אבל כוס ☐ של ההגדה אם אין
מברכין במה דיהא נכר שבא בשביל עצמו· ונהגו
להביא שלֹש/מצות ופורס האמצעית לשנים כמו
שאמרו הכל מודים בפסח שמניחה פרוסה בתוך
שלימה ובוצע דבעינן לחם עני/מה דרכו של עני
בפרוסה אף כאן בפרוסה· ואם תאמר בחדא f.27a
**ופלגא סגיא** ☐ למה צריך שתי שלימות מלבד
הפרוסה· יש לומ' משום שבת כאשר יבא יום
ראשון של פסח בשבת שצריך שתי מצות/שלימות
בשביל מצה [צ״ל שבת] ופרוסה משום פסח
דבעינן לחם עני· ויש מברכין ☐ על הפרוסה
המוציא ועל השלימה משום דברכת המוציא
לגבי אכילת מצה כברכה כברכת היין לקדוש מה
התם תרייהו אחר/כסא הכא נמי תרייהו אחר
מצה· ולדברי הכל אין לבצוע השלימה עד
שיבר''(')/על הפרוסה על אכילת מצה כדאמרי'
מברך ואחר כך בוצע·וכיון שאינו יכול לאכול עד

f.26b right as a mandatory cup: so that the eating of the bitter herb, which likewise stands independently as a mandatory act, ought likewise to require a benediction [over fruit of the ground] in its own right. In rebuttal of that argument one may say that it is quite sufficient to recite over the lettuce the benediction: 'who commanded us to eat bitter herbs', for it to be obvious that its consumption constitutes a separate item. On the contrary, if the cup associated with the narrative core of the *Haggadah* were not to be marked by having its own benediction, how would it be palpably recognizable as an item in its own right?

It is customary to have three wafers of unleavened bread and to divide the middle one into two, as we say: 'All are agreed that on Passover one places a broken unleavened wafer inside a whole one when reciting the benediction over bread, since we need [to demonstrate that it is] "bread of poverty"' [*Deut.* 16, 3][19] – just as a poor man regularly has but broken pieces of bread, so should we [on Passover]. If it be argued f.27a that [for this purpose] one and a-half wafers are sufficient – why should we need two whole ones as well as a broken piece? – the answer is because of the Sabbath; when the first day of Passover falls on a Saturday, one requires two whole wafers to mark the Sabbath and a broken one because it is Passover, 'poor man's bread being of the essence'.

Some recite the benediction: 'who bringest forth bread from the ground' over the broken piece and [one of] the whole one[s], since the benediction: 'who bringest forth bread', alongside the other ('who commanded us to eat unleavened bread'), is like the benediction over the wine that precedes the Sanctification-benediction; just as in that case both are occasioned by the cup, so in this both are occasioned by the unleavened bread. All, however, agree that one ought not to break the whole wafer until one has recited the benediction: 'who commanded us to eat unleavened

bread' specifically over the broken piece; as it says: 'One recites the blessing first, and only thereafter breaks bread'.[20] And since one may f.27b not eat it until the [second] blessing, 'who commanded us to eat unleavened bread', has been recited, the act is still incomplete. The best practice is to hold both in one's hand while reciting the two benedictions, and then to break both of them.

This completes the established procedure regarding the four cups. I shall now proceed to expound a little of [the text of] the *Haggadah*.

[PART TWO: TEXTUAL COMMENTARY.]

*THIS IS THE poor [man's] bread that our fathers ate in the land of Egypt* [see f.21b]. This is a formal declaration to inform the children why it is that we divide the unleavened wafer into two, as a poor man does; since it was 'bread of poverty' [*Deut.* 16, 3] that our ancestors ate in Egypt, snatching a hurried meal and dividing their bread into two in order to share with their fellows, as people do when eating in frenzied haste and saying to each other: 'Let anyone who is hungry come and eat', as much as to say: 'If f.28a anybody has neglected to prepare food, I have some ready; so let him not delay'. Similarly: *if anyone is in need, let him come and celebrate the Passover – this year here, next year in the Land of Israel*. Meaning: 'There are grounds for rejoicing in this; for if we eat it in haste – next year we shall be in the Land of Israel, where we may eat it at our leisure. If this year we are [still] slaves, next year we shall be free.' That is an account of what our forefathers will have been saying in Egypt, and we consequently follow their example.

*ON ALL OTHER nights we do not dip food even once* [see f.22a] – that is, before the meal – *but on this night we dip food twice*. This is done for the sake of the children, in order that they may ask about the variation on the normal conventions of the evening meal. *WE WERE* f.28b *SLAVES to Pharaoh in Egypt*. The celebrant now

replies to the children, who had asked: *Why is this night different from all other nights?* The answer is because we were slaves, and that is why we eat unleavened bread and bitter herbs, just as they did, and that is the reason for our adopting a reclining posture, in the manner of free men. Should you [be prompted to] rejoin: 'Yes, they acted so because they themselves actually came out [of Egypt], but why should we do likewise?', [the answer is]: *If the Holy One, Blessed be He, had not brought our fathers out*, etc. Or again, should one say: 'Very well, let us eat unleavened bread and bitter herbs, but let us dispense with discussing the matter', [we are told that] *EVEN THOUGH we are all wise, it is a divine precept to tell the story*; how much the f.29a more, then, is it up to us to inform those who do not know about it, as Scripture says: '[When your children ask . . .] then you shall say, it is the paschal sacrifice to the Lord, because He passed over the houses of the Children of Israel in Egypt when He smote Egypt: but our houses He protected' [*Ex.* 12, 27]. It also says: 'And thou shalt relate to thy son' [*Ex.* 13, 8] etc., and again: 'When thy son asks thee' [v. 14]. It therefore rests with us to tell the whole story, beginning with what causes embarrassment and concluding with praise.[21] By doing that we have, it is true, fulfilled our obligation; however, *anyone who goes on discussing the exodus* after the meal *is to be commended. IT ONCE HAPPENED THAT RABBI ELIEZER, Rabbi Joshua* [see f.22b] etc. This [prolonged discussion] must have taken place after the meal; had it been before the meal, [the sages would have been ignoring] the f.29b talmudic record[22] [of the principle that]: 'on the nights of Passover one "snatches", that is hurries, [to get to the point where] unleavened wafers are eaten; for the sake of the children, in order that they should not fall asleep.' And even though [it is clear from the text of Scripture] that we are to remember the exodus by day, as it is written: 'In order that thou mayest remember the day of thy going forth from Egypt all the

---

ושותה בהסבה דרך חירות ואחר כך נטל כל
אחד ואחד ידיו לפי שהסיח דעתו/מהם בשעת
קריאת ההלל ונוטל שתי מצות השלים' והפרוס'
ומברך המוציא· ואחר כך על אכילת מצה ובוצע
משתיה·□ ונותן לכל אחד כזית· ואחר כך נוטל
המרור שהוא חזרת ומברך על אכילת מרור /
ואחר כך מצה ומרור כאחת ואוכלן בלא ברכה
זכר למקדש כהלל· ואחר כך אוכל כל מה
שרוצה לאכל ושותה/כל מה שרוצה לשתות·
ואחר שגומר סעודתו נוטל המצה הפרוסה
שתחת המפה ואוכל ממנה כזית ואין אוכלין □ f.24a
אחריו כלום כמו שאמרו אין מפטירין אחר
הפסח אפיקומן'· וכן לאחר מצה לפי שמצה זו
נאכלת באחרונ'/זכר לפסח ולמצה הבאה עמו
הנאכלין אחר החגיגה על השבע שנא' על מצות
ומרורים יאכלוהו· מיהו מרור □ בזמן הזה שהוא
מדרבנן לא הצריכו לאכלו בסוף דרי [צ"ל דדי]
לנו לאכלו בפעם אחת· ואחר כך מוזגין כוס
שלישי/ואו' עליו ברכת המזון· ואחר כך מוזגין
כוס רביעי וגו' עליו את ההלל· ומברך בורא פרי
הגפן ושותהו/ואחר כך מברך ברכה אחת מעין

שלש שהיא על הגפן ועל פרי הגפן· אבל על
האחרים אינו צריך מידי דהוה □ אנמלך דצריך f.24b
לברך אכל כסא וכסא וא"כ עפ"כ אינו מברך על
הגפן ועל פרי הגפן אלא בכסא דברכת המזון /
דעביד לברוכי עליה ומשתיה נטר ליה לברכה
אחרונה עד דמטי להוו כסא הכא נמי כוין
דאיכא כסא דהלילא קמיה □ דבעי למשתיה
ובריך עלי ומפטרי כולהו · וכל אלו ארבעה
כוסות צריך לשתותן בהסבה/דרך חירות· וכן
מצה צריכה הסבה אבל לא מרור לפי שהוא זכר
לעבדות· ובין /הכוסות הללו אם רצה לשתות
ישתה בין שלישי לרביעי לא ישתה· ומפרש
בירושלמי בשביל □ שלא ישתכר ולא יוכל f.25a
לגמור ההלל והלא משוכר הוא פי' והלא שתה
הרבה תוך סעודה· ואי' חוששין לשכרות /יין
שבתוך המזון אינו משכר אבל שלאחר המזון
משכר ונהגו עלמא דלא למשתי בתרייהו □ אלא
באחרונה בין שנזכר קודם הלל בין שנזכר לאחר/
הלל נוטל ידיו ומברך על נטילת ידים ובצע על
מצה משומרת ואוכל ממנה כזית ומברך ברכת

המזון ומפטיר דסדר / ברכות אינו מעכב· ואם
בשביל שאין שותין בין שלישי לרביעי הרי רביעי
זה במקום □ שלישי נכנס הברכה אמצעית שלא f.25b
כתקנה נעשית· ואם אחר הלל נזכר לא נדע מכוס/
חמישי של הלל הגדול שהוא אחר רשות וכל שכן זה
שהוא מצוה כמו שבארנו· ויש שואלין □ למה
אין מברכין במרור בורא פרי האדמה ואם תאמר
שברכת הכרפס פוטרו והלא ברכת היין של /
קדוש היום אינו פוטר כוס שני של ההגדה לפי
שההגדה מפסיק ביניהם וצריך לחזור ולברך
בורא פרי הגפן פעם שנייה הכא / נמי ליהוי
ההגדה הפסק בין הכרפס והמרור· יש לומר
שברכת הלחם של מצה שהוא □ המוציא פוטרו f.26a
כמו שאמרו פת פוטרת כל מיני מאכל· ואע"ג
דאמרי רפת אינה/פוטרת אלא בדברים הבאים
בתוך הסעודה פי' שבאין ללפת והמרור אינו בא
ללפת אפילו הכי כיון □ שבא שכח לבא בתוך
הסעודה כמו שבא ללפת דמי· ואם תאמר והלא
יין שלפני/המזון פוטר יין שלאחר המזון· וכן כל
מיני ירקות שלפני המזון פוטר כל שלאחר המזון/
ואפילו הכי של קדוש כוס של שלאחר המזון פוטר כוס של הגדה

days of thy life' [Deut. 16, 3], in regard to remembering it at night we find no corresponding text. That is why [the *Haggadah*] introduces [ben Zoma's exegesis]: *'The days of thy life' means what it says: but the inclusion of 'all' – 'all the days of thy life' – is to extend the obligation to cover the night.*[23]

*WHAT DOES THE WISE son say* [see f.23a]. He says: *What are the testimony, judgements etc. . . . that the Lord our God commanded us.*[24] This question is palpably that of an intelligent boy, who [may be deemed to] ask: 'Why is it that we dip food before the meal, and likewise why are we eating the parched corn and nuts prior to the meal itself?', these having been distributed [to the children] to stimulate their questions,[25] **f.30a** instead of coming after the meal as usual. [He will also probably have asked:] 'Why is it that we eat first a morsel of the paschal sacrifice and then the festival sacrifice, leaving the paschal sacrifice [to be finished later]?' He is not [to be considered to have] excluded himself in his use of the second person plural, 'you' [as the Massoretic text has him say],[24] since he also refers to the Lord 'our' God. By 'you' he means 'you who were alive and there at the time'. *Do you therefore tell him about all the established procedures for Passover* – explain them to him; that is, that one does not mark the end of the Passover meal with revelry:[26] this last being an answer to why it is that parched corn and nuts have appeared before the meal, since [on this occasion] they cannot do so after it.

*WHAT DOES THE WICKED son say? . . . 'to you', and not 'to himself'*. One may feel some surprise here, in that the verse which [the father] **f.30b** is [represented as] quoting back at him [*Ex.* 13, 8] is inconsequential: inasmuch as the answer to the foregoing question [from *Ex.* 12, 26] is provided in the following verse, whereas the answer that is proffered here [from *Ex.* 13, 8] is taken from a different context [with no question preceding, and thus open to the construction that it enjoins spontaneous instruction]. One would have anticipated that the answer would cite *Ex.* 12, 27. The explanation of the apparent

paradox is that whoever fixed the text of the *Haggadah* [as we know it] was not concerned with the scriptural answers to the textually corresponding questions, this being clear enough [from the Bible itself]. What he was concerned to enunciate was the way in which the language of the Torah envisages four [types of] son. In connection with the wise and wicked sons there is exegetical innovation, which elaborates from the text the appropriate answer to give to the wicked one. The figurative expression: *blunt his teeth* [see f.23b], is deduced from the choice of language in *Ex.* 13, 8, where the verb used is *we-higgadta* [cognate with *haggadah*, 'telling a story'], 'thou shalt announce', rather than the [flatter] *we-'amarta*, 'thou shalt say'.

**f.31a** *One might suppose that [instruction ought to be begun] from the first day of the month*. I now explain when is the appropriate time for [reading and discussing] the *Haggadah*. Arguably from the first of the month, when the process of redemption began.[27] Against that, however, stands the evidence of the text itself: 'Thou shalt inform thy son on that day' [*Ex.* 13, 8]. Granted that 'on that day' points to 14 *Nisan*, conceivably it envisages instruction being given during the daytime – while the people where slaughtering their lambs for Passover; the text, however, must be deemed to indicate a more specific time, through its wording: *ba'abur zeh*, 'because of "this"'.[28] *The only reason for my* [or rather, the divinely given text], *saying* ba'abur zeh, *'because of "this"'*, is to indicate that [it hints at the time when] *unleavened bread and bitter herbs have been placed in front of thee*, in other words, at the time of the meal itself.

*BLESSED BE HE that keeps his promise to Israel . . . calculated the chronology of providence* [see f.24b] from the birth of Isaac: from which date, until you went out of Egypt, four hundred years elapsed. Hence the wording of *Gen.* 15, 13: 'A sojourner shall thy seed be', in other words, after you have had issue.

*Inexorably directed by the Word of God* [see f.25a]; the Holy One, blessed be He, having said [to Jacob]: 'Fear not to go down to Egypt' [*Gen.*

**f.31b** 46, 3]; whence it emerges that he only went under compulsion, [having been reluctant to do so] until God said to him: 'I will go down with thee' [v. 4].

*Showing that [the Children of Israel] were marked out there* [meaning, 'in Egypt'] [see f.25b]. Identifiable by their style of dress,[29] in order to avoid being confused with [the Egyptians].

*And thou wast naked and exposed* [*Ez.* 16, 7]. That is, the climactic date [for providential redemption] had arrived, but [Israel] had no [merits achieved through the fulfilment of divine] precepts. God consequently gave them the precepts of the paschal sacrifice and [renewed] circumcision, so that they carried out the operation on 14 *Nisan*. That is the point of the plural in the text: 'Thou wast wallowing in thy blood' [literally 'bloods'] [*Ez.* 16, 6], indicating the two [reasons for the presence of] blood – the paschal sacrifice and the circumcision.[30]

*And God 'knew'* [see f.26b]. This refers to [enforced] *sexual abstinence*: since the verb to 'know' is idiomatically used in connection with marital relations. It says *wa-yeda'*, God 'knew' [or rather, revocalizing the word in the causative form, *wa-yoda'*, 'He secured the continuance of conjugal life'], as in: 'Elkanah knew his wife'. [*I Sam.* 1, 19]. Because of Pharaoh's decree: *Every son that is born shall ye cast into the Nile* [*Ex.* 1, **f.32a** 22], they had chosen to abstain from sex,[31] and indeed the Egyptians themselves promoted such abstinence by saying to them: 'If you go home to sleep you will not get up tomorrow morning, and will consequently be unable to produce your quota of bricks'. They would therefore compel them to spend the night in the open country, whither their wives would bring them food and would lie down amid the slag-heaps under the apple trees. When the time arrived for their delivery they would go out to the fields and give birth there. The Holy One, blessed be He, would assign angels to wash [the infants]; and these would give each child two lumps of some rich nutriment. When any approaching Egyptians were about to come upon them the earth would

---

ביד כל אחד ואחד שתי חתיכות / של שומן
וכשמגיעין המצרים באים עליהם והארץ
בועלתם [צ"ל בולעתם] והם מביאין שוורים
וחורשים עליהם ולאחר זמן הם צצין כעשב /
השדה ובאים לבתיהם ערדים וזהו
שכתני רבבה כצמח השדה. **ובזרוע** נטויה זו
**f.32b** **החרב** שהרגו □ **הבכורות** אבידם בחרב כמו
שכתני למכה מצרים בבכוריהם. זו גלוי שכינה
שיכול לעשות על ידי שליח ונגלה/הוא בעצמו
שנא' או הנסה אלהים. ובאותות זה המטה כי
במטה נעשו האותות. ובשם □ דצ"ך עד"ש
באח"ב להביאם בסדר. [כנראה טעה המעתיק והקדים.
עיין שורה 4 למטה] ביד חזקה שתים. לפי שהיה יכול
לומר ביד וכתי' חזקה]/ללמדך וכן במורא גדול
שלא אמ' ובמורא לבד / וכן ובאותות ובמופתים
שהיה יכול לומ' ובאות ובאות. ובמופת. **ר' יהודה**
היה נותן בהם סימנין דצ"ך עד"ש באח"ב □
**f.33a** לכך חלקן בלשון הזה לפי שד"צך הם מכת
הארץ. וע"דש מכות מקריות. באח"ב / מכות

האויר □ ושתף מכת בכורות עמהם לפי שאין
להם זוג אך התשעה חלק □ ויש□ מפרשין לפי
שבספר תלים לא נמנו כסדר זה ועל כן בא
להודיענו כי כן היו כסדר הכתובין בתורה./ועל
הים לקו חמשים מכות. שאם לקו באצבע עשר
מכות לכל היד שהם חמש אצבעות / עולה
חמשי' שבים נאמ' את היד הגדולה. **אלו**
הוציאנו ממצרים וכו'. לא רצה לומר שלא יעשה
בהם □ נקמה שכבר הבטיח לאברהם וגם את
הגוי אשר יעבודו דן אנכי. אלא לא עשה בהם
שפטים כי אם במקצתם **ולא** / נתן לנו את
ממונם □ ולא רצה לומר מבזת מצרים שכבר
הבטיח אברהם ואחרי כן יצאו □ ברכוש גדול
אלא מכת [צ"ל מביזת] הים רצה לומר **ולא**
קרע לנו את הים דיינו שיכול להצילנו ונלך
לדרכנו. **ולא** / העבירנו [צ"ל העבירנו] בתוכו
בחרבה אלא במעט מים או במעט טיט אך/הלכו
ביבשה בתוך הים. **ולא** שקע שכל שיכול לסגור הים
**f.34a** אחרינו והמצרים ישוב לדרכם. □ **ולא** ספק

צרכנו □ שהיו להם כמה בהמות והוא נתן להם
בשר ועוד / שהיה להם ממון הרבה ונוכל
לקנות כל צרכנו מן הגוים הקרובים אלינו. **אלו**
**קרבנו** □ לפני הר סיני. להראות לנו כבודו דיינו /
ולא נתן לנו את התורה הוא בעצמו כתב
הדברות/אלא על ידי משה כשאר התורה או
שלא יוסיף לנו המצות כלם אלא מחצה או
שליש המצות כמו שמעינו שנתן לאדם/הראשון
מצות והוסיף לאברהם אבינו מילה והוסיף
**f.34b** ליעקב גיד הנשה. אלו נתן לנו וכו'. □ **ולא**
הכניסנו לארץ ישראל וכו'. וא"ע'פ שנשבע
לאבותינו לתת לנו ארץ כנען רוצ' לומ' / יתן
לבנינו אך הדור שיצאו ממצרים די להם במה
שלא נגזר עליהם למות כדור שראו הנפלאות
ונכנסו לארץ. **ולא** הכניסנו וכו' / בית /המקדש
דיינו שהרי יש לנו משכן ובנין בית המקדש
נוספו עשרה / נסים. **רבן גמליאל** היה אומר'
**f.35a** וכו' כלומר אע"פ שיאכל פסח מצה ומרור □ לא

swallow them up, and they would then bring along their oxen and plough the ground above. After a while the infants would sprout like grass, and would make their own way home in droves; that is the meaning of the text: 'I made thee numerous as the young shoots in the field' [Ez. 16, 7].

f.32b 'WITH AN OUTSTRETCHED ARM' refers to the sword [see f.27a], inasmuch as the Egyptian firstborn slew their own fathers with the sword. The text of Scripture [Ps. 136, 10] implies as much, since it can be rendered [albeit in not the most natural way]: 'to Him that smote Egypt by [the hand of] their firstborn.[32]

['And with a most terrifying display'] refers to the revelation of God's very Presence [see f.27b], inasmuch as although He could have effected it by means of an emissary, He revealed Himself, as Scripture says: 'Or did ever [any] god attempt to take for himself a nation from within a nation ... as God did in Egypt, under your very eyes?' [Deut. 4, 34].

'And with signs' refers to [Moses'] staff, by means of which the signs were effected.

'With a strong hand' points to two plagues. Since the mention of [God's] 'hand' alone would have sufficed, the pleonasm must have been intended to make a point. Similarly: 'a most terrifying display' [in Hebrew: u-be-mora' gadol, literally: 'and with great fearfulness'], where 'fearfulness' does not stand alone; and again 'signs and wonders', in the plural, instead of the singular in each case.

RABBI JUDAH used to make a mnemonic of the initials [of the Ten Plagues] DṢK 'DSh B'ḤB.
f.33a He grouped them thus since the first three ['Blood' (Hebrew dam), 'Frogs' (ṣephardea'), 'Lice' (kinnim)] initials (DṢK) were plagues to which the land is subject; the next three ['Wild beasts' ('arob), 'Murrain' (deber), 'Boils' (shehin)] initials ('DSh) were extraordinary visitations; while ['Hail' (barad), 'Locusts' ('arbeh), 'Darkness Prolonged' (hoshekh)] initials B'ḤB are climate-linked. The Smiting of the Firstborn [bekhoroth] is combined with the others [initials B'Ḥ] because the last plague is

isolated, whereas the [preceding] nine can be divided [into three groups].[33] Some explain Rabbi Judah's mnemonic as due to the circumstance that in Ps. 78, 44f the plagues are not listed in this order: his object, therefore, was to point out to us that the pentateuchal order is the factual one.

And at the sea they suffered fifty plagues [see f.28a]. If, through the 'finger' of God [Ex. 8, 15], they suffered ten plagues, through the complete 'hand' of five fingers mentioned at the sea ('the great hand' [Ex. 14, 31]), the total would [logically] amount to fifty.

HAD HE BUT brought us forth from Egypt [see f.29a]. The author did not see fit to
f.33b continue: 'without exacting vengeance on them', since [God] had already promised Abraham: 'Moreover the nation to whom they shall be enslaved I Myself will judge' [Gen. 15, 14]. [The author] therefore said: without inflicting judgements upon them (meaning on all of them, rather than merely on some of them).

WITHOUT giving us their wealth [see f.29b]. Similarly, he avoided saying: 'without giving us any of the spoil of Egypt', since [God] had promised Abraham: and after that they shall go forth with much property [ibid.]. What he specifically referred to was the spoil at the sea.

WITHOUT dividing the sea for us, it would have been adequate for us; in other words, He could have delivered us [in some other manner], and we should have proceeded on our march.

WITHOUT taking us through it on dry land. Meaning [it would have been quite adequate] if there had been but a little water or a modicum of mud; but: 'They went on dry land in the midst of the sea' [Ex. 14, 29].

WITHOUT submerging [our foemen]. Meaning it would have been sufficient to dam the waters in our rear, and for the Egyptians to have retreated.

f.34a WITHOUT providing our needs. For they had numerous cattle, yet He gave them [quail] meat. Furthermore, they had plenty of money, and we (sic) could have purchased all our needs from the nations near to us.

HAD HE BROUGHT US NEAR to Mount Sinai [see f.30a] merely to display to us his Glory, it would have been adequate for us, without giving us the Torah. Meaning [without] writing the Ten Commandments with his own hand, instead of [communicating them] through the agency of Moses, like the remainder of the Torah. Alternatively, without giving us the whole corpus of precepts, but rather a half or a third of them, in the same way as he gave Adam [six] precepts,[34] added circumcision as a precept for Abraham [Gen. 17, 10f], and prohibited Jacob from consuming the ischiatic nerve in meat [Gen. 32, 33].

f.34b Had He given us the Torah WITHOUT bringing us into the Land of Israel. Even though He had sworn to our patriarchal ancestors that He would give us the land of Canaan: in other words, He might have given it to [their, or] our descendants, while for the actual generation of the exodus their own experiences might have been deemed sufficient. For that generation included many persons younger than twenty – and consequently exempt from God's decree that it must die in the wilderness [Num. 14, 29] – who both witnessed the miraculous events and entered the Promised Land.

WITHOUT bringing us in ... to the Temple. There was, after all, a tabernacle; and at [rather 'from'] the building of the Temple ten additional miracles occurred.[35]

RABBAN GAMALIEL used to say [see f.30b] etc. means that even though someone has eaten
f.35a unleavened bread and bitter herbs, he will not thereby have fulfilled his obligation; since we see that the Deity laid emphasis on the 'telling' or 'recounting' of the story, and He Himself included, in connection with unleavened bread, the verse: 'They baked the dough as unleavened cakes' [Ex. 12, 39], since that is a reason for [our eating unleavened bread] all seven [days].

As if he personally had come forth from Egypt [see f.31b], since the text reads: '[Thou shalt tell thy son ... because of that which] the Lord did for me, when I came forth from Egypt' [Ex. 13, 8]. The formulation could well have

---

תירא מרדה מצרימה ☐ נמצא שמוכרה ירד | f.31b
לשם עד שאמ' לו אני ארד עמך מלמד שהיו
מצויינין שם· שהיו מצויינין ב'/במלבושיהם כדי
שלא יתערבו בהם ואת ערום ועריה כלו'
שהגיע זמן הקץ ולא היה בידם מצות ☐ ונתן
להם פסח ומילה שמלו ביום ארבעה עשר בניסן·
וזהו שכתו' מתבוססת בדמיך פי' בשני/דמים
פסח ומילה· וידע אלקים זה פרישות דרך ארץ
דבדרך ארץ כתי' לשו') ידיעה כדכת' וידע
אלהים· / וידע אלקנה ומתוך גזירת כל הבן
הילוד היו פורשין מנשותיהן ועו[ד] שהמצרים
מסבבין שיפרשו ☐ מנשותיהן ועוד שהמצרים | f.32a
מסבבין שיפרשו [כפל המעתיק מתוך טעות] שהיו
אומ' אם תלכו לישן בבתיכם לא תקומו מחר
ולא תוכלו לתת סכום /הלבנים והיו מלינים
אותם בשדה ונשותיהן מביאין לעת מזון
ושוכבות בין שפתים תחת התפוח ומגמגעין
לעת לדתן היו ☐ הולכות לשדה ויולדות שם
והק"ב"ה מזמן להם מלאכים ורחצים אתם ונותנין

/קדש· והיה לו להביא פסוק ואמרתם זבח פסח
הוא שהוא מענה על השאלה· ויש לומ' כי מסדר
ההגדה☐ לא חשש להזכיר הפסוקים בתורה על
השאלות כי זה דבר פשוט כשישיב להם כמו
שכת'· אך בא/להודיענו איך דברה תורה כנגד
ארבעה בנים· ובחכם וברשע חדוש שאינו כתו(')
בתורה אך אנו דורשין/ממנו תשובה לרשע·
והקהה את שניו נפקא לן מדכתי' והגדת לשון
דלא אמר ואמרת לבנך יכול ☐ מראש חדש | f.31a
וכו' עתה אפרש אי מתי זמן ההגדה יכול מראש
חדש שהתחילה הגאלה ת"ל ביום ההוא/אי
ביום ההוא יכול מבעוד יום כששוחטין פסחיהם
ת"ל בעבור [צ"ל + זה] לא אמרתי אלא שיש
מצה ומרור מונחים לפניך פירו'☐ בעת
האכילה· ברוך שומר הבטחתו לישראל· מחשב
את הקץ מלידת יצחק כי מלידת/יצחק עד
שיצאתם ממצרים ארבע מאות שנה וזהו שכתו'
כי גר יהיה זרעך וכו' / כלומ' משנולד לך
זרע אנוס על פי הדבר שאמ' לו הק"בה אל

את יום צאתך מארץ מצרים כל ימי חייך אך
בלילה לא מצינו לכך מביא ימי חייך ☐ הימים
כל להביא הלילות· חכם מה אומ' אומ' מה
העדות והמשפטים וכו' צוה יי/אלקינו אתנו
שאלה זו נכרת שהיא מחכם ששואל מדוע אנו
מטבלים קדם/סעודה ומדרע אנו אוכלין קליות
ואגוזים קדם סעודה שמחלקין להם כדי שישאלו
כי דרכן לבא אחר סעודה· ומדרע אנו אוכלי' | f.30a
כזית מן הפסח תחלה ואחר כך החגיגה/ומניחין
הפסח אחריו· ולא הוציא עצמו מן הכלל
כשאמר אתכם אחר שאמר יי אלקינו אמר
אתכם ☐ שהייתם בימים ההם· ואף אתה אמור
לו כהלכות הפסח· פרש לו הלכות הפסח· אין/
מפטירין אחר הפסח אפיקומן זו תשובה לקליות
ואגוזים שהם באים אחר סעודה לפי שלא
יכ(ל/לו)/לבא אחר סעודה· רשע מהו והוא אומ'· לכם
ולא לו· עתה יש לתמוה כי הפסו' הזה שהביא | f.30b
אינו על השאלה· כי פסוק מה העבודה הזאת
לכם בפרשת משכו· ופסוק והגדת לבנך בפרשת

been: 'when our fathers left Egypt'. And although at an earlier point in the *Haggadah* [see f.22a] it has already been said that: 'Had the [Holy One, blessed be He] not brought our fathers out of Egypt [we should still be slaves]', it reiterates it here in order to indicate the indispensability of the recounting of the story. And the verse: 'And us did He bring forth thence' [*Deut.* 6, 23] adduces, in virtue of that statement, an apparent superfluity, since [the text of the *Haggadah* has] already [see f.26b] quoted the verse: 'And the Lord brought us out with a strong hand and an outstretched arm, with great fearfulness, with signs and wonders' [*Deut.* 26, 8]. [The superfluous element must therefore be intended to inculcate the obligation to rehearse the story.]

f.35b

THEREFORE are we in duty bound to give thanks, to praise [see f.32a] etc. Since we all [regard ourselves as actually having] come out of Egypt, there is incumbent upon us the obligation to utter a song, even as our ancestors did [*Ex.* 15, 1].

*Praise ye, servants of the Lord* – not slaves of Pharaoh. *From the rising of the sun to its setting.* Because it was through the exodus that God's Name became known throughout the world.[36] *His Glory is over the heavens.* Hitherto, people had been of the opinion that God does not exercise providential care over the inhabitants of the world; now, however, *exalted over all nations is the Lord, his Glory is over the heavens.* WHO IS LIKE UNTO THE LORD our God? Great as is his eminence, his capacity to assume a humble character is equally great:

f.36a

inasmuch as He Himself came down to wreak vengeance on Egypt, for the sake of mere slaves, a despised people. That is the point of the text: *He raises up the poor from the dust.*

*With nobles* [see f.32b], namely Moses and Aaron. *The nobles of his people,* meaning the elders. *He maketh the one who was barren in her house the [joyful] mother of children.* The Egyptians thought that they had abandoned conjugal relations; but when they went out [of Egypt], they saw that she was the mother of children, for many a group of little children came forth with us. For this we have good

reason to praise [Him] and say: *Praise ye the Lord, give praise,* etc.

In this psalm (113, 5–9) we find five instances of an [apparently] superfluous *yod*,[37] namely the endings of *ha-magbihi, ha-mashpili, meqimi,*

f.36b

*le-hoshibi* and *moshibi,* [the numerical value of which is five times ten, totalling fifty] corresponding to the fifty plagues which [the Egyptians] suffered at the sea.

THE END

---

[1] The application of the term *Hallel* ('[psalms of] praise', specifically *Pss* 113–118) to the order of the *Haggadah* as a whole, and not merely to the psalmic insertion (ff.32a–b; 33b–36a), is a solecism occurring in the body of this commentary also (see f.22a). An example will also be found in the related MS BL Or. 1404. It is not noted in Ben Yehudah's *Dictionary*. On the authorship of the commentary, see p. 22. [2] This traditional term reflects the ancient practice by which wine was watered down prior to serving. [3] Literally: 'they disturb', I am grateful to Dr S. Lowy for explaining this curious usage. [4] See p. 7. [5] Since this egg, like the bone, is not to be eaten, the remark is curious; it has no doubt been prompted by the custom, which relates to Roman table etiquette, of commencing the meal with eggs (see Horace, *Satires* I, 3, 6, 'ab ovo usque ad mala'). [6] See pp. 22f. [7] Unlocated; cf. R. Ḥanan'el on *Babylonian Talmud, Pesaḥim* 114b. [8] Source untraced. [9] See n. 2. [10] *Babylonian Talmud, Pesaḥim* 104a. [11] *Mishnah, Berakhoth* I, 5; cf.f.22b. [12] *Mishnah, Pesaḥim* X, 8, cf. f.23a. For a brief discussion of *afiqoman* see p. 36, n. 13. [13] See n. 2. [14] The text reads *dhwh 'nmlkh.* [15] Cf. on *Pesaḥim* X, 1 (towards the end). [16] Text is: *lo' neda'.* [17] These two paragraphs are somewhat obscure, and one may suspect that the text is not intact. [18] Cf. *Mishnah, Berakhoth* VI, 5. [19] *Babylonian Talmud, Berakhoth* 39b. [20] Ibid. [21] *Mishnah, Pesaḥim* X, 4. [22] *Babylonian Talmud, Pesaḥim* 109a. [23] *Mishnah, Berakhoth* I, 5. [24] See p. 36, n. 12. [25] See n. 2. [26] See n. 12. [27] *Ex.* 12, 2. [28] *Zeh,* 'this', probably has the force of a relative pronoun here ('because of *that* which'). Since this is an uncommon usage, as against the regular biblical particle *'asher,* 'who', 'which', it has prompted exegetical exploitation. [29] *Midrash Leqaḥ Ṭob, Wa-'era* 6, ed. S. Buber, f.16a, where see n. 10. [30] *Pesiqta de-R. Kahana, Wa-yehi ba-ḥaṣi ha-laylah,* ed. S. Buber, f.63a–b. [31] The source of the elaboration of the biblical story that here follows is in the *Babylonian Talmud, Soṭah* 11b, and *Midrash Ex. Rabbah* I, 12, ed. Wilna, f.4a. [32] *Midrash Psalms, in loc.,* ed. S. Buber, f.260b; *Pesiqta de-R. Kahana, Wa-yehi ba-ḥaṣi ha-laylah,* ed. S. Buber, f.65a. [33] Text is: *'akh ha-tish'ah ḥilleq.* [34] *Babylonian Talmud, Sanhedrin* 56b. [35] *Mishnah, 'Aboth* V, 5. [36] Cf. *Midrash Ex. Rabbah* 27, 4, ed. Wilna, f.48b. [37] I.e. the so-called 'ḥireq of compaction (*compaginis*)', see W. Gesenius, *Hebrew Grammar* (Oxford 1910) 90 *l-m,* p. 253.

---

f.37b

# The Pentateuchal Passages read on Passover

The pentateuchal readings – *parashiyyoth* – appear in this manuscript in a small but clearly legible hand, with vowels and accents, in the upper and lower margins of ff.37b–53b, as detailed below. The full heading, which is translated above, is followed by an Aramaic doggerel composed of the translation of the first prominent word in each Hebrew section, furnishing a mnemonic: 'draw [out]' (*Ex.* 12, 2); 'bullock' (*Lev.* 22, 27); 'sanctify' (*Ex.* 13, 2); '[lend] silver' (*Ex.* 22, 24); 'hew' (*Ex.* 34, 1); 'in the wilderness' (*Num.* 9, 1); 'let go' (*Ex.* 13, 17); 'firstlings' (*Deut.* 15, 19).

The eight words may be versified as follows:

*Draw* on the *bull* you tend;
   *make holy* what you *lend;*
*Sculpt* in the *desert* rocks;
   *release* your *firstling* stocks.

סדר פרשיות של פסח משׁך תורא · קדּשׁ
בכסּפּא · פסל במדׄברא · שלח בוכרא ·

יום ראשון קורין  On the First Day one reads
*Ex.* 12, 21–25 (f.37b) · vv. 26–33 (f.38a) · vv. 33–41 (f.38b) · vv. 41–50 (f.39a) · v. 51 (f.39b)

פרשת יום שני  Reading for the Second Day
*Lev.* 22, 26–23, 2 (f.39b) · vv. 2–10 (f.40a) · vv. 10–17 (f.40b) · vv. 18–24 (f.41a) · vv. 24–32 (f.41b) · vv. 32–39 (f.42a) · vv. 39–44 (f.42b)

פרשת יום שירה  Reading for the [Seventh] Day, when the Song of Moses is read
*Ex.* 13, 17 (f.42b) · v. 17–14, 3 (f.43a) · vv 3–10 (f.43b) · vv. 10–17 (f.44a) · vv. 17–23 (f.44b) · vv. 23–28 (f.45a) · v. 28–15, 2 (f.45b) · vv. 2–7 (f.46a) · vv. 7–10 (f.46b) · vv. 11–15 (f.47a) · vv. 15–16 (f.47b) · vv. 16–19 (f.48a) · vv. 19–21 (f.48b) · vv. 21–26 (f.49a)

אם יבא יום אחרון של פסח בשבת מתחילין מן עשר תעשר  [Reading for the Eighth and Last Day.] If it falls on a Sabbath, one begins from *Deut.* 14, 22 [, but if on a weekday, from *Deut.* 15, 19]. *Deut.* 14, 22–26 (f.49b) · v. 26–15, 3 (f.50a) · vv. 3–8 (f.50b) · vv. 8–13 (f.51a) · vv. 13–20 (f.51b) · v. 20–16, 4 (f.52a) · vv. 4–11 (f.52b) · vv. 11–16 (f.53a) · vv. 16–17 (f.53b)

---

ירד □ לעשות נקמה במצרים מפני עבדים ועם
נבזה זהו · מקימי מעפר דל· עם נדיבים · זהו /
משה ואהרן· עם נדיבי עמו· הם הזקנים· מושיבי
עקרת הבית אם □ הבנים· שהיו המצרים סבורים
שהם בטלים מפריה ורביה· ובצאתם ראו כי
היא אם הבנים· כי כמה חבורות בנים קטנים
יצאו עמנו ועל זה יש להלל ולומר· הללויה הללו
וכו'/ ומצאנו בזה המזמור חמשה יודין יתירות
המגביהי· המשפילי· מקימי· להושיבי· מושיבי· □
כנגד חמשים מכות· שלקו על הים·/
ת"ם ונש"לם

f.36a
f.36b

חזר ואותנו אלא לעכובא· **לפיכך** אנו חייבין
להודות להלל וכו'/אחר שאנו כנלו [צ"ל כאלו]
יצאנו ממצרים עלינו חובה לומ' שירה כמו
שאמרו אבותינו· □ הללו עבדי ייי ולא עבדי
פרעה· ממזרח שמש עד מבואו· כי על [צ"ל + ידי]
יציאת מצרים נודע שמו בעולם·/ על השמים
כבודו· עד עתה היו סבורים שאנו [צ"ל שאינו]
משגיח על יושבי תבל ועתה רם על כל גוים ייי·
על השמים כבודו [טעה המעתיק והכפיל] **מי כייי**
אלהינו כלומ' כשם שמעלתו גדולה כך
עינותינו [צ"ל · ענותנותו] גדולה שהוא בעצמו

יצא ידי חובתו מפני שאנו רואין שהמקום הקפיד
באמירה ובהגדה· והביא במצה הפסוק ויאפו
/ את הבצק מפני שהוא טעם למצה כל
שבעה· כאלו היה [צ"ל + יוצא] ממצרים שנ'
עשה ייי לי בצאתי ממצרים שיכול [לומ' בצאת
אבותינו ממצרים· ואע"פ שבתחלה הגדה אמר
ואלו לא הוציא את·/אבותינו ממצרים וכו'
חזר כאן לעכובא ומפסוק דואותנו הוציא /
משם נפקא מיותר שהרי כתוב למעלה מזה
הפסוק ויוציאנו ייי אלהינו ביד חזקה ובזרוע
נטויה ובמורא □ גדול ובאותות ובמופתים אמאי

f.35b

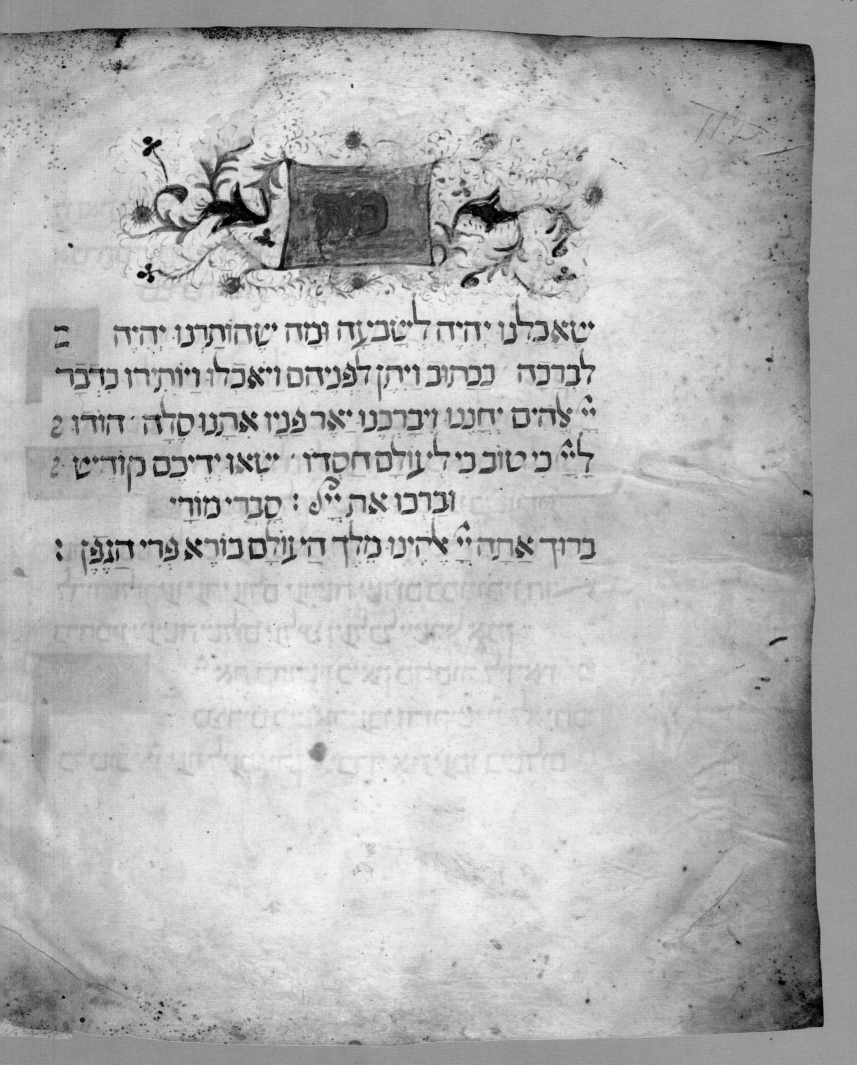

שאכלנו יהיה לשבעה ומה ישוחותרנו יהיה

לברכה נכתוב ויתן לפניהם ואכלו ויותירו כדבר

להם יחננו ויברכנו יאר פניו ארתנו סלה · הודו

לײ כי טוב כי לעולם חסדו · שאו ידיכם קודש

וברכו את ײ : סברי מורי

ברוך אתה ײ אלהינו מלך העולם בורא פרי הגפן :

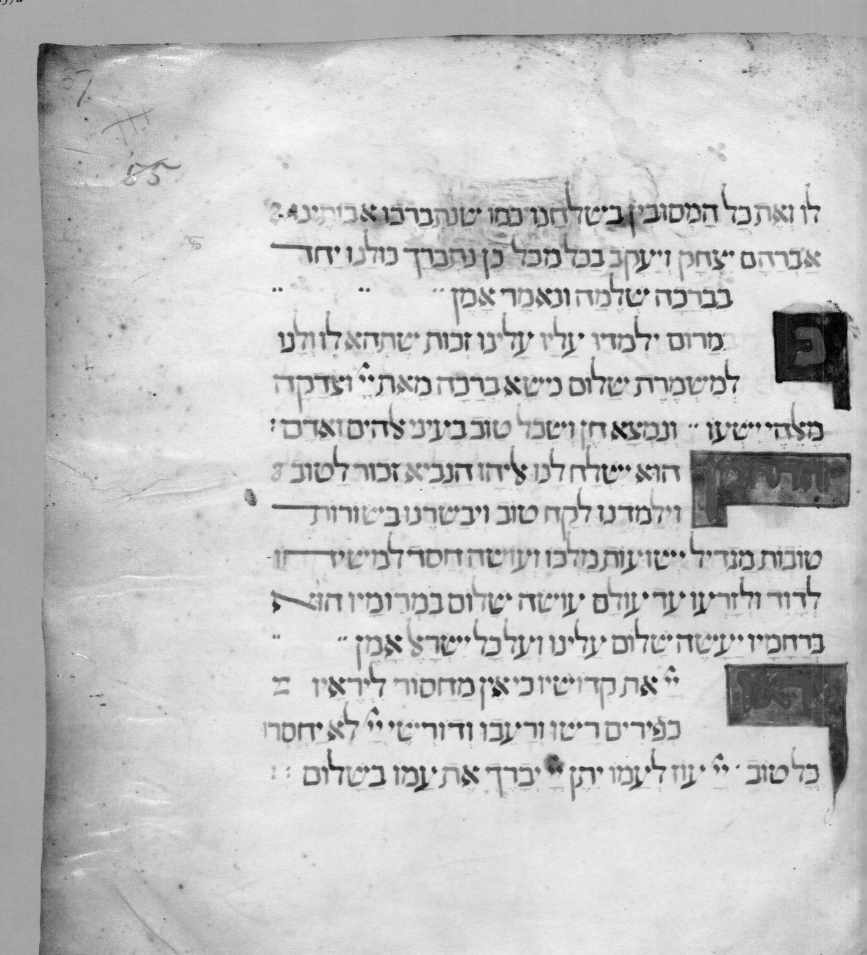

לו ואת כל המסובין בשלחנו כמו שנתברכו אבותינו

אברהם יצחק ויעקב בכל מכל כן נתברך כולנו יחד

בברכה שלמה ונאמר אמן

מרום ילמדו עליו עלינו זכות שתהא לנו ולו

למשמרת שלום וישא ברכה מאת ייי וצדקה

מאלהי ישעו ונמצא חן ושכל טוב בעיני אלהים ואדם

הוא ישלח לנו אליהו הנביא זכור לטוב

וילמדנו לקח טוב ויבשרנו בשורות

טובות מגדיל ישועות מלכו ועושה חסד למשיחו

לדוד ולזרעו עד עולם עושה שלום במרומיו הוא

ברחמיו יעשה שלום עלינו ועל כל ישראל אמן

את קדושיו כי אין מחסור ליראיו

כפירים רשו ורעבו ודורשי ייי לא יחסרו

כל טוב ייי עז לעמו יתן ייי יברך את עמו בשלום

עולמים ..

הוא יפרנסנו בכבוד ולא בביזוי ..

בהיתר ולא באיסור ..

הוא ירים קרננו למעלה מעלה ..

ויפיל כל שונאינו לנטה מטה ..

הוא יצילנו מדינה של גהנם ..

הוא ישלח ברכה מרובה בבית זה

ועל שלחן זה שאכלנו עליו ..

הוא יפתח לנו שערי תורה שערי

אורה שערי תשובה שערי פרנסה

שערי כלכלה שערי רוח שערי

חיים שערי מזונות שערי גן עדן

הוא יברך אדני מורי ורבי בעל

הבית הזה את ביתו ואת כל אשר

ובנה ירושלם עיר הקדש במהרה בימינו בנין עולם

בָרוּךְ אַתָה יְיָ בונה ירושלם:

בחיינו אמן במהרה בימינו תבנה עיר

ציון ותיכון העבודה בירושלם ··

אתה יְיָ להינו מלך העולם לעד הא    ב

אבינו מלכנו אדירנו בוראנו גואלנו    ק

קדושנו קדוש יעקב רוענו רועה    ה

ישראל הא המלך הטוב והמטיב לכל    שבכל יום

ויום הוא מטיב לנו הוא גמלנו הוא גומלנו הוא

יגמלנו לעד חן וחסד ורחמים וריוח והצלה והצלח    ז

והרוחה ושלום וברכה וכל טוב ··

הוא יתברך בשמים ובארץ ··

הוא ישתבח ויתפאר בנו לנצד

נצחים ויתהדר בנו לעולם ולעולמי

ב‏ וֵאלֹהֵי אֲבוֹתֵינוּ יַעֲלֶה וְיָבֹא וְיִגַּע

יֵרָאֶה וְיֵרָצֶה וְיִשָּׁמַע וְיִפָּקֵד וְיִזָּכֵר

ב‏ זִכְרוֹנֵנוּ וּפִקְדוֹנֵנוּ וְזִכְרוֹן אֲבוֹתֵינוּ

וְזִכְרוֹן מְשִׁיחֵנוּ מָשִׁיחַ בֶּן דָּוִד עַבְדֶּךְ

וְזִכְרוֹן יְרוּשָׁלַם עִיר קׇדְשֶׁךְ וְזִכְרוֹן כָּל עַמְּךָ בֵּית יִשְׂרָאֵל

לְפָנֶיךָ לִפְלֵיטָה לְטוֹבָה לְחֵן לְחֶסֶד וּלְרַחֲמִים לְחַיִּים ב‏

וּלְרָצוֹן אֶת יוֹם חַג הַמַּצּוֹת הַזֶּה וְאֶת יוֹם טוֹב מִקְרָא א‏

קֹדֶשׁ הַזֶּה‪:‬

זָכְרֵנוּ

א‏לֹהֵינוּ בּוֹ לְטוֹבָה וּפָקְדֵנוּ בוֹ לִבְרָכָה

וְהוֹשִׁיעֵנוּ בוֹ לְחַיִּים טוֹבִים בִּדְבַר

יְשׁוּעָה וְרַחֲמִים חוּס וְחָנֵּנוּ וַחֲמוֹל

וְרַחֵם עָלֵינוּ וּמַלְּטֵנוּ מִכָּל צָרָה וְיָגוֹן וְהוֹשִׁיעֵנוּ כִּי אֵלֶיךָ

עֵינֵינוּ כִּי מֶלֶךְ חַנּוּן

וְרַחוּם אָתָּה‪:‬

יום השביעי השבת הגדול והקדוש הזה כי יום זה גדול
וקדוש הוא מלפניך לשבות בו ולנוח בו באהב רצמצ
רצונך כרצונך הנח לנו יי אלהינו ואל תהא צרה ויגון בו
מנוחתנו והראנו בנחמותיך ובנחמות ירושלם עירך
ככתוב כאיש אשר אמו תנחמנו כן אנכי אנחמכם ובירו
ובירושלם תנוחמו ברוך אתה יי מנחם עמו ישראל בבנין
ירושלם ואמן

יי אלהינו ואלהי אבותינו יעלה ויבא
ירושלם עירך ועל ציון משכן כבודך
ועל מלכות בית דוד משיחך ועל הבית הגדול והקדוש
שנקרא שמך עליו אלהינו אבינו רוענו זוננו פרנסנו
וכלכלנו והרויחנו יי אלהינו מהרה מכל צרותנו ואל נא
תצריכנו יי אלהינו לא לידי מתנות בשר ודם ולא לידי
הלואותם ולא נבוש לעולם ועד

נודה לך יי׳ אלהינו על שהנחלת לאבותינו ארץ חמדה

חמדה טובה ורחבה ברית ותורה חיים ומזון

על שהוצאתנו יי׳ אלהינו מארץ מצרים ופדיתנו מבית

עבדים ועל בריתך שחתמת בבשרנו ועל תורתך שלמד

ועל חקיך רצונך שהורעתנו ועל אכלה ועל מזון שאתה זן

ומפרנס אותנו בכל יום ובכל עת ובכל שעה ובכל זמן :

על הכל יי׳ אלהינו אנו מודים לך ומברכין את

שמך יתברך שמך בפי כל חי תמיד לעולם

ועד כאמור ואכלת ושבעת וברכת את יי׳

אלהיך על הארץ הטובה אשר נתן לך ברוך אתה יי׳

על הארץ ועל המזון :

נחמנו יי׳ אלהינו בציון עירך ושמחנו מלכנו

בבנין בית בחירתך מהרה תחזירנה

למקומה : רצה והחליצנו יי׳ אלהינו במצותיך ובמצות

תחלה על שלשה חברי מזרך לשם יכן היה שלשה ׃ מברך שהשלמו ונאכל ׃ ואם עשרה חבריו ׃׃
מברך היה שלשלמו ובאכלו חייבו ׃ ועשרים ושלשה חייר ׃ מברך לאלהינו שהשלמו ונאכל ומזוט
חייבו ׃ וכן חומר לששעם חברי זיוברך ׃ וכביל חכן חול ׃ מברך היה לאלהין שהשיוחה במשלו
שחבלו ונשל ׃ ויחיל חול ׃

ברוך משביע רעבים ברוך משקה

צמאים ברוך הוא ברוך שמו ברוכה מתנתו לעד

ולנצח ׃

אתה יי אלהינו מלך העולם הזן

את העולם כלו בטובו בחן בחסד

וברחמים נותן לחם לכל בשר כי

לעולם חסדו ובעמנו וטובו הגדול תמיד יעלינו לא

חסרנו ולא יחסר לנו מזון לעולם ועד בעבור שמו

הגדול כי הוא זן ומפרנס לכל ומטיב לכל ומכין מזון

לכל בריותיו אשר ברא כאמור פותח את ידיך

ומשביע לכל חי רצון ׃ ברוך אתה יי הזן את הכל ׃

על ארצנו ועל נחלתנו ׃

צולת בכי חרבי · נבהל · עם נאנח וגה · נבהל

עבד לצל אדניו ישאף בצלך · הושב ורב עוניו תכלה כנרלך · נמכר בער מעניו מהר גאלך

נסגר בעד עול · יום יעמיק במשאל · ישאל

מיד זאב ולביא · את עבדך גאל · ישאל

## נאולה

זה קום ונלה צפו · גי זמני · טלי יקר ידעפו · אזבני · יען לך דלפו

שוב לכני · תקם דברך וחיה · צרי ללב מתוחיה · ראשי תרשן וכוסי רויה · גם

יעל השבי אסבלה · יצל כתפי · אמרים בני תהלה · כי צגיפי · הוא מינאות אחד לה · יד למופי

אשים ואשב כשביה · ואשיב למולצר שמרך יה · כחין וכהנית מסיע ושריה

קוצים בתוך כרמך יהתסירם · תמליך בני יעוך · ותסירם · יהיו כאז יעבך · אל תמירם

הוסף כאו צר שנה · הך שעירת שאיה · כינהפך לי בקשת רמיה

בתא ארוסה הפגה · אום יקרה · חנם מכורה הקנה · שהפזורה · בכסות ועונה יענה · ושארה

אל נא תהי העכיה · טרף לנורי לביא · וגל אסירה בארץ נטויה

## נאולה

ימין יעזך אי ואי חסדך · האם מפרות קצרה ה ידך · גם

נטע נעמן · איך הזיר כרסמו · נטשתו וצפצפה שמו · ויבט מקורו · וסר טעמו

יענישיעך · שאו ואת שרך · תרוה ותשקה · בטל אידך

חמידך בחידך · קראתו בכור · צרפתו בכור · אך זשמתו בכור · הלעד ישימו · ובו יעצור

נבזות וכבשם · ואין גערך · ארום יעבירו · והוא עבדך

ומה לך בני · אם בן יעבד · אליפזהבכה קט וזהיה לשור · ויונק תהי חיל · מלכים ושור

ארס וזעב · וערי איעך · בעץ וארזם · תרד זלא ירדך

כבשר ישועה כנשר יעלה · ברנה ותורה · וקול צלצלי · תרוזה האבץ לכב נחלה

קרב משבי · צורך יפרך · והוא גואלך · והפורך

לך

כשעריך ויחגך וחגיתים והא אל בינה והאל אשר בקרבך כי קום אשר יכחל ... אליך לשכן שמו שם: וזכרת כי עבד היית במצרים
ושמרת ועשית את החקים האלה: יען השמר תעשה לך שבעת ימים כאסרך

| | |
|---|---|
| והיתה כיום עלותו ממצרים מסלה יעלה דרך אישור | לשאר עמו אשר ישאר מאשור |
| חסדי ה' אזכיר יקרמני | ארוממך יום מכל עם תרוממני |
| אודך כי אנפת בי ותרחמנ | ישב אפך ותנחמני |
| טוב להודות לה' על כל אשר ראו עיני | ומאשר שמעו אזנים אשר היה לפני |
| אשאל אבי ויגדני ואמרו לי זקני | כי עזי וזמרת יה ה' |
| אזרה ואזמר זכר עשה לנפלאותיו | ספרו כנים את כבודו ותהלותיו |
| לדור אחרון יעוז ונוראותיו | הודיעו בעמים עלילותיו |
| כי גאות עשה מדרש לכל שואל | מודעת זאת בכל הארץ ישורון אין כאל |
| צהלי ורני יעלי ארץ ארא | כי גדול בקרבך קדוש ישראל |
| תביט כעיני אלי עולם | תקשיב כהיום שיח יעקב ופלולם |
| תכיאם לנכוח מקטנם ועד גדולם | כי עזרת אבותינו אתה הוא מעולם |

## נאולה

| | |
|---|---|
| רחמי ידיד כליל | הוד אחזה ואדל · על דל |
| מלכי וצור לבבי | עת אשקרה כדל · על דל · נב' |
| כי גוי וצורי רום פן יעברו | צרי כצאת הדרי מני ונעזרו · אל ישמחו לשברי אויכי ויאמרו |
| רמה ימין פסיל | על עזכי היגדל · נכבל |
| מהיות לא לנביא | מדתך חדל · נבהל |
| נפשי בתוך לבאים · דומם ונאלם | אשכב נשוא חלאים צר לי בכהלם · אותי והן פראים יצאו |
| מי יענה כסיל | אמר לבד מנו · נאל |
| באתי זשם כתבי | מלתך לא · נאל |
| שוקד עלי שקריו נתעב ונאלח | שוקטי על שמריו יען רצן זלה · קום וחטוף סתריו ואהרך |
| קום ישדרה שביל | ונתיב אמת ומינגל · גרגל |
| כנם יהי שביבי | צדק אשר תגל · נרגל |
| שוא העבר ונרש לין מזכילך | נטע נטיעה ונשרש שרשי בטלך · איך אויכי ישרש נזע |
| אך אשמעה צליל | פריי כפי צללל · צלצל |
| סר וזעי פרובי | נצל ונאצל · צלצל |
| תועה באורחותיו הדרך כאורחך | צועק בתוכחותיו הפדה בכחך · בוכה למשפחותיו תנך פוריך |
| קומה שמחה וגיל | יסם נצבו וקהל · נבהל |

יצדיקך ירך ... ושמדיתם בתוך אתה ובנך ... ואמתך ... ועבדך ... והלוי והגר והיתום ... אשר בשעריך ... שקענה ...
...

בערב ביום הראשון לספר · · לא תוכל לזבח את הפסח באחד שעריך אשר יי′ · · כי אל המקום אשר יבחר יי′ אלהיך
לשכן שמו שם תזבח את הפסח בערב כבוא השמש מועד צאתך ממצרים · ובשלת ואכלת במקום אשר יבחר יי′ אלהיך ופנית

## אהבה

נָאוָה בִינָה וְהָאִזֹּרִי · · · · כִּי עֹוד מֵעַט הִּתְעֹוֵרי
אִם מִכְּאָב לֵב הַצֹּרִי · · · · · גִּלְעַד צֳרִי וּקְחִי צֹרִי · · · · גַּם
נַחֲלָה וּמִיגֹון אֲשֶׁר · · · גְּבִרֹו וְכַנֵּר נִצְבֹּו · · · רֹוחַ צָהֳלִיבָּה יָעַד · · · · רֵעַ וְחָרֹוב יֶחֱרְבוּ
לֹא תֵאָטֵר פִּיהָ בְּאֵר · · · יַעַל עִם בְּתוּכֵה שָׁבּו · · מַהֵלֵךְ בְּסֹודֵךְ הִּפָּצֵרי · · אֹו עִם אֲרִי הִתְעֹורֵרי
מִתֹּוךְ גֹּוי הָאֲרִי · · · דְּבַשׁ אֲרִי דֹּרִי מֹורֵךְ אֲרִי
הֹוסֵן אַבִּיר הַמַּחֲרִיב · · לֵב הֵחֲלִיא יַאֲרִיךְ · · · וּלְרֹאשׁ שְׁתִילַי יֶעֱנֶף בְּלִיל
לֹא אֶעֱצַב אִם יִתְעַצֵּב · · · אֹותִי וְלֹא אֹהֱלֶה לֵחִיל · · לְבִי יְדִיד כָּא בַּחֲרִי · · · יַעַתְרְדַפֵנִי כְּחֵרי
כִּי כַאֲשֶׁר מַרְיָא · · · אֹובֵל לְטַבֹּוחַ עַל בְּדִי
מַלְכִי בְּךָ אֶבְטַח וְלֹא · · · עַל בִּלְתְּךָ עֹוד אֶבְטַחָה · · הָאֵת אֲשֶׁר אֶרֶץ מָלֵא · · כָבֹוד וְיָרֵךְ טְפָחָה
וּכְלֵי שְׁחָקִים הַעֲזֹו · · · נֶפֶשׁ בַּדֹּרַךְ תִּשְׂמָחָה · · שָׁלְחָה צָרִין יָפָה פְרִי · · הָאַר כְּגִלְעַד הַצֳרִי
לַיעֹוזר בְּעֵת צַר צֹורְרִי · · לִהְיֹות לַמְגֵדֵּל יעֹוזֵרי

## זולת

אַחַר עֶשֶׂר מַסָּעֹות כְּבֹא שִׁמְשֹׁו בַּצָּהֳרַיִם · · · · · · · נֶעֱזַר כִּי נָגַע מִשְׁפָּטֹו עַד לַשָּׁמַיִם
יָעִיר הַיֹּום בְּנָב לַעֲמֹוד לְהַשְׁחִית יְהוּדָה וְאֶפְרַיִם · · · · וְנֹופֵף יָדֹו הַרַבָּת צִיֹּון וּגְבָעַת יְרוּשָׁלָ◌ם
כְּקֶפֹּץ מִלְּפָנֵיו אֶרֶץ כַּאֲשֶׁר מֵאַז קָפָצָה · · · · · · · · · · · · לֹא כְּמִפְּנֵי דֹּרְךְ מִבְּאֵר שֶׁבַע יָצָא
זֶה לְטֹוב וְזֶה לְרַע לֹו כָּל אִישׁ לְדַרְכֹּו יָצָא · · · · · · · · · · · · הִנֵּה הָאָדֹון יי′ צְבָאֹות מְסָעֵף פֶּארָה בְּמַעֲרָצָה
גִּבֹּורַי קָרָאתִי לְאַפִּי וְגַם קָדֵשִׁי · · · · · · · · · · · · · · · · · וְנִקַּמְתִי מֵאֹויְבַי וְלִי יֹוכִילֹו וּמַלְכִּים שַׁי
וְאַרְצָה בְּבֵית מִקְדָּשֵׁי לַחְמִי וְאִשֵּׁי · · · · · · · · · · · · · · · · וְיָצָא חֹטֵר מְגֵזַע יִשַׁי
דִּבְּרוּ אֻקִים יֹאמַר צוּר עַד דֹּר עָרֶץ · · · · · · · · · · · · · · · · וְהָרִיחֹו בְּיִרְאָתִי יי′ וְלַקְּרֹוִיזְ זָקֵרץ
יִשְׁפֹּוט בְּצֶדֶק דַּלִים בְּבֵית יֹוסֵף וּפֶרֶץ · · · · · · · · · · · · · · וְהֹוכִיחַ כְּמִישֹׁור לְעַנְוֵי אָרֶץ
הֲמֹונִים הַמֹּונִים יַפִּיל בְּלֵב אֹויְבָיו חִצָּו · · · · · · · · · · · · · · וְגָדֵר וְאֵין פֹּורֵץ וְאֵין גֹּודֵר פִּרְצֹו
וְהָיָה צֶדֶק אֵזֹור מָתְנָיו · · · · · · · · · · · · · · · · · · · · · · · וְהָאֱמוּנָה אֵזֹור חֲלָצָו
וְשִׁעְשַׁע יֹונֵק מִבֵּית לֶחֶם יְהוּדָה · · · · · · · · · · · · · · · · · · וְעַל חוּר פֶּתֶן וְעַל מְאֹום שַׁחַל עָדָה
וְיָעַל מֵאֶרֶת צִפְעֹונִי אֲשֶׁר נַפְשֹׁו צָדָה · · · · · · · · · · · · · · · גַּם מֹלֵרֹו הָרָה
זֶה אֵלִי וְאַנְוֵהוּ עֵת נָפְלוּ אֹיְבָיו אַשֹּׁור · · · · · · · · · · · · · · · כִּי יָשִׂים בַּעֲרָבָה בְּרֹאשׁ הַדֶּדֶּר וְתַּאַשֹּׁור

בְּקֹור וְזִלְעָפֹות לֹא יָאַרֹוךְ · · שֶׁשֶׁת יָמִים לְמִצֹו וּמִיֹּום הַשְּׁבִיעִי עֲצֶרֶת לָךְ · · · · אֵלֶיךָ לֹא תַעֲשֶׂה דְרֹאַהֹי · · · · ·
שֹׁובֵעַ שְׁבַעְנַע תָּסֹפֵר לָךְ מַהְקְהֵל תָּחֵל לֹסְפֹּר שֶׁבַעָה שֶׁבַעֹות · · וְעֲשִׂיתָ רַב שֶׁבֶעֹות דְּ◌··· ·◌··
אֵלֶיךָ מֵמְּטָה אֵ וּדְבַק יָדְּךָ אֲשֶׁר אֵעֵן כָּאֲשֶׁר יי′ אֱלֹהֶיךָ יְבָרֶכְךָ · · אֱלֶיךָ אֱחָר וּבֵרַךְ יְבָרֶכְךָ וְעָבַדֶיךָ וְאָמַרְתְּ וְהָיוּ אֵטַ···

מאכלנו שנה פטנה פריקוס אשר יבחר אתה וביתך ׃ וכי יהיה בו ליום פסח או עזר כל מנפ רע לא תזבחנו לה׳ אחיך ומשעריך שעיר
מאכלנו העולם וטהרהור יחדיו כעבי וכאנל ׃ רק אתדמו לא תאכל על הארץ תשלכנו כמים ׃

הן ידי ישיער בלי קצרו ׃ מנאולי עמך ׃ אם עני ומי פדות צערו ׃ רב פדות עמך
אין גבורת שמך אשר גברו ׃ אייך צעמך ׃ אם לי עזרי זרוער מער ׃ אין לב מצטער
מיקשים תשובכם מישור ׃ מחשבים לאור

## מאורה

אתמחזה הזר צ הצילנו ׃ שור וענה רב טוב שגמלנו
יום יחלה חרד לזמן סחר ׃ יעל עלי כי סוף ליל שחר ׃ ואיר יעלה כיום אנט שחר
מה תאלה ותיצר צרת מחר ׃ סוב תחזה צליסך כלנו ׃ יוס יחנה צר כמיעט כלנו
צפי נאון קנער יונת אלם ׃ כי שתלאון אנשי חול צלם ׃ והמון שאון זרים כסעיף חולם
ולחיק סאון רוען פתע שלם ׃ ובשוטמי רעב האכלנו ׃ את שור בני עריזן האכילנו
חו בלי לאות אל דורות יאתיו ׃ אתמפלאות צורי לנונטין ׃ מי יאוראות כיום מתים חיו
ויהי לאות כיניעים ישליו ׃ יחז בזה דור מכור העלנו ׃ ממשכני עפר מותגלנו
קבל כפה סנור לימות יעצב ׃ ולשוב צפה יום כי לכל קצב ׃ וכעס כפה מלבי תעצב
מה לד רפה יה קוס נא התיצב ׃ ערב חזה עס תוך אפל בלקר פנה ׃ אל ואר לנו

## אהבה

הי ידעתם ידירי הצבי ברח ׃ ממלוני מתי ישוב מעני
יגיד לכם כרוכי ׃ אחרי נשא לבי ׃ איך אשא מיצבי
לא יד עבעת שהעלה עמו ׃ כל שלשוני ׃ על מינטש ינוני
צר לי צד על נרודו ׃ סר מיעלי כבורו ׃ אור יפעתו והודו
איעים שפתיו יטפו נפת ׃ עלי לשוני ׃ ויעקיו על נרוני
שעשועי איך זנחם ׃ חנותי אם שכחם ׃ וידירות בין בנחם
הראני באמון עתא אשר מזפתיו ׃ שם כמוני ׃ ויוצא את המוני
קרע יס סוף לעיני ׃ הראה הזרו לפני ׃ דבר דודיו באזני
ולחרד אהבי שר אליחין ׃ קזל פעבוני ׃ ולריח קנגוני
רבות מיום נרודך ׃ נשאתי על כבודך ׃ ובכל זאת אעבדך
עד עולם וצאת מיעבך רפשי ׃ אין רצוני ׃ אהבתי אתארני

אויחדרט תאכליב ונעניית לפסח לה׳ אלקיך כי בחדרט הוציאך ה׳ אלקיך ממצרים לילה ׃ וזבחת פסח לה׳ אלקיך צאן ובקר במקום אשר יבחר ה׳ לשכן שמו שם ׃ לא תאכל עליו חמץ שבעת ימים תאכל עליו מצות לחם עני כי בחפזון יצאת מארץ מצרים למען תזכר היום
יובר את יום צאתך מארץ מצרים כל ימי חייך ׃ ולא יראה לך שאר בכל גבולך שבעת ימים ולא ילין מן הבשר אשר תזבח

ריקם · הענק תעניק לו דישאיך ינגדנוב ימיחזקה אשר ברכך · שלחך תסן לו · וזכרת כי עבד היה וגברן ויצבים ויפדך · על · שחק על
בן אזכי מזגבך את הדבר הזה היום · והיה כי יאמר אליך לא אצא מעשך כי אהבך כי ארלבך כי טוב לי עשך · ולקחתפאר

מה לדור הזה רועה בין עפרים לעזוב קרביה לשכון ביצרים שוב לחיק רעה תעטוולה
הגעלה דוד צחלי נד מעעבי כד פרוב ממשח ינה אור שכבי

## מאורן

יום האזה ינלה יחישה וסות נאוה זה אותי הלבישה ובן נעוה
מכסלי יובישה שוכנים בכור שביב ימשכון יי באור פנך יהלכון
צוה קנות קנינך נקראו ותוסיף פנת פנים לך יראו אל מעינות מיישינ יצמאו
מדור לדור על שמך יתמוכון ופנים ליור מי רוק לא יחשוכון
חזק רפה לבך מקול צורר ועין ופה דובר סרה סורר אל שואפי ראשרדלים שוט עובד
הפיקזור זרים חין ידוזכון הסח לחור צפעונים ישכון
כרוש רעיה צאן מאוריעת וערר רעה אלנוה הודיעת ואות שינה יום קולי שמיעה
מעבן בכור מפיך יהברכון ותחיש דרור ונאולים ילכון

## מאורה

יזכרו פלאך צבא מרום על נלילי זבול סובכים חוג
בפאתי דרום הולכים על גבול נס ארמה בצדקך ברום לעשות כל יבול
יום ליום נוראות ימין נאור דור לדור
מלאכותם מלאכתך לגמור חק ולא יעבור
העמדתם ברום שמי ערץ לעדות אזרחים ותצום על בני ארץ להיות זורחים
אך שניהם כפי אשר תרן נוכבים שוחתים עת תצוה צבאך לקרור יחשכו משחור
ותשו ימך בבית הבור ישבעו ממרור
וערי מה הגנוז אתה אשכבה להטים בין ארוז וערב אשר שתה בעדי שופטים
הם ציעירי אבל אני ינתה נעוהם מצור ועינירך נצור צור לבת צור ושכנה מצור
וחצר כל הנה חצר חיצור וחצרך בצור
דברה יעל לך מיחליך מדברי רחמים שכחם כדרר פעלה לעני זועמים
המחכים שנת נאודיך אל נאום מבשרים לאמר בעבור קל מבשרים לאמר בא שנת הדרור
וכבית קרשך בהר המור מצאתך דרור

הכר צע ונכרית פאונו ובכרלה וחיה עבד עולם ואף לאמתך תעשה כן · לא יקשה בעינך בשלחך אתו חפשי מעמך כי משנה
שכר שכיר עבדך שש שנים וברכך יי אשר בכל אשר תעשה · כל הבכור אשר יולד בבקרך ובצאנך יצרך תקדיש ליי אלהיך · לפני יי אלהיך
תאכלנו כל הבכור אשר יולד בבקרך ובצאנך הזכר תקדיש ליי אלהיך לא תעבד בבכר שורך ולא תגז בכור צאנך · לפני יי אלהיך

52

58

מיהיה אומר יחזור לו · השכר לך לב בן יהיה וזכר עם לבבך בלבבך לאמר חירבת שבת שבע השמיטה שנה שנה השמיטה וראה עניין יראה האריך
האכיל ולא תתן לו והרא על ידך אל לו · והיה כך חטא · בתין התכלו ולא ידע לעבד בידיך לי כי בגלל הדבר הזה יברכך

שות שתי השערה ·

## קדיש

אלי הלי עד מעוני · תשכח זיר זעמך
תגביר ומרב זדוני · הסתיר פני נעמך
מבור שבי העלני · יצורי לחם לוחמיך · אל תחשוב לי עוני · ויקדמו רחמיך
מה האריך עוד זמני · בשבי יעצור זעמיך · ולמען לא למעני · תקדיש ותעריץ שמך

## אופן

יה שכינתך · בינת אנשים
אף אמונתך · בקהל קדושים

אופני פלאו · ושנאני מרומו · כוכבי רום צבאו · שואלים אימקומו · שמים כסאו · והארץ
הדומו · מעריצים לשמו · נערצים בסוד קדושים ·
נאמני ארץ · לוכשי חרדה · גודרי פרץ · נוצרי תעורה · אף המה במרץ · מעריצים בתודה
כי כל העדה · כלם קדושים ·
יהלו במפעל · שחקים עת כראם · ומוסרי יעולם · על בלי מה תלאם · ומלאכיו בבן יעל ·
הכינם וקראם · סורו נא מעל · אהלי אנשים ·
חרוף ינון נאנחים · היו תלחי שמחים · וישירו פתחים · אשר אבל ונצחים · וכהנים
המשוחים · אז יעלו זבחים · ואכלו פסחים · בקדשי הקדשים ·

## מאורה

הסתו ארה · ארח מעצבי · וגן פריפרה · פרח ויגל לבבי ·
נעורי יחרו הנרדים · ציץ וצמח פרדס המדים · שש ושמח · בהסר לבי ידידים
שוב צבי מדרח · ברחם כרובי · באשתה דקח · ייני עם חלבי ·
חלפתונות יוסחלפו ערוגות · בהרדס סונות · ברקמות ארוגות · מכל פוגות · הנבודאנות ·
מנדלות מרקח · נוטפות מור סביבי · האנוזטרח · דליו על מסיבי ·
ועלי תורה · נטה בין צללים · משמאל קרה · משמאל אהלים · כוס כי ען פטרה · ממעשים

שידיך בקל מעשיך וזכר מישלה נדך · כי לא יחדיל אביון מקרב הארץ על כן אמיר מקרב לאלר · פתח תפתח את ידך לאחיך
לעניך ולאמיך בארצך · לד אחיך העברי או העברה ועבדך · שש שניך וכשנה השביעה תשלחנו חפש מעמך · וכי תשלחנו חפשי מעמך לא תשלחנו
כי יזכר

רב סכלי והבלי | עם רוע מעללי | מחבלי
ואני תפלה | לפעלי | אם הבאיב ונחלה | כמעלי | רחמיו וסגלה | לכלמי
יעיר ישוב נצורי | עם מכצר ושורי | ינהלי
יעיר יכיר פתילי | אות חשקי זרגלי | אהלו

אמרו בני אלהים כמה | אתן לפעלי
צדק ונם אני מכם מה | לבני שאול ולי

בינות אמונתך שוא | חדר ויושבי מזקשיו | יטיב לאוהבו
אם תכספי לו וקדושיו | ומאוס בעזבין | תרדי ותעלי
ממך ובך באר למזמה | תרלי באין רלי
ראשית יסור היותך צורך | פועל ולעשות כל צורך | בך נתכנו כלי
גם וכן קחי לך דרך | בך תריעי אלי | צורות אמת בלי נהמה | עשות באין כלי
אנלי יחשבו כי שמה | כליש כלי כלי
מעון אשר בידו רוחי | אליא אשברה | הוא יחקור וידע שיחי | עד לא אדברה
אכן אני כפי כל כחי | כבוה אעורדה | כי ארדכה בדרכי צרמה | שלום באהלי
יהיה ואריר לי אעטה | צורי וגואלי

נש הרופים דחופים לקרא | בשמך יצאו | תחדרך | לכבוד
שמך כבמסגר הובאו | זכבתי כלאים רחבאו
נש שרידים חרדים לא נשאו ראשם | תשגבך | והיום יצאו לבקש על נפשם
מן החורים אשר התחבאו שם
נש נוהים רוהים בפרך מזנים | תנגן לשמך | בקר אם הגיע לפתח ים מעים
עת | להשליך אבנים
נש יחידים בודדים בין גוי נבל ומתנקש | תיחדרך | באמרו אלי לאלילי הצבת מוקש
זרמו מידך | אבקש
נש רעוצים רצוצים סובלים חמת צר בעדה | תרומנך | וקול עם לא יחטיאו חטערה

הן אור צפנתיו בישרא     עלה כיום זורח     צלה למלוכה ולכהנה     כימי שמש וירח
כרם נטיעתי ושמרתי     כלו שורק פורה     והנפנים סמדר     נתנו ריח
להעירותך רביד     טביעתי חיל שוטנך     והעברתי חילך
על שפתיך שוררי     כבודה בת המלך     הראיני את מראיך     השמיעני את קולך
ובשמיעי שירך     ומדברך הנאוה     ואמרך נעשה ונשמע     ליצר עיר ומצוה
חשקתי קרבתך     ולשכון יעמך כנוה     כי קולך ערב     ומראך נאוה
יום מתן לוחות     נזרת ספיר זר     שועלים השחיתו הכרם     ופרצו גדר הנגדר
וימירו כתבנית שור     הכבוד זה הדר     מחבלים כרמים     זכרמינו סמדר
כרם חילך     כתקפו וחילו     אשיב ואקשיב     לשיחו וקולו
ואם צר מכרו     ואויב כעלו     אחרי נמכר נאלה     תהיה לו
תביט בעניינו     יהי יעזלם     תקשיב בהיום שיח עמך     ופלזלם
תביאם בנכולם     מקטנם ועד גדולם     כי יעזרת אבותינו אתה הוא     מעולם

## נאולה

ימים רבזאות     וחדשים מאות     איחל ותלאות     לתוחלתי באות
ואבן כדאות     ישועותי רזאות     וחשות כצבאות     ידי משואות     ונפלו מנאות
לחכלך כפאות     ועריך מוצאות     ועיניך רזאות     איה נפלאות     וצדק נראות
נואלם חזק     לי     צבאות     גם

צערי אוני     לקרותי צרו     ולפירי אוני     בכליותי צרו     כמו ששוני
בנוס ותנות יעורו     וצרות וזעני     ימס לי עדני     ועדן צאני     ביד שביסגרו
ושערי פרזוני     מעבור נסגרו     ועלמה נעדרו     יעתידות נבאות     נוֹאֵם
חזיוני צפי     וזהזי איך צפי     מיתוך זפי     אם יעליהם צפי     ריגבי לשופי
בקשיה החלפו     ומסכו בצופי     רזש ולענה יצפו     ויאכל פי     אשרידן אפו
זכר אהבת יופי     כלילו שיפי     והעירה מראות     פלאות הבאות     נוֹאֵם
קרב כדריצון     לבן כאף רחקת     ולאטר יעה יצא     לטבח התקת     ועלמתי לצון
פרוק כאופרקת     וכונן עם היצון     מפנוס היעתקת     הלא ראשו קיצון     בניבך צדקת
וחקה הקדמכת     בדין והתיעלמת     כנהקם עתה     ליונה הדרחת     ולמכון שכנת
יעיבה יערבת     השבכר ירנת     ליעורבי מ שאות     ונוֹאֵם

וָאִישׁ מַהֵר אֵלֶה ׀ לַעֲלוֹת וְיַנְהַר ׀ וְאֵט לְכָל אֹסְהַר ׀ שָׁלוֹמִים כַּנָּהָר ׀ וּמִמַּחֲנֶה תַחֲנֶה
אֲנִי אַחַלְּצֵהוּ ׀ כִּי ׃

עַם נֶלְהָטוֹ וְנַלְהָב ׀ בָּאֵשׁ עוֹזְרֵירַהֲב ׀ וְאֹכְלִי כְּשַׂר הַכְּהָב ׀ וְנָאַקְיס עוֹד הַכְּהָב ׀ מַרְבֶּה מַחְכָּה
לַעֲתֵי עֲלוֹת הַדָּהָב ׀ מְקוֹמוֹ וְהַרוּמוֹ ׀ כְּפוֹרְ אִסַר וְזָהָב ׀ וּכְאַב בֵּן יֶאֱהַב ׀ אֲנִי אֹהֲבֵי אָהַב
כִּי נַעַר יִשְׂרָאֵל וָאֹהֲבֵהוּ ׀ כִּי

## אהבה

מִי יִתְּנֵנִי כִּימֵי צֵאֶה יַרְגֵּנִי ׀ אֶקְרָא וְיַאֲמֵר הִנְנִי ׀ נָם
אֵיךְ חַלְּלֵנִי ׀ דּוֹדִי וּבִי נִכְלָה נַפְשׁוֹ ׀ אֵיךְ הֶעֱלֵנִי ׀ מֶנַּף וְכִיצֵעֵנוּ וְאֵשׁוֹ אֶטַע הֲלָנִי ׀ וָאֶפְנֶה בַּמָּקוֹם
קָדְשׁוֹ ׀ וַיְקַדְּשֵׁנִי ׀ וַיֹּאמֵר צוּר יֹרְנִי ׀ בִּינוּ לְבִינִי ׀ וְכָל יַקִּיר רָאֵתָה עֵינִי ׀
בְּנַחֲלָתִי ׀ אֶרֶץ טְהוֹרָה הֶרְאֵתָנִי ׀ כַּאֲשֶׁר שָׁאַלְתִּי ׀ וּבֵית זְבוּל שָׂם בָּמָתִי ׀ לְצַמַּנְתִּי עַמּוֹ שָׁלוֹם הָיִיתִי
וַיְפָרְנֵנִי ׀ יַעַן אֲשֶׁר לֹא אִירָפֵנִי ׀ וַיִּשְׁכָּחֵנִי ׀ הַצּוּר אֲשֶׁר לֹא יְנַשֵּׁנִי ׃

רוֹעֵי לְפָנִים ׀ אַיֵּה זְרוֹעַ תִּפְאַרְתּוֹ ׀ אֵין קֵן לַשָּׁנִים ׀ מֵאָז כְּצִיּוֹן יָעִיר שִׁבְתּוֹ ׀ שׁוֹמֵר אֱמוּנִים נָתַן
גֵּר עֹבְדִי בִלְתּוֹ ׀ הֵן יְהַקְרֵנִי ׀ אִם אֵיבָר כֻּלּוֹ שֵׁנִי ׀ אֵיךְ יְטִישֵׁנִי ׀ עַד כֹּה וְלֹא יַנְאֵלֵנִי ׀
מָדְיָה וְזוּתִי ׀ חֶסֶד וּמִשְׁפָּט אֲשַׁרֵה ׀ אֶשְׁכַּח יְגוֹנֹתִי ׀ וּמַלְכִּי אֲאֲסֵרָה ׀ אָרֹךְ שְׁבוּתִי ׀ וּבְרִירַת
נְעוּרִים אַזְכִּירָה ׀ הִיא תְצַדֵּנִי ׀ מַזֶּה וְלֹא אִיבֵיעֵלֵנִי ׀ וַיְשׁוּבְבֵּנִי ׀ אִישׁ וְעוֹד יֹאֱהָבֵנִי ׀

## זולת

יוֹם נַפְלָא בֵן יָעֲמֹס ׀ נִפְלָאת בְּעֵינַי ׀ הֲסַבָּה ׀ כְּמַרְאֶה מִתּוֹךְ הַסְּנֶה רוּחַ לְבָשַׁתַּהּ
וַיָּבֹא בִּמְלֶאכֶת וַתַּן ׀ לְכַלָּה חוֹלַת אַהֲבָה ׀ קוֹל דּוֹדִי הִנֵּה זֶה בָּא

הַנֹּהֵג עַל נְעוּרִים ׀ שֵׁם מֶרְכָּבֹתָיו וִישׁוּעוֹת ׀ דִּבְּרוֹתָיו בְּמַרְבִּים ׀ בְּרוּחַ הַקֹּדֶשׁ שֶׁנָּסֹעוֹת
קוֹל הוֹלֵךְ לְמֵישָׁרִים ׀ וְאֹזֶן מֹשֶׁה שׁוֹמֵעוֹת ׀ מֹרְדָּן עַל הַטְּהוֹרִים ׀ מְקַפֵּץ עַל הַנְּבֹעוֹת
וְדֹמֶה דוֹדִי לִצְבִי ׀ עֲלֵי מֵיצָרִיב וּמִשְׁכָּבִים ׀ פָּעַם יְרַכֵּר לְפַרְיָה ׀ וּפַעַם יַאֲמֵן לֵב מַחְכָּבִים
בְּמֵזוּפַת אַחַר מוֹפֵת ׀ לְהַצִּיל מֵכִּים מִמַּכִּים ׀ מַשְׁגִּיחַ מִן הַחֲלּוֹנוֹת ׀ מֵצִיץ מִן הַחֲרַכִּים
רַגְלִי עֲלֵי יָדֵךְ ׀ וּמִי זֶה כִּי יֵדַע מֶלֶךְ ׀ וְזֶה יִתְפָּאֵר פַּרְיָה ׀ וְהִנֵּה רֹאשׁוֹ מוּשָׁלֵךְ
קוּמִי לָךְ רַעְיָתִי ׀ יָפָתִי וּלְכִי לָךְ ׀ כִּי הִנֵּה הַסְּתָו עָבַר ׀ הַגֶּשֶׁם חָלַף הָלַךְ
הָלַךְ זְמַן עֲבָדוֹת ׀ וְתַם קֵץ לַחַיֵּנוּ ׀ וְעֵת הַזָּמִיר לָזַמֵּר ׀ שָׁם ל ׀ יַקְיַצֵּנוּ
וְהַזְּמָן תּֽר וְגוֹזַל ׀ בָּא ׀ לְהַחֲיֵנוּ ׀ וְקוֹל הַתּוֹר נִשְׁמָע ׀ בְּאַרְצֵנוּ

# מאורה

יזכרו פלאך צבא מרום · על · גלילי זבול · סובבים חוג כפאת ·
הולכים על גבול · נס אדמה כצרקך תרום · לעשות כל יכול · יום ליום נוראות ימין נאור ·
ספרו דור לדור · מלאכתם מלאכתך לגמור · חק ולא יעבור ·
העמדתם ברום שמי ערץ · לעלות אורחים · ותצום עלי בני ארץ · להיות זורחים ·
אך שני כפי אשר תרץ · נובהים שוחחים · יצת תצוה צבאך לקרור · יחשכו משחור ·
ותשו עמך כבית הבור · ישבעו ממרור ·
ויעדי מה וגואלי אתה · אשבבה לוהטים · בין ארום וערב אשר שתה · כערי שופטים ·
הם ציערי אבל אני עתה · נעוהם שוקטים · צור לבת צור ושכנה מצור · וגזרך נצור ·
והצר כל הנה הצר חצור · והערך כצור ·
ודברה על לב מחליך · מרבי רחמים · שכחת כהדר פעליך · ליעני זועמים ·
המחכים שנת נאוליך · אלנאום נאמים · בעבור קול מבשרים לאמר · בא שנת הדרור ·
וכבית קרישך כהר המור · מצאה כן דרור ·
הן ידי ישדך בלי קצרו · מנאול עמך · אם עוני ימי פרות עצרו · רב פרות עמך ·
אי נטרות שכך אשר גברו · אי יקר נצמך · אם לעוזרי זרועך היעור · אי לך מעצור ·
מעקשים הטובבכם מישור · מחשכים לאור ·

# אהבה

יפה נוף דרוי נוף · וזו מחנהו · בלוין לוע אריה ונוראהו · זוחל מיחל ·
ליעת בא נאלהו · להונן לכונן · מכון נוהו · כמיצר ויום צד · אני מחסהו · להצל תעל ·
יגל ציר מחלהו · ארך ימים אשביעיהו · כי כי חשק ואפלטהו ·
צבי עם הוים · בגלות ונצבר · סנר ונסגר · ליום נכר ומכר · צופה למרפא · זכו תגמולו ושני ·
בריתה הור יוזכר · וחזן יכר · לכוש נר וזכר · כר רוזה ואכר · וכר וכרכר · שי יובל ואשכר ·
וכפרי יבכר · אני בכור אתננהו · כי ·
חרל אזן ורואון יעמים ונבזה · שסו וכוו · ערה הוזה וכוזה · יחפש צר וחזה · השמן אסר זה ·
אם אפס חוזה · ומזה בן מזה · הן אזכור מחזה · ספר כריתות אי זה · וסור לו זה אזה · לבל לקר וכזה ·
כיום הזה שר זה · אי ואנוהו · כי ·
קרת נסער כסער · וכנות יצהר כתדהר · אחיש ואלביש הוד בני היצהר · וישרינ מהר · יצר לות פלשתי ·

יעבר
ויטע עבדו

תלי אכלו
לכון

יעב זו קעת
בהיר
נר לתך

יעבר
ויטע עבדו

# קדיש

שיר יחדש במקדש · לשם הזה הנקדש ·
יתגדל · ויתקדש · נמ ·

ראשון בלי · סבה · כאין חקר ואין קצבה · נדלתו מארדבה · רזק מתח כמו קבה
היות סוכב עלי יעקבה · וזערך עד בלי נגבה · זיו יזעו כיצין לבה · הסנו לוכרב חבה
ויתקדש שמיה רבה · שיר

טהור יעין כרום ישכון · יקר בית זכול ייעו לתכון · כבודו חיש שב יסכון · לקראתו אני אכון
מלכות אזי תכון · נוה היכל התיכון · סכיכ הדכיר יהינכון · כחייכון וביומכון ·
שיר יחדש

עליון כרום שחקים סדר · פלאו אמת מאר נהדר · צוה היות חק נגדר · קורא כשם הנאדר
ריח הכל ולא נעדר · שמו ליזד היות נאדר · תקפו כפי כל נסדר · זיתנשא ויתהדר ·
שיר יחדש ·

# אופן

יחיד בגאונו וחסדו · משביח נגלים ורכיס
נוטה שמים לכדו · ורורך על במותים · נמ ·

מהרכ מספר בכלפה · ובכל לשון רכ נאונך · אם תמחין או אסתרפא · אין דכר בלתי רצונך
ולטובך כל חי מצפה · כי תשקיף כומ מיעענך · שמך צור מעוז וענדו · איפה מישנב יזו ואים
נמוגו הרים בפחדו · ובנערתו יחריכים

כינו זאת וראו כמחזה · הרעת מי הכל מכונן · שזא שקר הוכר וחזה · שכל את דריו מיענן
הכל בא מא ואין זה · בלתי כונת מכונן · זה התכל הזא העמידו · ונכורות נגל נ ובעזים
רוחו יום וליל מנירו · ומשלו מיסו ועריס ·

מענהן חק ליסודות · ויכינם אל הפעלה · מי הכן כמה הגדורות · נגלים על קו יעלה
חיות כנפיהם פרורות · אופנים וצבא המלה · מי זה ממר שם כסודו · ומוד ר נכהם ויעבים
האיר יעולם מכבודו · ונבול שם בל ייעברים ·

לך אפרש כפי להלל · הא שומיע תפלה · אבא כנכורות למלל · להם בלבכי מסלה
מה אזכיר אומה אהלל · ודך רומיה תתהלה · יה נפשך כלחי בירו · נזר אמר כם זהחים
ינן עלינו בהודו · מכטירתנו כהמותים ·

לשכיך
מחדש לנ
לעולם

פעלה
מונני ידיך
ייעד · כי כא

ומ דלה
סוס

נותן נשמה לעם עליה · רוקע

## מחדך

שֶבָּס אֲשֶׁר אֵין לו עֵרֶך · נִשְׁמַת כָּל חַי תְּהִי תְבָרֶך
אֲחֵר זֶה עַל כָּל נֶעֱלֵית · נִשְׂגָב וּמִכָּל נִפְלְאת · וְכָסוּד פְּלָאִים נֶעֱלֵית
שָׂמַתָּ בְּלֵב שָׁרִים מֵרֶך · יוֹם תֵּתֵּך בְּיָם סַדֶּרֶך
כִּי יַד גְּבוּרוֹת הוֹדַעַתָּ · וּמִצוּר נְהָרוֹת בָּקַעַתָּ · פִּי מָן וְעָפַת הִשְׂבַּעַתָּ
אָז כָּל מְקַנְאַי לִי אַבָרֵך · קָרְאוּ וְכַרְיוֹ עֲלֵי בְרֶך
רַבַּת יְרִיבַי כֵּן נָקַם · הַשֵּׁב נְמוּלָם אֶל חֵיקָם · תְּשׁוּבַ וְלֹא תָשׁוּב רֵיקָם
קוֹרֵא בְכָל לֵב וּמְבָרֶך · לִשְׁמָךְ וְכִשְׁמָךְ יִתְבָּרַך
מַה לָּך צְבִיָּה נִצָּבֶת · הוּמָּה כְּיוֹנָה עוֹזָבֶת · קֶנֶה וְהִנֵּה נִצָּבֶת
אַל תֵּרְגְּזִי יַצּוּר עַל אָרֶך · שְׁבִי עַד רֹאשִׁי כִי בָא אוֹרֶך

## נשמת

נִשְׁמַ יוֹצְאִים לְאוֹרוֹת מַחֲשָׁכוֹת · תִּיחַדָּך · מְרוֹמֵם עַל כָּל בְּרָכוֹת
יָרוּן נָטָה עֲלֵיהֶם · הִרְגִּיז מַמְלָכוֹת
נִשְׁמַ שָׁרִים מְהַלְּלִים כְּמַהֲלֵיהֶם · הַשְׁנֶּבֶך · יוֹם הֶעֱלִיתָם מִנּוֹף וְכָל אֲשֶׁר לָהֶם
שָׂמַח מִצְרַיִם בְּצֵאתָם כִּי נָפַל פַּחְדָּם עֲלֵיהֶם
נִשְׁמַ חוֹנְנִים חֵן לֵוִי וְהִלְלוּ מִשַּׁמְיִים · חַבְרָיו מְשׁוֹרֵרֵת · כְּמִצְרַיִם נִרְיָעִים
חָרוֹן אַפּוֹ עֶבְרָה וָזַעַם וְצָרָה · מִשְׁלַחַת מַלְאֲכֵי רָעִים
נִשְׁמַ קוֹרְאִים אֵלַי בַּצָּרוֹת · קְדוֹשׁ יַעֲקֹב הַקָּדוֹשׁ · מוֹצִיא אֲסִירִים בַּכּוֹשָׁרוֹת נֶאְזָר בִּגְבוּרוֹ
קוֹלָי יָחוֹל אַיָּלוֹת · וַיֶּחֱשֹׂף יְעָרוֹת
נִשְׁמַ בְּנֵי עֲבָדֶיךָ שׁוֹכְנֵי חֶבְרוֹן · נוֹרָאוֹת הַסֵּפֶר · לְדוֹר אַחֲרוֹן
נָחִיתָ כַצֹּאן עַמֶּךָ · בְּיַד מֹשֶׁה וְאַהֲרֹן
נִשְׁמַ יִשְׂרָאֵל עַמָּךְ בְּכָל אַרְצוֹת שֶׁבְיָם · תִּיחַדָּך · אֵלֶּה מִצָּפוֹן וְאֵלֶּה מִיָּם
אוֹמְרִים זֶה לָזֶה פִּינוּ מָלֵא · שִׁירָה כַּיָּם
וּלְשׁוֹנֵנוּ רִנָּה
וכו'

יאחד     עליהם אימתה     תמל
ינד יעבר     ידבי     כאבז     מגדל זרועך
עד        עמך

48

46

דֵי לוֹ סְתוּם קֵץ וְחָתוּם יַעֲלֶה וְיָבֹא נוֹאֵל

# רְשׁוּת לְיוֹם שְׁבִיעִי שֶׁהוּא יוֹם שִׁירָה לֹ
### יְהוּדָה הַלֵּוִי ז"ל

| | |
|---|---|
| צוּר מִלְסַפֵּר לוֹ שִׁירִים כְּיַם אֶבְכֶּה | יְקָרָה תְהִלָּתְךָ גַּלֵּי מְשׂוֹשׂ לִבִּי |
| נִלְאוּ וְלֹא מָצְאוּ עֶרְךָ לְמִשְׁנֶי | הִנֵּה לְשׁוֹנוֹת מִקְצָתָם לְהַגִּידָם |
| אַךְ לֹא כְפִי גָדְלְךָ כִּי אֵין יְכֹלֶת בִּי | וַאֲנִי כְּפִי כֹחִי אַגִּיד קְצָת נֶרְדְּךָ |
| צוּרִי לְמַעַן כִּבְךָ אֶשְׁכְּחָה עָצְבִּי | רַבַּן לְךָ לִבִּי וַאֲשַׂמְּחָה לְמָאֹד |
| שִׁירִי וְכָל יֵעוֹר יִשְׁרוֹ רוּחִי בְּתוֹךְ קִרְבִּי | הַיּוֹם לְךָ תֵעָרוֹךְ נַפְשִׁי וְתִיטַכְלָךְ |

## רְשׁוּת

| | | |
|---|---|---|
| יַעֲנִים אֱלֵי צִדִּי | יְהִי מֵאֲטִישׁ פַּחְדִּי | לְמָתַי זְרוֹעֲךָ |
| וְשַׁקִּי עָלַי גִּלְדִּי | זְנוּחָה כְּבֵית אֶבְלִי | לְמָתַי נְטַשְׁתַּנִי |
| וְהָדָר וְהוֹד תֵּעָרִי | לְהַעֲבִיד תֵּעָטֶה | וְאֶתְמַחְרְבָתִים |
| לְעֶבֶד בְּיַד עַבְדִּי | הֱיוֹתִי לְמֶלֶךְ עַל | יְנוֹחַם לְכַבִּי יַעַר |
| | | מְלָכִים וְהִנֵּנִי |

## מַחְרָךְ

| | | |
|---|---|---|
| מַצִּיב גְּבוּלֶיהָ גֹּם | רוֹקַע אֲרָמָה | כֹּל הַנְּשָׁמָה תְּהַלֵּל כְּמַלְיָה |
| כָּל עוֹף וְחַיָּה אֵלָיו יְשַׁכְּרוּ | אַנְשֵׁי נְשִׁיָּה נֵדְלוֹ יְסַפֵּרוּ | דְּרִי עָלֶיהָ לִשְׁמוֹ יְזַמְּרוּ |
| רוֹקֵעַ | כְּאֶשְׁכּוֹל וְסוֹכְלָיָה | תּוֹלֶה אֲרָמָה |
| עָלָיו גְּבִיר מֹשֶׁה | עֲמוֹ אֲצִילָיו | עָסֶר בְּפָעֳלָיו בְּיַם וְהוּא מֹשֶׁה | אֶתְמַהֲלָלָיו אַזְכּוֹר וְלֹא אֶנְשֶׁה |
| רוֹקֵעַ | מַבְחַר קְהָלֶיהָ | דֶּגֶל אֵיוּמָה |
| שַׁבְתּוּ שְׁחָקִים אֶרֶץ הָרוֹם | שׁוֹכֵן אֲרָקִים הַשֵּׁם כְּמַלְוֹלָיו | יְחוֹשׁ וַיָּקִים אָמְרוּ וּמִפְעָלָיו |

עס זו      נחית בחסדך      יבלומי עדי ארן
קדשך די      נהלת בעזך אל גוה      גאלת
כלמה ואז      די אדה יטבי      שמעו עמים ירגזון

הוֹלְכֵים וּמִדַּבֵּר · סוֹחֲרֵיִים וְדָרוֹם · מַחְטִיא אִישׁ בְּדָבָר · שׁוֹב וַהֲבֵט לַמָּרוֹם ·
סוֹב שָׁמְרֵי תַם וְנֵבֵר · נֵס יְנוֹסֵס וְיָרוֹם · הַךְ צְבִירֵם וּנְשָׁפָה · יַד לְכֹהֵן וְנָבִיא ·
כִּי לְהוֹצִיא אֲסוּרֵים · נֹצֵיחֵי וְאָבִי ·

## נאולה

דְּלֵי מְאֹד בִּשְׂרִי · שַׁח כְּאוֹב דְּבָרֵי לְמַחְלֵי · גַּם
יְהֶמֶה לִבֵּי · יַעֲלָנֵדּוֹ כְּרוּבֵי וְנַץ · קִצְּרוּ יָמוֹתֵי בִּיצַר צְבִי · נַתְנוּ נְאוֹתֵי לְאוֹיְבֵי · אוֹיְבֵי סָבִיבֵי בְּעָרוּ שְׁבִיבֵי
אַרְכוּ שְׁנוֹתֵי בְּבֵית שְׁבִי · מִי כְּבִינְהָרֵי · לְיוֹלֵי אוֹרֵי · וְנַחֲלֵי ·
וְנַחֲלֵי · כֹּעֲרֵים לְמוֹלָם יְהַלֵּלוּ · יְכַעֲרוּ לְפֶסֶל וְזִכְסְלוֹ · צוּרוֹ נֵעֲדָר כְּחַיִל · וְכַשְׁלוֹ · שֶׁאוֹנֵיכַ כַּבִּיא לְיוֹנְחֵיו
בְּהַלְלֵי · אַת שְׂמֹךְ וְצָרֵי · קָם כְּמֹאסְרֵי לְקַלְלֵי ·
רֹעֵנּוּ רִשְׁיָעֵים כִּיזָּבְמָחָה · וַיַּעֲדַת מְרֵעֵים כְּקִשְׁרָחָה · נֹדְרֵים וְנֵעֵים לְאָטֹנְחָה · אֵעֲלוֹ זֶכְשׁוֹב
יָעוּר לְחֵיק אָהוּבֵי · כְּאֹהֶל אִשְׁכָּחָה מְרוֹדֵי · שָׁם כְּשִׁיר מָרְדֵי · וְכֹל כְּלֵי ·
מִשְׁכְּנוֹת · מֵחֲנוֹת סַנְבָּלָה קָנוּ תְּשַׁנֶּה · מִשְׁפָּטֵי נְאֻלָּה לְךָ קָנָה · יוֹצְרֵי וְאָבִי ·
צִיר שָׁלַח וְנָבִיא · לָנוּ הֲלֵי · יֹשֵׁב שֹׁכֵן כְּהֲרֵרֵי · קוֹם הֶיֵה כְּעֶזְרֵי · לָנוּ ·

## נאולה

אֶחְשׁוֹק וְלֹא אֶרְעָ מְקוֹם · יֵעֹפֵר וְסַתֵּר אָהֵלוֹ
מֵי לִי וְיוֹרֵנֵי · הָרוֹם · רֵן לֵי וְזוֹמַר דַּרְךָ מִצָּלוֹ ·
בִּנְעוֹת צַלְעֵי נַחֲלֵי · חַשְׁקוֹ כְּתַנּוּר יְכַזְּרוֹ · לִשְׁטֹף לְחַיָּי נַחֲלֵי · יֵעֵי כְּיָמֵים יְסַצְּרוֹ ·
יוֹרֵעֵי כְּאֹב לְבֵי נַחֲלֵי · יַעַל לֵב קָשֶׁה לְכָדְבָרוֹן · אַחְלֵי שְׁאוּ אֵלֵיו שָׁלוֹם · נֹדְרֹש לְמֵי לֹא שׁוֹאֲלוֹ
יֵלֵךְ לְנוּדוֹ וְהֹלֹם · יֶלְאָה סְכֹלוֹ לוֹ סְכֹלוֹ ·
רֵיכוֹת יְפַת מַרְיכָאוֹ · אֶשְׁמֹעַ וְלֵי מַה מַתְקוֹ · אֵס כְּשֶׁכִּי אֶרְאֶה יָעֵן · אוֹ בֵי צְעִירֵים יִשְׂחָקוֹ ·
עֹד קֵטֹ מִיעֵט וּלְמַעַן · רַחֲמֵי יָרֹיר יֶתְאַפְּקֹן · יִקְרָא בְּקוֹל יִקְרַב הֹלֹם · יַעֲר לֵי עֲבֹד שֶׁסְּפָלוֹ
אֶבְנֶה כְּאֹבְנֵי יְהֹלֹם · כְּסָאוֹ וְתַחַשׁ אָנְצֵלוֹ ·
הוֹעַם קָנִיתוֹ נַחֲלָה · הַבֵּן קְרָאתוֹ בֶן בְּכוֹר · יַד לֵיוְעֵים בּוֹ מְשָׁלָה · יָשֵׁב עֲבַחֶרְפָּה מִמְּרוֹר ·
יִזְעַק כְּרֹב הַמַּחֲלָה · אָבִי חֲסָדֶיךָ זְכֹר · זִכְרָה אֵיהֵי לוֹ כְּתֹם · לִכּוּ וְיֹשֶׁר פְּעָלוֹ ·
זְכֹר יְיָ · לְאָרוֹם · יֹסֵף וְטוֹזַר מֵיעָלוֹ ·
מָה טֹוב נְשָׂא כְּשֶׁבֵי שְׁבָא · לֵיעָנוֹ וּבֹזֹ כֹּה וְאָרָם · לֹא יֵעָל נֵמוֹל יַד רְוָחָה · כִּי אָם לְחַטֹּק יָרָם ·
לֵיעֲבֹד לִשְׁמֹךְ אֶתְאַבָּה · יֹעֲבֹד לְאֶלֵעֲזָר יְחָרָם · יַעַל וְיָפֵתַּר הֹלֹם · אַל בֵּן מַכְרָתוֹ וְהֹלֹא

ואם ארכו הימים ‎ והקץ יתמהמה לה איחל ‎ כי חסדו בן קמים ‎ ישועה ישית חומות וחיל יעיר
רוח רחמים ‎ לקבץ שארית גלותה החל ‎ יאספם אחד מעיר ‎ ושנים ממשפחה ‎ מנגבה ומזרחה
סביב אשא עני ‎ ובני יבאו מרחוק ‎ הן אשיב לשכני ‎ נמולם ויום ההוא ירחק חוק ‎ יגלו רעיוני
ופי ימלא רנה ושחוק ‎ ירום ראשי על אויבי ‎ ותשמח נפש שחה ‎ כי היתה הרוחה
פצחי בתירנה ‎ וכל ישרי לבות הרנינו ‎ תהיו לראש ולפנה ‎ למען תשכילו ותאמינו ‎ דרך מלאך
והאלכם צדה הכינו ‎ לא כמנוסה וחפזון ‎ ולא בינון ואנחה ‎ תצאו כי בשמחה

## נאולה

נרך וזכרכם צן בני ‎ קמשון ימל ‎ וקמל ‎ ועלי נחלים ‎ ההרס הנן ונמל
תלצוסות אלמנותם ‎ כל עצי ערן וצצו ‎ מהדר זיו מחלצותם ‎ עלצו רוזרים ויעלצו
תור וסיס עלי משמרותם ‎ פערו פיהם ופצו ‎ שם יתנו עוז לקוני ‎ זה כמצרה הל זה בצלצל
עלי ערכים בין צללים ‎ צפצפו שירים ומהלל

וערונות הורדים ‎ תעטה סות הור מאדם ‎ יעלסו עץ רמון דודים ‎ שתו וכר לבן אדרדם
מעלות ריח נרדים ‎ יעלוזו יער וערדם ‎ כעבור ריח צפוני ‎ הבשמים יזלו טל
טל להרביע עמלים ‎ טלי שכחרי ש יעמל

מפאת מזרח לעיני ‎ בא מאור שמש וזרח ‎ מעצי ערן בני ‎ צץ שתיל רען כאזרח
אשמעה קורא באזני ‎ ציץ לישי צץ ופרה ‎ אהבי ראה בעיני ‎ יעל מיעטו חס וחמל
באדרור ושנת נאולים ‎ לאסיר תקוה וגאל

## נאולה

| | | | נט |
|---|---|---|---|
| ישא רוכה ומרפא ‎ | ישצ רי אל כאבן ‎ | חזקוני דברים ‎ | יעלו על לבכי |
| הזמן רכ מסכות ‎ | יהפוך לבקרים ‎ | לתמורות ארכות ‎ | להליפות שערים |
| הסרה מידו ורבות ‎ | יחטיאו שערים ‎ | עוד אקנן בעגפי ‎ | ההדסים בשובי |
| עוד אנופף וארים ‎ | יד עלי ראש מריבי ‎ | | |
| וחליפות וצבא ‎ | הטבעו ביצורים ‎ | יש לשעה קרובה ‎ | יש לימים ספורים |
| עתו נחת ושובה ‎ | עת לה שפל והרים ‎ | העמד מצפה ‎ | צור לכבוד ולצבי |
| אהבת הנעורים ‎ | עוד תחרש אהובי ‎ | | |
| ודכו כמסלה ‎ | כוכבי רום ועלו ‎ | בית דלי כתולה ‎ | אזרו עז ומשלו |
| עתדם יום נאולה ‎ | אכבו זנתלו ‎ | שוב ורצא בני ‎ | חנ מדומים מסבי |
| | | אל פצלים נזורים ‎ | על יצורי ולהכיא |

# אהבה

ארך זמני כמה וכמה סר הזד ופנה שמש ובא נהר גרוני
יבש בצמא לדכר אמונה שנכתבה
בשכי איחל יער בארדברי ימים ושנים אין לירמי יראו זזוחל שכתי בצירי לקחמיעס
כל נעמי איך צרי נהל עמו רבירי ואמר לבנים מי צור ומי חוזכס פלוני פתה בערמה
אהכם ועלה שוא כי יצא אקם להניא לכ אח ואמה אך זאתרדעונא כי נבזכה
רוככי אנשים באו לדנל אמרה כבורה תוך בית שבי בני גרושים מבית זבולי ויקר וחמדה
וארץ צבי הפשי קדשים ואמרולי בא יום פקרה שפלי שכי אנאארני רחם איומה
מחיות ישנה לא שנכה בכאב ועוני נשאה כלמה ברד כחונה היא יושכה
הרכות דברים יעכו נבירה יעלה באזני קול צעקך שכ כספרים חזות שמורה שפטך יי
ומחוקקך איש אזארים ידי מהרה לשפור חרוני יצלרוחקך וברבנאוני לעשות נקמה
בככי יערינה אתי צבה לשמי תתני שירה נעימה כי עת התנה הנקרבה
מר ואהלים קנה וזקרה עם קנמון בשכתרקחי נסוצלליס כזום והפדה אותך נבידכו
עוד תשמחי והמון נבלים שמוך לנדה בחרבו ישיס סחי יום צר חרוני אהבה קרומה
אזכר ליונה ואשובכה הורכת המוני נס אקראה מה יפתומה נעמת אהבה

# זולת

צור המקורא בצור ישראל קומה לעזרת קהל ישראל נגמי
אי לפנים ימך דרמה הבטלבנך בכורך למה נמכר לעבר ביד האמה איהרבכך בתורתך כי לי עברים בני ישראל
כי אש קנאות לכבי תעיר כי נעבדתי בפתה איש שעיר נהפך דכרוב יעבור צעיר
כי איך קדוש וביד מתנ יצעק לפניו ואין לו נואל
רכ ונעי וידי רפה אחרה רוג כל ילדי הרפה לא אפתחה פי עם מחרפי שפה
נרדס ומה יינשה ישרי צר עת אשר יעמד מיכאל
מזם גלותך נות אהבתי שבעת מרזרים וחרב ביתי אכן ביעזור אני לא באתי
אכן כשובך לעיר ההר גדול בקרבך קדוש ישרי

# גאולה

ידעתי חינואלי ואליו משפט הגאלה בקרם עושי ביעלי ואנכי אקרא כלה
יכון את היכלי והעיר תכנה על תלה ציון הידורש אינלה כמי עטקט נשכחה וקוראלה

אל תוך הים · ויהי באשמרת הבקר וישקף יי' אל מחנה מצרים בעמוד אש ויגן ויהם את מחנה מצרים · ויסר את
אופן מרכבותיו וינהגהו בכבדות ויאמר מצרים אנוסה מפני ישראל כי יי' נלחם להם במצרים ·

ררך לבית מלכי סלולה · דרך גאולים לעבור · ישפל מרום נגבעה וצלה · תחרב וקול קורא אדרור
ארצי ימים סוף גבולה · וביד פלשתים יעבור · חבוש עלי ראשי פארי · יקר כבורי על דבר
יעמדי למחזיק בית אסורי · לא מצעדה רגלי כצר ·

הוכן לך כסא משיחי · קום נא שבה עליו לדור · כי לא בחיל אך ברוחי · בהמון לאמים תצור
ערדי תנהל בית מנוחי · מפי אריה תציל ונזר · ישוב שאר עמי בחירי · בית יי' יעקב ישוב שאר
ולא אהבת חסדו בזכרי · אקרא דרור ממאסר ·

## אהבה

יעלה צבי תכסוף · לישוב לארץ · הצבי · יה נרחה תאסוף · מקצה מנורי
השבי · וזרוזך תחשוף · לדוש כאת אויבי · וכלי נדור תסיר · עפרה ליזפר שכבה
מבור יענותה שיר · תיטיב לבקש אהבה ·
ולהר מרום ציון · תתאו ליעפרה הדדור · לדביר ואפריון · קנה זקרה מר רדרור · תעטוף לא יעליון
לאסיר יעני תקרא דרור · ודברך יאיר · יעני בחזות נכתבה · למשוך שאר תשאיר · יעד
ביעבותות אהבה ·

| | | |
|---|---|---|
| ספרי נביאיך · | כלם כצדק נבאו · | מכל עמים נפלאו · |
| כי יעז פלאיך · | תראם ובך יקראו · | מרום לטוב תכיר · אמרה כבודה ערכה |
| דודי יהי מעיר · | עלי ורגלו אהבה · | |
| פצחי שאירנה · | בתי וקולך צהלי · | כי יעוד לראש פנה · תהיי וכבור תנחלי · |
| בוכה ומתאנה · | מהלך צרי תנצלי · | רומי ואל תבכי · עת להניחך קרבה · |
| | | חסר משכתיך כי · ינוה כמות אהבה · |

## אהבה

חולת צבי למה · לבך כים סוער · לבי כאש נערכה · ובאש נדור בוער · ואני
בלי נומה · ישן ולבי יער · וליד ידידי ובועלי · אשא כמו עני עיני · נם
רבו משנאי · הסמנדרלו חלי · בין נוף ובין כבל · כל ימי צבי · ואדום וישמעאל
הם לקחו ידי · אחר מלובש מעילי · וינטה שני שני
יום יום ביעולמוני · אשא לך יען · מאן ליעזרני · יכא ומאין בא · וחביאני אל ביתהין
אם אנוע אז בחיל · אשתה והחייני ייני ·
ויעתי ונכהלתי · בין סורדים סרים · רעיה כבר חשתי · לאביר לאכזרים · אל תרא אני כתי
המון זרים · האומרים בגללי · כי אוביך אני ואיני ·
יונה צאי מפה · מזוקשך והנצלי · כי אמרי ליצר נגאלה · באו ימי גילי · זכר ולא אשכה
דודי בריתו לי · כי אהבה נקשרה לי · בין דודי אהבני וביני ·

אִם בָּרַח מִבֵּית מְסַבִּי · זוּלָתִי אֵל עַם הַנִּגְלָה ·
הֶבְהִילוּנִי הַתְּלָאוֹת · מֵשֶׁכְתִּי לִסְבֹּל רְצוֹנִי · עַל שֶׁכַּמִּי מֵאָז נְשׂוּאוֹת · אֵין חֹדֶשׁ כִּרְבוֹת יְגוֹנִי
לִבִּי אֵל קֵץ הַפְּלָאוֹת · לִכְבוֹדִי שְׁמֹר זְמַנִּי · אֵל יָדְךָ אָנוּס לְעֶזְרָה · אַהֲבָה לֹא לַשֶּׁכֶר סֻלָּה
נָצוֹחַ אֶחֱזַק בְּחַרְבִּי · חֵין עֶרְכִּי וּבַשִּׁיר הַפְּלֵה ·
מוֹעֲדוֹת פְּנֵי לְדַרְכִּי · אֵל אֶרֶץ יַחֲדֵשׁ מְלוּכָה · וּמְבַשֵּׂר אוֹחִיל וּמַלְכִּי · תְּשַׁלֵּם תּוֹחֶלֶת הַמְּשׁוּכָה
זֶה פִּרְיִי כָּתוֹק לְחִכִּי · מְסוֹרֶת וּבְרִית עֲרוּכָה · וּבְאָזְנִי אֶשְׁמַע בְּשׂוֹרָה · חִישׁ אֵנִיד אַהֲבָה וְחֶמְלָה
זֶרַע אַבְרָהָם אֲהוּבִי · עוֹד וְהָיִיתֶם לִי סְגֻלָּה

## אהבה

יָהּ לַמְיַחֲלִים הָרֵס יַד יְמִינְךָ וְלִיאֵן · כִּי בְּךָ שׁוֹאֲלִים בְּנֵיסָהָאֱמוּנִים בְּחֻקֶּיךָ עֲ
כִּי יַד גּוֹאֲלִים · קְצֵרָה יַד יְמִינְךָ וְהִנְּנִי · אוֹמֵר אֲהָלַי יֻכַּנוּ שְׁבִילִי · לְפָנַי יָ וְאוּלַי
יֵרָאֶה בַקְצֵר · יַד כָּל גּוֹאֲלִי
הִנֵּה הָעֶבֶד · הַבֵּן שְׁנָתַתּוּ תְּמוֹל נַגְבִּיר · וְנָתוּ וּבְעֶבֶד · כָּל צוּרָךְ וְהָיְתָה לְךָ דְּבִיר
מָתַי מְכַבֵּר · פָּה אֶשְׁמִעָה בְּשׂוֹרָה בְּהַעֲבִיר · קוֹל כִּשְׁאֵר מָתַי טַל אוֹרוֹת לְמָתַי מָתַי אוֹ מָתַי
אֶשְׁמְעָה בַחֹצֵר · קוֹל לַמְשָׁרְתִי
וְאֵלֶּה הָרָאוֹת · קוֹרוֹת יְדִי דָפוֹנֵי וּמוֹצָאוֹת · כִּי הַשּׂוֹנְאוֹת · עוֹד כִּשְׁאֵר פָּלְטִי מְקַנְאוֹת
כָּתִמּוֹל מַפְלָאוֹת · יָדְךָ בְּעֵדִי שִׂים לְטוֹב לְאוֹת · תַּשְׁאִיר אַחֲרַי · מֵבֵרְכַת נְעוּרַי אָנֹכִי בְּצָרַי
דִּישׁוֹן וָצֹר · וִשְׁאַר יְצוּרַי
דּוֹדִי נִצַּפְּנוּ · לָךְ דּוֹדִי זִעַד אַן אֵכֹן זְמָן · יוֹם יַנְתְּנוּ · לָךְ יוֹם תִּהְיֶה לִי לְרַחֲמָן
יוֹם קוֹל יִתְּנוּ · צוֹפַיִךְ לָךְ כִּי יָשָׁר וְנֶאֱמָן · אֵלַי אוֹבְדִי · אֶסְפּוֹ לִי חֲסִירַי כִּי לַנְצוֹר לְשׁוֹנִי
בָּאוּ בְּנֵצֶר · יֵשַׁע מוֹצָרַי
הֵן אָס אַחֲרוֹן · פְּזַמַּי מֶרְכָּבוֹתַי וְנַעֲצָרוֹ · יַחַד נִכְמְרוּ · נִחוּמַי עֲלֵיכֶם וְגָבְרוּ · אַהֲבָה עוֹרְרוּ
כִּי הַנֵּה נִמּוֹלוֹתַי יְעוֹרְרוּ · חֵן לַמְאַהֲבַי · וְנִקְמוֹת לְעַזְּבִי · כִּי נֶטֶר לְאוֹיְבִי · אֲנִי זְנוֹצֵר חֶסֶד לְאוֹהֲבִי

## אהבה

יְשׁוּב צְבִי יָשׁוּב לַחֲדָרַי · יֵשֵׁב יְעָלְיָן כִּסְאָ יָקָר · רַב כַּמָּה יוֹת הַמַרְמֵס חֲצֵרַי · מִשְׁלֹחַ חֵלֶּ
הַיַּעַתְּלָךְ · לִתְמוֹךְ מִשָּׂנָאִי · שֵׁבֶט מְלוּכָה לֶעָצוֹר · עָלַי וְצוּר הַזָּקִי בְּקָרְאִי · יָעִיר חֲסָדָיו לַעֲזוֹר
יָדַע רְחוֹקִים יוֹשְׁבָאִי · כִּי אֵין לְנָעִים מַעֲצוֹר · לִבְנוֹת בְּיוֹם רְצוֹן גַּרְדִי · אַקְרָה זְסוֹחֲרַת וְדֶר
לִכְבוֹד שְׁמוֹ נָבָח דְּבִירִי · יִשְׁתַּחֲווּ מֶלֶךְ וָשָׂר
וְאֲשֶׁר בְּיוֹם מוּסַר יְדִידוּת · חֶשְׁבּוֹ לְהָפֵר הַבְּרִית · יֵעָטוּ בְיוֹם נָקָם חֲרֵדוֹת · רַמְעָם כְּמֵי נַחַל כְּרִית
רִגְעוֹ וְחִישׁ לָמוֹ עֲתִידוֹת · וּלְפוֹעֲלַי יָשָׁב דְּרוֹרַי · אֶשְׁמַע מֵחֲצֵר בֶּחָצֵר · קַרְכְּ וּמַהֵר יוֹסֵף דְּרוֹרִי
קֹדֶשׁ וְיַעַל הֲרֵי מְגוּרַי · רִנָּה וְקוֹל נוֹגֵן וָשָׂר

הם שואבים המה מריקים · ומרוצתם היא כלהם · אם כל חונ סובב בצדו · תכניתם עמד בעינו
ישפך עליו מעברו · כל מעשהו מרצונו

רומם צומח ומרגיש · יתילדו על משפחתם · נוש יפר לביא ודיש · תכניתם חתום בחותם
וצרור ספר אמות ונאביש · מיסור ארבע תולדותם · כלם נזונים באזרו · ומכלכל הכל בחנו
כל מין על ארץ יסדו · נורלם תפיל ימינו

הונע הורם חי מדבר · מתוך כל מרכב בשכלו · יש אחד חיל יגבר · העם בחר · נחלה לו
וקדושות שלש יחבר · כשרפים וצבא זבולו · מחנה מול מחנה יצרו · כל פעל הו למענו
נקדשים כלם ליעבדו · להתכתר אל נאונו

## מאורה

ישן בכנפי הנדוד · נרדם בפאתי · מאסר אשכון והורידד מאר · רומס בלב זין
הושב לבבי לצבי · רוחי בקרבי אוהבי · לא חונ ומוצק אדרשה · בינות בתרי יעמוד
הס יד לכסא היקר · מה לי לאחד קרוב ודור · מה יעשר מלך ושר
ואשר בירוח הצרי · מה לפתגים יחרד · ומה לקול אן או מריא · יפחד באדירים ירד
ישלי בסתר יוצרי · וכצל כבודו מ עמד · מי זה אשר בסוד · לבי ויבין מחקר
ישביתה סעיפי מעבור · מלכי ברעיון נאדר
דורי לרודי נצפנו · אף הזא נתננו בכור · לומחשבותי נתנו · אם איעבור או איעצור
אליו יעלילות נתכנו · ישלה פרות או ויעצר · חפשי אני כי איעבור · אשחק ליום מצוק וצר
לא הור מלוכה אחמור · לאחן וכבוד אחסר
הנה לתאבה נכספה · לשכון בהיכל קרשך · לעמוד לשרת אשאפה · לא לאכל צוף דבשך
וענד נרית לא ארדפה · רק ל עבור מקדשך · ישעי וכל חפץ יסוד · היסוד וכו אישן עזר
הוא כל ומאתו כבוד · הכל ואור לא ינעדר

## אהבה

יום רצון לשוב למשרה · הוחלתי ושנת נאולה
יתחדש רוחי בקרבי · לא נואש לימי נאולה · נם
מתעורר לבי לתקוה · לא בראות חפץ מכוקש · שפל מתלב שבנאוה · ואני מעמים מקורש
לאחלה נפשי ורוה · אם מכאוב תמיר מחודש · ישנולה ילבש נבורה · ושבותי מי נטה תהלה
מצאתי נאמן לבכי · כירפאתו על נקלה
שלותי כימי נעורי · ובבית יעולמים כבורי · נרדתי מבית מנורי · לא ירד אפור בידי
לא מצאתי חזון נכירי · מיום הרחקתי נדורי · איה דור ברח לחברה · אנ יחפץ לעשות נדלה
אם ברח מביתמסבי · זולתי אל עם הנגלה

בך יעל לבני ישראל וככיס הם באקהן פער ועל הם הדבר והזקתי את לב פרעה וירדן אחריהם ואכבדה בפרעה ובכל היל
פריס כראמי ליעשי כן ויגד למלך מצרים כי ברח העם ויהפך לבב פרעה ועבדיו אל העם ויאמרו מה זאת עשינו כי שלחנו את

נשמ חתן יעומר בכתר תוך ערת לאמו תחננך והצא עטרתו לראות כעין עמו
כעטרה שעטרה לו אמו

נשמ כלת יפת מכלל תרננך יעל אהבת שיר וכל מהלל
שקר החן והבל היופי אשה יראת ה היא תתהלל

נשמ קהלות עומרים בבית מאויס הקדישך הם ובניהם נועם ופרים או ואופינו מלא שירהכס

**נשמת**

נשמ ישראל עמך ישישו ביום תיחדך ישישנס יונק יתנו לך
תהלה נצחה ישמחו ויגלעו לפני זהיס וישישו בשמחה

נשמ ורוח שרי ונס נפש נוגני תויערך וחיה תבועני נס יחידתי רוזני יגל לבב אל ה
נשמ ישרידים שוחחים במצוות וחקים תשונבך ישישס ושמחים ביום שבת ופסח נדולים
ויונקים שמחו בי ונילו צריקים

נשמ פליטי ישורון ותלי תושיה תפארך באו ונחדש הוריה פתחו לי שערי צרק אבא בס אורה
נשמ כרורים בכל קצוות פזורים בכל מסלה הברכך עת תשמיעס בגלה
קול שישון וקול שמחה קול חתן וקול כלה

נשמ קוראים לך זמר ביום קרוא מקראות הקדישך קול שישון יהנו בקול תשואות
קול אומרים הודו את ה צבאות

נשמ פועלי רצונך בכל מאויס זמרתך יזמרו פועלי ישועות חיזוקים או ואופינו מלא שירהכס

**קדיש**

ינדל יקר נורא מספרו חדל ינדליקר כי כל כבוד מזשל תהל בכבוד ודל ינדל יקר
צעיר קצר ימים כומי עמד נגדך ינדליקר ומי לעמוד יוכל מולמי צור נבכל ינדל יקר
חלקך ניעס ביתו שיס ויערוך הורו ינדל יקר ויעל שפת לשון המיר יקרו דל ינדל יקר
קבל כבר פהמ חזות הדרך ינדל יקר ליעדוך לשכב יית קדש ותנדל ינדל יקר

**אופן**

יוצר מסתתר בוצרו אך רחוק בינו וביו מלאה הארץ כבודו אך אפס מקום לשכנו נם
האציל מרוחו שכלים נבדלים יעל מהלקותס מיעלותו והמה כה עלולים מאור קדשו תוצאותם
כל אחד יש לו פינלים ממשלים אל מיעלותס זה אלוה ישלח דברו ישפיע אורמ יענו
כל מיענו כהמורו הפצו הדמות לקונו

וכרוחו שפרה שחקים רצים אל יעבר פניהם איכרא מזעק חזקים מוראו יעל לבביהם

ישראל מיעבדינו ויאמר את הדבר ואחזיר אחר ונבלי לחה דבכו עליהם וכל לרכב מצריס ושר שכב יד ככו ויחזק ה
לב כל ערה כלב מצרים וירדן כי מצרים אחרי בני ישראל ובני ישראל ייאים ביד רמה ויררף מצריס אותם וישינו על הים כל
סוס פרעה ורכבו וחילו ויל ביד הים לפני זירת לפני בעל צפן ופרעה הקריב וישאו בני ישראל את עיניהס והנה מצרים נסע אחריהם

# רשות לשבת חלו שלמוער

נגילי וכולרא הדרך ונבעתי ונלי תהום שתקו בצאתך ונצמתו · ואיך תעמודנה
הנפשות בסודך מקור אש מלהטות קלעים ונצנתו · אבל יאמין לבם בך אם האמצמו
ונלו אדירו אי כבודך ושרתו · ולכן לך הנשמה מהללת אהים לך נאוו תהלות ויאותו ·

## רשות

שלום לבן דודי הצח והאדרמון · שלום לך מאתרקה כמו רמון
לקראת אחותך צאנא אל להושייעה · וצלח בכן ישי ברבת בני עמון
מהלך יפיפה כי תעוררי אהבה · ותצלי צלי קולך באהרן בקול פעמון
היעת אשר תחפון אהבה אחישנה · בעתה וזעליך ארד כטל חרמון ·

## רשות

שפלרוח שפל ברך וקומה · ברכ פהר ואימה · לפניך אני
נחשב בעיני · כתולעת קטנה בארמה · מלא עולם אשר אין קץ לנדלו · הכמוני
יהלך וכמה · הדרך לא יכילון מלאכי רום · ועל אחתאני כמה וכמה
לך תגדיל להורות הנשמה · הטיבות והגדילת החסדים

## מחרך

דר חביון באפרין יחד שרנה · וכמרומו פרות ליצאו · יטו
צאר נורא עלילה · ויושיעס וירגיעם וישמיעם בעיר תהלה · קול ששון קול שמחה ·
קול חתן וקול כלה · ושאנים ורעננים תשו לעד אמונך שמחתם וחרותתם · הצו
משמי מעונך · ויחלו ויעלו בך חברת המונך · ויאירו ויזהירו כמו נרות הנולה ·
ישמור ל בישרא חתגי זה הענעים · יחיהו וירבהו כסור רעיך מיורעים · ושבחתו ותאותו
כמלא צור תמים רעים · וכה לחי באזרחי יהי שלום לאין תכלה · הורי צלה בכל משלה
ידיך והונך · ורב שמחה ואין אנחה בביתך ומיעונך · עם כלה מהוללה · ותפק אתרצונך
ותפריח ותצליח · ותעלה מעלה מעלה · קול

## נשמת

נשמ ירידים הנשכימים עם החתן · לכא תישרך · ויושבים כמפה וכפה
סכיכו · ביום חתנתו · וביום שמחת לבו ·
נשמ כלת אהבים יפת קומה וצורה · תהללך · טוב מסחר כסף סחרה
אשר תחיל מימצא · ורחוק מפנינים מכרה ·

אלך לאורו חשך ורק אותי הפלא · נס כיעבורו נפשי בכלעדיו כחלה
לעורברי יען עזכני אלוף נעורי מאזאהבני כי חטא אשורי עתה סככני
ההכי כיעבורו עבר עלינפשי נחלה נס סר בשורו טובי ומכתי נחלה
מיעוז ומגדל לדלולא תבזה לנצור עליורל שפה ולא תחזה חילי עקברל מצרועם
כלזה לארכביוצרו הפרברית ובזות אלה נס לא אשורו הטה ולא נתן תפלה
היעיר ויעורר אהבה כלולות ללבן וברר קצי ישועתי וכאו ישורר פי שיר ידידותי
יוסקם דברו הטוב ליעם מנו היעלה · זרע עבחירו · יעקב אשר אהב כסלה

## זולת

אומר ליעפון תני חילי וצכאותי · ישכון בחצרותי וימין יעני
ביתי וחומתי · יעלה ויבא בעיר עני ורזכ בעיר ואני כתך הרכיב אבא בכנורשיר ליעד
כאו ימיני לו לא יכלו ימי עולם יהו זנונים כלא היו וכל חילם כי מושכנת אהלו יבנה
יעלי תלם הדור אשר טיעמו עפת ומן נאמו נוראו פלא שכו יעשה להפלא כמו תשבי
רעיה צאומשבי לצבי ולעטרת כימי נעורים שבי ביקר ותפארת כצבי לארץ צבי שובי
מפזרת יגדל כבור אחרית ידל מחדלברית ביי אריך מיענת יקח בידי נחנת ואני תפלתי
מחסי כאב מחצי רפא תרפא חיל הסר חמת לוחצי יש אוהבי הנחיל רי מוערים וחצי
מויעד פרות אוחיל קורא בשמך יענע עדר מכרתו קנה נדר חרסתו בנה חדר נטשתוחנה
חושה ליעזרתי · עזרת

## גאולה

כלימי צבא · אוחיל טוב גמולי · ליעלו וצבאי כיתו שיענ אולי נם
יחריד לכנרכה גוישוקט וגוטח יעתלנגדו אבכה הואירוזושמה גיענה ומחכה ומנצה
מנצה · איעמור בכלאי מתנשא כחילך ליעצור כמשנאי אס תיעצור בחילך
צהלו ריעיוני מתבונן לקן ימים אס לארך שני נסערתי בידר קמים מקדשי ארמוני
אבכה לי כמורמים יעור מיעטמקנאי תחיל כחבלי ביעלותנרכאי כמאסר חבליך
חרבך מושיעי הורי יעלצרך אלבשבט פשע תוכיח בחירך הררי שיעשויעי כון
כהדריך אשברה צמאי מיערן נחליך עלמכון מקראי יראו פיעליך
קן פדותי אחר זאני יעלבריתך אבטחה במצר כי אשא חמתך אמצאה לי מבצר
לשקוד יעל דלתיך יערכ בכנשאי צור ויכון כסא והלכו נאוליך

## מאורה

יעלת אהבים שמחי ורני · כי עור המונך ישקטו נה ·
בנוה הרומי · וכבית מעוני · שמחה ירנן · עם נאנח · נם ·
ישוב צביח אל בית מעוחו · ברח ועלה מן הרכיד · גולה ונדח מצר אניחו · רעת משנאיו להעבי
כונן אכונן כסא משיחו · מיסוער ים ימסול נכיר · קול צעקתו עלה באזני · מנטי אח ונאלה
ירגע בעירי עירי ואזני · ירון כנבור נלכר כפח
ומי ינוחו ישכחו ושביו · אשיב ונרחו אקבצה · בצנך מלוכה יענוף וזעירו · יערה וחילו אחפשה
לא אזכרה עוד חטאו ומריו · וכלי פשעיו אנפצה · אוכלי יניע עמי וצאני · אשים כאפס רסן זחח
תשוב צביה הדר נאוני · תערה עריחן זם וחח
סורה אדני סורה לכלה · מיום היותה החשקה בך · תשיח בלבבה לך מסלה · תסור ותשמר נתיבך
ציון תכונן תשים תהלה · בך ישכנו עם קרוכך · תשתה יעסיסי צופו וייני · על נהרין רטוב זולח
תרח כשמי וקנמוני · יושר לך שיר ארום וצח ·
פלא הדרך תשוב ליעולם · ממשלתך היה מרור לדור · נשגב ידי ער נשא ונעלם · מורא חקל א עבור
האר אפל תדכא ונכלם · תשים לפני מחשך לאור · ליעשותר צונך הפק רצוני · לאור כאורך יעני פקח
יום בו אצל צל קול פיעמוני · קומה וזה צלה אורי זרה

## מאורה

שמעי בת ורואי · למה כנלה הך תשתאי · נם ·
יגתי שמעי · בין צוריך קול מבשרת · כי יצא ישיעי · ישע אשר היה מש שברת · התבונני וריעי
כי לך אגל אהבה מסתרת · אם יעור תשאי · יעל השבי רנ ע הכי · שמהובי · רי צר אל הלא ·
וחכי לנ אלה · כי לך ברית ניעור זכרתי · כי לא לנקלה · בשבי פלא יכך הנכרתי · כי שה מארד לה
בין דלת יעתק נורים שמרתי · משני שונאי · אציל כרל אזן נדל · מכא וכ ורל · מכל א ואו
סביכ פני ורואי · יען זכתי הזר בניכתי · כצפור תדאי · או כדרור לשוב להתפארתי · כי אקרא הלך
א · תמלכנון כלה אתי · יערכתי כסא · ביקר שבו לשמוכו · תשביוכ · איכלה בואי
פלא היישיע · אם אחרו מבא זה חכמה · ולדי יירשיע · אם נברו יעל אשתי מרמה · כל זאת יעל פשיע
יעמו אשר יעל מיעלו מרמה · כי רת מקראי · שכחבני באסור יעני · אם אב כאני · איה מוראי ·
פני דרכי · ציון ושמחתי בבאיס · יתהזקו חוכי · ישע העלה ההחיות לכנרכאיס · ינחם בוכה
מחיש נמול אשיכ יעל נאיס · יעל צורי רי תנאו · כי בארר ור לשוס כבור מחשך לאור · ולאור יתגאי

## אהבה

כי אל לחררו · הדור מאד מרור · נעלה · ריעיה לזכרו · ובאהבתו אותה חולה ·
שכת בצלו אחמור · ולא אשי · אישי וזר נלו · שאהבה נפשי · קרס בחלו · נרו יעל יראשי

וענטו... שבעת ימים הקד... בא אשה של ה... ב'יום השמיני כי קרא קד... יה... א יה... ה חדש לכם ... והקרב... בו לבך חריה לה... ה'... ה... ב מל... את כת יעלה... ל פל אבכ... ה לא תיעשו... א אד...
מ זונ... ה... ה אש... הקה...א... אהם כי קרא קד... ש לכם ל להקריב... ה אשה לה...ה... יה ומנ... ה זבח ומ... יום כי... מ... ל בר וש... לת... יו... מלבד מ... ו ... יכם
ולבכד כל נד... יכם אש... הקג ל ל'... ה · אך בי דר י שה ... ע... ר יום ל'... מ... אתם את תב... את האר...ן תהו... את דנ'... ה שב... ת... יכם · כיום

נשמ פועלי רצונך בכל מאזים · ההרדך · קול יתנו למשביה שאון ימים זדכים
אומרי · ואלופינו מלא · שירה כים

## אופן

יקרו להלל יה מהלליך · ואין מי יעז יפעליך · ויהו יום וליל · מפלאות שמך
כי אתה מהולל · כל כ נ כ מליך · רבות עשית בעצם גדלך · יי אהי אין ערוך אליך · נם
יוצפה לכל אך · באין יען צופה · ופעל טאין יר · ודובר מאין פה · וחי לא כחי · אנ ש למהר נ פשה
ומאז נודעת · בשם מורן ורופא · ועשה טוב וזרע אך שניהם יפה · ונצפה בשכל ולא בעין
נצפה · כי מפעליך · יעדון עליך · יי אהי

חכם בחכמה נפלאה נפלאות · ודיעת פליאה מנ נפלאת · ומבא במחקר חכמים נעלית
מזה יעלא · אשר לא מלאת · ויחל וכלה אם לא כלית · נכטה ואולם בפלאך נגלה
ודם באין מקום ויעלב מלאת · אתה התכבלהו והוא לא יסכלך · יי אהי

קהושט מקורא · ומשרתיו קרושים · טהורי יעצם כי עצם תרשישים · פלאי צורה · ולא כתבנית איש
לבלתי שלוטכם · יסור חמ ש ה רגשים · ומחנות נפריטות לארבעה ראשים · להלל נגשים
לקרש קרשים · ויחד מקדישים · בתוך היכלך · יי אהי

## מאורה

אשפילך · לבו עיני · שפל ושח
יענ נך · פקח · וראה בעני · כי רב יגי · ים נאנח · נם
בן כי שבי ינ ונ לאה · ויעקב וישבי מ ממרור · לא יעצר רוח נכאה · כי אן לנוס מ מעצר
לאמר הבכר בן שנאה · על בן אהובה הבכור · תחלוף דבר פין ארני · לי ואנ בידך כאה
כי אחזה מקרש מ עני · מורש ביד יעבד ואה
רחקו אבותי מרצונך · חטאו וחטאם נשאו · ונאות יקרים נשאו
אבי היומתו כהרונך · בנים אבותם חטאו · ארבק בך לו הקטלנו · מ עמך לא אארה
אם אשכחה אחר בשנ · עמי ביעב נבל שבח
הנני בך אבטח ואחסה · כי כלתך אין לי במי · אם לא לך אומר ועשה · אצעק המון זעקי למי
האצעקה ליען ויעשה · אתה לבר ארון קנני · אבן הישמע נאמי · שימה בפי מהג וחה
ורצע במרצ ע באזני · אשא מקום נזם זחה
מושך בשבי ע על נדודים · צורי משוך אלי יצרי · ביכו ש קציר ו טל חסרים · הורד והעלה לופרי
חדש ימי קרם זדודים · קרב והרחק בית תמרי · כימי צו ה ישמרני · לי שערי ישע פתה
אקרא ואתה תענני · באמתך אורך שלח

וּלְשִׁיר הַיּוֹם בֵּית־קְהָתִי · וּלְכֶם מְלוּכָה אֶפְרָתִי · תְּהִי
אֱלֹהֵינוּ וֵאלֹהֵי אֲבוֹתֵינוּ בְּטַלְלֵי אוֹרָה תְּאַדֵּר אֲדָמָה · בְּטַלְלֵי בְרָכָה תְּבָרֵךְ אֲדָמָה · בְּטַלְלֵי גִילָה
תָּגֵל אֲדָמָה · בְּטַלְלֵי דִשְׁאִים תְּדַשֵּׁן אֲדָמָה · בְּטַלְלֵי הֲמֻלָּה תְּהַדֵּר אֲדָמָה · בְּטַלְלֵי וֶסֶת
תְּעַדֵּן אֲדָמָה · בְּטַלְלֵי חַיִּים תְּחוֹנֵן אֲדָמָה · בְּטַלְלֵי טוֹבָה תְּטַהֵר אֲדָמָה · בְּטַלְלֵי יְשַׁע תִּישַׁר
אֲדָמָה · אֱמֶת שָׁאַתָּה הוּא יְיָ אֱלֹהֵינוּ וֵאלֹהֵי אֲבוֹתֵינוּ מוֹרִיד הַטַּל · אָנָּא יְיָ אֱלֹהֵינוּ הוֹרִידֵהוּ
לְאוֹרָה לְטוֹבָה לִבְרָכָה לְחַיִּים לְשׂבַע מִכָּל־בַּל חַיִּים · וכו׳

# רְשׁוּת לְיוֹם שֵׁנִי שֶׁל פֶּסַח

יְדַעְתִּיךָ בְּשֵׁם נִשָׂא וְנָאֶה · וְשֵׁרַתִּיךָ כְּמִפְעָל וְלֹא כְמַרְאֶה · צְפָנֶיךָ דֵעָתְךָ הֲלֹא וְחֲכָמִים
וְרֵעָה נִשְׁגָּבָה נִפְלֵאת וָתֵּלֵא · חֲקַרְתִּיךָ וְהִנֵּה בֶן זְמַמִּי · בְּעֵין לֵב אֶמְצָאָה אוֹתְךָ וְאֶרְאֶה
קְשׁוּרַת כְּסָאֲךָ נֶפֶשׁ נִפְתָּחָה · וְאִם שָׁכְנָה בְּגוּף דַּכָּא וְנִכְאֶה · כְּבוֹד נִרְאָה וְלֹא רוֹאֶה הַיְשִׁינַ
כְּבוֹד רוֹאֶה וְלֹא נִרְאֶה וְרוֹאֶה

# רְשׁוּת

שַׁעַר אֲשֶׁר נִסְגַּר קוֹמָה פְּתָחֵהוּ · וְעָבִי אֲשֶׁר כָּרַח אֵלֵי שִׁלְּחֵהוּ · לְיוֹם בּוֹאֲךָ עֲדִי תָלִין כְּבֵין שָׁדַי
וְשֵׁם רֵיחֲךָ הַטּוֹב עֲלֵי תַנִּיחֵהוּ · מִזֶּה דְמוּת דוֹדֵךְ כָּלָה יְפֵפִיָּה כִּי תֹאמְרִי אֵלֵי שִׁלְּחָה
וְקָחֵהוּ · הַהוּא יְפֵה עַיִן אָדֹם וְטוֹב רוֹאִי · הוֹדִי וְרֵעִי זֶה קוּם נָא מְשָׁחֵהוּ

# נִשְׁמַת

נִשְׁמַ חָנֵּנִי חַן הַמִּצְוֹת לַיְיָ יַחְסְנֵךְ · חֶסְנָךְ יָהּ הִצַּלְתָּ הֲמוֹנִי וְהִצַּלְתָּ מוֹנִי
חָסְרִי יְיָ אַזְכִּיר · תְּהִלּוֹתַי יְיָ ·
נִשְׁמַ שׁוֹאֵף יִתְמַן הַשֵּׁם אַרְבּוּ בְּקִרְבּוֹ · תְּשַׁבַּחַ הַצּוּר נִשְׁפָּט עַם בְּנֵי נֹף בְּצוּר חַרְבּוֹ
שָׁלַח מֹשֶׁה עַבְדּוֹ · אַהֲרֹן אֲשֶׁר בָּחַר בּוֹ ·
נִשְׁמַ לְאֹם מִצֵּל מִקּוּץ הַכְאֵב צִדּוֹ · תִּלְבָּבֵךְ · לְעֹשֶׂה נִפְלָאוֹת גְּדוֹלוֹת לְבַדּוֹ
לְמַכֵּה מִצְרַיִם בִּבְכוֹרֵיהֶם כִּי לְעוֹלָם חַסְדּוֹ ·
נִשְׁמַ מִעֲנֶה כֹחַ מְצָאוּ רְוָחָה · מָרוֹם מֵפִיק הֲנָחָה תַּחַת אֲנָחָה
מוֹצִיא אֲסִירִים בַּכּוֹשָׁרוֹת · אַךְ סוֹרְרִים שָׁכְנוּ צְחִיחָה ·
נִשְׁמַ פְּדוּיִם פְּרִיתָם מִכַּף מְעַבִּידֵם תְּפָאֲרֵךְ · פְּעֻלָּתְךָ בִּימֵיהֶם לְהַנְעֵרֶם
פְּעֻלָּה לַחוֹסִים בָּךְ · נֶגֶד בְּנֵי אָדָם

לביא עליהם · וְהֵנֵף יִסְכֹּן אֹתָם וְהִלְּחֵם הַכֹּהֲנִים אֶל הַפְּתָח בְּנֻעֵם הַכֹּהֲנִים בְּעֵנֶג חַיֹּם הַשֵּׁל קִדְוַשׁ לַחְדָשׁ קָדוֹשׁ לאסֹן · וְקָרָא אֹתְכֶם בְּעֻנְגֵם חָדוֹשׁ קֹדֶשׁ יִהְיֶה
לָכֶם כֹּל מְלֶאכֶת עבַדָה לֹא תַעֲשׂוּ שַׁבָּת קֹדֶשׁ קְבָלַת בְּרֵיבְה וּנְסִיבָה לְעֹרֵב הֶחָדָשׁ וּמְהֵרָתָם אֶת הַקָּרִיב אַךְ אֹתָם לֹא תַעֲרִיב בְּקָרַב לַשֵּׁרֵת וְאֹנֶק ···
לֹא יִתְקְטֹרֶ · וַיְדַבֵּר לֹא יַעֲבֹד אֹתָם אֹתָם אֶחָרִי · וַיְדַבֵּר יְיָ אַל משֶׁה לֵאמֹר צַו אֶת · כְּנִי

ביום הילך כבחדרי קדש מרחם משחר לך טל ילדותך

## פזמון

| | | | |
|---|---|---|---|
| גם | לך טל ילדותך | וכימי שחרותך | יטיב אחריתך | יהמראשיתך |

יחדש כקדם ימי ושני וכימי עליו ימי זקונו ובקרב במקהלות מונו יהיה שאריתך
חוכים לצל ענך ישאפו ולזמן הרים עסים יטפו ורשן נאות מדבר יערפו טלי המלתך
קיים חזון טעם מליך ובקרב שנים חיה פידיך לעם קריביך ונלוו עליך וכטל אורות טלך
וכימי יחוומתיך

בטל פלן מלא מאנר פרי ען השדה ימנר למען פרש כפיו וסגד הפוגך בבזל קשתנד
בטל צרק הופעו ורדוש צנומים שים ריען כברוש בכסלו צבא שכן כמראש צבי ארן רן
ותירוש כבתו וישבן ישרל בטח כדר ען יעקב אל ארן דון ותירוש אף שמיו יערפוטל
בטל קצוי צפון חשר קוזוך רבת העשר למען קנא ותועים אשר הקשט במזל נדי אשר בטל
רזה כל נאות החציר רבות אספיק קין וכציר בטכתרועון ולא להעציר רדת כיעבטלבחסקציר
כבתו כה אמר יי אלי אשקטה ואביטה במכוני כחם צח עלי אזר כיעבטל בחם קציר בטל
שפע שרב הכסף שוררי ומעיקי שסף למען שנים את לאסף תשעשע במד דלי יוסף בטל
תענה נצב כשואל תשוב תרחמנו ותואל בשכט תביא לציונו תהיה כטל ישרל כבתו
אהיה כטל לישרל יפרח כשושנה ויוך שרשיו כלבנן בטל שכיוצה לישמאו ומין לקרב לעתן
הימין למען מליציס מצר הטמין תהדר כמזל דנים בגמן בטל הפרה שרשי ופרחי
קח שוירעתי בחנ פסחי כאדר טפול נתן לסחי ואף יערף כמטר לקחי כבתו יערף
כמטר לקחי תזל כטל אמרתי כשעירים עלי דשא וכרביבים עלי עשב

## פזמון

| | | | |
|---|---|---|---|
| גם | ופרי עצי ואדמת | להזו וברך תבואתי | בער טל פני צור | יום הפילי תחנתי |
| | | | תהינא לרצון תפלתי | תזל כטל אמרתי | התלתי |
| תהי | ומבחר אמרים תשורתי | כשי הקריב נשמתי | לכונן וחק לחם ביתי | יום בער טרפי ומחיתי |
| | | | ידרי הושיט בעמירתי | לקחת את מנחתי | |
| יום יום תריק ברכתי | וער לאמרדי בשפתי | בטלך לעוכב שאלתי | צמחי יערונות הנובכת | |
| תהי | | ושקוי לעצמי וגופתי | והתצו רפאות כל שנתי | |
| ומיומי טוב מחרתי | תשמר ועתי חרישתי | ותשלים ימותי תקות | חק שביעות הקצירתי | |
| תהי | | וביום החם חמתי | וכזמן ביזם קור קרתי | |
| והשב כהני עבודתי | תשובב וכנס גולתי | ויסד אבני פנתי | קצי תגלה ושביתי | |

ישראל ואמרתה אלהם מועד אשר תקראו אתם כי קראי קד ש אלה הם מועדי : ששת ימים תעשה מלאכה וביום השביעי שבת...
עברון כיקרא חד ש צ ר דרבה ש לא תעשה שדי העל ל : קבל כושכותיכם : אלה מועדי י :

**פזמון**

**פזמון**

מבטח כל היצור ומעזם וצלם המכין טרף ומזון לכלם שנתינו תעטר
בעב מלקוש מושלם והשמים יתנו טלם נט

קמה למלאת ברסיסי ברכה לחם לאכל כמרפא וארוכה היתה הזני נסוכה כמאורות בהלם
ירינפו נאות מרבר ותחנורנה גיל ופטזורי ציצים תאזורנה פתיניל ירנורב חסרך כמלם
ישניב כבתו וקרוש שמו ינטל לישול היה כטל נהלשה מנטל תתן אמת ליעקב חסד לאברה
שה אוכר בקש על שמך נקטל ושארית יעקב בתוך עמים כטל כשושנה יפרח שרשם וזלזלם
יער מושלים אשר כאשפות מטל יקב מעפר להחיזהו בעב טל ולמשכו נקרם בעבות אהבה מהלם
ישבעו עציו יי בישפלה וכהר ומלאו הגרנות בר והיקבים תירושו ויצהר תרנה פרזות ויושבות על
יי ארננו מה אדיר שמך רגל יעדתך דורשי נחומך וברך את עמך את ישרא כלם
בטל טהר יעלז אכר טרפי עמק וכל כר למען טכוס להקריב אשכר תטליל במזל
אריה יששכר בטל ישין תמיר יוטל יציך לקוחי מקטל באב יעלזו עם מנטל
ביום ותעל שכבת הטל ככתו ותעל שכבת הטל והנה על פני המדבר דק מחספס דק ככפור
על הארץ בטל כר ונבעניליון כעשך כען יחילון למען כביר אין ללון תבלכל
במזל כתולה זבלון בטל לזכד חסד קרמון למשולת פלה רמון באלול תשלג ליונה כצלמון
לררת כטל חרמון ככתו כטל חרמון שיורר על הררי ציון כי שם צוה יי את הברכה חיים ער היעולם

**פזמון**

**פזמון**

אנא הרק ממעל על בלי דרי ברכתך על נאות מרבר ושרה בעל מטל השמים מעל
אנא ישאו בשיר קולם נפוצים כשנער ובעילם יצאת הארצות ליכולם והשמים יתנו טלב
אנא צעיר מטלטל זה כמה עבר נוטל ועצור בבטן שאול הוטל מתי יוליר אנלי טל
אנא חבוש מחלה ויציר לנותר כעוללות כציר ויבא לחבשם כנשם ציר וכעב טל כהב קציר
אנא קומם לררל הררד ופצה לטרוד מטורר וטל ישעך למז הורר בטל חרמון שיורר
כטל מרוה קיין מערן מיהל ערן וערנין ופלו ערן למען מעלה טלה מערן תבלט
במזל מאזנים דן בטל נכון לנדן אמון נובכ ים חכיוש וטמון בתשרי נתיבי
מסלותי ירומן נבלתי יקומון ככתו יחיו מתיך נבלתי יקומון הקי צו ורנ נו שוכני יעפר כי
טל אורות טלך וארץ רפאים תפיל בטל שנשב שוכן זבולי ספיחי ושחיסי יבולי
למען סלסל שיר לא י תסער במזל עקרב נפתלי בטל עברים זבוליך עשה אות
למיחליך במרחשון ערוב לשואליך עמך נרבות ביום חילך ככתו עמך נרבות

מיקדאי קד ש אשר תקראי אלהם במוערם : פלק ש חדראשון בארבעה עשר לל ל ש ל אין העשך ביב לפסח ל ל יי : ובדכ קרשה עשר יום דחדש ל תנה חב הי עש הי ל ל : שבעה ל יים כרי ב מצות תאכלו : פטם קראשון כי קרא חך א קב ש יהיה לכם כל דרך אבקה עבדרי לא תעשו : ויקר קקבה אשר תדי לאי תעשי ... בייל הערביע ביך ש צ ר דל אברת שבברי ל : לדכר ל אל משה לאמר ... דפר אל בני

ויהי בעצם היום הזה הוציא יי את בני ישראל מארץ מצרים על צבאותם
וידבר יי אל משה לאמר שור או כשב או עז כי יולד והיה שבעת ימים תחת אמו ומיום השמיני והלאה ירצה לקרבן

| | | | |
|---|---|---|---|
| ואני נרד | פוחזים רקים לצלעי שמחו | אמרו האה | כי ימי הודי כמו צל כרחו |
| אל מסלתי | יעזרוני רחב בעמי שחחו | זהדרי שח | כונה רגלי והרס רגלך |
| אתגאלתי | שוב שבותי נוי ונולך | | |

## מן למוסף לטל
### לר' שלמה אבן גבירול ז'ל

| | | | |
|---|---|---|---|
| בטללי רסיסים | לחוצת פתרוסים | מרורה הנוכב | שזופת שמש |
| לכל החוסים | ביצר ריצון עמוסים | מגן הוא | הא היענה |

## מחיה

| | | | |
|---|---|---|---|
| נחלת צביינו | לקרמותה תשובב | להחיות נוינו | שלח רוחך |
| תשוב תחיינו | הלא אתה | ימצא פריינו | ממך טוב לכל |

## רשות לטל

אמץ נדוש כהדוש מתכן למען אב
להשך בן האמץ במזל טלה הראובן במיצר נרש נעורה
בניסן כרך יעס כמהיס בברכת ויתן לך האלהים ככתו ויתן לך האלהים מטל השמים ומשמני
הארץ ורב רגן ותירוש בטל נבורה עורר ושעון נאודיס ממסנר צפעון למען
נכיר נעקר במיען תנון במזל שור שמעון בטל דרשן ציה הרפך דלי ומרורי בעשר
ספק כאייר דרוש אוכד זהפק קול דורי רופק ככתו אני ישנה ולבי ער קול דודי
רופק פתהי לי אחותי רעיתי יונתי תמתי שראשי נמלא טל קויצותי רסיסי לילה בטל העמק משבו
ני הרגיעני ביום שלוי למיען הוחק ככם תוי ההדר במזל תאומים לוי בטל ויער
למישור ויעקוב ושפוי נעצמות כאין נרקוב בסיון וסת חזות הקוב והיה שארית יעקב
ככתו והיה שארית יעקב בקרב עמים רבים כטל מאת יי כרביבים עלי עשב אשר לא יקוה לאיש
ולא ייחל לבני ארם בטל רזון שוזקק יסורה זקוף יונת סתר לכורה למיען צרלקח
תעודה תזנק במזל סרטן יהורה בטל חונ הצפון לנלום הוסיך טהר
כיהלם כתמוז חפוץ לשמר לעילום חזיון כי זרעה שלום ככתו כי
זרע השלום הנפן תתן פריה והארץ תתן יבולה והשמים יתנו טלם והנחלתי את שארית העם הזה
את כל אלה

שָׁרְשֵׁי וּכַדִי בִּידֵי לוֹחֲמִי אֶצְעַק כְּמָר כְּלוּבְכַדּוּר יָמֵי וְחֶלְדִּי אֶבְכֶּה עַל מְרוֹם גִּבְעָה וְהַר
שִׂמְחִי יְיַּלְתַּ הַחֶזְרֹנִי כִּי עוֹד כָּל מַעְיָנֶךְ תַּעֲנֶי בַּתִּי סִקְלִי דַּרְכֵּךְ וּפְנֵי לַעֲלוֹת לֶהָצֵר קָדְשַׁי וַחֲמֹרֵי
לִשְׁמוֹעַ בְּקוֹל נוֹגֵן וְשָׁר שַׁבָּה תִּלְבְּשִׁי רִקְמָה וְתֶעְדִּי זָהָב וַחֲלִי כֶּתֶם וְזֵר
פָּתַחְתִּי שִׁבְיָה מֵאֹסְרָךְ זָרַח כְּשֶׁבִי שְׁמֵשֶׁךְ וְאוֹרֵךְ קוּמִי נָא שְׁבִי כִּי בָא דּוֹרֵךְ לֹא אָסִיר אֲמָתִי
מֵעַם נִגְעֲנָה וְנֶאֱסָר אֵזְכֹּר אַהֲבַת נוֹעַר לְעֶבְדִי מִגְּאוֹן אַשּׁוּר מֶלֶךְ וְשַׂר

## זולת

אָז כְּהִגְדַּלְתָּ לְיָמִים קְדוּמִים בְּדִבְרָךְ לִיעַנּוּ דְּבָרֶיךָ הַנְּעִימִים
גִּדַּל אַנְדְּרָךְ וְהָיָה זִכְרָךְ לְעוֹלָמִים זֵכֶר צַדִּיק לִבְרָכָה דַּרְכֵּי אוֹרַיְיָךְ וְעַל כָּל חוֹזִים
אֲרוֹמִמְךָ הֵכִין לְהַעֲלוֹת תָּגֵן בְּרָשְׁתָּךְ וְחֶרְמָךְ וְהוֹצֵא מִמַּסְגֵּר צְמֵא וְעָמֵךְ וְאֶנְדְּלָה
שְׁמַךְ וְהָיָה בְּרָכָה זֵרַזְתַּנִי יוֹצְרִי וְשֵׁרַתַּנְתִּי כוֹת מֵעָלַי הַבְלֵי חֶפְרָא אֲחֵזוּנִי וַתִּשְׁתַּף
נַפְשִׁי עָלַי טֶרֶף פֶּן יִטְרְפֵנִי כְּשָׁמְעוּ אֶת יֶתֶר מִלִּי וְהֵבֵאתִי עָלַי קְלָלָה וְלֹא בְרָכָה
יְדַעְתִּיךָ בְּשֵׁם אַתָּה וְאַהֲרֹן אָחִיךָ שְׁנֵיכֶם כָּבוֹד וְהָדָר לְעֵינֵי עַמִּים אַנְחִילְכֶם לָכֵן נָא
כְּשֵׁמִי וְאֶת הַמַּטֶּה הַזֶּה קְחוּ בְיֶדְכֶם וְלָתֵת עֲלֵיכֶם הַיּוֹם בְּרָכָה מִלִּים יַעַרְכוּ פָנַי נָכֹה
כְּשָׂפָה נְבוֹנָה נְרִיבֵי עַמִּים שָׁלַח עִם אֹיְבֵי קָרָם מֵעוֹנָה סִבְלוֹתֵיהֶם הֵסֵר כִּי רַב לְקַחְתָּם
לְמִקְנֶה וְיַעְתָּה קְחָה נָא בְרָכָה יַעֲנֶה תַּגֵּן בֵּרְנוּ חֲמָתוֹ וְקֹלוֹ פָּעַר פִּיהוּ מִי זֶה הָאָרוֹן
וּמֵחֲמַת מַעֲשָׂיו וּמֵהַנְדְּלוֹ צָאוּ מֵעָלַי כִּי לֹא אֶשְׁמַע לֵינַצּוֹ וּלְקֹלוֹ וְלֹא חָפֵץ בִּבְרָכָה
קָדוֹשׁ הִפְלָא צוֹרְרִים וְהֶחֱרִימָם רֵאשִׁית אוֹנִים חֲצוֹת לַיְלָה הֵמִית יַעַרְתָּמָם שׁוֹרֵרוּ
תְּהִלּוֹת גְּאוּלִים לְמִי יַעֲשֶׂה אֲשֶׁר זֶמֶם וּמְרוֹמְמֶךָ יַעַל לְכָל בְּרָכָה

## גאולה

יוֹם פְּרוֹתִי כְּיַעֲדוּ כָל שֹׁטִי יִעְצְבוּנִי יָד רָפָה שְׁמֵמָתִי וְרַחֲמַי נֵטוּ זַר חֶשְׁבּוֹנִי
אַפְּפוּ עָלַי וְרִשְׁפֵי שׁוֹלְלֵי הֶאֱדִיכוּנִי אֹזֶן מִעַל מְרוֹם כִּסֵּא נִגְדָּךְ הֵט לְשַׁוְעָתִי
חַסְדָּךְ הַפְלֵא וְהוֹשִׁיעַ חֲבָלָךְ צוּר יְשׁוּעָתִי
וְהָדַרְךָ יֵחֱזֶה בֶן נֶאֱמָן יָגֵל שְׂמֹךְ יִבְטַח יְחַשֵּׁב דָּתֶךָ לַחֲכוּ צוּן וּמִן גַּם בָּךְ יִשָּׁמֵעַ
אֵיךְ שָׁכַחְתּוֹ כְּשֶׁבִי אַכְרְחַמָּן נֶגֶד יְצַרְךָ טַל יְשׁוּעוֹת לַחֲסָדִים טָלֶךָ בָּךְ תְּהִלָּתִי
עֲנֵנִי הוֹדָךְ וְסִתְרַת צִלָּךְ שִׂים הִתְהַלָּתִי
סוֹת גְּבוּרָתָךְ וְקִנְאָתָךְ לְבַשׁ וְתַחֲגֹּר חֵמוֹת וּלְדַמְיָתָ נִגְעָה אַל תֶּחֱרַשׁ יִעְטֶה אֵימוֹת
מֵהֲמוֹן צוֹרֵר מְחָרֵף נָאַשׁ יַחֲשֹׁב מִרְמוֹת דַּל בְּיוֹם יַפְגְּשָׁךְ וְשָׁאַלַךְ אֵת שְׁאָלָתִי
יֶהְגֶּה וְשָׁמַע בְּיוֹם אֶקְרָאֶךָ אֵת קְרִיאָתִי

וְכִלּוּ עָלָיו אוֹכְלֵי אָז יֹאכַל בּוֹ ... מֹושָׁב וְשֵׁתִי לֹא יֹאכַל בּוֹ ... בְּכַיִת אֶחָד יֵאָכֵל לֹא תוֹצִיא מִן הַבַּיִת מִן הַבָּשָׂר חוּצָה וְעֶצֶם לֹא תִשְׁבְּרוּ בוֹ ... 
יִצְרָךְ קָהָל ... יִשְׂרָאֵל יַעֲשׂוּ אֹתוֹ ... וְכִי יָגוּר אִתְּךָ גֵּר וְעָשָׂה פֶסַח לַייָ הִמּוֹל לוֹ כָל זָכָר וְאָז יִקְרַב לַעֲשֹׂתוֹ וְהָיָה כְּאֶזְרַח הָאָרֶץ וְכָל עָרֵל לֹא יֹאכַל בּוֹ ...
תּוֹרָה אַחַת יִהְיֶה לָאֶזְרָח וְלַגֵּר הַגָּר בְּתוֹכְכֶם ... וַיַּעֲשׂוּ כָל בְּנֵי יִשְׂרָאֵל כַּאֲשֶׁר צִוָּה ייָ אֶת מֹשֶׁה וְאֶת אַהֲרֹן כֵּן עָשׂוּ

ומורים ומהללים · ומי הוא זה שואלים

# מאורה לשבת ופסח

יושבה בכנעים ציץ פרחך · הניצי ועצי פרחך · לחך · ושאי מנדך ותפורך · להיות מטיעם
והפיחי כשמי ריחך · ריח רוקח מרקחך · והעלי שמשך אור זרחך · והאירי פני מזרחך
והלכו גוים לאורך · נגם · ומלכים לנגה זרחך ·
צפון היערי רוחך · ותימן הביאי נרדך · נולתכוזך המון שיחך · התנערי כינער שוחך ·
חיאני אס אשכחך · יער ארי ח מריחך · קומי והעלי מנוחך · קוטי שובי למנוחך · נוחך
חיל דוהך וצבא משחך · יצר מדרך פיעך לוחך · וארצה ישתחוו נכחך · ושי יובילון לבית
פשטי אבלך ומזרחך · לכשי יזועוי רי החך · העני אצמיח צמחך · ועככתי נר למשיחך
קרבן זכרך וניחוחך · ייצלו לרצון על מזבחך · ומשבר שומרי מסחך · יעומדים בתוכן נצוחך
כשיר הרש יתענ שיחך · כשבתך וכחנ ופסחך · ולאי יבא שמשך נצרך · ולא יאסף יעוד ירחך
ככתו והלכו גוים לאורך ומלכים לנגה זרחך · ונ לא יבא עוד שמשך וירחך לא יאסף זכו

# מאורה

ירוחם בך יתוס אסיר תקוה · ולבו כנחלי היגני נבוה
יחכה ונפשו ומ חנו תרוה · ויחלום בשובך את שבות חילך · כאסיר פרות חלם · גמ
המון רחמי נכמר לכן צעיר · בטרס חפין האהבה איעיר · הקולך בני זה בן כני שעיר ·
כאוב מארמה אשמעה קולך · ושאגת כפיר קולם ·
והיה כיוס תגמול וישלומים · אנופף מטר נכם וטל רחמים · להפליא יעצות בינך ובין עמים
רצוני וברכתי יהי טלך · ווזעמי יהי טלם ·
דברי לך נאמן ולאי ישנה · אשר הם סודריס הרסו אני אבנה · התצעק וצופה לך בקולי יענה
אסיר אויבי קומה ראה צלך · להיס וצר צלם ·
הטוב אמרך נאשט ואל יעזרך · ותדאני עלי שכרך והואי שכרך · מיעט קט ותראה בעירוך נרך
ימי אבלך ושלמו והיה לך · יי לאור עולם ·

# אהבה

יונה נכספה · למיצא מנוחה · חפש שאפה בת נאנחה · עד אן בשבי
תהיה זנוחה · תקרא איך אני · אשא לכדי פירור ואני כבואסר · וכני צוריך שכים לעדי · צלי
ולטו ישיעך איא צפה · מתי מחלת לבי תרפא · תצמית אויבי נפשי ותספה · שוקדים ליעקור

ותתן סי אמרי אליכם פניכם ביום הנעטרה היא את לכם ... ואמר לה ... ובתקפה הוא ... אשר פסל ... על דבר פני ישראל ... פני ... את ר עדיך ואת כהניהו
... ויקד העם וישתחוו ... ויכפרו ... עשו בני ישראל כאשר צוה יי את משה ואהרן כן עשו  ויהי

נשמת שרידי איומה נשים במקרב · תשגבך · ישגיא כה הקהל בכל מזמור נערב
שש אנכי על אמרתך · כמוצא שלל רב

נשמ פרויים חשבת רוחם משחת כלי · תפארך · פאר פאות תמורת צל יגיל נבדי
פרה בשלום נפשי · מקרב לי

נשמ בחוגים בקרב עם כמוסך שוגג · תברכך · ברוך שהחיינו וחלצנו מכף מונג
בקול רנה ותודה · המון חוגג

נשמ רוזנים כמועד וחוגגים כפסחם · תרננך · רס המרצה בנוף כל פטר רחם
ראשית אונים · באהלי חם

נשמ ירידים יקראו מקרא קדש כבמועדם · תיחדך · יום חג פסח כמקהלות סודם
יודו ליי חסדו · ונפלאותיו לבני אדם

נשמ צבאות ישורון שירות לך ישנגו · תצדקך · צור כל המשורר שירתך ירננו
צפון וימין אתה בראתם · תבור וחרמון בשמך ירננו

נשמ חוקרים מימים ימימה הקיך בשכל · תחסנך · חק יום כיום מראש ועד הכל
שבעת ימים · מצות תאכל

נשמ קוראים לך הלל ביום הפלאת פלאות · תקדישך · קדוש בחדשך עתידות הבאות
קול אומרים הורו · יי צבאות

נשמ פועלי רצונך בכל מאוים · תפארך · פאר לך יעציהו פועל ישועת חוקים
אומרי ואופנו ומלא · שירה בכם

### אופן

יחיד מקדם לכל פלאיו נגלים · וחרלו לחודם · ומבא תוך מלים · כי חי מתרוזם
ימין כצללים · וכפו ואדם · הרריו לא מסולים · כי מי כשחק יערוך ליי · ירמה ליי כבני אלים
צפה ביען מפלאות עורך · ודע כי מאין באוך וסורך · מהתכבטה בחיין ותאמין שורך · וכסורמי
ליעפר סודך · וכבר קן · ומזריע מוסרך · שוכן ומכשורך הכר יוצרך · דרך ירך · לחיים ושכילים
חיסוף מתוכנתו למות מטניתו ולא בן יום יצגתו בארץ מולדתו · כי כפחר שתהו יהלך לו כתוא
ולרפאים רדהו ומתים כמשפחתו · ויקח משכרתו שם כפי מרכלתו · ויאכל צידו פתו כבר אנתתהתו
ומיעלתו ושבתו · כתוך מפיגלים

קרושים חשמלים יתנו מהללים · למפלא פיגלים · גדולים לא נקרלים · ולנותן ובכבלים לעשירים ודלים
ומחליא ובוחלים בריאים וחולים · ומחלומשלים · וצופה נסמילים · בקרב מקהלים קול זמר ומיעל

כחני הלוית ... כל עד יש ... מדרים ... מדרי ... על ... בו ... על הישב ... על בקיה הטוריה בשור אבל ... כל בקרה ... קרלי נכבדו בטוכם · ונתנו צרי ...
... עברינו וכל לדרות ... והיו ... עוקה גרולה בכל ארץ ... אין בית אשר אין שם ... ויקרה ... ללה ... ואתכם ... קומי ... עלי
... נס אתכם נס ... ולכי ... עברו את יי · בדרכיכם · נס ... נס ... גם כהורבו גם בהורבה באהר ... ונתנה ... גם אומו ... החזקתם ... ... ועלי

# רשות ליום ראשון של פסח לריי צחק ז״ל

| | | | |
|---|---|---|---|
| ושמחת פסחיה | בזכרה זמן חנה | תען כשיחיה | זנה מענה פה |
| נצח נצחיה | ותיחלה לעד | תשיב לנוחיה | ערכת איחי |
| תמורת זכחיה | חלף נסכיה | במעל טפחיה | הפצה להורות לך |
| נוטפות רקחיה | פתחה וידיה | דור צל פתחיה | קמה כשמעה הקול |
| יערכות שבחיה | רוחה ונשמתה | ומספר ידחיה | חשבון זמן קצה |

## מחדך

| | | | |
|---|---|---|---|
| תברך את שמך גם | נשמת כל חי | כל ימי עולמך | כיום ולחי |
| כסאך תהלות | ויתנו פעלות | ענך יום ולילות | ירוצצו לעלות |
| ולך אין מכלכל | כל יציר כהתימך | שר ושופט שמך | |
| נשמת | את כל תכלכל | עירום מנעל | צפתה יען שכל |
| כי על אחר מאות | ואין מקום עולמך | את פעלך עולמך | |
| נשמת | וכהם חותמך | אך פעלך את | נפלאו מראות |
| לא בפעל כוכב | מלוכה כי תרכב | כי יהם מכך | |
| נשמת | אלהים מי יקימך | בשגבך וכקומך | קומך נמושכב |
| מאתו זדמך | אך כשרך וזעמך | יהי בלילך ויוכך | נר לזכרו לחמך |
| נשמת | כנפן ברמך | ופוריה אמך | |
| כלתך לההרם | כימיר ירם | בן מקנה כרם | תשמור מזרם |
| נשמת | תנה לי את כרמך | ולאמר מי יקומך | |

## נשמת

נשמ׳ ישראל עמך שארית עמוסה · יום צאת עם ײ מפרך ומעשה · היהדרך יבאו וינידו צדקתו · ליום נולד כי יעשה · נשמ׳ ורוה פרוזי ממלכות האליל · תעדך ובן תחדש לך תמורת שי וכליל · ושמחת לב כהלל

ל״ב שכל יהודיתכם ושרתות הפכה · ולהיתם אגדת אזוב וטבלתם בדם אשר בסף · והגעתם אל המשקוף ואל שתי · המזוזות מן הדם אשר בסף · ואתם לא תצאו איש
מפתח ביתו עד בקר · ועבר יײ לנגף את מצרים וראה את הדם על המשקוף ועל שתי המזוזות ופסח יײ על הפתח ולא יתן המשחית לבא אל בתיכם
לנגף · ושמרתם את הדבר הזה לחק לך ולבנך עד עולם · והיה כי תבאו אל הארץ אשר יתן יײ לכם כאשר דבר ושמרתם את העבדה הזאת

יְבָרְכוּךְ וְצַדִּיקִים עוֹשִׂי רְצוֹנֶךָ וְעַמְּךָ יִשְׂרָ

בֵּית רִנָּה יוֹדוּ וִיבָרְכוּ וִישַׁבְּחוּ וִיפָאֲרוּ וִירוֹמְמוּ

אֶת שִׁמְךָ מַלְכֵּנוּ כִּי לְךָ טוֹב לְהוֹדוֹת וּלְשִׁמְךָ

נָעִים לְזַמֵּר כִּי מֵעוֹלָם וְעַד עוֹלָם אַתָּה

בָּאֵ מֶלֶךְ מְהֻלָּל בַּתֻּשְׁבָּחוֹת ׃

וְלוֹקֵחַ אֶת הַכּוֹס וּמְבָרֵךְ ׃ בָּאֵ אמֵ בּוֹרֵא פְּרִי הַגָּפֶן ׃

וְשׁוֹתִין כָּל אֶחָד כּוֹסוֹ וּמְבָרֵ ׃ בָּאֵ אמֵ עַל הַגֶּפֶן וְעַל פְּרִי

הַגֶּפֶן וְעַל תְּנוּבַת הַשָּׂדֶה וְעַל אֶרֶץ חֶמְדָּה טוֹבָה וּרְחָבָה

שֶׁנָּתַתָּ לְעַמְּךָ יִשְׂרָ לֶאֱכֹל מִפִּרְיָהּ וְלִשְׂבּוֹעַ מִטּוּבָהּ רַחֵם

עַל עַמֶּךָ וְעַל הֵיכָלֶךָ כִּי אַתָּה טוֹב וּמֵטִיב לַכֹּל בָּאֵ עַל

הַגֶּפֶן וְעַל פְּרִי הַגָּפֶן ׃ וְאַחַר כָּךְ לֹא יֹאכְלוּ וְלֹא יִשְׁתּוּ אֶ

מַיִם ׃ וּמִי שֶׁיִּרְצֶה לִשְׁתּוֹת כּוֹס חֲמִישִׁי יֹאמַר הַהַלֵּל

הַגָּדוֹל ׃ וְהוּ וּתְקוּנוֹ מַתְחִי מִן הוֹדוּ לַיְיָ כִּי טוֹב ׃ עַד הוֹדוּ

לֵ הַשָּׁמַיִם וְכוּ ׃ וְעוֹ עַל כָּל פָּסוּק נַפְסוּק אוֹ יְהַלְלוּךָ יְיָ אֵ

עַד מֶלֶךְ מְהֻלָּל בַּתֻּשְׁבָּחוֹת ׃ וּבוֹרֵא פְּרִי הַגָּפֶן ׃ וְאוֹמֵ עַל

הַגֶּפֶן וְעַל פְּרִי הַגָּפֶן ׃

צרק אבאכם אודה יה ׳ זה השער ל‎
צדיקום יבאו בו ׳ אודך כי עניתני ותהי לי ל‎
לישועה ״ אודך ׳ אבן מאסו הבונם היתה‎
לראש פנה ״ אבן ׳ מאת ״ היתה זאת‎
היא נפלאת בעינינו ׳ מאת ״ זה היום עשה‎
יי ׳ נגילה ונשמחה בו ׳ זה ״‎
יי ׳ הושיעה נא ״‎

אנא‎

אנא‎

יי הצליחה נא ״‎

ברוך‎

הבא בשם יי‎
ברכנובם מבית‎

יי אל ויאר לנו אסרו חג בעבותים עד קרנות‎
המזבח אלי אתה ואודך אלקי ארוממך‎

הודו‎

ליי כי טוב כי לעולם חסדו‎
יהללוך יי כל מעשיך וחסידיך‎

קָרָאתִיָה עֹנֵי
בַּמֶּרְחַבְיָה יֹלִי
לֹא אִירָא מַה

מזרהם צור

יַעֲשֶׂה לִי אָרֶם יֹלִי בְעֹזְרַי וַאֲנִי אֶרְאֶה
בְּשֹנְאַי טוֹב לַחֲסוֹת בַּיֹי מִבְּטֹחַ בָּאָרָם טוֹב
לַחֲסוֹת בַּיֹי מִבְּטֹחַ בִּנְדִיבִים כָּל גוֹיֵם
סֹבָבוּנִי בְּשֵׁם יֹי כִּי אֲמִילָם סַבּוּנִי גַם סְבָבוּנִי
בְּשֵׁם יֹי כִּי אֲמִילָם סַבּוּנִי כִדְבֹרִים דֹּעֲכוּ
כָּאֵשׁ קוֹצִים בְּשֵׁם יֹי כִּי אֲמִילָם דָּחֹה דְחִיתַנִי
לִנְפֹּל וַיֹי עֲזָרָנִי עָזִּי וְזִמְרָת יָה וַיְהִי לִי לִישׁוּעָה
קוֹל רִנָּה וִישׁוּעָה בְּאָהֳלֵי צַדִּיקִים יְמִין יֹי
עֹשָׂה חָיִל יְמִין יֹי רוֹמֵמָה יְמִין יֹי עֹשָׂה חָיִל
לֹא אָמוּת כִּי אֶחְיֶה וַאֲסַפֵּר מַעֲשֵׂי יָה יַסֹּר
יִסְּרַנִּי יָּהּ וְלַמָּוֶת לֹא נְתָנָנִי פִּתְחוּ לִי שַׁעֲרֵי

הללו עבדי יֹי ולא עבדי פרעה
על השמים כבודו
על השמים בכבודו

כמזרח שמש עד מבואו
עד עתה היו כברין שאנו משועה על יושבי תבל
אחינו כלנו כשם שמעלתו נדולה כך

כי על יציאת מצרים נודע שמו מעולם
ועתה רם על כל נוים
עינותינו נדולה שהוא בעצמו יר ד

נדרה נא לכל עמו יקר בעיני יי    המותה
לחסידיו אנא יי כי אני עבדך אני עבדך בן
אמתך פתחת למוסרי לך אזבח זבח תודה
ובשם יי אקרא נדרי ליי אשלם נגדה נא לכל
עמו בחצרות בית יי בתוככי ירושלם הללויה
הללו את יי כל גוים שבחוהו כל האמים    כי
גבר עלינו חסדו ואמת יי לעולם הללויה

**הודו** ליי כי טוב כי לעולם
חסדו
**יאמר** נא ישראל כי לעולם
חסדו
**יאמרו** נא בית אהרן כי לעולם
חסדו
**יאמרו** נא יראי יי כי לעולם חסדו

יִשְׁמַ֥ע יְיָ אֶת־קוֹלִ֖י תַּחֲנוּנָ֑י כִּי הִטָּה אָזְנ֖וֹ לִ֥י

וּבְיָמַ֥י אֶקְרָ֑א אֲפָפ֙וּנִי חֶבְלֵי־מָ֔וֶת וּמְצָרֵ֥י

שְׁא֖וֹל מְצָא֑וּנִי צָרָ֥ה וְיָג֖וֹן אֶמְצָ֑א וּבְשֵׁם יְיָ

אֶקְרָ֑א אָנָּ֥ה יְיָ מַלְּטָ֥ה נַפְשִׁ֑י חַנּ֖וּן יְיָ וְצַדִּ֑יק

וֵאלֹהֵ֖ינוּ מְרַחֵ֑ם שֹׁמֵ֖ר פְּתָאִ֥ים יְיָ דַּלּ֖וֹתִי וְלִ֥י

יְהוֹשִׁ֑יעַ שׁוּבִ֥י נַפְשִׁ֖י לִמְנוּחָ֑יְכִי כִּי יְיָ גָּמַ֥ל

עָלָ֑יְכִי כִּי חִלַּ֥צְתָּ נַפְשִׁ֖י מִמָּ֑וֶת אֶת־עֵינִ֖י מִן

דִּמְעָ֑ה אֶת־רַגְלִ֖י מִדֶּ֑חִי אֶתְהַלֵּ֖ךְ לִפְנֵ֥י יְיָ

בְּאַרְצ֑וֹת הַחַיִּ֖ים הֶאֱמַ֥נְתִּי כִּי אֲדַבֵּ֑ר כִּי עָנִ֖יתִי

מְאֹ֑ד אֲנִ֥י אָמַ֖רְתִּי בְחָפְזִ֑י כָּל־הָאָדָ֖ם כֹּזֵ֥ב

לַיְיָ כֹּ֥ל מָ֥ה אָשִׁ֖יב

תַּגְמ֑וּל֖וֹהִי

עָלָ֑י כּ֥וֹס יְשׁוּע֖וֹת

אֶשָּׂ֑א וּבְשֵׁ֥ם יְיָ אֶקְרָ֑א נְדָרַ֖י לַיְיָ אֲשַׁלֵּ֑ם

ולא
הכניסנו וכו'
המקדש ש גימלי עשרי
אנ$ שיאכל פסח מ'עה וכדרור
ב"ח
נסיר
שלא נגזר עליהם לנוע במדבר שד אן הנכלאות ונכנסו לארץ
שהרי יש לני מישקן ובכנין ביח
היה אומר ∙ וכו'
כלומר
וכמישי

להם ולא יריחון ידיהם ולא ימישון רגליהם

ולא יהלכו ולא יהגו בגרונם כמוהם יהיו

עשיהם כל אשר בוטח בהם ישראל בטח

ב... עזרם ומגנם הוא בית אהרן בטחו ב...

עזרם ומגנם הוא ירא יי בטחו ב... עזרם

ומגנם הוא

יי זכרנו

יברך את בית ישראל יברך

בית אהרן יברך יראי יי הקטנים עם הגדולים

יסף יי עליכם ועל בניכם ברוכים

ליי עשה שמים וארץ השמים שמים

ליי והארץ נתן לבני אדם לא המתים יהללויה

ולא כל יורדי דומה ואנחנו נברך יה מעתה

ועד עולם הללויה

אהבתי כי

נקמה שכבר הבטיח לאברהם וגם את הגוי אשר יעבודו דן אנכי · לא לא עשה כהם שפטים כי אם במיקעתם
ולא רצה לומר לכזה מיעריב שכבר הבטיח אברהם יאחרי כן יצאו · נתן לנו את גיונינס

שְׁתֵּיהֶן בְּיַחַד וְאֵין צָרִיך לְכָרֵך · וְאוֹכְלִין סְעוּדָתָן · וְאַחַר
נָמַר סְעוּדָה נוֹטְלִין יְדֵיהֶם · וְיִקַּח הַמַּצָּה שֶׁהֵנִיחַ תַּחַת
הַמַּפָּה וְאוֹכְלִין מִמֶּנָה כְּזַיִת · וְאֵין מַפְטִירִין אַחֲרֶיהָ אֲפִיקוֹמָן
וּמְבָרְכִין בִּרְכַּת הַמָּזוֹן · וּמוֹזְגִין כּוֹס רְבִיעִי וְגוֹמ עָלָיו אֶת הַהַלֵּל

שְׁפוֹך

חֲמָתְךָ עַל הַגּוֹיִם
אֲשֶׁר לֹא יְדָעוּךָ וְעַל
הַמַּמְלָכוֹת אֲשֶׁר
בְּשִׁמְךָ לֹא קָרָאוּ יי
יי לָאלֵנוּ כִּי לְשִׁמְךָ
תֵּן כָּבוֹד עַל חַסְדְּךָ
וְעַל אֲמִתֶּךָ לָמָה

לֹא לָנוּ

יֹאמְרוּ הַגּוֹיִם אַיֵּה נָא אֱלֹהֵיהֶם וֵאלֹהֵינוּ בַשָּׁמַיִם
כֹל אֲשֶׁר חָפֵץ עָשָׂה · עֲצַבֵּיהֶם כֶּסֶף וְזָהָב
מַעֲשֵׂה יְדֵי אָדָם · פֶּה לָהֶם וְלֹא יְדַבֵּרוּ עֵינַיִם
לָהֶם וְלֹא יִרְאוּ · אָזְנַיִם לָהֶם וְלֹא יִשְׁמָעוּן אַף

ברכוש גדול לא מבית היב רעה לומר
העפירתני כתיבו בחרכה לא כמינט
שינו שיפול לסנור היט אחריני והמעריב ישוכי לרהכס
ליפי או כמינט טיט אך
הלכו ביבטה כתוך היב

ממצרים והגיענו הלילה הזה לאכל בו

מצה ומרור כן יי אלהינו ואלהי אבותינו יגיענו

למועדים ולרגלים אחרים הבאים לקראתי

לשלום שמחים בבנין עירך וששים בעבודת

ונאכל שם מן הפסחים ומן הזבחים

לכשניע ודמם על קיר מזבחך לרצון ונודה

לך שיר חדש על גאלתנו ועל פדות נפשנו

ברוך אתה יי גאל ישראל

אתה יי אלהינו מלך **ברוך**

העולם בורא פרי הגפן

ושותין בהסבת שמאל ואחר כך נוטלין ידיהם

ומברכין על נטילת ידים ויקח מצה שליש'

פרוסה מן הכל ומברך על הפרוסה המוציא ועל השלי'

על אכילת מצה ויקח מן החזרת ומטבל בחרסת ומברך

כאו אמ'ה אקכו על אכילת מרור ויקח מצה וחסא וכורך

מאשפות ירים אביון להושיבי עם נדיבים

אם עם נדיבי עמו מושיבי עקרת הבית

**בצאת** הבנים שמחה הללויה

ישראל ממצרים בית

יעקב מעם לועז היתה

יהודה לקדשו ישראל ממשלותיו הים

ראה וינס הירדן יסוב לאחור ההרים

רקדו כאילים גבעות כבני צאן מה לך

הים כי תנוס הירדן תסוב לאחור ההרים

תרקדו כאילים גבעות כבני צאן מלפני

ארון חולי ארץ מלפני אלוה יעקב ההפכי

הצור אגם מים חלמיש למעינו מים

**ברוך** אתה יי אלהינו מלך העולם

אשר גאלנו וגאל את אבותינו

ואותנו הוציא משם למען הביא אותנו   אל
הארץ אשר נשבע לאבותינו   לפיכך אנו
חייבין להודות להלל לשבח לפאר לרומם
להדר לעלה ולקלס למי שעשה לאבותינו
ולנו את כל הנסים האלו והוציאנו מעבדות
לחירות ומיגון לשמחה ומאבל ליום   טוב
ומאפלה לאור   נדול ונאמר
לפניו הללויה   הללו
עבדיי הללו   את
שם יי   הי שם

## הללויה

מבורך מעתה ועד   עולם ממזרח שמש עד
מבואו מהלל שם יי רם על כל יי על השמים
כבודו מי כיי אלהינו המגביהי לשבת המשפילי
לראות בשמים ובארץ מקימי מעפר   דל

f.31b

# מרור זה שאנו

שום מה על     אוכלין על

המצרים את     שום שמרדו

במצרים שנ     חיי אבותנו

חייהם בעבוד     וימררו את

ובכלנים וכל     קשה בחמר

עבודה בשדה את כל עבודתם אשר עבדו

בהם בפרך " בכל דור ודור חיב ארס

לראות את עצמו כאלו הוא יצא ממצרים שנ

והגדת לבנך ביום ההוא לאמר בעבור זה

עשה יי לי בצאתי ממצרים " לא את אבותנו

נ הקבה בלבד גאל אא אף אותנו עמהם שנא

לל׳ אֲשֶׁר פָּסַח עַל בָּתֵּי בְּנֵי יִשְׂרָאֵל בְּמִצְרַיִם כְּנַנְפּוֹ
אֶת מִצְרַיִם וְאֶת בָּתֵּינוּ הִצִּיל וַיִּקֹּד הָעָם וַיִּשְׁתַּחֲווּ

## מַצָּה זוֹ שֶׁאָנוּ

אוֹכְלִין עַל
שׁוּם שֶׁלֹּא
בְּצֵקָם שֶׁל
לְהַחֲמִיץ עַד
הקב"ה וּנְאַלְם מִיַּד

שׁוּם מַה עַל
הִסְפִּיק
אֲבוֹתֵינוּ
שֶׁנִּנְלָה עֲלֵיהֶם
מֶלֶךְ מַלְכֵי הַמְּלָכִים

שֶׁנֶּא' וַיֹּאפוּ אֶת הַבָּצֵק אֲשֶׁר הוֹצִיאוּ מִמִּצְרַיִם
עֻגוֹת מַצּוֹת כִּי לֹא חָמֵץ כִּי נֵרְשׁוּ מִמִּצְרַיִם וְלֹא
יָכְלוּ לְהִתְמַהְמֵהַּ וְגַם צֵדָה
לֹא עָשׂוּ לָהֶם ׳

בערב האכילה ... מחושב איד חקן מלידה יצחק כי מלידה ... שומר המטחדי לישראל
יצדיק ע"דהיי שיינ ... יאמצ ממצריב ... ארבע ... כי גר יהיה ... ולפי ... כלום מפועלי
לך זרע ... אנום על לי חדפר שומ דו הקבה אל תירא מדידה מצרימ ...

ברוך

הוֹצִיאָנוּ מִמִּצְרַיִם · עָשָׂה בָּהֶם שְׁפָטִים · עָשָׂה

בֵאלֹהֵיהֶם · הָרַג בְּכוֹרֵיהֶם · נָתַן לָנוּ אֶת מָמוֹנָם

קָרַע לָנוּ אֶת הַיָּם · הֶעֱבִירָנוּ בְתוֹכוֹ בֶּחָרָבָה ·

שִׁקַּע צָרֵינוּ בְתוֹכוֹ · סִפֵּק צָרְכֵּנוּ בַּמִּדְבָּר אַרְבָּעִים

שָׁנָה · הֶאֱכִילָנוּ אֶת הַמָּן · נָתַן לָנוּ אֶת הַשַּׁבָּת

קֵרְבָנוּ לִפְנֵי הַר סִינַי · נָתַן לָנוּ אֶת הַתּוֹרָה ·

הִכְנִיסָנוּ לְאֶרֶץ יִשְׂרָאֵל · וּבָנָה לָנוּ אֶת בֵּית הַבְּחִירָה

לְכַפֵּר עַל כָּל עֲוֹנוֹתֵינוּ

**רַבָּן** גַּמְלִיאֵל

הָיָה אוֹמֵר כָּל מִי שֶׁלֹּא אָמַר

שְׁלֹשָׁה דְּבָרִים אֵלּוּ בַּפֶּסַח

לֹא יָצָא יְדֵי חוֹבָתוֹ וְאֵלּוּ הֵן פֶּסַח מַצָּה וּמָרוֹר פֶּסַח

שֶׁהָיוּ אֲבוֹתֵינוּ אוֹכְלִין בִּזְמַן שֶׁבֵּית הַמִּקְדָּשׁ

קַיָּם עַל שׁוּם מָה עַל שׁוּם שֶׁפָּסַח הַקָּבָּ"ה עַל בָּתֵּי

אֲבוֹתֵינוּ בְמִצְרַיִם שֶׁנֶּאֱמַר וַאֲמַרְתֶּם זֶבַח פֶּסַח הוּא

האכילנו את המן

נתן לנו את השבת

נתן לנו את השבת

קרבנו לפני הר סיני

קרבנו לפני הר סיני

נתן לנו את התורה

נתן לנו את התורה

הכניס לארץ ישראל

הכניס לארץ ישראל

בנה לנו בית המקדש

וכמה טובה כפולה ומכפלת למקום עלינו

שהוציאנו ממים ההם
מפטירין אחר הפסח אפיקומן
לבא אחר סעודה

ואף אתה אמור לו כהלכות הפסח אן
זו תשובה לקליות ואנוזי' ש
מהו אומר
לכם ולא לו

פרש לו הלכות הפסח
שה פאים קרבן סעורה לפי שלאכל
עתה יש לרמייה כי הפסו הזה שהיא כ

רשע

עשה בם כ׳ היהם
הרג בכוריהם
הרג בכוריהם
נתן לנו את ממונם
נתן לנו את ממונם
קרע לנו את הים
קרע לנו את הים
העבירנו בתוכו בחרב
הציב כתוכו בחרב
שקע צרינו בתוכו
שקע צרינו בתוכו
ספק צר כם ארב שנ
ספק צר כם אר שנ
האכילנו את המן

מה אומ אומ מה העדות והמשפטי׳ וכו׳  עדה
זו גזרות שהיא מחכם שטות מדוע אני מטבלין קרב׳
קליות ואגוזים קדם סעודה שמחלקין להם כדי שישאלו

הימים כל להביא הלילות
שקינו אהנו
סעודה ומרדינ אנו אוכלין

יודעים פירכי ואכורהם זבח פסח היא לה אטר פסח על בתי כו ישראל במצריים בנגפו את מצ בוואלו בר וג
העציל ונגמר ונענח ליבגך ונאמ כי יטאך בנך ריש לנו לספר הליונטף

הַקָּבָּה עַל הַמִּצְרִים בְּמִצְרִים הָיְתָה שֶׁל
חֲמֵשׁ מַכּוֹת שֶׁנֶּא יְשַׁלַּח בָּם חֲרוֹן אַפּוֹ עֶבְרָה
וָזַעַם וְצָרָה מִשְׁלַחַת מַלְאֲכֵי רָעִים אַפּוֹ אַחַת
עֶבְרָה שְׁתַּיִם וָזַעַם שָׁלֹשׁ צָרָה אַרְבַּע מִשְׁלַחַת
מַלְאֲכֵי רָעִים חָמֵשׁ אֱמוֹר מֵעַתָּה בְּמִצְרַיִם
לָקוּ חֲמִשִּׁים מַכּוֹת וְעַל הַיָּם לָקוּ מָאתַיִם
וַחֲמִשִּׁים מַכּוֹת

# כַּמָּה מַעֲלוֹת

הוֹצִיאָנוּ מִמִּצְרַיִם
עָשָׂה בָהֶם שְׁפָטִים
עָשָׂה בֵאלֹהֵיהֶם שְׁפָטִים
עָשָׂה בֵאלֹהֵיהֶם

עתה משיב התינוקות שישאלוה
נשתנה הלילה הזה מכל הלילות כי עבדים היינו
לפרעה במצרים
ועל כן

## כַּמָּה

לָקוּ בָאֶצְבַּע עֶשֶׂר מַכּוֹת
אֱמוֹר מֵעַתָּה בְּמִצְרַיִם
לָקוּ עֶשֶׂר מַכּוֹת

## רַבִּי יוֹסֵי

וְעַל הַיָּם לָקוּ חֲמִשִּׁים מַכּוֹת
אוֹמֵ' מִנַּיִן שֶׁכָּל מַכָּה וּמַכָּה
שֶׁהֵבִיא הַקָּבָּ"ה עַל

הַמִּצְרִים בְּמִצְרַיִם הָיְתָה שֶׁל אַרְבַּע מַכּוֹת
שֶׁנֶּאֱ' וְשִׁלַּח בָּם חֲרוֹן אַפּוֹ עֶבְרָה וָזַעַם וְצָרָה
מִשְׁלַחַת מַלְאֲכֵי רָעִים עֶבְרָה אַחַת זַעַם
שְׁתַּיִם צָרָה שָׁלֹשׁ מִשְׁלַחַת מַלְאֲכֵי רָעִים
אַרְבַּע אֱמוֹר מֵעַתָּה בְּמִצְרַיִם לָקוּ אַרְבָּעִים
מַכּוֹת וְעַל הַיָּם לָקוּ מָאתַיִם מַכּוֹת"

## רַבִּי עֲקִיבָא

אוֹמֵר מִנַּיִן שֶׁכָּל
מַכָּה וּמַכָּה שֶׁהֵבִי

אנו אוכלין מצה ומרור כאשר אכלו הם ועל הם כהקבה דרך חירות
ואם תאמר אם
הם עשו שיצאו שיצאו אנן מה זה לנו שאן דא חירא מקבה את ה' אבותינו
ואם תאמר
באכל מצה ומרר ולא נספר הענין
כלנו חכמי' ם מצוה לספר וכל שכן שיש לנו לחירוי עלמ'
וא פי

בְּיָד חֲזָקָה שְׁתַּיִם וּבִזְרוֹעַ נְטוּיָה שְׁתַּיִם וּבְמוֹרָא
גָּדוֹל שְׁתַּיִם וּבְאוֹתוֹת שְׁתַּיִם וּבְמוֹפְתִים שְׁתַּיִם "
אוֹ עֶשֶׂר הַמַּכּוֹת שֶׁהֵבִיא הַקָּבָּ"ה עַל הַמִּצְרִים
בְּמִצְרַיִם אוּ הֵן דָּם צְפַרְדֵּעַ כִּנִּים עָרוֹב דֶּבֶר
שְׁחִין בָּרָד אַרְבֶּה חֹשֶׁךְ מַכַּת בְּכוֹרִים ר׳
יְהוּדָה הָיָה נוֹתֵן בָּהֶם סִמָּנִין ר׳ דְּצַ"ךְ עַדַ"שׁ בְּאַחַ"ב
הַגְּלִילִי אוֹמֵר מִנַּיִן
אַתָּה אוֹמֵר שֶׁלָּקוּ
הַמִּצְרִים בְּמִצְרַיִם עֶשֶׂר

מַכּוֹת וְעַל הַיָּם לָקוּ חֲמִשִּׁים מַכּוֹת בְּמִצְרַיִם
מַהוּ אוֹמֵר וַיֹּאמְרוּ הַחַרְטֻמִּים אֶל פַּרְעֹה אֶצְבַּע
אֱלֹהִים הִיא וְעַל הַיָּם מַהוּ אוֹמֵ וַיַּרְא יִשְׂרָאֵל אֶת
הַיָּד הַגְּדוֹלָה אֲשֶׁר עָשָׂה יְיָ בְּמִצְרַיִם וַיִּירְאוּ
הָעָם אֶת יְיָ וַיַּאֲמִינוּ בַּייָ וּבְמֹשֶׁה עַבְדּוֹ "

וְהַמִּצְפּוּנִין הַמִּזְבֵּחַ יִטּוֹל שְׁתֵּיהֶן בְּיָדוֹ בְּשָׁעָה שֶׁיְבָרֵךְ שֶׁרַתֵּ שֶׁיְבָרֵךְ אֲכִילָה הֲוֵי כְּפִי שֶׁלֹּא נִגְמְרָה הַמְּלָאכָה נִשְׁלְמוּ הִלְכוֹת דְּ כּוֹסוֹת וְעַתָּה אֶפְרֹשׁ כִּעִנְיָן כֵּן הַגָּדָה בָּרְכּוֹת יֹאחֵר כָּךְ יְבַעֵעַ מִשְׁתֵּיהֶן

## וּבְמוֹרָא

בְּיָד נְטוּיָה עַל יְרוּשָׁלַיִם
גָּדוֹל זֶה גִּלּוּי שְׁכִינָה כְּמָה
שֶׁנֶּאֱמַר אוֹ הֲנִסָּה אֱלֹהִים
לָבֹא לָקַחַת לוֹ גוֹי מִקֶּרֶב גּוֹי בְּאֹתֹת וּבְמוֹפְתִים
וּבְמִלְחָמָה וּבְיָד חֲזָקָה וּבִזְרוֹעַ נְטוּיָה וּבְמוֹרָאִים
גְּדוֹלִים כְּכֹל אֲשֶׁר עָשָׂה לָכֶם יְיָ אֱלֹהֵיכֶם בְּמִצְרַיִ

## וּבְאוֹתוֹת

לְעֵינֶיךָ
זֶה הַמַּטֶּה
כְּמָה
שֶׁנֶּאֱמַר
הַמַּטֶּה
הַזֶּה
הַקַּח בְּיָדְךָ אֲשֶׁר תַּעֲשֶׂה בּוֹ אֶת הָאֹתֹת

## וּבְמוֹפְתִים

זֶה הַדָּם כְּמָה
שֶׁנֶּאֱמַר וְנָתַתִּי
מוֹפְתִים בַּשָּׁמַיִם
וּבָאָרֶץ דָּם וָאֵשׁ וְתִמְרוֹת עָשָׁן דָּבָר אַחֵר

זוֹ יְרִידָה לְתִינוֹקוֹת לַמֶּה אָטוּ מְחַלְּקִין הֲמִצְרַ
עַנְיָא דִּי אֲכָלוּ אַבְהָתָנָא בְּאַרְעָא דְּמִצְרַיִם
לִשְׁנִים כְּדַרְכּוֹ שֶׁל עָנִי דְּלָהֶם עָנִי אֲכָלוּ אֲבוֹתֵינוּ בְּמִצְרַיִם דֶּרֶךְ הַפָּזוֹן וּמְחַלְּקִין חֵלֶף לְשֶׁבַח לְהַבְרֵיאֵיהֶם
פָּאדב שֶׁאוֹכֵל בִּמְרוּעָה וּבַחִפָּזוֹן וְכָל אֶחָד וְאֶחָד אוֹמֵר לַחֲבֵרוֹ כֹּל דִּבְפַּן יֵיתֵי וְיֵכוֹל כָּלוֹם מִי שֶׁלֹא אִיתָהֵן

לפיכך צריך שתי שלימות מלבד הפרוסה יש לום משום שבת כי כאשר יבא יום ראשון של פסח בשבת צריך שתי מיצרין
שלימות בשביל מיצה ופרוסה משום פסח דבעינן לחם עני ׃ ויש מפרבין

כל לילה הזה והכיתי כל בכור בארץ מצרים
מאדם ועד בהמה ובכל אלהי מצרים אעשה
שפטים אני יי׳ וְעָבַרְתִּי
בארץ מצרים
אנו ולא מלאך
והכיתי כל בכור אני ולא שרף ובכל אלהי מצרי
אעשה שפטים אני יי׳ אני ולא השליח אני

חזקה
הנהיד
בשדה

יי׳ אני הוא ולא אחר בָּהּ
זה הדבר כמה שנ׳
יי׳ הונה במקנך אשר

כבד מאד וּבִזְרוֹעַ
נטויה
זו החרב
כמה
שנא׳ וחרבו
שלופ

כבד מאד
כבסוסים כחמורים כנמלים כבקר וכצאן דבר

על הפרוסה המויכיא ועל השלימה משום דבריכה המויעא לנבי אכילת מיצה בברכה סבריכה היין לקדוש לך הים תקיילהו אמר
פסא הפא גני תירי ירון אחר מיצה ולדברי הכל אין לביענא השל יודד עד טיבד
על הפרוסה על אכילת מיצה כדאמרי מבריך ואחר כך בוצע וכוון שאינו יכול לאבו ו ער

יֵשׁ לוֹמַ׳
אֲבָל כֵּי׳

וַיַּרְא אֱלֹהִים אֶת בְּנֵי יִשְׂרָאֵל וַיֵּדַע אֱלֹהִים

**זֹאת** עֲמָלֵנוּ אֵלּוּ הַבָּנִים כְּמָה
שֶׁנֶּ׳ כָּל הַבֵּן הַיִּלּוֹד

הַיְאֹרָה תַּשְׁלִיכֻהוּ וְכָל **זֹאת**

לַחֲצֵנוּ זֶה
הַדְּחַק כְּמָה

שֶׁנֶּ׳ וְגַם
הַדֹּחַק כְּמָה

הַלַּחַץ אֲשֶׁר רָאִיתִי אֶת

מִצְרַיִם לוֹחֲצִים אֹתָם **וַיּוֹצִיאֵנוּ** יְיָ מִמִּצְרַיִם

בְּיַד חֲזָקָה וּבִזְרֹעַ נְטוּיָה וּבְמֹרָא גָדֹל וּבְאֹתוֹת
וּבְמֹפְתִים **וַיּוֹצִיאֵנוּ**

מִמִּצְרַיִם לֹא
עַל יְדֵי מַלְאָך וְלֹא

עַל יְדֵי שָׂרָף וְלֹא עַל יְדֵי הַשָּׁלִיחַ אֶלָּא הַקָּבָּ׳ה

כְּעַצְמוֹ וּבִכְבוֹדוֹ שֶׁנֶּ׳ וְעָבַרְתִּי בְאֶרֶץ מִצְרַיִם

כְּמִסְכְּלוֹתָם וַיִּבֶן עָרֵי מִסְכְּנוֹת לְפַרְעֹה אֶת פִּתֹם
וְאֶת רַעַמְסֵס ' וַיִּתְּנוּ עָלֵינוּ עֲבוֹדָה קָשָׁה כְּמָה
שֶׁנֶּא' וַיַּעֲבִידוּ מִצְרַיִם אֶת בְּנֵי יִשְׂרָאֵל בְּפָרֶךְ ﾟ

אֶל יְיָ אֱלֹהֵי אֲבוֹתֵינוּ ﾟ **וַנִּצְעַק**
כְּמָה שֶׁנֶּא' וַיְהִי בַיָּמִים
הָרַבִּים הָהֵם וַיָּמָת מֶלֶךְ
מִצְרַיִם וַיֵּאָנְחוּ בְנֵי יִשְׂרָאֵל מִן הָעֲבוֹדָה וַיִּזְעָקוּ
וַתַּעַל שַׁוְעָתָם אֶל הָאֱלֹהִים מִן הָעֲבוֹדָה ﾟ

יְיָ אֶת קוֹלֵנוּ כְּמָה **וַיִּשְׁמַע**
שֶׁנֶּא' וַיִּשְׁמַע אֱלֹהִים
אֶת נַאֲקָתָם וַיִּזְכֹּר
אֱלֹהִים אֶת בְּרִיתוֹ אֶת אַבְרָהָם אֶת יִצְחָק וְאֶת
יַעֲקֹב אֶת עָנְיֵנוּ זוֹ פְּרִישׁוּת **וַיַּרְא**
דֶּרֶךְ אֶרֶץ כְּמָה שֶׁנֶּאֱמַר

ואף אחר הלו' מכר לא נרע מכיס
שלי שי נכנס דברכה אמעעית שלא בהקנה נעשיר
חמישי של הלל הגדול שהוא רטוח וכל שכן זה שהוא מעוה כמי שבארנו
יש שאלין

מצוינין שם גדול ועצום כמה שנא' וכני
ישראל פרו וישרצו וירכו ויעצמו כמאד מאד
ותמלא הארץ אותם " ורב
כמה שנא' רבבה כצמח
השדה נתתיך ותרבי
ותגדלי ותבאי בעדי עדיים שדיים נכונו ושערך
צמח ואת ערום ועריה " וירע
אותנו המצרים כמה שנ
הבה נתחכמה לו פן
ירבה והיה כי תקראנה מלחמה ונוסף גם הוא על
שונאינו ונלחם בנו ועלה מן הארץ "
ויענונו
אותנו המצרים כמה
שנא' וישימו עליו שרי
מסים למען ענותנו

למה אין מברכין במרור כדא לרי האדמיה * והלא ברכה אחין של
קדוש היום היה איגו פוטר כוד שני של המגרה לי שהמגרה מלמעיך ביניהם ועריך לחזור לרי הנכי מעד שניה הכא
נכי ליהוי הדגרה הלמסקין כן הכרלם והמרור * יש לומר שברכת הלהם של מצה שהוא
ואם תאמר שברכת הכרלכ ליטרו
נה

אֲרַמִי אוֹבֵד אָבִי וַיֵרֶד מִצְרַיְמָה וַיָגָר שָׁם בִּמְתֵי

מְעָט וַיְהִי שָׁם לְגוֹי גָדוֹל עָצוּם וָרָב

וַיֵרֶד מִצְרַיְמָה אָנוּס עַל פִּי

הַדִבוּר וַיָגָר שָׁם מְלַמֵד

שֶׁלֹא יָרַד לְהִשְׁתַּקֵעַ אֶלָא

לָגוּר שָׁם שֶׁנֶאֱמַר וַיֹּאמְרוּ אֶל פַּרְעֹה לָגוּר בָּאֶרֶץ

בָּאנוּ כִּי אֵין מִרְעֶה לַצֹּאן אֲשֶׁר לַעֲבָדֶיךָ כִּי

כָבֵד הָרָעָב בְּאֶרֶץ כְּנָעַן וְעַתָה יֵשְׁבוּ נָא עֲבָדֶיךָ

בְּאֶרֶץ גֹּשֶׁן בִּמְתֵי מְעָט

בְּמָה כְּשִׁבְעִים נֶפֶשׁ

יָרְדוּ אֲבֹתֶיךָ מִצְרַיְמָה וְעַתָה שָׂמְךָ וַיְהִי

אֱלֹהֶיךָ כְּכוֹכְבֵי הַשָׁמַיִם לָרֹב

שָׁם לְגוֹי מְלַמֵד שֶׁהָיוּ יִשְׂרָאֵל

אגמלך דעאריך לפריך אבל מיא ואעלב אינו כפריך על חנפן ועל פרי חנפן    לא בכסא דברכה   המזו
דעביד לפרוב עליה ומטרה ית נטר ליה לברכה אחרונה עד דמטי להדיוא כסא חכא נמי טין דאיכא כסא דמליא קמ״ה

שׁוֹמֵר הַבְטָחָתוֹ לְיִשְׂרֵ׳ בָּרוּךְ הוּא שֶׁהַקבה

מְחַשֵּׁב אֶת הַקֵּץ לַעֲשׂוֹת כְּמָה שֶׁאָמַר לְאַבְרָהָ

אָבִינוּ בֵּין הַבְּתָרִים שֶׁנֶּ׳ וַיֹּאמֶר לְאַבְרָם יָדֹעַ

תֵּדַע כִּי גֵר יִהְיֶה זַרְעֲךָ בְּאֶרֶץ לֹא לָהֶם וַעֲבָדוּם

וְעִנּוּ אוֹתָם אַרְבַּע מֵאוֹת שָׁנָה וְגַם אֶת הַגּוֹי

אֲשֶׁר יַעֲבֹדוּ דָן אָנֹכִי וְאַחֲרֵי כֵן יֵצְאוּ בִּרְכֻשׁ

גָּדוֹל

וְהִיא שֶׁעָמְדָה לַאֲבוֹתֵינוּ

שֶׁלֹּא אֶחָד בִּלְבַד

עָמַד עָלֵינוּ לְכַלּוֹתֵינוּ אֶלָא

שֶׁבְּכָל דּוֹר וָדוֹר עוֹמְדִים עָלֵינוּ לְכַלּוֹתֵינוּ

וְהַקבה מַצִּילֵנוּ מִיָּדָם

צֵא וּלְמַד

מַה בִּקֵּשׁ לָבָן הָאֲרַמִּי

לְיַעֲקֹב אָבִינוּ שֶׁפַּרְעֹה

לֹא גָזַר

אֶלָּא עַל הַזְּכָרִים לָבָן בִּקֵּשׁ לַעֲקוֹר אֶת הַכֹּל שֶׁנֶּ׳

דכען למפשתיה וכריך על׳ ומפטרי׳ פולחו     וכל אלו ארבעה כוסות צריך לשתוקן כהסבה ויבן

דרך חירוך    ובן מצה צריכה הסבה אבל לא מרור לפי שהיא זמר לעבדות   ומפרש בירוש׳ לפי בשבכן

כבוסות הללו אם רעה לשתותי ישתה בין שלישי׳ לרביעי לא ישתה

שֶׁיֵּשׁ מַצָּה וּמָרוֹר מוּנָּחִים לְפָנֶיךָ

**מִתְּחִלָּה** עוֹבְדֵי עֲבוֹדָה זָרָה הָיוּ

אֲבוֹתֵינוּ וְעַכְשָׁו קֵרְבָנוּ הַמָּקוֹם לַעֲבוֹדָתוֹ שֶׁנֶּאֱמַ׳
וַיֹּאמֶר יְהוֹשֻׁעַ אֶל כָּל הָעָם כֹּה אָמַר יְיָ אֱלֹהֵי
יִשְׂרָאֵל בְּעֵבֶר הַנָּהָר יָשְׁבוּ אֲבוֹתֵיכֶם מֵעוֹלָם
תֶּרַח אֲבִי אַבְרָהָם וַאֲבִי נָחוֹר וַיַּעַבְדוּ אֱלֹהִים
אֲחֵרִים וָאֶקַּח אֶת אֲבִיכֶם אֶת אַבְרָהָם מֵעֵבֶר
הַנָּהָר וָאוֹלֵךְ אֹתוֹ בְּכָל אֶרֶץ כְּנַעַן וָאַרְבֶּה אֶת
זַרְעוֹ וָאֶתֵּן לוֹ אֶת יִצְחָק וָאֶתֵּן לְיִצְחָק אֶת יַעֲקֹב
וְאֶת עֵשָׂו וָאֶתֵּן לְעֵשָׂו אֶת שֵׂעִיר לָרֶשֶׁת אֹתוֹ
וְיַעֲקֹב וּבָנָיו יָרְדוּ מִצְרָיִם

**בָּרוּךְ**

דך כברך כזא פרי הגפן ושותה כהסבה דרך חירות · ואחר כך נטל בכל אחד ואחד ידין לפי שהסיח דערתי
מהם כש ער קריאה ההלל ונטל ונטל שתי מצוה השלי וחלרוס וכרך המוצא · ואחר כך על אכילת מצה וכריעע ושתייה

הזאת לכם ולא לולפי שהוציא את עצמו
מן הכלל כפר כי אף את הקהה את
שניו ואמור לו בעבור זה עשה יי לי בצאתי
ממצרים לי זלא לו וזהיה שם לא היה נגאל

חכם

מהוא אומ מה זאת ואמרת
אליו בחזק יד הוציאנו יי
ממצרים מבית עבדים ו

ושאינו יורע לשאל את פתח לו שנא והגדת
לבנך ביום ההוא לאמר בעבור זה עשה יי לי
בצאתי ממצרים

והגדת

לבנך יכול מראש
חדש תל כי ביום ההוא
אי ביום ההוא יכול

מבעוד יום תל כי בעבור זה לא אמרתי אלא בשעה

ונתן לכל אחד כזית
ואחר כך נטל המריר שהוא חזרת ומכדך על אכילת מרור
ואחר כך מצה זמרור כאחד ואוכלין בלא ברכה זכר למקדש כהלל · ואחר כך אוכל כל מזון שרוצה לאכל ושותה
כל מה שרוצה לשתות · ואחר שגמרו סעוריהן נוטל המצה הפרוטה שהנחה המפה ואוכל ממנה כזות ואין אוכלין

יהרי זה משבח ‏‎ ‏‎ ‏‎ ‏‎ ‏‎ ‏‎ ‏‎ ‏‎ ‏‎ ‏‎ ‏‎ ‏‎ ‏‎ ‏‎ ‏‎ ‏‎ ‏‎ ‏‎ ‏‎ ‏‎ ‏‎ ואוכ לעבר שהוא במקום זגר הנסים ‏‎ ‏‎ ‏‎ ‏‎ ‏‎ ‏‎ ‏‎ ‏‎ ‏‎ ‏‎ ‏‎ ‏‎ ‏‎ ‏‎ ‏‎ ‏‎ ‏‎ ואחר

כך מברך אשר גאלנו וכו ‏‎ ‏‎ ‏‎ ‏‎ ‏‎ ‏‎ ‏‎ ‏‎ ‏‎ ונודה לך שיר חדש על גאלתנו ועל פדיות נפשנו בלי ישריאל

וכן יחיך העולם הזה וכל ימיחיב להביא

לימות המשיה בָּרוּך

המקום ברוך

הוא ברוך שנתן

תורה לישראל

ברוך הוא כנגר ארבעה בנים דברה התורה

אחד חכם ואחר רשע ואחד תם ואחד

שאנו יודע לשאול חָכָם

מה הוא אומר מה

העדות והחקים

והמשפטים אשר

צוה יי אלהינו אותנו אף אתה אמר לו כהלכות

הפסח אין מפטירין אחר הפסח אפיקומן רָשָׁע

מה הוא אומר מה העבודה

עירורית בשמירתהם על שכפט ומתחיל לומ הנרזד ‎ ‎ וכשריצה לומ כיצה זו מנביה הימינה וכשאומ
כריר זה מנביה המרירי ומתחי לומ הלל עד למינינו מים ואינו מכירך על החלל מפני סאין קוראין אותי כולל לא כמילקן

כד׳ אֱלִיעֶזֶר    ור׳
יְהוֹשֻׁעַ וּר׳ אֶלְעָ
בֶּן עֲזַרְיָה    ור׳

# מֹשֶׁה

עֲקִיבָא וּר׳ טַרְפוֹן שֶׁהָיוּ מְסֻבִּין בִּבְנֵי בְרַק וְהָיוּ
מְסַפְּרִין בִּיצִיאַת מִצְרַיִם כָּל אֹתוֹ הַלַּיְלָה עַד
שֶׁבָּאוּ תַלְמִידֵיהֶם וְאָמְרוּ לָהֶם רַבּוֹתֵינוּ הִגִּיעַ
זְמַן קְרִיַת שְׁמַע שֶׁלְ שַׁחֲרִית

# אָמַר ר׳ אֶלְעָזָ

בֶּן עֲזַרְיָה
הֲרֵי אֲנִ
בֶּן שִׁבְעִ
שָׁנָה וְלֹא זָכִיתִי שֶׁתֵּאָמֵר יְצִיאַת מִצְרַיִם בַּלֵּילוֹ
עַד שֶׁדְּרָשָׁהּ בֶּן זוֹמָא שֶׁנֶּאֱ לְמַעַן תִּזְכֹּר    אֶת
יוֹם צֵאתְךָ מֵאֶרֶץ מִצְרַיִם כָּל יְמֵי חַיֶּיךָ    יְמֵי
חַיֶּיךָ הַיָּמִים כָּל יְמֵי חַיֶּיךָ הַלֵּילוֹת וַחֲכָמִים אוֹ

יהית תרח גדול · ואחר כך נוטל י'ה · בן המצ'ה לוברס לשתים ומטמין האחת מהן תחת המפה לאפו כמנה כוזית
כל אחד ואחד בארדינה · והכנ'ג · שומר היה את המצה זכר למשארוח צרורות בשמלותם · וסנהג

וכלין שאר ירקות הלילה הזה מרור שבכל
הלילות אין אנו מטבלין אפלו פעם אחת הליל
הזה שתי פעמים שבכל הלילות אנו אוכלין
בין יושבין בין מסבין הלילה הזה כלנו מסבין

עברים
היינו לפרעה במצרים
ויוציאנו י'י' אלינו משם
ביד חזקה ובזרוע נטויה

ואלו לא הוציא הקבה את אבותינו ממצרים הרי
אנו בנינו ובני בנינו משועברים היינו לפרע

ואפלו
במצרים כלנו חכמים כלנו
נבונים כלנו זקנים כלנו
יודעים את התורה מצוה
עלינו לספר ביציאת מצרים וכל המספר
ביציאת מצרים הרי זה משבח

לכיסה קורם שיאמר החלל כדי שיאמר עלוה הא לחמא עניא · ומנהג ליטול לך הסל הזרוע והב'צה כדי שלא · יבא
להגביהה כשיאמר פסח שהיה אבותי אובלי' · ונראה כאוכל קדשים בחוץ · ואחר כך מוזגין כוס שני וכדב'מ'וכין
הסל שיש עליו המצוה כדי שיראו התינוק ות וישאל לו · ומנהג להגביה הסל על לבת'ל' זכר למשארוח שם

כך מביאין הקערה ומברכין אשר קד'שנו    על אכילה הזבח    וכשנכרי לאכל החגיגה לפי אין הפסח ואוכל
ובזמן שהל'לה י כניס בשבת אין צריך לא תכשיל אחד שאין חגיגה דוחה שבת ובכל
אתו על השמע

רָאֵלֹ חֲמָא עַנָיָא

אֲכָלוּ אַבָהָתָנָא בְּאַרְעָא דְּמִצְרַיִם כָּל דַּכְפִין
יֵיתֵי וְיֵכוּל כָּל דָּ מַאֹן צָרִיך יֵיתֵי וְיִפְסַח הָא שַׁתָּא
הָכָא לְשָׁנָה הַבָּאָה בְּנֵי דְּעָא דְּיִשְׂרָאֵל הָא שַׁתָּא
הָכָא אֲנַן עַבְדֵי לְשָׁנָה הַבָּאָה בְּאַרְעָא דְיִשְׂרָאֵל

בְּנֵי חֹורִין
הַלַיְלָה    מַה נִּשְׁתַּנָּה

הַזֶּה מִכָּל
הַלֵּילוֹת שֶׁבְּכָל הַלֵּילוֹת אָנוּ אוֹכְלִין חָמֵץ     אוֹ
מַצָּה הַלַּיְלָה הַזֶּה כֻּלּוֹ מַצָּה שֶׁבְּכָל הַלֵּילוֹת אָנוּ

השמש אין צריך לעלות הביצה כי אם הזרוע לבדין לפי שהחגיגה אינה צריכה לחיות על    ירושלמי    שלך לוקחין ביעא
ודרעא כלו ביעא רחמנא לפדרק יתכא דרעא דאתפרע ביימא    והכונה לעלות הזרוע על הנחלים לפי שהפסח    אין
צולין אותו אלא בשפוד של רמון מפני חטעם שאמרו חכמים ז'ל בפסח שני    ואם באנו להפש אחר שפוד של

מכל העמים ושבתו מועדי קדשך בשמחה ` וכששון
הנחלתנו ברוך אתה יי ` מקדש השבת וישראל והזמנים `
ברוך אתה יי ` אלהינו מלך העולם שהחיינו וקיימנו והגיענו
לזמן הזה ` ` ואם חל להיות במוצאי שבת ` אומר בורא
פרי הגפן ` ` אשר בחר בנו ` ברוך אתה יי
אלהינו מלך העולם בורא מאורי האש ` ברוך אתה יי
אלהינו מלך העולם המבדיל בין קדש לחול בין אור לחשך
בין ישראל לגוים בין יום השביעי לששת ימי המעשה
בין קדושת שבת לקדושת יום טוב הבדלת ואת קדשת
את המבדיל בין קדש לקדש ` שהחיינו ` וסימן יקנהז
ושותין כהסבת שמאל ` ` ונוטלין ידיהם ומגביהין את הקע
ואומ ההגדה ` `

מברכין על ארבע כוסות על הנכן לא בסוף כוין שדעתו לשתות עוד
אחד זכר לחנינה יבאא עד הפסח כד ` ש ` לא הלפסח תאכל על השבע
כתד ` לח פינאין הלפסח ומבדכין אשר קדשנו ` על אכילת הלפסח ואוכל ` ממנו כל אחד כזית ואח
והרסת זכר לטיט ולתבן וזרו עו פיעה
שכך היא מגוה טאכל שבח דמקד ` ט
קיע

ידיהם ומברכין על נטילת ידים · ונוטל מן הכרפס
ומטבל בחרוסת · ומברך · ברוך אתה יי אלהינו
מלך העולם בורא פרי האדמה · ואכל ויתן לבני
ביתו · ויקח שתי כיצים ויכצע האחת לשתים
וישים חציה על השלימה · וההציה האחרת יניח
תחת המצה ויסיר מן הסל שני תבשילין כגן זרוע
וביצה · ומוזגין כוס שני ומגביהין את הסל זאו
ההגדה **ואם** חל להיות בשבת או
השמים **ויכלו** והארץ וכל צבאם
ויכל אלהים ביום השביעי מלאכתו אשר עשה וישבת
ביום השביעי מכל מלאכתו אשר עשה ויברך אלהים את
יום השביעי ויקדש אותו כי בו שבת מכל מלאכתו אשר
ברא אלהים לעשות **ברוך** אתה יי אלהינו מלך
העולם אשר בחר בנו מכל ורוממנו מכל
לשון וקדשנו במצותיו ותתן לנו יי אלהינו באהבה שבתות
למנוחה ומועדים לשמחה חגים וזמנים לששון את יום
השבת הזה ויום חג המצות הזה זמן חירותינו באהבה מקרא
קדש זכר ליציאת מצרים כי בנו בחרת ואותנו קדשת

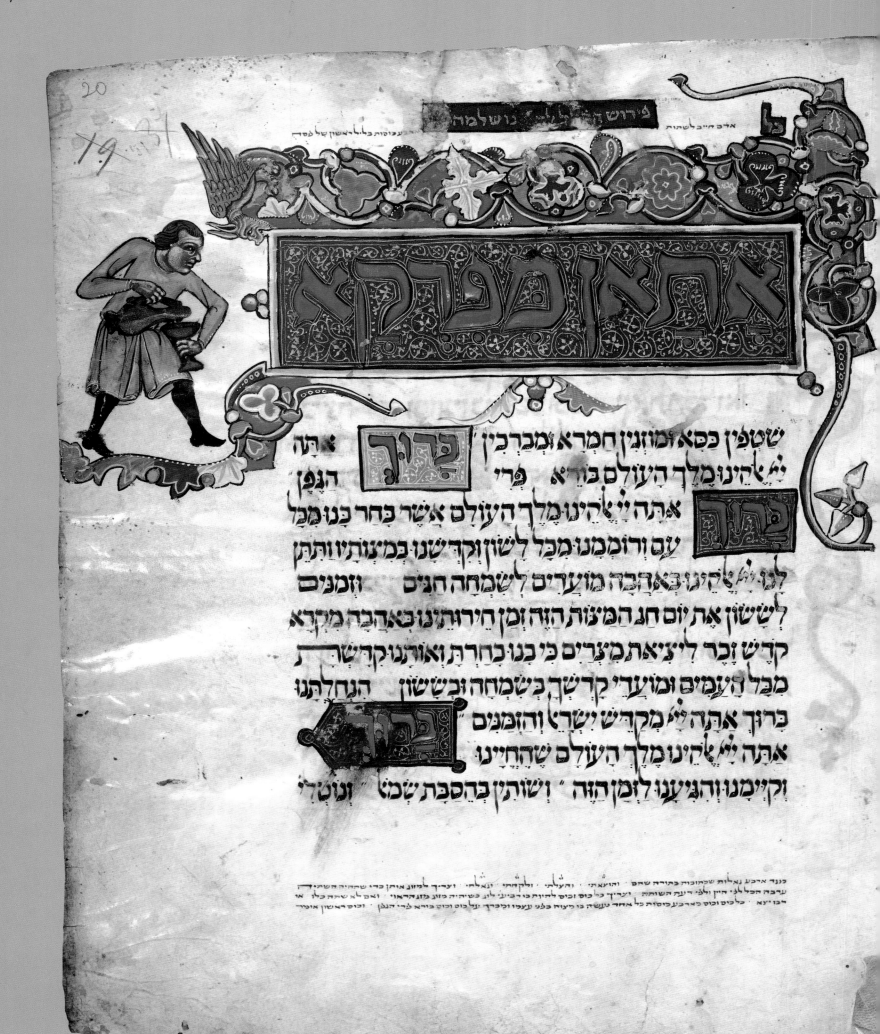

# את"ז מפ"ק"א

שטפין כסא ומוזגין חמרא ומברכין

ברוך

אתה יי' אלהינו מלך העולם בורא פרי

הגפן

פתח

אתה יי' אלהינו מלך העולם אשר בחר בנו מכל

עם ורוממנו מכל לשון וקדשנו במצותיו ותתן

לנו יי' אלהינו באהבה מועדים לשמחה חגים וזמנים

לששון את יום חג המצות הזה זמן חירותנו באהבה מקרא

קדש זכר ליציאת מצרים כי בנו בחרת ואותנו קדשת

מכל העמים ומועדי קדשך בשמחה ובששון הנחלתנו

ברוך אתה יי' מקדש ישראל והזמנים

ברוך

אתה יי' אלהינו מלך העולם שהחיינו

וקיימנו והגיענו לזמן הזה ' ושותין בהסבת שמא ' ונוטלי

כנגד ארבע גאלות שכתובות בתורה שהם והוצאתי ' והצלתי ' וגאלתי ' ולקחתי ' וצריך למזוג אותן כדי שתהיה השתיה
ערבה הכל לפי היין ולפי דעת השותה ' וצריך כל כוס וכוס להיות בו רביעי' לוג כשתהיה מזוג מ?? ??האו ' ואם לא שתה כל ?? או
??וציא ' כל כוס וכוס כארבע כוסות כל אחד נעשה בו מצוה בפני עצמו ומברך על כל כוס וכוס בורא פרי הגפן ' וכוס ראשון אומר

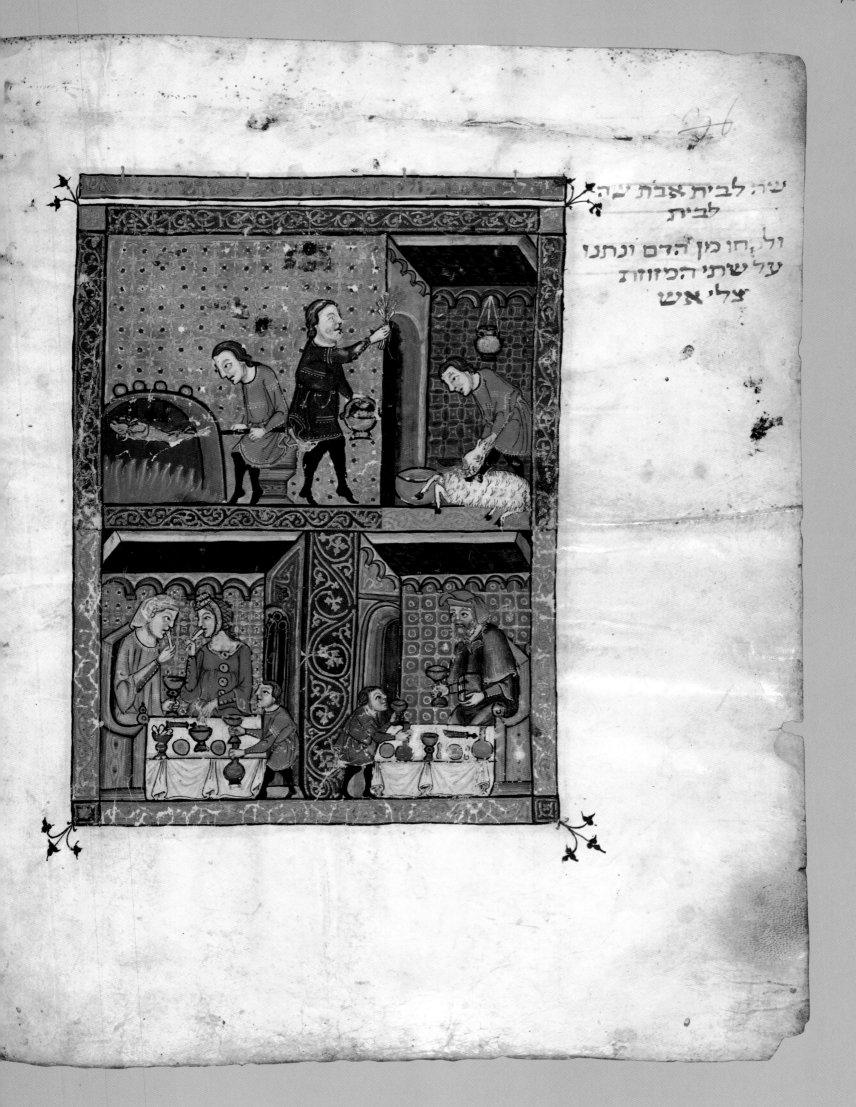

שה לבית אבת שה
לבית

ולקחו מן הדם ונתנו
על שתי המזוזת
צלי אש

ויער יי את מצרי
בתוך הים
ובני ישראל הלכו
ביבשה בתוך הים

34

רעמסס צררות בשמלותם על שכמם וחמשים יצלו בני ישראל

ויאסר את רכבו ואת עמו לקח עמו

18

יק

ותהי צעקה גדולה
במצרים כי אין בית
אשר אין שם מת

ויש נתן את חן העם
בעיני מצרי וישלום
ויצלו את מצרי

ויעל הארבה על
כל ארץ מצרים וינח
בכל גבול מצרים

ויהי חשך אפלה
ולכל בני ישראל
היה אור במושבותם

יהיו שחין אבעבוע
פרח באדם ובבהמה
פיח כבשן
וזרקו משה.

ייר הברד בכל ארץ
מצרים את כל אש
בשדה

ויך הברד בכל ארץ מצרים את כל אשר בשחה

עֲרֹב כָּבֵד בֵּיתָה פַּרְעֹה וּבֵית עֲבָדָיו וְגוֹ׳ יָמֵי עַפְרִיסֶ

וּבֵית עֲבָדָיו

וְשַׂמְתִּי פְדֻת בֵּין עַמִּי וּבֵין עַבֶּ—— נֶשֶׁן

בְּסוּסִים בַּחֲמֹרִים בַּגְּמַלִּים בַּבָּקָר וּבַצֹּאן וְכִי כְבֵּד מְאֹ

בְּסוּסִים בַּחֲמֹרִים בַּגְּמַלִּים בְּבָקָר וּבְצֹאן דֶּבֶר כָּבֵד מְאֹ׳

פרעה חרטמים
ויעל הצפרדע
ותכס את ארץ מצרי

ויט אהרן את ידו במטה
ויך את עפר ואי ץ
ותהי הכנם

פרעה

ויבלע מטה אהרן
את מטותם
חרטמים

פרעה יצ'וצא המימה
דם
משה
אהרן

14

פרעה
כה אמר י'י אלדי
ישראל שלח את עמי
חרטמיב

תכבד העבודה
נוגש
יקושישו להם תבן
לבנם

ויפגשהו בהר האלדי
וישק לו
ויגד משה לאהרן
את כל דברי יי

ויעש האותות לעיני
העם ויאמן העם
ויקדו וישתחוו

14

73

הבאנא ידך בחיקך
והנה ידו מצורעת
השב ידך
והנה שבה כבשרו

מדין
ויקח משה את מטה
האלקים בידו
ותקח צפרה צר
מצרים

משה היה רועה
של נעליך מעל רגלי

מה זה בידך
ויהי לנחש
ויהי למטה בכפו

13.

12

XIX

# ליל שמורים

קראו נורא עלילה     כי בן שכר מוטות עלה

רעוץ ירעץ אום מדכא ואכלה     שנית בן נגאלה

בא״ גאל ישר״

# ליל שמורים

שמעו לעם אהובים     אשר הציל מיד להבים

תשועה היא לבתרבים     בנחת בשלום כלי פחד

שוכבים    ופרוש עלינו סכת שלומך ועל ירושלם עיר קדשך בא״ הפורש סכת שלום

בִּימֵי חַג פֶּסַח פֶּסַח

שֶׁת לְכָל בֵּית וָלָיִל · בְּצֵאת כְּחַצוֹת לָיִל

בִּימֵי חַג פֶּסַח פֶּסַח

תָּכֵן וְחָקַק לְאֹם · לְהַרְאוֹתֵינוּ נִפְלָאוֹת בְּכָל יוֹם

בִּימֵי חַג פֶּסַח פֶּסַח

תְּהִלָּה לְשׁוֹכֵן שְׁחָקִים · תַּקְפוֹ הֵנִיעַ לַקְּרוֹבִים וְלָרְחוֹקִים

תַּקֵּף עֻזּוֹ בַּיָּם מְחוֹקְקִים · תּוּשְׁבָּחוֹת מְשׁוֹרְרִים

וּמְשַׂחֲקִים · מֹשֶׁה וּבְנֵי יִשְׂרָאֵל · עַד · לְפָנֶי נֹשֶׁה

# לֵיל שִׁמּוּרִים

סִימָן הוּא לֶעָתִיד לָבֹא · עָלָיו כִּי בֹא יָבֹא
פָּקוֹד יִפְקוֹד עַם קָרוֹב · צוּרֵנוּ הוּא נָגִילָה וְנִשְׂמָחָה
בּ " · זֶה אֵלִי עָנוּ וְאָמְרוּ

בִּימֵי חַג פֶּסַח פֶּסַח

נְגִינוֹת יָהִיר יַפִּיל וְנִיל עַמּוֹ יַכְפִּיל

בִּימֵי חַג פֶּסַח פֶּסַח

סִנָּר זֵרִים לַדֶּבֶר וְרָפָא עַמּוֹ מִשֶּׁבֶר

בִּימֵי חַג פֶּסַח פֶּסַח

עָבַר כְּלֹא נוֹי שָׁמוֹר וְנָקַם עַמּוֹ כְּאָמוֹר

בִּימֵי חַג פֶּסַח פֶּסַח

פַּחַד בָּתֵּי מִצְרַיִם מֵבִין צַוֵּי נוֹצְרִים

בִּימֵי חַג פֶּסַח פֶּסַח

צְפִירַת צַר בַּעֲלוּקָה כָּנַס לְאֹם הַחֲזֻקָה

בִּימֵי חַג פֶּסַח פֶּסַח

קֶשֶׁר לְצֵר אֲבָדָה וְנֵץ יְדִידִים מֵעֲבוֹדָה

בִּימֵי חַג פֶּסַח פֶּסַח

רְמִים זֵרִים הֲרַסְתָּ וְרֵעֲתִי אֵרַסְתָּ

כִּי יְמֵי חַג פֶּסַח פֶּסַח ··

זֶמֶר בְּנַף נָתַן     לִגְאוֹל בְּנֵי אֵיתָן
כִּי יְמֵי חַג פֶּסַח פֶּסַח ··

חֶרֶב חַדָּה עַל אֱדוֹם     בְּיַד צַח וְאַדוֹם
כִּי יְמֵי חַג פֶּסַח פֶּסַח ··

טְבִיחַת נְגֵי כוּשׁ     וְהוֹצִיא עַמּוֹ בִּרְכוּשׁ
כִּי יְמֵי חַג פֶּסַח פֶּסַח ··

יְדִידוּת קֵן שְׁדוּרָה     כִּנֵּס לְאֵזֶם נְהוּרָה
כִּי יְמֵי חַג פֶּסַח פֶּסַח ··

כָּרַת לִשְׁמוֹ נִסִּים     וְהוֹצִיא עַמּוֹ מִבֵּין פַּתְרוּסִים
כִּי יְמֵי חַג פֶּסַח פֶּסַח ··

לוֹחֲצֵינוּ יִלְחַץ     וְיִרְפָּאֵנוּ מִמַּחַץ
כִּי יְמֵי חַג פֶּסַח פֶּסַח ··

מִלֵּא הֲרִיקָה     וְהִסִּיעַ גֶּפֶן שׂוֹרֵקָה

מחרא · אסור · לאכל כלום אחר הלל מאריה צריכה · נצרה לבר אם תרצא ועד שך בעמרא כאולפך · זכן דיך מים ותשמיח לחלוק לעילון תריסה
כיס · קדיס על נפש ניעלפ · יושר · הליטות וציין דברי הוושעיה · איום לתגביר ואפלר יחרך כנפש דעניה · שוכבי
כיתרה ואז אשורר · ולמסיך רב העולה לכה · לסועד חזה סעה חיה

הַדְּרָשׁוֹת הַמְדַיְּנִין פְּשׁוּכִים · בְּכָה יָאבְלוּ בְּנֵי יִשְׂרָאֵל אֶת הַלֶּחֶם · שֶׁיִּתְעַסְּקוּ בְּעֶזְרָה וְעוֹרְכֶת וְאוֹפֶה כְּוָלֵי וּמְבַקְּעוֹל ·
קְטַן וְחָדָשׁ וְיִשְׁטְחוּ אַל יְבוּשׁוּ מֵדְיֹבֵי וְהַלֵּל · קָבוּן מִי הַגָּפוֹת · קְרָאוּ · יְשַׁלְּכוּ בְּמָקוֹם סְדָרִין וּמַצִּ'לְוֹל · נְכוֹיָה וְהַלֵּלֹל ·

בָּרוּךְ אַתָּה יְיָ אוֹהֵב עַמּוֹ יִשְׂרָאֵל · שְׁמַע יִשְׂרָאֵל · אֱמֶת וֶאֱמוּנָה

יַעַד וּמַלְכוּתוֹ · בְּרָצוֹן קִבְּלוּ עֲלֵיהֶם וְאוֹמְ

# לֵיל שמורים

אָכְלוּ פְחוֹזִים נִפְלָאוֹת חוֹזִים · בִּימֵי חַג פֶּסַח פֶּסַח

בָּאנוּ לִשְׁמוֹר הַדּוֹרוֹת · פְּנֵה לָנוּ לְהוֹרוֹת

בִּימֵי חַג פֶּסַח פֶּסַח

נֵזֶר עֲנָוֵי אֱמוּנִים · אַרְבַּע עֲמָאוֹת נֶאֱמָנִים

בִּימֵי חַג פֶּסַח פֶּסַח

רַת שָׁבוּעִים יִמָּלֵא · וְזוּם נָקָם יִגָּלֶה

בִּימֵי חַג פֶּסַח פֶּסַח

הַרְגְּנֵנִי חֵם · וּבֵן בְּכוֹר וָרֶחֶם

בִּימֵי חַג פֶּסַח פֶּסַח

וַיַּעַד לִשְׁפּוֹט מַרְשִׁיעִים · לְהַעֲלוֹת מוֹשִׁיעִים

רָאוּ · לְהָיוֹת הָעֵדָה פָּאַרְבָּעָה וְשָׁלֹשׁ מִיטִין וְלַקֶּשׁ בַּ'רְבָה לְהַלָּיְלָה · רֵאשִׁית הַעֲשִׂיָּה לַהֲבָרִיוֹת שְׁתֵּי חַלּוֹת תְּרוּגְיָה ·
הֶחָשׁוּ שֶׁרָא וְלֶעְנוּס אָדָם הַטִּין דָּשׁוֹב עַד מִרְמִי רְטַיֵּב · פֶּ'עֶג וְהֶהָדַר וּפְכָה טְרֵיב · שָׁמְרוּ
שֶׁתִּקַּנְתָּה הַנָּשִׁים וְחֵירוֹת פָּאַנְשִׁים עָזָיֵב · שֶׁעֲבַד לְחַוֵּר קַשְׁתָּיו תָּחַר יָד פֶּ'צֵיֵב וְסִכְלֵיהֶם ·

מאהליכם · ועיניך אל תחוס אל פליכם · יין · עלי להשריכו
במים חיים ברחו כך פרלטו כרולע · צריכת · תחרך אכן יש פר מים הרים ודי אתו תתום כאשר עליו · והוציאתי

# סדר הפסח

ערב הפסח מתפללין תפלת מנחה שמנה עשרה ואין נופלין על פניהם
לערבית פותח שליח צבור ברכו כמו שבת · וכשיניע ומכביר כן יום וכן לילה קרי"ט זה הקבל אומ

## ליל שמורים

אורתו אל חצה · כחצות הלילה בתוך מצרים
כיצא · נבור על אדום יחזנו כחצה · הורמעריב
ערב נזמרנו בנפש חפצה · בא"י המעריב ערבים

אהבת עולם כות · וכו

## ליל שמורים

הוא זה הלילה · ועתדנו כחצות הלילה · זה אשר
לו יום ונם לילה · חק אהבתו יזכור לניני חלק לילה

את פלע · פקורי · הכליכ קרכונים בדכ הדבק כאשר לרשתי · לכה הלדע עני שמיר בעשויר אשר הזהרתי למחזון לה · יתיה דר לאלר טוב לי כי נני ירפ מנעתי · קטעניב כאשר אי יר · צריכות כיצות חרק לכה שני כלים מיצנה וכ הטפה זכיים · ציוני שלא לישי לשמש לן יהדיקנצו העריות ברמם · עזיני לעד

**יחד** מצה וחזרת שניה · בכרך אחד בריך · ואכלהו צרב · ולא יפטיר אחר מצה
אפיקומן קשתה זרך · ידיו נטל ומזג כוס שלישי לאכד על מזונו הנגערך
יהי שם יי מבורך

**צפנתי** כוס רביעי לגמור הלל וברכת השיר · ואחריו ברכה אחרונה לכל שקוני צבעתי
לשהותבין הכוסות הללו יער השלישי שתיתי רד · צמאתי בין שלישי לר ביעי
מנעתי מיין ושכר מאויי · כן אברכך בחיי

**חביתי** נרמות כמוסות · והבטחות מאז צפונות · חסדים חדשים לבקרים למיחלים רבות אמונת
חליפות שמלות תלבישגי בגדי ישועות אחרונות
ולא תזכרנה הראשונות

**קבץ** להר צבי קדש · נפוצות יהודה ואפרים · קרן ישועה תצמיח לשוכבים בין שפתים
קול נשאו צופי · צפה כימי צאתך מארץ מצרים
וראה בטוב ירושלם

**פזמון**

| | | |
|---|---|---|
| זמרה עם נכאה | ורפה ידים | לרם על כל ונאה · רוכב שמים |
| | יעתרך למראה · זהר וקרנים | מציון וראה בטוב ירושלם |
| רצה בן דלי וחזלה | כמוסר אב מיסר · ואל תקון בכלא | ובמאסר אזסר |
| זאם מבוזז מלא | את ומטוב חסר | מנך חיט יעלה · את שבטו ויסר |
| | ראה רגלי מיסר | כאחד הצביים · מציון |
| חפשי יהנך | מאשר בך עוד | ליעבד יקנך · לו ובכן הכבד |
| וישיב כהניך | לובשי בגדי כר | והיה מחניך · אזי קרוש ונכבד |
| | והסונר לכולבד | ימחין מתנים · מציון |
| יהיו לך רחמי | אהי הצבאות · צנה מרזמי | בך חצי קנאות |
| וישלח ציד חזמי | ליעפר הצבאות · לרוזתך כמימי | ישוגעות נפלאות |
| | כימי צאתך מ · ה · ארץ מצרים · מציון |

**ככתו** כימי צאתך מארץ מצרים אראנו נפלאות · ונ יברכך יי מציון וראה בטוב ירושלם כל ימי חייך · ונ כי הנני בורא שמים חדשים וארץ חדשה ולא תזכרנה הראשונות ולא תעלינה על לב · ונא כי אם שישו וגילו עדי עד אשר אני בורא כי הנני בורא את ירושלם גילה ועמה משוש · קדיש · יעד ואמרו אמן

אֿרֿבֿעֿ וֿלֿהֿלֿוֿת כָל הַבֿיֿש וֿלֿשֿרֿוֿן פֿ כְהֿלֿת שֿט לֿהֿכֿמֿיֿאֿיֿם לֿרֿיֿום    יְכֿהֿרֿי שֿמֿא יֿוֿם כֿעֿגֿ יֿרֿקֿתֿא לֿגֿרֿא וֿאֿיֿום

וֿהֿתֿבֿ חֿרֿהֿי עֿד נֿטֿוֿרֿה ...    כְשֶׁתֻּצֵא    בֿדֿך אֿם קֿוֿדֿם לֿשֿלֿשֿים יֿום וֿמֿגֿעֿיֿל בֿמֿיֿד וֿהֿכֿלֿאֿים    כֿד אֿכֿרֿה

יְכֿטֿל    כֻלֿבֿו הֿוֿלֿך לֿמֿצֿוֿה וֿנֿזֿכֿר לֿחֿמֿיֿן אֿם אֿיֿנֿו יֿכֿול לֿחֿזֿור עֿד כֿה וֿעֿד כֿה    יֵלֶךְ

לֿשֿחֿוֿטֿ אֿת פֿסֿחֿו וֿלֿא יֿתֿמֿהֿמֿה עֿד יֿהֿי כֿשֿלֿם סֿכֿו    יֿמֿול בֿנֿו וֿיֿסֿעֿור בֿבֿית חֿמֿיֿו

מֿמֿתֿקֿי חֿכֿו    וְיֿאֿחֿז צֿדֿיֿק דֿרֿכֿו

הָפוֹךְ    יָדֶךְ אֿם תֿלֿך לֿשֿבֿיֿת הֿרֿשֿוֿת וֿשֿוֿב לֿבֿעֿר בֿחֿזֿקֿה    הֿמֿצֿיֿל מֿן הֿגֿוֿיֿם וֿמֿן הֿנֿהֿר

הֿמֿפֿלֿת וֿמֿן הֿדֿלֿיֿקֿה    הֿחֿמֿיֿן תֿבֿטֿל בֿלֿבֿך וֿלֿבֿעֿר כֿל עֿיֿקֿר אֿין חֿזֿרֿתֿך זֿקֿוֿקֿה

וְלֿבֿא וֿהֿיֿה צְדָקָה

הַמְלָאכות    הַמֻּתָּרוֹת בֿאֿרֿבֿעֿה עֿשֿר עֿשֿה עֿל פֿי חֿכֿמֿיֿך    הַחַיָּטִים וֿהֿסֿפֿרֿים וֿהֿכֿוֿבֿסֿים

עֿוֿשֿים כֿדֿרֿכֿם בֿעֿמֿמֿיֿך    הֿזֿרֿים שֿנֿתֿנֿו שֿלֿא לֿעֿשֿוֿת עֿד חֿצֿוֿת נֿהֿוֿג כֿמֿנֿהֿג מֿקֿוֿמֿיֿך

וֿלֿא הֿטֿוֿש תֿוֿרֿת אֿמֿך

לְעָבֿךְ    סָמוּך לְמִנְחָה לֿא יֿאֿכֿל אֿדֿם עֿד שֿחֿשֿיֿכֿה    לֿא יֿאֿכֿל עֿד שֿיֿסֿב בֿשֿמֿאֿל הֿדֿרֿך

חֿירֿות נֿסֿוֿכֿה    לֿא יֿפֿחֿתֿו לֿו מֿאֿרֿבֿעֿ כֿוֿסֿות לֿמֿסֿבֿתֿו הֿעֿרֿוֿכֿה

וֿנֿתֿתֿי אֿוֿתֿם וֿסֿכֿיֿבֿוֿת גֿבֿעֿתֿי בֿרֿכֿה

וְשֵׂיעוֹר    כָל כוֹס רְבִיעִית כֿמֿזֿיֿנֿה יֿפֿה כֿאֿשֿיֿשֿך    וֿכֿלֿס צֿרֿיֿכֿים הֿסֿבֿה לֿך וֿלֿבֿיֿתֿך בֿנֿיֿך

וֿשֿמֿשֿיֿך    וֿהֿמֿרֿוֿר אֿין צֿרֿיֿך הֿסֿבֿה כֿי כֿן הֿוֿרֿו יֿשֿיֿשֿיֿך

וֿאֿכֿלֿתֿ כֿשֿאֿצֿרֿיֿך בֿכֿל אֿוֿת נֿפֿשֿך

יַיִן    וֿקֿדֿוֿש הֿיֿום סֿדֿר עֿל כֿוֿס רֿאֿשֿוֿן כֿמֿעֿנֿך    יֿטֿבֿוֿל טֿבֿוֿל רֿאֿשֿוֿן בֿבֿרֿכֿת פֿרֿי

הֿאֿדֿמֿה בֿאֿחֿד מֿכֿל יֿרֿק גֿנֿך    יֿעֿקֿרֿו הֿשֿלֿחֿן לֿעֿוֿרֿר כֿשֿאֿלֿתֿם אֿרֿבֿעֿ בֿנֿיֿך

כֿשֿתֿלֿי וֿתֿיֿס סֿבֿיֿב לֿשֿלֿחֿנֿך

בָּא    שֿלֿחֿן שֿנֿיֿה בֿמֿצֿה וֿחֿזֿרֿת וֿחֿרֿסֿת וֿשֿנֿי תֿבֿשֿיֿלֿין מֿצֿוֿתֿו    בֿמֿזֿיֿנֿת הֿשֿנֿי וֿכֿאֿן הֿבֿן

טֿוֿאֿל כֿפֿי דֿעֿתֿו שֿאֿלֿתֿו    בֿגֿנֿוֿת מֿתֿחֿיֿל וֿמֿסֿיֿם    כֿשֿבֿח וֿדֿוֿרֿש עֿד שֿנֿוֿמֿר פֿרֿשֿתֿו

טֿוֿב אֿחֿרֿית דֿבֿר מֿרֿאֿשֿיֿתֿו

רֶמֶז    בֿהֿגֿבֿהֿתֿו מֿצֿה זֿו וֿמֿרֿוֿר זֿה    עֿל שֿוֿם מֿה לֿמֿלֿל    רֿצֿף בֿשֿרֿו שֿלֿא לֿהֿגֿבֿיֿהֿו שֿלֿא

יֿרֿאֿה כֿקֿדֿשֿי שֿמֿיֿם כֿמֿחֿלֿל    רֿנֿן שֿבֿח וֿהֿוֿדֿאֿה לֿשֿם עֿם שֿנֿי פֿרֿקֿים מֿן הֿהֿלֿל

וֿשֿפֿתֿי רֿנֿגֿוֿת יֿהֿלֿל

בֵּרֵךְ    אֿשֿר גֿאֿלֿנֿו וֿגֿאֿל אֿת אֿבֿוֿתֿיֿנֿו    וֿשֿתֿה כֿוֿסֿו רֿוֿיֿה    בֿטֿבֿוֿל שֿנֿי נֿטֿל יֿדֿיֿו וֿבֿרֿך

עֿל נֿטֿיֿלֿתֿו שֿנֿיֿה    בֿרֿך שֿתֿים וֿכֿצֿע בֿצֿוֿע אֿחֿד בֿתֿוֿך שֿלֿיֿמֿה מֿן הֿרֿצֿה

יֿצֿפֿון לֿישֿרֿים תֿושֿיֿה

יָדוֹ    שֿלֿח לֿחֿזֿרֿת וֿבֿרֿך בֿרֿכֿת מֿרֿוֿר לֿטֿעֿם    יֿטֿבֿוֿל בֿחֿרֿסֿת וֿיֿזֿהֿר בֿירֿקֿת שֿלֿא

וֿשֿקֿיֿעֿם    יֿסֿוֿרֿתֿו פֿטֿום קֿהֿה וֿנֿבֿוֿל עֿבֿה    בֿמֿיֿנֿי תֿבֿלֿין כֿתֿוֿבֿו אֿתֿקֿעֿם

כֿטֿיֿט חֿוֿצֿוֿת אֿריֿכֿם אֿרֿקֿעֿם

שֿאֿלֿתֿה חֿיֿיֿב לֿבֿעֿרֿס וֿכֿהֿלֿמֿת יֿקֿדֿרֿאֿס    לֿוֿה    כֿל שֿאֿוֿר וֿכֿל חֿמֿץ שֿגֿתֿד רֿ כֿיֿס אֿו בֿדֿרֿבֿר וֿאֿמֿרֿם וֿבֿרֿשֿוֿתֿד אֿל אֿכֿם    חֿרֿס

וֿרֿוֿד תֿשֿאֿס    וֿגֿתֿבֿ    לֿהֿנֿי    תֿאֿכֿים שֿתֿגֿרֿד בֿמֿצֿוֿ גֿבֿה    לֿעֿשֿוֿת מֿחֿי רֿה בֿרֿגֿיֿהֿם מֿרֿירֿו לֿחֿבֿרֿ לֿי עֿעֿן

וֿיֿטֿאֿה    חֿמֿין שֿחֿכֿבֿ גֿי אֿו יֿצֿאֿו וֿלֿפֿסֿד לֿבֿטֿוֿתֿו בֿעֿגֿ אֿתֿו דֿאֿה    בֿעֿגֿ

| | | |
|---|---|---|
| קְבַל | אַפּוּ שֶׁבִּשְׁלוּ וְחָלוּט בְּמַיִם רוֹתְחִין חֲלָטוּהוּ · קַמָּח שֶׁנָּפַל לְתוֹכוֹ דְּלוֹ טוֹרֵד | |
| | הֻתַּר בַּמֵּימָז שֶׁהֵטִיפוּהוּ · קִיְּמוּ וְהוֹרִים שֶׁלֹּא לְלָתוֹת וְשֶׁלֹּא לַחְלוֹט · וְאֵין | |
| | לִפְרוֹין גֶּדֶר נְדָרוּהוּ · אֵת אֲשֶׁר כְּבָר עֲשׂוּהוּ | |
| רְקִיק | הַשָּׁרוּי יוֹצְאֵין בּוֹ · וּכְבָשֵׁל אַל תְּבַשֵּׁל כְּמַהֲלָכְיךְ · דְּיֵן לְמַצָּה מִשְׁמֶרֶת | |
| | וּלְהַשָּׁלִים חֲטִים מַחְמִיצוֹת קִנְכַּב עַל יָדֵי חֲנִיכְיךָ · רַחֵק מִבַּלַּתְּקֵדֵרוֹת קְמַח | |
| | וְחָמֵץ וְקָמָח בַּחֲרֹסֶת וְחָרַד לֵאל יְהוּ בְּמַעֲרָכֶיךָ · הַמַּיִם תִּהְיֶה עִם יְיָ אֱלֹהֶיךָ | |
| שְׁפּוֹךְ | כְּמוֹרֵד מִי תַשְׁמִיטוֹ שֶׁלֹּא נְחַתּוֹז · לִרְחִיצַת כֵּלִים וְיָדַיִם · שֶׁהֵם מַחְמִיצִים וְנִמְצָאת | |
| | יַעֲכֹר בִּשְׁהִיָּתָם · עַל מִצְוֹת לְהוֹי הַשָּׁמַיִם · שֶׁאֵל לַלּוּשׁ יַעֲשֶׂה מַיִם קָרִים כְּמִצְוֹת | |
| | עֲמוּסֵי יְרֵיבַיִם · לֹא אָמַר לָנוּ הַמָּיִם | |
| תִּזָּהֵר | הָאִשָּׁה שֶׁלֹּא תָלוּשׁ בַּחַמָּה · וּכְחַמִּין וּכְחַמֵּי חַמָּה · תִּרְחַק מִן הַמֵּעַן וּמִמַּיִם | |
| | הַגְּרוּפִים · וְאַל תַּנַּח יָדָהּ מִתְּנוּרָהּ יַד שֶׁתִּהְיֶה כְּלֹא כַבַּדָּה תַּמָּה · תִּקְחֶדָה שְׁתֵּי כֵלִים | |
| | לִקַּטֵף וּלְנַצֵּן · וְאִם עָבְרָה וְלָשָׁה תִּשָּׂא עָוֹן וְאַשְׁמָה · פְּתֵיתוֹת וְכָל יְרֵעֶתָה פֶּה | |
| אֵלּוּ | עוֹבְרִין בְּפֶסַח · אַרְבַּעַת מִינֵי מְדִינָה וּשְׁלֹשֶׁת מִינֵי אֻמָּנֹת · אָבָר כַּתָּה הַכְּבָלִי | |
| | וְשֵׁכָר הַמָּדִי וְזֵיתוֹס הַמִּצְרִי · וְחָמֵץ שְׂעֹרִים אֲדֹמִיֹּת · אָפְסוֹ וְזוֹמָא שֶׁל | |
| | צַבַּעִין וַעֲמִלָן שֶׁל טַבָּחִים וְקִלֵּן שֶׁל סוֹפְרִים הַמַּשֵּׁיר לְטַפּוּל מַנּוֹת עֲנִיֹּת · עָבְדוּ | |
| נִמְצָא | בָּצֵק בְּסִדְקֵי עֲרִיבָה · בְּכָל מָקוֹם אוֹ פָחוֹת שֶׁלֹּא בְּמָקוֹם לִישָׁה חַיָּב לְבַעֲרוֹ · נָתַן עָבָרֵן קְמַח | |
| | נִרְאֶה פָּחוֹת מִכַּזַּיִת · שֶׁלֹּא בְּמָקוֹם לִישָׁה מוֹתָר לְהַשְׁאִירוֹ · עָד מְהֵרָה יָרוּיִן דְּבָרָו | |
| | לָעֲרִיבָה הוֹךְ שְׁלֹשָׁה לַפֶּסַח אַתָּה חַיָּב לְבַעֲרוֹ | |
| יוֹם | אֶחָד אוֹ שָׁעָה אַחַת הַבַּר · אִם לְתוֹכָהּ יְעֹרֹת יְנַעֵר · יַנִּיחַ רְטִיָּה וְאֶסְפְּלָנִירֵת | |
| | וּמְלוּגְמָא שֶׁנַּסְרָחָה וְקִלְוֹר לְעַיִן מִצְטַעֵר · יָרְדָה פַּת לְעִפּוּשׁ אִם לֹא נִפְסְלָה | |
| | מִכְּלֹב שֶׁפְּזוֹ פּוֹעֵר · זָהֶה לְאָדָם לְבַעֵר | |
| זִמּוּן | שְׁלֹשָׁה נָשִׁים לַתַּנּוּר אֶחָד · יְעֹסוּקוֹת וְתָבִּעֲשֶׂה כְּהִלְכָתָהּ · זוֹ לֹשָׁה וְזוֹ מְקַטֶּפֶת | |
| | וְזוֹ אֹפָה כְּמִצְוֹתָהּ · זֹאת חֲזַרְבֶן חֲלִילָה עַד שֶׁתִּגְמֹר כָּל אַחַת אֲפִיָּתָהּ · נָשִׁים בָּאוֹת מְאִירוֹת אֹתָהּ | |
| רֵאשִׁית | עֲרִיסוֹתֵיכֶם שֶׁבַּעַה רַבָּעִים קַמֵחֲזְעוֹר · לַפֶּסַח וְלַחֲדָשָׁה הַתְּרוּמָה · רָאתָה נִדָּה וְנִטְמָאת | |
| | עָסְתָה בְּיוֹם טוֹב · לֹא תִקְרָא אֵלֶּה שֵׁם יַעַד שֶׁתֵּאָפֶה בִּשְׁמָהּ · רֹאשׁ קְרִיאַת הַשֵּׁם | |
| | מְבָרֶכֶת שֵׁם הָאֵל כִּאֵימָה · פִּיהָ פָּתְחָה בְּחָכְמָה | |
| חֲרֵיֹסוּת | בָּצֵק אִם כָּיוֹצֵא מֵחֲמִין · אוֹ בְּכַרְמֵיל הַתַּעֲלַם · הֶקַּה אַחַת לַשִּׂיאוֹר בְּקַרְדָּנִי | |
| | חֲנַכִים · וּלְסִידּוֹק כְּהַבְּרֵת לָאֹכֵל · חַל אַרְבָּעָה עָשָׂר בְּשַׁבָּת חֹזְדִין | |
| | וּתְרוּמָה בִּיעֹרֵים יַחַר בְּזִמַנָם יַשְׁלָם · כִּי יְרֵא אֱלֹהִים יֵצֵא אֶתכֻּלָּם | |

**טמון** כמפלת שנפלה עליו הרי הוא כמכוער וכלבו יבטלנו טפחים יותר משלשה כדי שהכלב לא יחפשנו טהרת כלי השמיש ברותחין כבלעו ככה יפלטנו חיל בלע יקיאנו ומבטנו יורישנו

**יורה** וקומקמוסין ומיחם וכל כלי שבאור מהזכהב ישטף כלי יעם שפודין של ברזל וכלי נחשת מוזהב יחר יעם יעץ פרור וסכינין כרותחין ובכל כלרא שזןהב גם הנצב אחר הלהב

**כפת** וקערות שליעץ או שלמתכת שפוך עליהם מזורה לקערה כחס על שברון כלי חרס ועל קדרתו יענו צרה פלו ימי הפסח התרה ונאסרה וחזרה והתרה אחת מהנה לא נשברה

**לאכול** כל ארבעו ותהלות כל חמש היו הנחוין לשרוף בתחלת שש ולזרות לרוח יחפרו להטילים לבל ימצא יהי נבזה נפוץ ולא שם לו יעל פני חוץ

**מותר** בחגאתו אחר זמנו אם מקדם זמנו חרבו שעה משלנכרי אחר הפסח אכילתו והנאתו לא נמנעה משלישראל אסור אם בעיניו יעמד ולא כתיע וזבת משוקצה חטאים תרדף רעה

**נשתמש** בכלי חמיץ בצונן מותר להישתמש בומצה נודעבית שאור וכלי קונא באסור בהלבו קרוצה נרמה אוכלמצה ביערב הפסח משיע שעזות ולמיעלה לבא על ארוסתו לישמצה אוהב פשיע אזהב כמצה

**סופגנין** ודובשען ואסקרטין ממצוותמצה מניעזה שלך סלת נקיה והדראה הוזהרו ואפלו כמדצתו של שלמה המלך סריקן המצונזירין אין עושין כיאס לחם עני וחלך אל תתהדר לפני מלך

**יעסה** כל יעיקר אין לשין בשמן ורביעוין עוגתמצות הוזהרו כחלב בשני וכלבר כצורת עין ערך לחם פראשון בכל אלה אין כי כוזבים

דרריך מיין

**פרוס** חטה ושיעורה וכסמת שבלת שועל ושיפון לרמך פנה לחהזרת ועול שין המכה וחרחבינה זמרור למיניעמיך פרוסה קחתלברך שם סמכין מזוניך ומטיעמיך יברך את לחמך ואת מימיך

**צויה** שלא לשרות מורסן לתרנוגלין אבל חולטין יעצרה אשה למרחץ לא תשרה מורסן בבירה כרהטים צומרת ושטפה על בשרה יבש ואין ליעסין עלגבי מכה החטים אלה היעדות והחקים והמשפטים

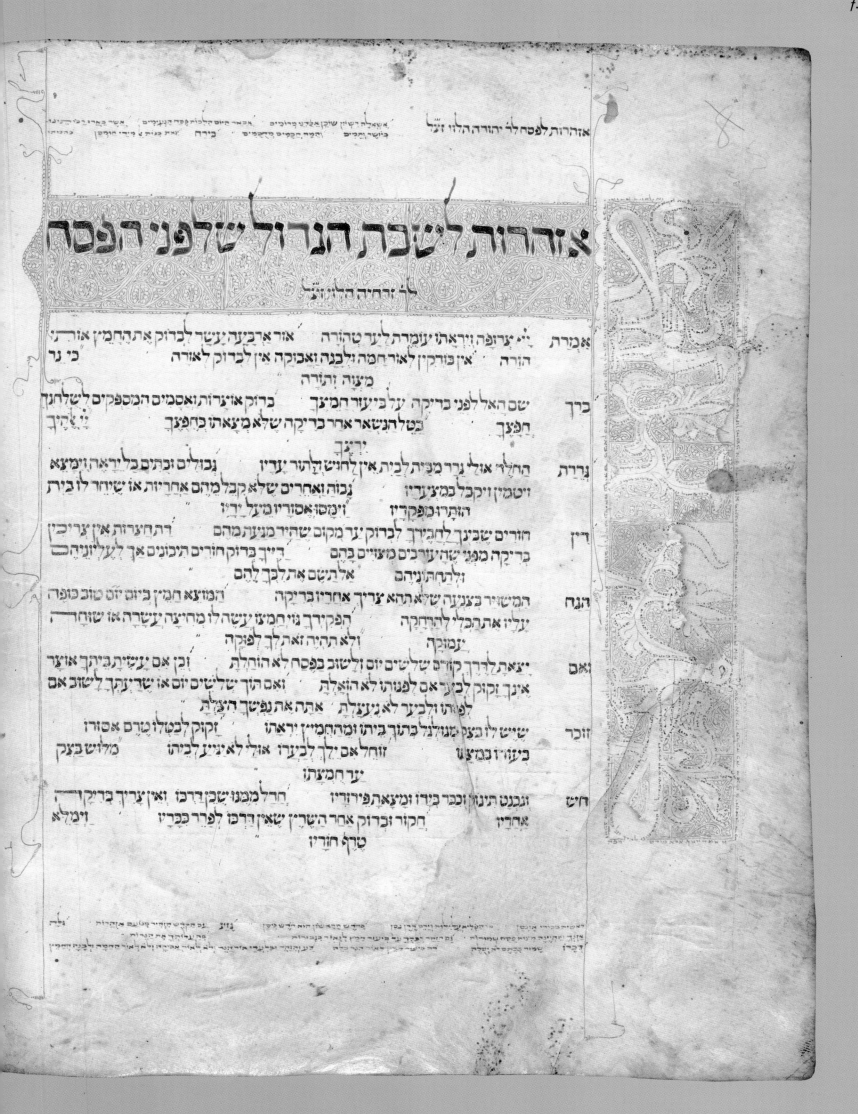

אזהרות לפסח לר' יהודה הלוי זצ"ל

# אזהרות לשבת הנרות שלפני הפסה
## לר' זכריה הלוי ז"ל

אמרת יי' צרופה וזראתו יעמרת לעד טהורה · אור ארבעה עשר לבדוק אתה מן אורה הורה · אין בודקין לאור חמה ולבנה ואבוקה אין לבדוק לאורה · מצוה זהורה

ברך שם האל לפני בדיקה על ביעור המיץ ברוק אוצרות ואסמים המספקים לשלחנך חפצך בטל הנשאר אחר בדיקה שלא תמצאהו כחפצך יצוינך

נרות התחל אול נרו מבית מבית אין לחוניט ולתור ידיו נכולים וכתיב כל ידיאה ומצא זיטמין ויכבל כמ'צעריו נכוה ואחרים שלא קבל מהם אחריות או שיחד לו בית התירו כפקדרין וימסו אסוריו מעל ידיו

דין חורים שבינך לחבירך לבדוק יער מקום שהיר מנעת מהם דתה חצרות אין צריכין בדיקה מפני שהעורבים מצויים בהם דייך בדוק חורים תיכונים אך לעליונים ולה חתהניהם אל תשם את לבך להם

הנה המשוי בצנעה שלא תהא צריך אחריו בדיקה המוצא חמץ ביום יום טוב כופה עליו את הכלי להדחקה הפקירב נוי חמצו יעשה לו מחיצה יעשרה או שוחר ימוקה ולא תהיה זאת לך לפוקה

ואם יצאת לדרך קודם שלשים יום ולשוב בפסח לא הוחלת וכן אם עשית ביתך אוצר אינך זקוק לבער אם לפנותו לא האלת ואם תוך שלשים יום או שדעתך לשוב אם לפיתו ולבער לא הנצלת אתה את נפשך הצלת

זוכר שייט לו בצק מנו'על כתוך ומחמין יראתו זקוק לבטלו טרם אסודו ביעור ונמצאו זוחל אם ילך לביערו אולו לא הניע לביתו מלוש בצק יער חמצתו

חוש וגבנט תינו וכבר בידו ומצאת פירודין חדל ממנו שכן דדכו ואין צריך בדיקה אחריו הכור וברדוק אחר השרץ שאין דדכו לפרר כפריו וימלא טרף חוריו

ראשית כברידי אונטן ... עס הקדש הודיר קונם אזהרות ... נלה
הזהב ותחנה ... עד יזהר ... מן גבודה את הנרות
דכרו שמור ... דע יהנסד ... לבני הכפץ

5

מבית תעתע אדונים קשה קֹלֹ אֶרֶץ

אפרים ומנשה יֹ

מבית חשך אפלים קֹלֹ ב

לשנה הבאה בירֹ

בירושלם

יפתי ולכי לך :

ככתוב התאנה חנטה פגיה והגפנים סמדר

נתנו ריח קומי לך רעיתי יפתי ולכי לך : :

תם ונשלם

תהלה

לאל

עולם :

אמן

חזק

מבית סורד מגריז רעות    קל אר‎ץ
הרים ובקעות זול

מבית עולל דמה לסחבה    קל אר‎ץ
טובה ורחבה זול

מבית פצח צוארי חרוזי    קל אר‎ץ
הכנעני והפריזי זול

מבית צלמות בשכנות    קל אר‎ץ
אשר לא כמסכנות זול

מבית קצת חתן וחותן    קל אר‎ץ
אשר ייי להידעיתן זול

מבית רכתה חבלותיה    קל אר‎ץ
כנען לגבולותיה זול

מבית שדיחו ענבי רוט    קל אר‎ץ
דגן ותירוש זול

מכית חוף דלים עזל    קלו ארץ

אשר אעניה הברזל   יול

מכית טופל שקר וכזה    קלו ארץ

הגלער לאחוזה   יול

מכית יהיר און חורש    קלו ארץ

אשרי אלהידרו   יול

מכית כלא מצור חרמים    קלו ארץ

לחם וכרמים   יול

מכית לוחן על ובעלב    קלו ארץ

זבת חלב   יול

מכית מון דעתי דיני    קלו ארץ

אחזת יי   יול

מכית נכל אוכל עד    קלו ארץ

יער וארץ צעד יול

מבית און שבת מדני     קלי ארץ
אחזת י׳     יול

מבית בוגד ביתמטן     קלי ארץ
הכנעני והלבטן     יול

מבית גוי צוך כבט     קלי ארץ
זבת חלב ודבש     יול

מבית דולק חמתו בעדה     קלי ארץ
חטה ושיערה     יול

מבית הובדי שמים     קלי ארץ
נחלי מים     יול

מבית ווכח הקישה הארץ     קלי ארץ
הכנעני והחתי     יול

מבית זר לישחתך אבה     קלי ארץ
אשר לא יגעתבה יול

פֶּסַח מצרים ספי לא בא המשחית פֶּסַח

דורות עריין גבה לבו עד להש ֿחית

פֶּסַח מצרים פדויי מהרו לישלחם פֶּסַח

דורות צרי אך בי נלחם

פֶּסַח מצרים קדושים נתן לדרחן פֶּסַח

דורות תודה פני עניי טורחן

פֶּסַח מצרים ישאל האשה משכנֿ פֶּסַח

דורות שפחה התר שת גבירתה

פֶּסַח מצרים תורתו מצה ומרור פֶּסַח

דורות תקרא לישבויים דירור

ככתוב ייען מישח יי אותי לבישר ענוים שדֿ

ישלחני לקרוא לישבוים דרור ולאסירים

פקח רוח קומי לך רעיתי יפתי ולכי לךֿ

מבית

פסח. מצרים אסירי יצאו חפשים פסח
דורות בעלונו אדונים נפשים

פסח מצרים נאלת בזרוע עזך פסח
דורות דוממתי מפני זעמך

פסח מצרים הכית בה הסכל בכורה פסח
דורות ולדי נוצצו לעבורה

פסח מצרים זבחו שה לבית אבות פסח
דורות חטפוהו זאבי ערבות

פסח מצרים טעמוהו חגור מתנים פסח
דורות ישבתי כיושבת אבנים

פסח מצרים כתם דמו היה לאות פסח
דורות לבי סחרחר לתלאות

פסח מצרים מושיעם בזענו הציל. פסח
דורות נערו אריות ואין מציל

ר אֵה סֵפֶר יְלִיד סֵפֶר בְּצַלְמוֹ · פְּנֵי זֶה כִּפְנֵי זֶה בִּדְמוּתוֹ ·

פְּ אַר הַדּוֹר שְׁמוֹ יָצָא לְמֶרְחָק · רְחוֹקִים יוּכְלוּ עַתָּה רְאוֹתוֹ ·

אַ נִי אֶצְלוֹ מְיֻלֶּדֶת בְּמַשְׁבֵּר · וְעַל חֶלְקִי אֲנִי מוֹדָה בְּלִדְתּוֹ ·

לְ שׁוֹן שִׁירָה קָשַׁת־הָבֵין לָרַבִּים · בְּנֵי עַם כִּמְעַט שָׁכַח שְׂפָתוֹ ·

הֵ פַכְתִּיהָ וְתִרְגַּמְתִּי בְּשִׁירָה · לְשׁוֹן אַנְגְּלִית · וְכָל שׁוֹרֵר בְּבֵיתוֹ ·

לְ דַבֵּר כִּלְשׁוֹן עַמּוֹ יְבָרֵךְ · אֲשֶׁר עוֹלֵל וְלָקַח שְׁכָחָתוֹ ·

וְ יִשְׁתַּבַּח אֲשֶׁר עָזַר וְעוֹדֵד · עֲנָוִים בַּעֲשׂוֹתָם אֶת מְלַאכְתּוֹ ·

יְ רוֹמֵם אוֹהֲבֵי שִׁיר גַּם מְתַרְגֵּם · בְּהַקְפִּידוֹ כְּהִלְכָתוֹ וְדָתוֹ ·

# הגדה של פסח

סדר לימי חג הפסח

כתב יד ספרדי

מהמאה הי"ד למס'

שנמצא בספרית

ג'ון רייילנדס דמנצ'סטר

וכלול בו

פרשיות אזהרות

פרושים ושירי קודש

העתיקו

והוסיף עליו הערות

ודברי מבוא

רפאל

בן צבי מרדכי

הלוי

פרופסור אמריטוס
דאוניברסיטת לונדון